THE WORLD ACCORDING
TO TOMDISPATCH

THE WORLD ACCORDING TO TOMDISPATCH

America in the New Age of Empire

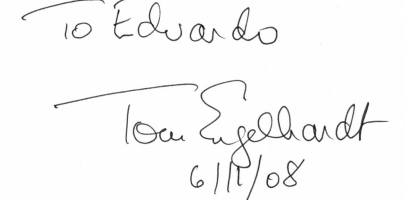

TOM ENGELHARDT

To Edwardo

Tom Engelhardt

6/1/08

VERSO

London • New York

First published by Verso 2008
Copyright in the collection © Verso 2008
Copyright within the contributions © the individual contributors 2007
All rights reserved

The moral rights of the authors and editor have been asserted

1 3 5 7 9 10 8 6 4 2

Verso
UK: 6 Meard Street, London W1F 0EG
USA: 180 Varick Street, New York, NY 10014-4606
www.versobooks.com

Verso is the imprint of New Left Books

ISBN-13: 978-1-84467-257-8

British Library Cataloguing in Publication Data
A catalogue record for this book is available from the British Library

Library of Congress Cataloging-in-Publication Data
A catalog record for this book is available from the Library of Congress

Typeset in Bembo by Hewer Text UK Ltd, Edinburgh
Printed in the USA by Maple Vail

CONTENTS

Introduction: "E" as in Expeditionary
by Tom Engelhardt ix

I HOW IT ALL BEGAN
1 *Tom Engelhardt* 9/11 in a Movie-made World 3
2 *Tom Engelhardt* The Billion-dollar Gravestone 14

II IMPERIAL PLANET
3 *Jonathan Schell and Tom Engelhardt*
  The Empire That Fell as It Rose 25
4 *Chalmers Johnson* No Longer the "Lone" Superpower 36
5 *Greg Grandin* The Wide War: How Donald Rumsfeld
  Discovered the Wild West in Latin America 59
6 *Noam Chomsky* What If Iran Had Invaded Mexico? 71
7 *John Brown* "Our Indian Wars Are Not Over Yet":
  Ten Ways to Interpret the War on Terror as a Frontier Conflict 77
8 *Adam Hochschild* A Pseudostate Is Born 82
9 *Tom Engelhardt* Twenty-first-century Gunboat Diplomacy 86
10 *Dilip Hiro* The Sole Superpower in Decline:
  The Rise of a Multipolar World 96

III INVISIBLE VICTIMS OF THE "WAR ON TERROR"
11 *Chalmers Johnson* The Smash of Civilizations 107
12 *Judith Coburn* Unnamed and Unnoticed: Iraqi Casualties 116

13 *Ruth Rosen* The Hidden War on Women in Iraq 126
14 *Ann Jones* Not the Same as Being Equal: Women in Afghanistan 134
15 *Karen J. Greenberg* Guantánamo Is Not a Prison: Eleven Ways
to Report on Gitmo without Upsetting the Pentagon 141
16 *Dahr Jamail* "I Am Now a Refugee":
The Iraqi Crisis That Has No Name 147

IV UNDER THE BOMBS
17 *Tom Engelhardt* Degrading Behavior: The Middle East
and the Barbarism of War from the Air 159
18 *Rasha Salti* Siege Notes 173
19 *Behzad Yaghmaian* Will American Bombs Kill My Iranian Dreams? 184

V THE PETRO-INDUSTRIAL COMPLEX
AND ITS DISCONTENTS
20 *Michael Schwartz* The Prize of Iraqi Oil 201
21 *Michael T. Klare* The Pentagon vs Peak Oil:
How Wars of the Future May Be Fought Just to
Run the Machines That Fight Them 214
22 *Chad Heeter* My Saudi Arabian Breakfast 220
23 *Mike Davis* The Other Hurricane: Has the Age of Chaos Begun? 225
24 *Bill McKibben* Sucker's Bets for the New Century:
The US after Katrina 229

VI NAME THAT WAR
25 *Tom Engelhardt* George Bush's War of the Words 235
26 *Juan Cole* Pitching the Imperial Republic:
Bonaparte and Bush on Deck 248
27 *Mark Danner* Words in a Time of War:
Taking the Measure of the First Rhetoric-Major President 257

VII BRINGING IT ALL BACK HOME
28 *Nick Turse and Tom Engelhardt* Corporations of the Whirlwind:
The Reconstruction of New Oraq 275
29 *Arlie Hochschild* The Chauffeur's Dilemma 284

30 *Ira Chernus* Democratic Doublespeak on Iraq:
    Questions Unasked, Answers Never Volunteered   291
31 *Steve Fraser* The Perfect Storm of Campaign 2008:
    War, Depression, and Turning-point Elections   298

VIII BACK TO THE FUTURE?
32 *David Rosner and Gerald Markowitz*
    Katrina Started at Ground Zero   307
33 *Rebecca Solnit* On Not Forgetting New Orleans   313

    Acknowledgements   322

    Note on Sourcing   325

    About Tom Engelhardt   326

    About Tomdispatch   327

    List of Contributors   328

    Index   333

INTRODUCTION: "E" AS IN EXPEDITIONARY

The Internet teaches its own lessons, often painfully quickly. In April 2005, I followed an urge, as I often did in those days. Our President, who would soon claim to be spending his spare time absorbing meaty books like *King Leopold's Ghost, Lincoln: A Life of Purpose and Power*, and *Mao: The Unknown Story*, was then largely known for reading *The Pet Goat* to schoolchildren while the 9/11 attacks were taking place and for being fond of *The Very Hungry Caterpillar*. So I took a plunge into humor and wrote a mock children's ABC book that I dubbed "George's Amazing Alphabet Book of the Contemporary World, or Al-Qaedas All Around." I claimed that the manuscript, produced by George W. himself, had been leaked to my website by "a senior official in one of our intelligence agencies."

Maybe it wasn't Jon Stewart-worthy, but I posted it anyway as my commentary of the week and thought no more about it until the first angry emails began appearing in the Tomdispatch mail box. A number of readers claimed I had been "gulled." I shoulda known! The President could never have written such a document! It had obviously been produced by the CIA! No, the Secret Service! No . . .

A perfectly sane friend rang up, wondering whether the manuscript could possibly be genuine—or was I pulling a leg or two? Irritated readers assured me that it was a total fraud and I a total fool for ever taking the word of that senior intelligence official.

I was stunned. I hadn't been trying to fool a soul, just make a passing point or two about our President and his people. Still, I got the message—an instant lesson in Bush era online reality. You couldn't out-absurd this administration. You couldn't write a "document" so extreme that some readers wouldn't mistake it for the real thing. That was the extremity of our moment—thank you, George!

Actually, back in November 2001, that very extremity had driven me online in the first place and into the waiting arms of what became Tomdispatch.com—after the assaults of 9/11; after we had been at "war" and George had become a "wartime" President with an ever-expanding idea of his own powers; after Americans had engaged in endless 9/11 rites in which we took all the roles in the global drama (except Ultimate Evil One); after we had become the planet's greatest victims, survivors, and dominators; after, with relentless, repetitive vigor, the heartland had donned hats and T-shirts proclaiming that they "loved" (or hearted) that former Sodom—to Los Angeles's Gomorrah—New York City; after the Patriot Act was reality; after the money—to "support our troops"—was already pouring into the Pentagon and allied private corporations; after a budding second Defense Department, the Office of Homeland Security, was a reality (it would be turned into a full-scale Department of Homeland Security in November 2002); after the Bush administration had begun planning for a detention camp at Guantánamo Bay, Cuba, that would become the jewel in the crown of an offshore Bermuda Triangle of injustice; after Secretary of Defense Donald Rumsfeld and other top officials had made clear their urge to "take off the gloves" and commit just about any act imaginable, from kidnapping to torture, against anyone anywhere they believed to be a "terrorist"; after the newspapers I used to read in the still commanding world of print had narrowed their coverage, upped their "patriotism," and were beating the drum for George Bush's Global War on Terror.

Tomdispatch was a happenstance, the unplanned creation of a man too old by half for the medium he stumbled into. It came into existence out of a simple urge not to sit still, not to continue my life as it had been while our already shaky world was being ravaged. Between November 2001 and 2004, it went from a private, no-name group email for perhaps twelve friends and relatives to an official site in cyberspace, backed by the Nation Institute, and featuring a range of provocative writers and thinkers.

Sometime in 2004, the year after the site gained its name, I went out to lunch with a Mexican political cartoonist. In what still passed for real life I was working, as I had been for almost thirty years, as a book editor in the publishing business, and we were discussing a project we planned to do together. At one point, trying to explain his life and world to me, he said: "You know, for Mexicans the PRI years"—he was talking about the one-party-state era in his country—"were shameful times . . ." He paused and then leaned across the table confidentially. ". . . But we political cartoonists," he said, "we were like pigs in slop."

In the same confessional mode, what were indisputably the worst years of most of our lives turned out to be a small, late-in-life odyssey for me. Call it "A" for adventure.

Tomdispatch is—as I often write inquisitive readers—the sideline that ate my life. Being in my late fifties and remarkably ignorant of the Internet world when it began, I brought some older print habits online with me. These included a liking for the well-made, well-edited essay, an aversion to the endless yak and insult that seemed to fill whole realms of cyberspace, and a willingness to go against, or beyond, every byte-sized truth of the online world where, it was believed, brevity was all and attention spans were virtually nonexistent. Tomdispatch pieces invariably ran long. They were, after all, meant to reframe a familiar, if shook-up, world that was being presented in a particularly limited way by the mainstream media.

Soon enough, the site became a good deal more than my private venture. I began to recruit writers (whose books I had edited over the years) to produce pieces on whatever was bothering them about Bushworld. If you didn't happen to be a champion of global empire, then that world was your critical oyster. Initially, they wrote for nothing but the pleasure of helping a friend, offering an interpretive hand to others, and possibly the pure amazement of seeing their pieces virally wing their way into previously unknown worlds. Tomdispatch became, as this book reflects, a cooperative venture of friends, colleagues, and e-acquaintances who, like the incandescent writer Rebecca Solnit, I first bumped into online. It also gradually became a tiny rallying point for dissident thinkers, especially those who felt the urge to write the missing collective history of that moment as it was happening.

Finding myself on a mad, unipolar imperial planet, I plunged into an alphabet soup of mayhem and chaos. Let me try, then, to offer you my shorthand version of the world according to Tomdispatch, the world you're about to revisit in this book.

An Expeditionary Service in an Expeditionary World

In late October 2007, when top-level volunteers for duty in Iraq from the US State Department had long since thinned out, Secretary of State Condoleezza Rice threatened to assign diplomats to posts in Baghdad and the provinces whether they wanted to go or not. This had not happened since the days of the Vietnam War. At an angry "town hall" meeting of career diplomats, a foreign service officer named Jack Croddy denounced the plan. He called it a "potential death sentence." "It's one thing," he said, "if someone believes in what's going on over there and volunteers, but it's another thing to send someone over there on a forced assignment."

David Satterfield, Rice's deputy, responded: "I certainly understand very much that this is extremely difficult for people who have not contemplated this kind of service." Then he reportedly added, "This is an expeditionary world. For better or worse, it requires an expeditionary service."

An expeditionary world. An expeditionary service. How typical of those muscled-up, faintly un-American phrases—think "homeland," "regime change," "enhanced interrogation techniques," "extraordinary rendition"—that the Bush administration has made part of our vocabulary. These were years when American men (and a few women) put on the pith helmets they had last seen in imperial adventure films in the movie theaters of their childhoods, imagined themselves as the imperial masters of a global Pax Americana (as well as a domestic Pax Republicana), and managed to sound as if they were surging across the planet with Rudyard Kipling at their side.

In the good old days of 2002–3, before a ragtag insurgency in Iraq managed to lay low the plans of the leaders of the Earth's "sole superpower," the administration's neoconservative followers and assorted pundits, openly touting empire (and "freedom"), spoke glowingly of the United States as a new Rome or a new imperial Britain. The US was to be the last great power on which the sun could never—in fact, would never dare to—set. Commentator Max Boot was typical when he wrote of the US military, in 2002, that it "far surpasses the capabilities of such previous would-be hegemons as Rome, Britain, and Napoleonic France." Of course, back then, a barrel of crude oil was still in the $20 price range.

By that time, the leftover American internationalists, whose weak last hurrah was the Clinton interregnum, had been ousted. Clinton's eight years had, of course, taken place in the midst of a quarter-century-long Republican "revolution" that, in the name of "small government," had ramped up the powers of the national security state and the profile of the Pentagon, while slowly strangling services to the populace. From George W. Bush on down, the officials of the new administration would, however, prove extreme, even by the standards of that right-wing revolution. They were, in a sense, mutant versions of old, heartland Republican types turned inside out. They arrived triumphantly in Washington as armed, aggressive isolationists who couldn't swallow the concept of partnership either in Washington or in the world.

The phrase *du jour* was "unipolarity." In the wake of the Soviet Union's collapse, there was, it was said, only one great-power "pole" left on the planet and it was firmly embedded in Washington, DC. The job of the rest of the world was to accept that reality and bend a knee to it. Anything else would be considered a form of terrorism or, as the administration put it in one of its Ur-documents, the *National Defense Strategy of the United States of America*: "Our strength as a nation-state will continue to be challenged by those who employ a strategy of the weak using international fora, judicial processes and terrorism." *There* was an unholy troika for you, a genuine axis of evil.

When Bush's people sallied forth into the world, they did so without equals, and less as classic imperialists than as imperial looters (in conjunction with crony corporations like Halliburton, Bechtel, and Blackwater USA, to whom they slipped their no-bid contracts). Arm in arm with a mob of K-street lobbyists, congressional power brokers, and assorted right-wing think-tanks and media pundits, they were itching to take the world by storm. These were people who imagined no problems that couldn't be overcome by a shock-and-awe-style military strike abroad. They saw their toughest enemies, however, not overseas, but in Washington. As a result, they first seized the Pentagon, then Kiplinged the military and the intelligence services, sent the State Department into purdah, and set up the most secretive, yet leak-ridden, administration in American memory.

Unlike any previous administration, they arrived in office with an allied right-wing media already firmly in place—their own publishing houses, newspapers, and talk-radio shows, as well as their "fair and balanced" TV news. They felt no need to jolly up to, or interact with, the rest of the media. As Bill Keller, executive editor of the *New York Times*, put it in 2007, "We have endured nearly seven years of the most press-phobic government in a couple of generations." In the phrase of critic Jay Rosen, the intent of the

Bush administration was to "roll back" the media, pacifying and sidelining the major papers and TV networks; and, with the help of the assaults of 9/11, they were more than successful in doing so—for a time. Never, in fact, had an administration released less news to those covering them. (Most newspapers and the TV news, for instance, gave up even assigning reporters to cover Vice President Dick Cheney, a man so averse to providing information that his daily schedule was regularly unavailable, while reporters couldn't even find out the full roster of people working in his "office.")

The administration's method of ruling revolved around injecting regular doses of fear into the public bloodstream, while dominating an increasingly powerless Congress. If conquering Washington had been the only thing that mattered, the Republicans might have been titans for decades, though it's worth remembering that to do so they still needed a little help from their enemies— even ones they didn't deign to pay the slightest attention to on occupying the Oval Office. After all, they were only conquerors after September 11, 2001. On September 10 of that year, the media was still describing the administration as "adrift"; its Secretary of Defense was believed to have "cratered"; and the President's polling figures were visibly sagging, thanks to a public that viewed him "not as decisive but as tentative and perhaps overly scripted."

The President, who had just returned from an overlong, much-criticized vacation at his "ranch" in Crawford, Texas, was then being charged by figures in his own party and Republicans in Congress with being "out of touch" and out of ideas. Wielding, in Mike Davis's vivid phrase, hijacked "car bombs with wings," al-Qaeda solved that one fast. As the towers fell and that giant cloud of dust and ash rose toward the heavens, the Bush administration found itself swept along by the perfect storm toward its conquest of Washington.

When it came to conquering the world, however, the President's top officials would turn out to have an excess of faith and not a clue.

A Faith-based Administration

Let's start with that faith. Much has been made of the Christian fundamentalist beliefs of George W. Bush and the religious foot soldiers of the right whom his administration mobilized in the election campaigns of 2000 and 2004. But consider the possibility that the most fundamental belief of the top officials of his administration was, in fact, in the efficacy of force.

If the Republicans emerged from 9/11 as a fundamentalist regime, it wasn't really as a fundamentalist Christian one. After all, political strategist Karl Rove, Secretary of Defense Donald Rumsfeld, and the Vice President were not Christian fundamentalists, any more than were key Pentagon officials Paul Wolfowitz and Douglas Feith, for example. The administration's top officials may not, in fact, have agreed among themselves on when (or whether) End Time would arrive, but they all had a singular faith in the US military as the most awesome power projector in history.

They tended to hold individual American military commanders in contempt—unless they had a very big "Yessir" stamped on their foreheads—but when it came to the ability of the US armed forces to accomplish anything, romantics would be a mild word for what they were. They believed themselves uniquely in possession of an ability to project force in ways no other country ever had; and so, despite much talk of "democracy" and "liberty," a Hellfire-missile-armed Predator drone would perhaps be the truest hallmark of the early-twenty-first-century American civilization they presided over.

They were in awe of the force at their President's command, armed to the teeth with techno-toys, already garrisoning much of the globe (and about to garrison more of it), already on the receiving end of vast inflows of taxpayer dollars (and about to receive more of them), and already embedded in a sprawling network of corporate interests (and about to cede further control to such corporations). By the time the Bush administration took the helm of the warship of state, most of the globe had already been divided into US military "commands"—essentially imperial viceroyships—but they would finish the job, creating a command for the "homeland," Northcom, in 2002, and for the previously forgotten, suddenly energy-hot, continent of Africa, Africom, in 2007.

The President and his top officials put the lean, mean, high-tech all-volunteer military on a pedestal and worshiped it as the most shock-and-awesome institution around. Speaking of his war in Iraq in 2007, in a statement typical of his administration's military hyperbole, Bush said: "I'm confident we'll prevail because we have the greatest force for human liberation the world has ever known—the men and women of the United States Armed Forces." *The greatest force for human liberation the world has ever known.* This was a claim unimaginable from any past president. Then again, all the President's men had similar warm and fuzzy visions of achieving planetary dominion of a sort that had once, in American parlance, been the goal only of the most evil of foreign powers—the Nazis, Imperial Japan, or Stalin's Russia.

When it came to unleashing that force to achieve their aims, the President and his men turned out to be fervent utopians and blind believers. They were firmly convinced that, with it, they could reshape the Middle East, establish an unassailable position in the oil heartlands of the planet, roll back the Russians (yet further), and cow the Chinese.

And then, with 9/11, the Pearl Harbor of the new century, the administration suddenly had a divine wind at their backs, a terrified populace ready to be led, a supine Congress, and a pacified media. Everything they believed deeply in seemed just so . . . well, possible. In faith-based terms, the attacks of 9/11 were a godsend. Not surprisingly, top administration officials promptly began to prepare to act on behalf of an angry imperial god by bringing the world—particularly its energy heartlands—to heel.

First, however, the President's men created their sacred texts at the heart of which lay the doctrine of "preventive war." At the same time, the President began speaking out about the need to act forcefully to prevent the emergence of any possible threat to the country. As he put it in his 2002 State of the Union Address, "We'll be deliberate, yet time is not on our side. I will not wait on events, while dangers gather. I will not stand by, as peril draws closer and closer. The United States of America will not permit the world's most dangerous regimes to threaten us with the world's most destructive weapons." Meanwhile, in the office of the White House Counsel and in the Justice Department, acolyte lawyers were creating pretzeled legal memos that essentially redefined torture out of existence, clearing a path for any agent or interrogator in the field ready to take off those constraining "gloves." At home, these fundamentalist believers were also working to free the President from all restraints, intending to create a Caesarian commander-in-chief presidency as well as the first imperial vice-presidency in American history.

Because their faith was of the blind sort, however, they would misread the nature of what was powerful in our world; and so their fervent unipolarity would help give premature birth to a newly multipolar planet. Among other disastrous miscalculations, they would confuse the power that lay in the threat of loosing the American military with its actual ability to impose itself on places like Afghanistan and Iraq. They believed, like the monotheists they were, that a single God, personified by the military at their command, would sweep all before Him; that, with a "coalition of the willing" (by which they meant the submissive), they could take their God of force to the heathen at the point of a cruise missile, and that victory would be theirs. The pieces in this book indicate just how wrong this belief would prove to be.

Missing Stories on a One-way Planet

At his 2006 confirmation hearings for the post of CIA director, Michael V. Hayden (who absorbed the Bush ethos while running the super-secret electronic spying organization the National Security Agency) offered the following promise to Congress: "If confirmed as Director, I would reaffirm the CIA's proud culture of risk-taking and excellence, particularly through the increased use of non-traditional operational platforms . . . and the inculcation of what I would call an expeditionary mentality." That same year, the then Director of National Intelligence John Negroponte told the Marine Corps Intelligence Association, "We are developing an 'expeditionary' mentality in the field of science and technology."

That old-fashioned imperial idea of an "expeditionary mentality" abroad took on a life of its own in the Bush years. The answer to any problem was that "expeditionary mentality" and the armed expedition that went with it—and disaster ensued. For the adherents of the cult of force, the world of fantasy took over; the result was an empire of stupidity. If, for instance, you were to offer a reckoning of the Bush administration's "Global War on Terror," you might—at least in the world according to Tomdispatch—sum up its achievements thus:

With Guantánamo as the Devil's Island of the twenty-first century; with the extraordinary renditions, waterboardings, tortures, and abuses (and the perverse memos and photos that went with them); with the CIA's "ghost prisoners" and network of secret offshore prisons; with that Delta Force intelligence agent who stepped off a plane from Afghanistan holding the suspected head of al-Qaeda second-in-command Ayman al-Zawahiri in a "US Government" metal box (the head, it turned out, belonged to someone else);[1] with neither Osama bin Laden nor Zawahiri apprehended; with woebegone terror wannabes, the innocent, and small fry of every sort turned

---

[1] As journalist Ron Suskind tells the story in his book *The One Percent Doctrine*.

into Public Enemies numbers 1 to 1,000; with illegal spying and warrantless, limitless surveillance taking hold in "the Homeland"; with the Taliban rising from the grave and the original al-Qaeda (as opposed to name-stealing al-Qaedas elsewhere) finding a "safe haven" in the Pakistani tribal borderlands—the GWOT (as the Global War on Terror so inelegantly came to be known) could easily have been renamed something like the "misfire on terror" (MOT) or even, with an eye to what developed in Iraq and elsewhere, the "engine for terror" (EFT).

Among the administration's greatest achievements was launching what in the eyes of many globally came to look like a "crusade"—to use a word that slipped effortlessly out of the President's mouth soon after 9/11—against Islam. In the process, the President's neocon supporters demarcated an area extending from the western border of China, through the territories of the former Central Asian SSRs of the Soviet Union and the Middle East, down through the Horn of Africa and across North Africa (more or less coinciding with the oil heartlands of the planet), and dubbed it "the arc of instability." Then, from Somalia to Pakistan, they managed to set it aflame, transforming their own empty turn of phrase into a reality on the ground, an actual arc of instability, even as the price of crude oil soared above $100 a barrel.

For most of these years, much of this was remarkably ill-covered (if covered at all) in the mainstream US media. Almost no American reporter, for instance, considered it worth the bother to write about those massive "facts on the ground" in Iraq the permanent mega-bases—heavily fortified American small towns, sometimes 15–20 square miles in area, with multiple bus routes, PXs, brand fast-food outlets, and many of the amenities of home—that the Pentagon was building at the cost of multi-billions of dollars. Few American journalists in Iraq or Afghanistan bothered to look to the skies and consider the role of air power in the President's global war (even though air power had been the signature American way of war for well over half a century); almost all of them found the crucial issue of energy flows through the oil heartlands, and the vast reserves of oil in Iraq in particular, an embarrassment to mention in conjunction with the invasion and occupation of that country.

You'll note that the table of contents of *The World According to Tomdispatch* could be considered a running catalogue of the missing stories of these last years in the mainstream world. Some have finally been taken up there;

others, like those mega-bases or the real justifications for the invasion of Iraq, oil among them, still remain largely taboo at the time of writing.

From 2002 through 2007, Tomdispatch has focused on stories such as these. For instance, it's hard to remember today how little was being written about climate change in the mainstream back in the days before Al Gore made that "inconvenient truth" somewhat more convenient to consider. Or, at the outset, how little remarked upon were the Iraqi casualties of the President's war of choice (once known as a war of aggression), or the plight of Afghan women, once they had been "liberated" into further misery by the President's 2001 war against the Taliban. As you'll see in this book, Tomdispatch did not ignore the invisible victims, the "collateral damage," of the President's Global War on Terror.

Similarly, you could find articles in the mainstream complaining about cost overruns for the grandiose billion-dollar memorial to the dead of 9/11 being built at Ground Zero in my city of New York; but not one suggesting that what was really being memorialized there was a Bush moment that reflected ways Americans have, even in victimhood, exhibited an unseemly imperial hubris. Nor were you likely to find a piece on American politics that used the *D* word (for depression) in an analysis of the storm clouds gathering over our economic moment; or a discussion of the way in which the Bush administration first began to turn the US from a can-do into a can't-do nation, not with its disastrous handling of Hurricane Katrina's descent on New Orleans, but at Ground Zero on September 12, 2001. All of this hidden history and much more can be found in the pages that follow. Most of it was hidden in plain view; often, all you had to do was open your eyes to see it.

What underpins all the missing stories in this book is the imperial nature of the American world we've inhabited in these last years. For a brief period in 2002–3, the neocons and various right-wing pundits were openly beating the drum for "empire," but when Iraq started to go south and the US military visibly ran off the tracks, the words "empire" and "imperial" left the scene of the crime as well—except at websites like Tomdispatch.

And yet, in American thinking, this still remains an imperial planet. Try to imagine, for instance, Iranian President Mahmoud Ahmadinejad landing on an aircraft carrier in the Gulf of Mexico—as Vice President Dick Cheney did on the USS *John C. Stennis* on May 11, 2007, while it floated in the

Persian Gulf off Iran's coast—and saying, as Cheney also did: "With two carrier strike groups in the Gulf, we're sending clear messages to friends and adversaries alike. We'll keep the sea lanes open. We'll stand with our friends in opposing extremism and strategic threats . . ." and so on. If that had happened the other way round, it would have been cause for a declaration of war—and imagine what the press coverage would have been like. Cheney's address to the sailors of the *John C. Stennis* was, of course, reported as an unremarkable event on our still one-way planet. Tomdispatch has tried to make such moments seem a little more remarkable.

In these last years, the Bush administration's unbounded sense of imperial impunity and an older American belief that this country possesses a moral code exceptional among nations have proven a lethal cocktail. This curious perspective has led our administration to commit acts of horror in our name, while absolving us from thinking about how others might look on those acts—and, by extension, how they think about us. No such absolution will be found in this book.

Because, for years, so little on these and similar subjects made it into print or onto the TV news, there has been a special need and place for Tomdispatch (as well as other political websites and blogs). We started—and maintained—discussions that only slowly seeped into the mainstream world, even as readers from that world increasingly fled online. At the height of the Bush administration's power and narcissism, what Tomdispatch represented was perhaps an urge not to let *them* set an agenda for all of America, and for the planet.

Many worthy topics are missing both from my website and this book. I've largely kept Tomdispatch to my obsessions and areas of interest, to what one person, with the help of his friends, could make of a complex world. But within these bounds, I think you'll find here something like the beginnings of an alternative history of our desperate times, by some of the best minds around.

Tom Engelhardt
New York City
January 1, 2008

I

HOW IT ALL BEGAN

September 2006

1

9/11 IN A MOVIE-MADE WORLD

Tom Engelhardt

We knew it was coming. Not, as conspiracy theorists imagine, just a few top officials among us, but all of us—and not for weeks or months, but for more than half a century before September 11, 2001.

That's why, for all the shock, it was, in a sense, so familiar. Americans were already imagining versions of September 11 soon after the dropping of the first atomic bomb on Hiroshima on August 6, 1945. That event set the American imagination boiling. Within weeks of the destruction of Hiroshima and Nagasaki, as scholar Paul Boyer has shown, all the familiar signs of nuclear fear were already in place—newspapers were drawing concentric circles of atomic destruction outward from fantasy Ground Zeroes in American cities, and magazines were offering visions of our country as a vaporized wasteland, while imagining millions of American dead.

And then, suddenly, one clear morning it seemed to arrive—by air, complete with images of the destruction of the mightiest monuments to our power, and (just as previously experienced) as an onscreen spectacle. At one point that day, it could be viewed on more than thirty channels, including some never previously involved with breaking news, and most of the United States was watching.

Only relatively small numbers of New Yorkers actually experienced 9/11: those at the tip of Manhattan or close enough to watch the two planes smash into the World Trade Center towers, to watch (as some schoolchildren did) people leaping or falling from the upper floors of those buildings, to be enveloped in the vast cloud of smoke and ash, in the tens of thousands of pulverized computers and copying machines, the asbestos and flesh and plane, the shredded remains of millions of sheets of paper, of financial and office life as we know it. For most Americans, even those like me who were living in Manhattan, 9/11 arrived on the television screen. This is why what leapt to mind—and instantaneously filled our papers and TV reporting—was previous screen life, the movies.

In the immediate aftermath of the attacks, the news was peppered with comments about, thoughts about, and references to films. Reporters, as Caryn James wrote in the *New York Times* that first day, "compared the events to Hollywood action movies," as did op-ed writers ("The scenes exceeded the worst of Hollywood's disaster movies"), columnists ("On TV, two national landmarks . . . look like the aftermath in the film *Independence Day*"), and eyewitnesses ("It was like one of them Godzilla movies"; "And then I saw an explosion straight out of *The Towering Inferno*"). Meanwhile, in an irony of the moment, Hollywood scrambled to excise from upcoming big- and small-screen life anything that might bring to mind thoughts of 9/11, including, in the case of Fox, promotion for the premiere episode of *24*, in which "a terrorist blows up an airplane."

In our guts, we had always known it was coming. Like any errant offspring, Little Boy and Fat Man, those two atomic packages with which we had paid *them* back for Pearl Harbor, were destined to return home someday. No wonder the single, omnipresent historical reference in the media in the wake of the attacks was Pearl Harbor or, as screaming headlines had it, INFAMY, or A NEW DAY OF INFAMY. We had just experienced "the Pearl Harbor of the 21st Century," or, as R. James Woolsey, former CIA director (and neoconservative), said in the *Washington Post* that first day, "It is clear now, as it was on December 7, 1941, that the United States is at war. . . . The question is: with whom?"

The Day After
No wonder that what came instantly to mind was a nuclear event. No wonder, according to a *New York Times* piece, that Tom Brokaw, then chairing NBC's nonstop news coverage, "may have captured it best when he looked at videotape of people on a street, everything and everyone so

covered with ash . . . [and said] it looked 'like a nuclear winter in lower Manhattan.' " No wonder the *Tennessean* and the *Topeka Capital-Journal* both used the headline "The Day After," lifted from a famous 1983 TV movie about nuclear Armageddon.

No wonder the area where the two towers fell was quickly dubbed Ground Zero, a term previously reserved for the spot where an atomic explosion had occurred. On September 12, for example, the *Los Angeles Times* published a full-page series of illustrations of the attacks on the towers headlined: "Ground Zero." By week's end, it had become the only name for "the collapse site," as in a September 18 *New York Times* headline, "Many Come to Bear Witness at Ground Zero."

No wonder the events seemed so strangely familiar. We had been living with the possible return of our most powerful weaponry via TV and the movies, novels and our own dreamlife, in the past, the future, and even— thanks to a John F. Kennedy TV appearance on October 22, 1962, during the Cuban Missile Crisis to tell us that our world might end tomorrow— in something like the almost-present.

So many streams of popular culture had fed into this. So many "previews" had been offered. Everywhere in those decades, you could see yourself or your compatriots or the enemy "Hiroshimated" (as *Variety* termed it back in 1947). Even when Arnold Schwarzenegger wasn't kissing Jamie Lee Curtis in *True Lies* as an atomic explosion went off somewhere in the Florida Keys or a playground filled with American kids wasn't being atomically blistered in *Terminator 2: Judgment Day*, even when it wasn't literally nuclear, that apocalyptic sense of destruction lingered as the train, bus, blimp, explosively armed, headed for us in our unknowing innocence; as the towering inferno, airport, city, White House was blasted away, as we were offered Pompeii-scapes of futuristic destruction in what would, post-9/11, come to be known as "the homeland."

Sometimes it came from outer space armed with strange city-blasting rays; other times irradiated monsters rose from the depths to stomp our cities (in the 1998 remake of *Godzilla*, New York City, no less). After *Star Wars*'s Darth Vader used his Death Star to pulverize a whole planet in 1977, planets were regularly nuclearized in Saturday-morning TV cartoons. In our imaginations, post-1945, we were always at planetary Ground Zero.

Dystopian Serendipity

Increasingly, from Hamburg to Saudi Arabia to Afghanistan, others were also watching our spectaculars, our catastrophes, our previews; and so, as Hollywood historian Neal Gabler would write in the *New York Times* only days after 9/11, they were ready to deliver what we had long dreamed of with the kind of timing—insuring, for instance, that the second plane arrived "at a decent interval" after the first so that the cameras could be in place— and in a visual language American viewers would understand.

But here's the catch: what came, when it came, on September 11, 2001, wasn't what we thought came. There was no Ground Zero, because there was nothing faintly atomic about the attacks. It wasn't the apocalypse at all. Except in its success, it hardly differed from the 1993 attack on the World Trade Center, the one that almost toppled one tower with a rented Ryder van and a homemade bomb.

OK, the truck of 1993 had sprouted wings and gained all the power in those almost full, transcontinental jet fuel tanks, but otherwise what "changed everything," as the phrase would soon go, was a bit of dystopian serendipity for al-Qaeda: nineteen men of much conviction and middling skills, armed with exceedingly low-tech weaponry and two hijacked jets, managed to create an apocalyptic look that, in another context, would have made the special-effects masters of Lucas's Industrial Light & Magic proud. And from that—and the Bush administration's reaction to it—everything else would follow.

The tiny band of fanatics who planned September 11 essentially lucked out. If the testimony, under CIA interrogation techniques, of al-Qaeda's master planner Khalid Shaikh Mohammed is to be believed, what happened stunned even him. ("According to the [CIA] summary, he said he 'had no idea that the damage of the first attack would be as catastrophic as it was.' ") Those two mighty towers came crumbling down in that vast, roiling, near-mushroom cloud of white smoke before the cameras in the fashion of the ultimate Hollywood action film (imagery multiplied in its traumatizing power by thousands of replays over a record-setting more than ninety straight hours of TV coverage). And that imagery fit perfectly the secret expectations of Americans—just as it fit the needs of both al-Qaeda and the Bush administration.

That's undoubtedly why other parts of the story of that moment faded from sight. On the fifth anniversary of September 11, there will, for instance, be no memorial documentaries focusing on American Flight 77, which plowed into the Pentagon. That destructive but non-apocalyptic-looking attack didn't satisfy the same built-in expectations. Though the term "ground zero Washington" initially floated through the media ether, it never stuck.

Similarly, the unsolved anthrax murders-by-mail of almost the same moment, which caused a collective shudder of horror, are now forgotten. (According to a LexisNexis search, between October 4 and December 4, 2001, 260 stories appeared in the *New York Times* and 246 in the *Washington Post* with "anthrax" in the headline. That's the news equivalent of a high-pitched scream of horror.) Those envelopes, spilling highly refined anthrax powder and containing letters dated "9/11/01" with lines like "Death to America, Death to Israel, Allah Is Great," represented the only use of a weapon of mass destruction (WMD) in this period; yet they were slowly eradicated from our collective (and media) memory once it became clearer that the perpetrators were probably homegrown killers, possibly out of the very Cold War US weapons labs that produced so much WMD in the first place. It's a guarantee that the media will not be filled with memory pieces to the anthrax victims this October.

The 36-hour War
Indulge me, then, for a moment on an otherwise grim subject. I've always been a fan of what-if history and, when younger, of science fiction. Recently, I decided to take my own modest time machine back to September 11, 2001; or, to be more exact, the IRT subway on several overheated July afternoons to one of the cultural glories of my city, the New York Public Library, a building that—in the realm where sci-fi and what-if history meld—suffered its own monstrous "damage," its own 9/11, only months after the A-bombing of Hiroshima.

In November 1945, *Life* magazine published "The 36-Hour War," an overheated what-if tale in which an unnamed enemy in "equatorial Africa" launched a surprise atomic missile attack on the United States, resulting in 10 million deaths. A dramatic illustration accompanying the piece showed the library's two pockmarked stone lions still standing, guarding a ground-zero scene of almost total destruction, while heavily shielded technicians tested "the rubble of the shattered city for radioactivity."

I passed those same majestic lions, still standing (as was the library) in 2006, entered the microfiche room and began reading the *New York Times* as well as several other newspapers starting with the September 12, 2001, issues. Immediately I was plunged back into a hellish apocalypse. Vivid *Times* words and phrases from that first day: "gates of hell," "the unthinkable," "nightmare world of Hieronymus Bosch," "hellish storm of ash, glass, smoke, and leaping victims," "clamorous inferno," "an ashen shell of itself, all but a Pompeii." But one of the most common words over those days in the *Times* and elsewhere was "vulnerable" (or as a *Times* piece put it, "nowhere was safe"). The front page of the *Chicago Tribune* caught this mood in a headline, "Feeling of Invincibility Suddenly Shattered," and a lead sentence, "On Tuesday, America the invincible became America the vulnerable." We had faced "the kamikazes of the 21st century"—a Pearl Harborish phrase that would gain traction—and we had lost.

A thought came to mind as I slowly rolled those grainy microfiches; as I passed the photo of a man, in midair, falling headfirst from a World Trade Center tower; as I read this observation from a Pearl Harbor survivor interviewed by the *Tribune*: "Things will never be the same again in this country"; as I reeled section by section, day by day toward our distinctly changed present; as I read all those words that boiled up like a linguistic storm around the photos of those hideous white clouds; as I considered all the op-eds and columns filled with all those instant opinions that poured into the pages of our papers before there was even time to think; as I noticed, buried in their pages, a raft of words and phrases—"preempt," "a new Department of Preemption [at the Pentagon]," "homeland defenses," "homeland security agency"—already lurking in our world, readying themselves to be noticed.

Among them all, the word that surfaced fastest on the heels of that "new Day of Infamy," and to deadliest effect, was "war." Senator John McCain, among many others, on the spot labeled the attacks "an act of war," just as Republican Senator Richard Shelby insisted that "this is total war," just as the *Washington Post*'s columnist Charles Krauthammer started his first editorial that first day, "This is not crime. This is war." And they quickly found themselves in a milling crowd of potential war-makers, Democrats as well as Republicans, liberals as well as conservatives, even if the enemy remained as yet obscure.

On the night of September 11 the President himself, addressing the nation, already spoke of winning "the war against terrorism." By day two he used the phrase "acts of war," by day three "the first war of the twenty-first century" (while the *Times* reported "a drumbeat for war" on television), by week's end "the long war"; and the following week, in an address to a joint session of Congress, while announcing the creation of a Cabinet-level Office of Homeland Security, he wielded "war" twelve times. ("Our war on terror begins with al-Qaeda, but it does not end there.")

What If?

So here was my what-if thought. What if the two hijacked planes, American Flight 11 and United 175, had plunged into those north and south towers at 8:46 and 9:03, killing all aboard, causing extensive damage and significant death tolls, but neither tower had come down? What if, as a *Tribune* columnist put it, photogenic "scenes of apocalypse" had not been produced? What if, despite two gaping holes and the smoke and flames pouring out of the towers, the imagery had been closer to that of 1993? What if there had been no giant cloud of destruction capable of bringing to mind the look of "the day after," no images of crumbling towers worthy of *Independence Day*?

We would surely have had blazing headlines, but would they have commonly had "war" or "infamy" in them, as if we had been attacked by another state? Would the last superpower have gone from "invincible" to "vulnerable" in a split second? Would our newspapers instantly have been writing "before" and "after" editorials, or insisting that this moment was the ultimate "test" of George W. Bush's until-then-languishing presidency? Would we instantaneously have been considering taking what CIA director George Tenet would soon call "the shackles" off our intelligence agencies and the military? Would we have been reconsidering, as Florida's Democratic Senator Bob Graham suggested that first day, rescinding the congressional ban on the assassination of foreign officials and heads of state? Would a *Washington Post* journalist have been trying within hours to name the kind of "war" we were in? (He provisionally labeled it "the Gray War.") Would *New York Times* columnist Tom Friedman on the third day have had us deep into "World War Three"? Would the *Times*, on its front page on September 14, have been headlining and quoting Deputy Defense Secretary Paul Wolfowitz insisting that "it's not simply a matter of capturing people

9

and holding them accountable, but removing the sanctuaries, removing the support systems, ending states who sponsor terrorism." (The *Times* editorial writers certainly noticed that ominous "s" on "states" and wrote the next day: "but we trust [Wolfowitz] does not have in mind invading Iraq, Iran, Syria and Sudan as well as Afghanistan.")

Would state-to-state "war" and "acts of terror" have been so quickly conjoined in the media as a "war on terror" and would that phrase have made it, in just over a week, into a major presidential address? Could the *Los Angeles Daily News* have produced the following four-day series of screaming headlines, beating even the President to the punch: Terror/Horror!/"This Is War"/War on Terror?

If it all hadn't seemed so familiar, wouldn't we have noticed what was actually new in the attacks of September 11? Wouldn't more people have been as puzzled as, according to Ron Suskind in his new book *The One Percent Doctrine*, was one reporter who asked White House press secretary Ari Fleischer, "You don't declare war against an individual, surely?"? Wouldn't Congress have balked at passing, three days later, an almost totally open-ended resolution granting the President the right to use force not against one nation (Afghanistan) but against "nations," plural and unnamed?

And how well would the Bush administration's fear-inspired nuclear agenda have worked, if those buildings hadn't come down? Would Saddam's supposed nuclear program and WMD stores have had the same impact? Would the endless linking of the Iraqi dictator, al-Qaeda, and 9/11 have penetrated so deeply that, in 2006, half of all Americans, according to a Harris poll, still believed Saddam had WMD when the US invasion began, and 85 percent of American troops stationed in Iraq, according to a Zogby poll, believed the US mission there was mainly "to retaliate for Saddam's role in the 9/11 attacks"?

Without that apocalyptic 9/11 imagery, would those fantasy Iraqi mushroom clouds pictured by administration officials rising over American cities or those fantasy Iraqi unmanned aerial vehicles capable of spraying our East Coast with chemical or biological weapons, or Saddam's supposed search for African yellowcake (or even, today, the Iranian "bomb" that won't exist for perhaps another decade, if at all) have so dominated American consciousness?

Would Osama bin Laden and Ayman al-Zawahiri be sitting in jail cells or be on trial by now? Would so many things have happened differently?

The Opportunity of a Lifetime

What if the attacks on September 11, 2001, had not been seen as a new Pearl Harbor? Only three months earlier, after all, Disney's *Pearl Harbor* (the "sanitized" version, as *Times* columnist Frank Rich labeled it), a blockbuster made with extensive Pentagon help, had performed disappointingly at the multiplexes. As an event, it seemed irrelevant to American audiences until 9/11, when that ancient history—and the ancient retribution that went with it—wiped from the American brain the actual history of recent decades, including our massive covert anti-Soviet war in Afghanistan, out of which Osama bin Laden emerged.

Here's the greatest irony: from that time of triumph in 1945, Americans had always secretly suspected that they were not "invincible" but exceedingly vulnerable, something both pop culture and the deepest fears of the Cold War era only reinforced. Confirmation of that fact arrived with such immediacy on September 11 largely because it was already a gut truth. The ambulance chasers of the Bush administration, who spotted such opportunity in the attacks, were perhaps the last Americans who hadn't absorbed this reality. As that New Day of Infamy scenario played out, the horrific but actual scale of the damage inflicted in New York and Washington (and to the US economy) would essentially recede. The attack had been relatively small, limited in its means and massive only in its daring and luck—abetted by the fact that the Bush administration was looking for nothing like such an attack, despite that CIA briefing given to Bush on a lazy August day in Crawford ("Bin Laden Determined To Strike in US") and so many other clues.

Only the week before 9/11 the Bush administration had been in the doldrums with a "detached," floundering President criticized by worried members of his own party for vacationing far too long at his Texas ranch while the nation drifted. Moreover, there was only one group before September 11 with a "new Pearl Harbor" scenario on the brain. Major administration figures, including Vice President Dick Cheney, Defense Secretary Donald Rumsfeld and Deputy Defense Secretary Paul Wolfowitz, had wanted for years to increase radically the power of the President and the Pentagon, to roll back the power of Congress (especially any congressional restraints on the presidency left over from the Vietnam/Watergate era) and to complete the overthrow of Saddam Hussein ("regime change"), aborted by the first Bush administration in 1991.

We know as well that some of those plans were on the table in the 1990s and that those who held them and promoted them, at the Project for the New American Century in particular, actually wrote in a proposal titled "Rebuilding America's Defenses" that "the process of transformation [of the Pentagon], even if it brings revolutionary change, is likely to be a long one, absent some catastrophic and catalyzing event—like a new Pearl Harbor."

We also know that within hours of the 9/11 attacks, many of the same people were at work on the war of their dreams. Within five hours of the attack on the Pentagon, Rumsfeld was urging his aides to come up with plans for striking Iraq. (Notes by an aide transcribe his wishes this way: "best info fast. Judge whether good enough hit S.H. [Saddam Hussein] at same time. Not only UBL [Osama bin Laden]. . . . Go massive. Sweep it all up. Things related and not.")

We know that, by the 12th, the President himself had collared his top counterterrorism adviser on the National Security Council, Richard Clarke, and some of his staff in a conference room next to the White House Situation Room and demanded linkages. ("It was a very intimidating message which said, 'Iraq. Give me a memo about Iraq and 9/11.'") We know that by November, the top officials of the administration were already deep into operational planning for an invasion of Iraq.

And they weren't alone. Within the Pearl Harbor/nuclear attack/war nexus that emerged almost instantly from the ruins of the World Trade Center, others were working feverishly. Only eight days after the attacks, for instance, the complex 342-page Patriot Act would be rushed over to Congress by Attorney General John Ashcroft, to be passed through a cowed Senate in the dead of night on October 11, unread by at least some of our Representatives, and signed into law on October 26. As its instant appearance indicated, it was made up of a set of already existing right-wing hobbyhorses, quickly drafted provisions and expansions of law enforcement powers taken off an FBI "wish list" (previously rejected by Congress). All these were swept together by people who, like the President's men on Iraq, saw their main chance when those buildings went down. As such, it stands in for much of what happened "in response" to 9/11.

But what if we, in the most victorious nation on the planet, its sole "hyperpower," its new Rome, hadn't been waiting so long for our own thirty-six-hour war? What if those pre-existing frameworks hadn't been quite so well primed to emerge in no time at all? What if we (and our enemies as well) hadn't been at the movies all those years?

Movie-made Planet

Among other things, we've been left with a misbegotten "billion dollar" memorial to the attacks of 9/11 (recently recalibrated to $500 million) planned for New York's Ground Zero and sporting the kinds of cost overruns otherwise associated with the occupation of Iraq. In its ambitions, what it will really memorialize is the Bush administration's oversized, crusading moment that followed the attacks. Too late now—and no one asked me anyway—but I know what my memorial would have been.

A few days after 9/11, my daughter and I took a trip downtown, as close to Ground Zero as you could get. With the air still rubbing our throats raw, we wandered block after block, peering down side streets to catch glimpses of the sheer enormity of the destruction. And indeed, in a way that no small screen could communicate, it did have the look of the apocalyptic, especially those giant shards of fallen building sticking up like— remember, I'm a typical movie-made American on an increasingly movie-made planet and had movies on the brain that week—the image of the wrecked Statue of Liberty that chillingly ends the first *Planet of the Apes* film, that cinematic memorial to humanity's nuclear folly. Left there as it was, that debris would have been a sobering monument for the ages, not just to the slaughter that was 9/11 but to what we had awaited for so long—and what, sadly, we still wait for; what, in the world that George Bush has produced, has become ever more, rather than less, likely. And imagine our reaction then.

Safer? Don't be ridiculous.

May 2006

2

THE BILLION-DOLLAR GRAVESTONE

Tom Engelhardt

Recently, a number—one billion—in the *New York Times* stopped me in my tracks. According to a report commissioned by the foundation charged with building Reflecting Absence, the memorial to the dead in the attack on the World Trade Center, its projected cost is now estimated at about a billion dollars and still rising. According to Oliver Burkeman of the British *Guardian*, "Taking inflation into account, $1bn would be more than a quarter of the original cost of the twin towers that were destroyed in 2001."

For that billion, Reflecting Absence is to have two huge "reflecting pools"—"two voids that reside in the original footprints of the Twin Towers"—fed by waterfalls "from all sides" and surrounded by a "forest" of oak trees; a visitor will then be able to descend 30 feet to galleries under the falls "inscribed with the names of those who died." There is to be an adjacent, 100,000-square-foot underground memorial museum to "retell the events of the day, display powerful artifacts, and celebrate the lives of those who died." All of this, as the website for the memorial states, will be meant to vividly convey "the enormity of the buildings and the enormity of the loss." Not surprisingly, the near billion-dollar figure does not even include $80 million for a planned visitors' center or the estimated $50–60 million annual cost of running such an elaborate memorial and museum.

So what is Reflecting Absence going to reflect? For one thing, it will mirror its gargantuan twin, the building that is to symbolically replace the World Trade Center—the Freedom Tower. As the memorial is to be driven deep into the scarred earth of Ground Zero, so the Freedom Tower is to soar above it, scaling the imperial heights. To be precise, it is to reach exactly 1,776 feet into the heavens, a numerical tribute to the founding spirit of the Declaration of Independence and the nation which emerged from it; its spire will even emit light—"a new beacon of freedom"—for all the world to see and admire. Its observation deck will rise a carefully planned 7 feet above that of the old World Trade Center; and with spire and antennae, it is meant to be the tallest office building on the planet (though the Burj Dubai Tower, whose builders are holding its future height a tightly guarded secret, may quickly surpass it).

The revelation of that staggering billion-dollar price tag for a memorial whose design, in recent years, has grown ever larger and more complex, caused consternation in my city, led Mayor Michael Bloomberg to suggest capping its cost at $500 million, caused the *Times* to editorialize, "The only thing a $1 billion memorial would memorialize is a complete collapse of political and private leadership in Lower Manhattan," and became a nationwide media story. Because the subject is such a touchy one, however, no one went further and explored the obvious: that, even in victimhood, Americans have in recent years exhibited an unseemly imperial hubris. Whether the price tag proves to be half a billion or a billion dollars, one thing can be predicted. The memorial will prove less a reminder of how many Americans happened to be in the wrong place at the wrong time on that September day, or how many—firemen, policemen, bystanders who stayed to aid others—sacrificed their lives, than of the terrible path this country ventured down in the wake of 9/11.

If the latest opinion polls are to be believed, Americans have grown desperately tired of that path and, as a result, the whole construction project at New York's Ground Zero is likely to become emotionally obsolete long before either Reflecting Absence or the Freedom Tower make it onto the scene.

Memorials Built and Unbuilt

Let me offer a few framing comparisons.

1. Sometime in the coming week or two, the number of American soldiers killed in the Iraq and Afghan wars will exceed the 2,752 people who died in or around the World Trade Center on September 11, 2001 (including those on the two hijacked jets that rammed into the towers).

With a combined death toll of 2,739, the war dead have already crept within 13 of that day's casualties in New York. Here's a question then: Who thinks that the United States will ever spend $500 million, no less $1 billion, on a memorial to the ever-growing numbers of war dead from those two wars?

2. Or consider the prospective 9/11 memorial in this context:

The National World War Two Memorial (405,000 American dead): $182 million for all costs.

The Vietnam Memorial (56,000 American dead): $4.2 million for construction.

The Korean War Veterans Memorial (54,000 American dead): $6 million.

The USS *Arizona* Memorial at Pearl Harbor (2,390 American dead, 1,177 from the *Arizona*): $532,000.

The Oklahoma City National Memorial (168 American dead): $29 million.

The 1915 USS *Maine* Mast Memorial at Arlington Cemetery (260 American dead): $56,147.94.

The Holocaust Museum in Washington (approximately 6 million dead): $90 million for construction/$78 million for exhibitions.

The World Trade Center Memorial (2,752 dead): $494 million – $1 billion.

3. Or imagine a listing of global Ground Zeros that might go something like this:

Amount spent on a memorial for the Vietnamese dead of their Vietnam Wars (approximately 3 million): $0.

Amount spent on a memorial to the Afghan dead in the civil war between competing warlords over who would control the capital of Kabul in the mid-1990s (unknown numbers of dead, a city reduced to rubble): $0.

Amount spent on a memorial to the victims of the December 26, 2004, earthquake and tsunami in the Pacific and Indian Oceans (at least 188,000 dead): $0.

Amount spent on a memorial to Iraqis confirmed dead, many with signs of execution and torture marks, just in the month of April 2006 in Baghdad alone (almost 1,100), or the Iraqis confirmed killed countrywide "in war-related violence" from January through April of 2006 (3,525)—and both of these figures are certainly significant undercounts: $0.

The World Trade Center Memorial (2,752 dead): $494 million–$1 billion.

The Victors Are the Victims

The dead, those dear to us, our wives or husbands, brothers, sisters, parents, children, relatives, friends, those who acted for us or suffered in our place, should be remembered. This is an essential human task, almost a duty. What could be more powerful than the urge to hold onto those taken from us, especially when their deaths happen in an unexpected, untimely, and visibly unjust way (only emphasizing the deeper untimeliness and injustice of death itself). But where exactly do we remember the dead? The truth is: we remember them in our hearts, which makes a memorial a living thing only so long as the dead still live within us.

As an experiment, visit one of the old Civil War or World War One memorials that dot so many towns, undoubtedly yours included. You might (or might not) admire the fountain, or the elaborate statue of soldiers, or of a general, or of any other set of icons chosen to stand in for the hallowed dead and their sacrifices. I happen to like the Grand Army Plaza, designed by Augustus Saint-Gaudens and dedicated to the Union Army, that fronts on Central Park in New York City, my home town; but it is, in a sense, no longer a memorial. Decades ago, it turned back into a somewhat gaudy, golden decoration, a statue—as all memorials, in the end, must. The odds are that few today visit it to remember what some specific individual did or how he died. To the extent that we remember, we remember first individually in our hearts in our own lifetimes—and later, collectively, in our history books.

And, of course, for most human beings in most places, especially those who are not the victors in wars, or simply not the victors on this planet, no matter how unfairly or horrifically or bravely or fruitlessly their loved ones might be taken from them, there is only the heart. For those dying in Kabul or Baghdad, Chechnya, Darfur, the Congo, or Uzbekistan today, the emotions released may be no less strong, but in all likelihood there will be no statues, no reflecting pools, no sunken terraces, no walls with carefully etched names.

There has, in American journalism, been an unspoken calculus of the value of a life and a death on this planet in terms of newsworthiness (which is often, of course, a kind of memorializing, a kind of remembering). Crudely put, it would go something like: One kidnapped and murdered blond, white child in California equals 300 Egyptians drowning in a ferry accident, 3,000

Bangladeshis swept away in a monsoon flood, 300,000 Congolese killed in a bloodletting civil war.

Call that news reality in the United States. It's also true, as the recent World War Two memorial on the Washington Mall indicates, that Americans have gained something of a taste for Roman imperial-style memorialization (though, to my mind, that huge construction catches little of the modesty and stoicism of the World War Two vets like my father who did not come home trumpeting what they had done).

Reflecting Absence and the Freedom Tower, however, go well beyond that. Their particular form of excess, of the gargantuan, in which money, elaborateness, and size stand in for memory, is intimately connected not so much to September 11, 2001, as to the days, weeks, even year after that shock.

To grasp this, it's necessary to return to the now almost forgotten moments after 9/11, after the President had frozen in that elementary school classroom in Florida while reading *The Pet Goat*; after a panicky crew of his people had headed Air Force One in the wrong direction, away from Washington; after Donald Rumsfeld and George Bush (according to former counterterrorism tsar Richard Clarke) started rounding up the usual suspects—i.e. Saddam Hussein—on September 11 and 12; after the President insisted, "I don't care what the international lawyers say, we are going to kick some ass"; after he took that bullhorn at Ground Zero on September 14 and—to chants of "USA! USA! USA!"—promised the American public that "the people who knocked these buildings down will hear all of us soon"; after his associates promptly began to formulate the plans, the "intelligence," the lies and tall tales that would take us into Iraq.

It was in that unformed, but quickly forming, moment that, under the shock not just of the murder of almost 3,000 people, but of the apocalyptic images of those two towers crumbling in a near-mushroom-cloud of white dust, that an American imperial culture of revenge and domination was briefly brought to full flower. It was a moment that reached its zenith when the President strutted across the deck of the USS *Abraham Lincoln* on May 1, 2003 and, with that MISSION ACCOMPLISHED banner over his shoulder, declared "major combat operations" ended in Iraq.

The gargantuan Freedom Tower and the gargantuan sunken memorial to the dead of 9/11 are really monuments to that brief year and a half, each project now hardly less embattled in controversy, cost overruns, and ineptitude than the war in Iraq or the post-Katrina rescue-and-reconstruction mission. Each project—as yet unbuilt—is already an increasingly controversial leftover from that extended moment when so many pundits pictured us proudly as a wounded imperial Rome or the inheritor of the glories of the British empire; while the administration, with its attendant neocon cheering squad in tow, all of them dazzled by our "hyperpower" (as other Americans were horrified by the hyperpower of al-Qaeda's imagery of destruction), gained confidence that this was their moment; the one that would take them over the top; the one that would make the United States a Republican Party possession for years, if not generations, the Middle East an American gas station, the world an American military preserve, and a "unitary" commander-in-chief presidency the recipient of the kinds of untrammeled powers previously reserved for kings and emperors. These were, of course, dreams of gargantuan proportions, fantasies of power and planetary rule worthy of a tower *at least* 1,776 feet high, that would obliterate the memory of all other buildings anywhere, and of the largest, most expensive gravestone on Earth, one that would quite literally put the sufferings of all other victims in the shade.

As those two enormous reflecting pools were meant to mirror the soaring "beacon" of the Freedom Tower, so the American people, under the shock of loss, experiencing a sense of violation that can only come to the victors in this world, mirrored the administration's attitude. In a country where New York City had always been Sodom to Los Angeles's Gomorrah, everyone suddenly donned "I ♥ New York" hats or T-shirts and became involved in a series of repetitive rites of mourning that in arenas nationwide, on every television screen, went on not for days or weeks but months on end.

From these ceremonies, a clear and simple message emerged. The United States was, in its suffering, the greatest victim, the greatest survivor, and the greatest dominator the globe had ever seen. Implicitly, the rest of the world's dead were, in the Pentagon's classic phrase, "collateral damage." In those months, in our version of the global drama, we swept up and repossessed all the emotional roles available—with the sole exception of Greatest Evil One. That, then, was the phantasmagoric path to invasion, war, and disaster upon which the Bush administration, with a mighty helping hand from al-Qaeda, pulled back the curtain; that is the drama still being played out today at Ground Zero in New York City.

But those 2,752 dead can no longer stand in—not even in the American mind—for all the dead everywhere, not even for the American dead in Iraq and Afghanistan.

Perhaps it's time not just to cut back radically on that billion-dollar cost, but to do what we should have done—and, if we had had another kind of leadership, might have done—starting on September 12, 2001. Taken a breath and actually thought about ourselves and the world; taken another breath and actually approached the untimely dead—our own as well as those of others around the world—with some genuine humility.

I know that somehow this memorial will be built; that, for some, it will touch the heart. But I also know that someday, maybe even yesterday in a country that now wants to forget much of what occurred as it was railroaded into a never-ending war, whatever is built at Ground Zero will mainly memorialize a specific America that emerged from the rubble of 9/11. That was the America that had stopped being a nation and had become a "homeland," a country that should not have been using the numbers 1776 in any way.

Facing a building so tall, who has any need to approach a declaration of only 1,322 words, so tiny as to be able to fit on a single page, so iconic that just about no one bothers to pay attention to it any more. But perhaps, with that monumental invocation of its "spirit" in mind, it's worth quoting a few of the words those men wrote back in the year 1776 and remembering what the American dead of that time actually stood for. Here, then, from a great anti-imperial document, are some passages about another George's imperial hubris that you are less likely to remember than its classic beginning:

The history of the present King of Great Britain is a history of repeated injuries and usurpations, all having in direct object the establishment of an absolute Tyranny over these States. . . . He has erected a multitude of New Offices, and sent hither swarms of Officers to harass our people and eat out their substance. He has kept among us, in times of peace, Standing Armies without the Consent of our legislatures. He has affected to render the Military independent of and superior to the Civil Power. . . . He has combined with others to subject us to a jurisdiction foreign to our constitution, and unacknowledged by our laws; giving his Assent to their Acts of pretended Legislation. . . . For depriving us in many cases, of the benefit of Trial by Jury:

For transporting us beyond Seas to be tried for pretended offences . . . For suspending our own Legislatures, and declaring themselves invested with power to legislate for us in all cases whatsoever.

Someday, those reflecting pools and that tower will mirror so much of the rise as well as the fall of the Bush administration—not least of all its heck-of-a-job-Brownie incompetence and its inability to fulfill civil promises of any sort. Almost five years past the catastrophe of 9/11, after all the grandiose promises and the soaring costs, after all that "enormity," there is nothing 1,776 feet in the air, nor, as yet, any hint of a gravestone over the dead of the tragedy of that day.

II

IMPERIAL PLANET

August 2004

3

THE EMPIRE THAT FELL AS IT ROSE

Jonathan Schell and Tom Engelhardt

TE: Had anyone in Washington bothered to read Jonathan Schell's prophetic—or perhaps I should just say, historically on the mark—book *The Unconquerable World*, Iraq could not have happened and all the dreams of the neocons, hatched in the claustrophobic confines of right-wing think tanks and the corridors of power in Washington, would have evaporated into thin air. The book was a reconsideration of several centuries of the imperial "war system," as it built up through a series of extreme moments of violence in the twentieth century to a kind of global paralysis that nonetheless left the Earth and all its inhabitants in deadly peril. At the same time, it also laid out unerringly the successful resistance to that system, both by force of arms (in the form of national liberation movements) and by aggressively nonviolent means. In the process, *The Unconquerable World* uncovered a series of nonviolent pathways in history that seemed to lead into a possible future and so might someday beckon us further.

Because I edited the book, I had an advantage. I knew the moment we took Baghdad and the looting began that some kind of resistance movement (or movements) would drive our then triumphant president to the polls in November 2004, and I wrote that immediately.

In the course of our work together, we often discussed not just the imperial systems he was writing about, but the nature of the one we were living in. Here's our most recent exchange.

Dear Tom,

You'll remember that just before the September 11 attacks, when I was writing and you were editing my book *The Unconquerable World*, you were much readier than I to call American policies "imperial" and the United States an "empire." I hesitated; I hung back. After all, one theme of the book was that the age of empires was over. The newly expired twentieth century, I pointed out, was one huge boneyard of empires: the British, the French, the Portuguese, the Dutch, the Ottomans, the Germans, the Japanese, the Russians. Imperial rulers had repeatedly been amazed to find themselves over-matched by the localized, intense, and finally unquenchable forces of national resistance movements. More startling still, the success of those movements invariably depended mainly on political, not military strength. In some cases, such as Gandhi's independence movement against the British in India, and the Polish rebellion against the Soviet empire, the struggles succeeded without using violence at all.

The twentieth-century anti-imperial movement triumphed almost everywhere. No political creed, feudal or modern, was able to defeat it. Yet almost any political creed proved adequate for winning independence. Liberal democracy (the United States in 1776, Eastern Europe in the 1980s and 1990s), communism (China, Vietnam, Cambodia), racism (the Boers of South Africa), militarism (many South American states), theocracy (Iran in 1979 and Afghanistan in the 1980s), even monarchy (Germany in the first half of the nineteenth century) had all proved suitable for achieving self-determination. In these circumstances, it seemed almost unimaginable that the United States could really be aiming at that hoary old nightmare of the ages, the always-feared but never-realized ambition to win universal empire, otherwise known as "world domination" (as people used to say of the Soviet Union's goals in the Cold War years). In any case, didn't "imperialism" mean rule over other countries—viceroys issuing orders from grandiose palaces, occupying armies, colonial administrations—which were methods mostly avoided by the United States?

These differences regarding empire were quickly settled in your favor after September 11. I gave up my reservations. Like the empires of old, the United States set out to rule foreign lands—directly, as in the case of Iraq (I won't even pause to rebut the risible claim that that country was recently handed "sovereignty") or indirectly, as in Afghanistan. I joined you in speaking of American empire. We were hardly alone. In fact, if there was one thing that everyone suddenly seemed to agree on, it was that the US was an empire, and a global one at that. There were the right-wingers, like *New York Times* columnist David Brooks, celebrant of America's yuppie class, who called the United States the first "suburban empire," and William Kristol, editor of the *Weekly Standard*, who wanted the US to step up to "national greatness" and "benign" empire. (And which empire has not seen itself as benign?) There were the new realists, like the journalist Robert Kaplan, admirer of Henry Kissinger, who championed American "supremacy by stealth," and supplied US policy makers with "Ten Rules for Managing the World." There were the liberal imperialists—or, as I think of them, the romantic militarists—like Thomas Friedman of the *New York Times*, who wanted to bring democracy to the Middle East and elsewhere at the point of a gun. And then there was the left, which had long excoriated American imperialism and still did. Once, the left had stood alone in calling the US imperial and was reviled for defaming the nation. Now it turned out to have been the herald of a new consensus. Yesterday's left-wing abuse became today's mainstream praise.

And surely there was no word in the extant vocabulary but "imperial" for the post-September 11 policies of the Bush administration—for its unilateralism, its doctrines of preemptive war and regime change, its frankly avowed ambition to achieve global hegemony (although the administration itself continued to disavow the imperial label).

Yet the consensus was short-lived. As the debacle in Iraq unfolded, the note of the imperial trumpet grew uncertain. I also began to wonder again about my embrace of the language of empire. My old reservations started cropping up in new forms. For one thing, if, as so many mainstream commentators were saying, the United States was self-evidently an empire, when did it become one? Was it with the Louisiana Purchase in 1803, the Mexican-American war of the 1840s, the allied victory in World War Two, the collapse of the

Soviet Union in 1991 that left only the "sole superpower" standing? Or was it perhaps at some undetermined moment in the giddy decade that followed? Did any of the new mainstream imperial apologists notice the development, or alert anyone else to what was happening? Was I looking the other way when the transformation was announced? I am unaware that any candidate ran on an imperial program, or that any voters voted for one. Or did empire simply sneak up on the country—a stealth empire indeed—as in the case of the British empire, once famously said to have been acquired in a fit of absence of mind? Can a people rule the world without noticing it?

Such an account of American history involves a spectacular denial of agency—and of democratic responsibility—to voters and politicians alike. Moreover, an assumption that the imperial deed is already done deprives the public of decision-making power for the future. Why debate a decision already taken? American empire then acquires the tremendous weight of accomplished fact, and the only realistic question becomes not whether to run the world, but how to do so. Before the Iraq invasion, Michael Ignatieff of Harvard wrote that the United States was an empire "in denial." He wanted the United States to wake up and face its imperial responsibilities: "enforcing such order as there is in the world and doing so in the American interest," "laying down the rules America wants," "carrying out imperial functions in places America has inherited from the failed empires of the 20th century—Ottoman, British and Soviet." For "in the 21st century, America rules alone, struggling to manage the insurgent zones—Palestine and the northwest frontier of Pakistan, to name but two—that have proved to be the nemeses of empires past." This was reluctant, sorrowful imperialism. The British historian Niall Ferguson took the argument a step further, writing an entire book, *Colossus*, praising the fallen British empire and inviting the United States to step into its shoes.

These ideas seem to me to embody a grand misreading of events. Ignatieff and Ferguson appear to look at twentieth-century history as a contest among empires that was won by the United States, opening the way for it to run the world. As I see it, however, the United States is likely to prove the last of the long series of imperial tenpins that have been knocked down not by other empires but by local independence struggles. Once it has become clear to everyone that the American imperial bid has failed, and with it the entire age-old imperial enterprise, we can return to the mountainous real work of our time, which is to put together what we have never had but now must create—an anti-imperial, democratic way of organizing the world.

We're now almost three years into the out-of-the-closet American imperial timetable, and I doubt even the most eager imperialists can argue that things are going well. North Korea, a member of the President's "Axis of Evil" has reportedly become a nuclear power, in defiance of the explicit threats made by the global hegemon. Iran, another Axis member, is heading down the same path. The long-awaited recovery of the American economy, like the empire it is supposed to support, is stalling. American forces are stretched to the breaking point around the world. World opinion on all continents has turned against the United States. But the centerpiece of the imperial endeavor is of course the war in Iraq, as Ignatieff recognized in his pre-war essay, in which he wrote that Iraq was "a defining moment in America's long debate with itself about whether its overseas role as an empire threatens or strengthens its existence as a republic."

The war, launched in pursuit of a mirage (those missing weapons of mass destruction), is an unqualified disaster. But the most remarkable "intelligence failure" in Iraq was not to see weapons of mass destruction where there were none; it was to blind ourselves to the struggle of national resistance that history told us would have to follow American invasion and occupation. It was perfectly reasonable (though mistaken) to think that Saddam Hussein had revived his WMD programs. It was delusional to imagine that the people of a postcolonial country would happily accept a new occupation. No consultation with British or French or Israeli intelligence agencies was needed to grasp this lesson. It was writ large in the annals of twentieth-century history, including the voluminous records of the US defeat in Vietnam. The lessons of Vietnam remain important not because the Vietnamese nation resembles the Iraqi nation but because Vietnam was America's very own, protracted, anguished experience of the almost universal story of imperial defeat at the hands of local peoples determined to run their own countries.

Like every other chapter in the long history of the fight against empire, the war in Iraq has had its peculiar features. When the United States arrived in Baghdad, there was no preexisting popular resistance movement (or movements) in place—Saddam Hussein had seen to that— as there had been when the American military arrived in force in Vietnam. Neither was there any apparatus of an imperial puppet government at hand like Ngo Dinh Diem's in Vietnam. Instead, there was a double political vacuum. The consequence was anarchy, immediately visible in the looting of the country in the days following the conquest. Now, that vacuum is being filled on one side. Movements of national resistance have arisen in both the Sunni north and the Shia south. (The Kurdish population is friendly to the United States but not to the Iraq that the United States wants it to join.) On the American side, a former Baathist official and CIA asset, Iyad Allawi, does the bidding of the United States without benefit of popular support. The contest has assumed a form distressingly familiar from other anti-imperial movements. The local resistors are weak militarily but strong politically. The imperial masters are powerful militarily but nearly helpless politically. History teaches that in these contests it is political power that prevails. The shameful and piteous slaughter throughout southern Iraq of Iraqi Shias, the people the United States supposedly went to war to save, has the look of one of those victorious battles that loses the war.

But the full truth may be that the war in Iraq was lost before it was launched. The preemptive war was pre-lost. The problem was not the Bush administration's incompetence, great as that has been, but the incurable incapacity of any foreign conqueror to win local hearts and minds, on which everything, in the last analysis, depends.

Don't the recent fortunes of the "empire" as a whole reveal a similar pattern of political weakness underlying military strength? "Rise and fall"—these are terms inseparably connected to the story of empires, and the question at any given moment has ordinarily been where an empire is on this curve. But the place on the rise-

and-fall trajectory of today's American empire is not easy to calibrate. It seems to be rising and falling at the same time. It garrisons the globe, but accomplishes little. The emperor in Washington thunders his instructions to the five continents but is often disregarded. America's military power is "super," but its use seems to hurt the user. Perhaps the American empire was pre-fallen. It seems not so much to rise or fall as, all at the same time, to expand and contract, to thunder and retreat.

We should perhaps not be surprised by this merging of sequence. The handwriting announcing failure was not on the proverbial wall in the form of a prediction whose fulfillment had to be awaited, it was inscribed in every history book of the last hundred years. The verdict was delivered before the crime was committed.

I know the question is many-layered. Critics were calling economic globalization imperialism long before George Bush ever attempted regime change in Iraq, and they still have substantial reasons for doing so. But surely it would be as much a mistake to assume the triumph of an American imperial system while the issue is still in the balance as it was for the President to proclaim "mission accomplished" on the USS *Abraham Lincoln* shortly after American troops had taken Baghdad.

The new imperialists told us that the United States could run the world if only it snapped out of denial and got on with the job. The results are before our eyes. Is the United States then a globe-straddling empire? Not just yet—and maybe never.

Love, Jonathan

Dear Jonathan,

As you know, I'm less a theorist of empire than an anti-imperialist by gut and intuition. But when you have a country whose military, spying, and covert action budgets combined easily top the half-trillion-dollar mark; when both major political parties at their conventions feel the need to immerse themselves to their eyeballs in the blood-drenched flag and in glorious memories of past wars; when our country seems incapable of not fighting a war or launching a military "intervention" somewhere on our planet every few years; when the sun never sets on our 700-plus military bases and our intellectuals, incapable of explaining the existence of those bases in such numbers, fall silent on the subject; when our elected Congress, with the supposed power of the purse, finds itself incapable of saying no, even to the most outlandish budgetary requests of our unelected military; when our President decides to reorganize our basing structure and redeploy tens of thousands of troops globally over the coming decade so that we will be even better prepared to intervene in what is now called the "arc of instability," which more or less overlaps with the major oil-lands of our planet, and his opponent responds by launching a fierce attack on him before a military audience for removing some of our troops from the Korean peninsula after half a century; when, no matter which presidential candidate wins the November election, the Pentagon and our intelligence services are guaranteed to grow still larger and be even more lavishly funded; when our globe—the whole shebang—is divided into five commands (Pacom, Centcom, Southcom, Eurcom, and the newest Northcom, for North America itself), and the generals who head these commands act like global viceroys to whom our civilian diplomats must bow, while they themselves report only to the Secretary of Defense and the President; when our best-funded, blue-sky environmental research takes place in the Defense Advanced Research Projects Agency and involves hitching nature to weapons development; when our military planners consider our militarization of space a singular priority for the future control of the planet; when we already have superweapons in the planning stage for the half-century mark, but no significant planning in the works for dealing with global warming or energy dependence next year; when . . . but I know that you could add to this list as easily as I can . . . then, it seems to me, based on the if-it-quacks-and-waddles-it's-a-duck school of political philosophy, you're talking about an imperial presence—a military empire—of a very advanced and unbalanced sort, though I do agree with you that it is a distinctly unfinished, even ungainly, creature and one that, from the very imbalance of its overwhelming (and o'erweening) military muscle in relation to its political and economic muscle, shows signs both of overdevelopment and of collapse; or put another way, our empire, at least at the moment, quacks and waddles, but neither in unison, nor particularly well.

You know, Jonathan, it's important for us to remember that there was once quite another tradition in America. Whatever our country was in the 1950s, you and I, like so many of our peers, like so many American kids before us, were raised to believe that empire was a dreadful, un-American thing, and inconceivable for us. We were, of course, already garrisoning the globe, but there was that other hideous empire, the Soviet one, to point to. We absorbed, in any case, a powerful predisposition against the imperial, one that I can still feel in your letter (and in myself), one that was only fully cast off in this country in the era of the younger Bush, thanks to what the imperial Chinese once called a "rectification of names." But I still believe (as I know you do) that that belief was a valuable one, whatever the realities. I still believe that there are other, better, saner ways than garrisoning the globe; that it *is* un-American (un-my-America, anyway) to be doing what we're doing.

Of course, these days the minute you begin to write such things, you're promptly dubbed an "isolationist," though I'm distinctly an internationalist who doesn't believe that the leaders of this Earth should be left alone to commit crimes against their own or other peoples, or that any people should be left alone and powerless to face the disasters of our world. I just also know, again in my guts, that today nothing in our world can be made anything but worse by sticking to the imperial path.

What remains to be seen, as you say, is where exactly we are on the rising-and-falling "curve" of empire, or have we indeed managed to turn it into a single synchronous event, as you suggest? The Bush administration, with its torn-up international treaties, its strident insistence on the right to preventive war and US global domination, its urge to institutionalize an offshore gulag (and the legal thinking that must accompany it), and of course its occupation of Iraq, has followed an extreme and thoroughly militarized version of an American imperial dream. As Chalmers Johnson has, to my mind, effectively explained in his book *The Sorrows of Empire*, from 1945 on, the United States pursued an imperial policy predicated on the military base rather than the colony. We would set up our bases—little Americas—in other countries, get extraterritorial rights for our troops, and with our economic power at our backs and close ties with local elites, go about our global business. Iraq, it seems to me, represents a striking deviation from this path. It is the closest thing in our lifetimes to a straightforward colonial landgrab (whatever pretty words the neocons may have woven around it). And it is clearly failing, hence all the military and intelligence officials up in arms and angry indeed. A Kerry administration would undoubtedly try to return us to our older form of imperial creep. The question is: could it do so? Or rather, has the world so changed in the brief but wrenching interim that imperial policy in any form will prove bankrupt?

Part of our problem, I suspect, lies in conceiving of an empireless world; or put another way, one legacy of all those empires you wrote about, even though each of them fell before the unconquerable world, the people's world, that you speak of so eloquently, is that our only script for hundreds of years was imperially dominated. That was no less true of the rebels and revolutionaries who put all their energies into opposing empire (and so, as with all things we oppose fiercely enough long enough, became in one way or another imperially fused). The United States, having in our own moment reached the pinnacle dreamed of by all past empire builders, a global imperium, but in a thoroughly half-assed and half-baked fashion (as you point out), seems to be proving that the very idea of empire is indeed bankrupt (and by the time we're done, we may be quite literally bankrupt too). Trying to deal with this situation, I think we're hobbled by having no other script. We don't quite know what to do without the idea of empire. We simply can't imagine a functional world that lacks the imperial element, or if you prefer (as we Americans liked to say before we got so briefly but thoroughly into the imperial spirit), a global policeman. A world without its sheriff still seems a fearsome prospect to us. You might say—with a bow to the original *Manchurian Candidate* rather than its bankrupt modern cousin—that we've been imperially brainwashed in certain ways. Whether we hate the global policeman or love him, all we can imagine is a kind of chaos without him, not the possibility of new kinds of order as yet unimagined (and perhaps still unimaginable), as yet, as you've said to me many times, "to be invented."

So we sit on a powder-keg planet inside a great military machine that garrisons the globe from Thule, Greenland to northern Australia, from Qatar on the Arabian Peninsula to Okinawa in Japan, shivering with fear and ready, by default, to opt for the history of war and empire. Let me—since what do I have to draw on except my own experience?—for my final comments mention my work as an editor with another author, Adam Hochschild. His latest book, *Bury the Chains*, is a history of the British anti-slavery movement. What makes it so inspiring is that slavery was no less embedded in the eighteenth-century world where he begins than empire has been over the last century; the world was no less unimaginable without it, and those madmen and kooks—mostly Quakers—who first opposed it in England really did have to imagine the then nearly unimaginable. Yet within perhaps three-quarters of a century, with the help of endless, tireless organizing and, of course, a series of vast, bloody slave revolts in the Caribbean colonies of England and France, slavery had become the almost unimaginable thing.

The question, for us, is whether we have those seventy-five years, but perhaps that's a topic to be saved for another exchange.

Love, Tom

March 2005

4

NO LONGER THE "LONE" SUPERPOWER

Chalmers Johnson

I recall forty years ago, when I was a new professor working in the field of Chinese and Japanese international relations, that Edwin O. Reischauer once commented, "The great payoff from our victory of 1945 was a permanently disarmed Japan." Born in Japan and a Japanese historian at Harvard, Reischauer served as American ambassador to Tokyo in the Kennedy and Johnson administrations. Strange to say, since the end of the Cold War in 1991 and particularly under the administration of George W. Bush, the United States has been doing everything in its power to encourage and even accelerate Japanese rearmament.

Such a development promotes hostility between China and Japan, the two superpowers of East Asia, sabotages possible peaceful solutions in those two problem areas, Taiwan and North Korea, left over from the Chinese and Korean civil wars, and lays the foundation for a possible future Sino-American conflict that the United States would almost surely lose. It is unclear whether the ideologues and war lovers of Washington understand what they are unleashing—a possible confrontation between the world's fastest-growing industrial economy, China, and the world's second-most productive, albeit declining, economy, Japan: a confrontation that the United States would have caused and in which it might well be consumed.

Let me make clear that in East Asia we are not talking about a little regime-change war of the sort that Bush and Cheney advocate. After all, the most salient characteristic of international relations during the twentieth century was the inability of the rich, established powers—Great Britain and the United States—to adjust peacefully to the emergence of new centers of power in Germany, Japan, and Russia. The result was two exceedingly bloody world wars, a 45-year-long cold war between Russia and the "West," and innumerable wars of national liberation (such as the quarter-century-long one in Vietnam) against the arrogance and racism of European, American, and Japanese imperialism and colonialism.

The major question for the twenty-first century is whether this fateful inability to adjust to changes in the global power structure can be overcome. Thus far the signs are negative. Can the United States and Japan, today's versions of rich, established powers, adjust to the reemergence of China— the world's oldest continuously extant civilization—this time as a modern superpower? Or is China's ascendancy to be marked by yet another world war, when the pretensions of European civilization in its US and Japanese projections are finally put to rest? That is what is at stake.

Alice-in-Wonderland Policies and the Mother of All Financial Crises

China, Japan, and the United States are the three most productive economies on Earth, but China is the fastest growing (at an average rate of 9.5 percent per year for over two decades), whereas both the US and Japan are saddled with huge and mounting debts and, in the case of Japan, stagnant growth rates. China is today the world's sixth-largest economy (the US and Japan being first and second) and the US's third-largest trading partner after Canada and Mexico. According to CIA statisticians in their *Factbook 2003*, China is actually already the second-largest economy on Earth measured on a purchasing power parity basis—that is, in terms of what China actually produces rather than prices and exchange rates. The CIA calculates the US's gross domestic product (GDP)—the total value of all goods and services produced within a country—for 2003 as $10.4 trillion and China's as $5.7 trillion. This gives China's 1.3 billion people a per capita GDP of $4,385.

Between 1992 and 2003, Japan was China's largest trading partner, but in 2004 Japan fell to third place, behind the European Union (EU) and the United States. China's trade volume for 2004 was $1.2 trillion, third in the world after the US and Germany, and well ahead of Japan's $1.07 trillion. China's trade with the US grew some 34 percent in 2004 and has turned Los Angeles, Long Beach, and Oakland into the three busiest seaports in America.

The truly significant trade development of 2004 was the EU's emergence as China's biggest economic partner, suggesting the possibility of a Sino-European cooperative bloc confronting a less vital Japanese–American one. As Britain's *Financial Times* observed, "Three years after its entry into the World Trade Organization [in 2001], China's influence in global commerce is no longer merely significant. It is crucial." For example, most Dell computers sold in the US are made in China, as are the DVD players of Japan's Funai Electric Company. Funai annually exports some 10 million DVD players and television sets from China to the United States, where they are sold primarily in Wal-Mart stores. China's trade with Europe in 2004 was worth $177.2 billion, with the United States $169.6 billion, and with Japan $167.8 billion.

China's growing economic weight in the world is widely recognized and applauded, but it is China's growth rates and their effect on the future global balance of power that the US and Japan, rightly or wrongly, fear. The CIA's National Intelligence Council forecasts that China's GDP will equal Britain's in 2005, Germany's in 2009, Japan's in 2017, and the US's in 2042. But Shahid Javed Burki, former vice president of the World Bank's China Department and a former finance minister of Pakistan, predicts that by 2025 China will probably have a GDP of $25 trillion in terms of purchasing power parity and will have become the world's largest economy *followed* by the United States at $20 trillion and India at about $13 trillion—and Burki's analysis is based on a conservative prediction of a 6 percent Chinese growth rate sustained over the next two decades. He foresees Japan's inevitable decline because its population will begin to shrink drastically after about 2010. Japan's Ministry of Internal Affairs reports that the number of men in Japan already declined by 0.01 percent in 2004; and some demographers, it notes, anticipate that by the end of the century the country's population could shrink by nearly two-thirds, from 127.7 million today to 45 million, the same population it had in 1910.

By contrast, China's population is likely to stabilize at approximately 1.4 billion people and is heavily weighted toward males. (According to Howard French of the *New York Times*, in one large southern city the government-imposed one-child-per-family policy and the availability of sonograms have resulted in a ratio of 129 boys born for every 100 girls, and 147 boys for every 100 girls for couples seeking second or third children. The 2000 census for the country as a whole put the reported sex ratio at birth at about 117 boys to 100 girls.) Chinese domestic economic growth is expected to continue for decades, reflecting the pent-up demand of its huge population, relatively low levels of personal debt, and a dynamic underground economy not recorded in official statistics. Most important, China's external debt is relatively small and easily covered by its reserves; whereas both the US and Japan are approximately $7 trillion in the red, which is worse for Japan with less than half the US population and economic clout.

Ironically, part of Japan's debt is a product of its efforts to help prop up America's global imperial stance. For example, in the period since the end of the Cold War, Japan has subsidized America's military bases in Japan to the staggering tune of approximately $70 billion. Refusing to pay for its profligate consumption patterns and military expenditures through taxes on its own citizens, the United States is financing these outlays by going into debt to Japan, China, Taiwan, South Korea, Hong Kong, and India. This situation has become increasingly unstable as the US requires capital imports of at least $2 billion *per day* to pay for its governmental expenditures. Any decision by East Asian central banks to move significant parts of their foreign exchange reserves out of the dollar and into the euro or other currencies in order to protect themselves from dollar depreciation would produce the mother of all financial crises.

Japan still possesses the world's largest foreign exchange reserves, which at the end of January 2005 stood at around $841 billion. But China sits on a $609.9 billion pile of dollars (as of the end of 2004), earned from its trade surpluses with the US. Meanwhile, the American government and Japanese followers of George W. Bush insult China in every way they can, particularly over the status of China's breakaway province, the island of Taiwan. The distinguished economic analyst William Greider recently noted, "Any profligate debtor who insults his banker is unwise, to put it mildly. . . . American leadership has . . . become increasingly delusional—I mean that literally—and blind to the adverse balance of power accumulating against it."

The Bush administration is unwisely threatening China by urging Japan to rearm and by promising Taiwan that, should China use force to prevent a Taiwanese declaration of independence, the US will go to war on its behalf. It is hard to imagine more shortsighted, irresponsible policies, but in light of the Bush administration's Alice-in-Wonderland war in Iraq, the acute anti-Americanism it has generated globally, and the politicization of America's intelligence services, it seems possible that the US and Japan might actually precipitate a war with China over Taiwan.

Japan Rearms

Since the end of World War Two, and particularly since gaining its independence in 1952, Japan has subscribed to a pacifist foreign policy. It has resolutely refused to maintain offensive military forces or to become part of America's global military system. Japan did not, for example, participate in the 1991 war against Iraq, nor has it joined collective security agreements in which it would have to match the military contributions of its partners. Since the signing in 1952 of the Japan–United States Security Treaty, the country has officially been defended from so-called external threats by US forces located on some ninety-one bases on the Japanese mainland and the island of Okinawa. The US Seventh Fleet even has its home port at the old Japanese naval base of Yokosuka. Japan not only subsidizes these bases but subscribes to the public fiction that the American forces are present only for its defense. In fact, Japan has no control over how and where the US employs its land, sea, and air forces based on Japanese territory, and the Japanese and American governments have until quite recently finessed the issue simply by never discussing it.

Since the end of the Cold War in 1991, the United States has repeatedly pressured Japan to revise article nine of its constitution (renouncing the use of force except as a matter of self-defense) and become what American officials call a "normal nation." For example, on August 13, 2004, Secretary of State Colin Powell stated baldly in Tokyo that if Japan ever hoped to become a permanent member of the UN Security Council it would first have to get rid of its pacifist constitution. Japan's claim to a Security Council seat is based on the fact that, although its share of global GDP is only 14 percent, it pays 20 percent of the total UN budget. Powell's remark was blatant interference in Japan's internal affairs, but it merely echoed many messages delivered by former Deputy Secretary of State Richard Armitage, the leader of a reactionary clique in Washington that has worked for years to remilitarize Japan and so enlarge a major new market for American arms. Its members include Torkel Patterson, Robin Sakoda, David Asher, and James Kelly at State; Michael Green on the National Security Council's staff;

and numerous uniformed military officers at the Pentagon and at the headquarters of the Pacific Command at Pearl Harbor, Hawaii.

America's intention is to turn Japan into what Washington neoconservatives like to call the "Britain of the Far East"—and then use it as a proxy in checkmating North Korea and balancing China. On October 11, 2000, Michael Green, then a member of Armitage Associates—the former deputy secretary of state's consulting and lobbying organization—wrote, "We see the special relationship between the United States and Great Britain as a model for the [US–Japan] alliance." Japan has so far not resisted this American pressure since it complements a renewed nationalism among Japanese voters and a fear that a burgeoning capitalist China threatens Japan's established position as the leading economic power in East Asia. Japanese officials also claim that the country feels threatened by North Korea's developing nuclear and missile programs, although they know that the North Korean standoff could be resolved virtually overnight—if the Bush administration would cease trying to overthrow the Pyongyang regime and instead deliver on American trade promises (in return for North Korea's agreement to give up its nuclear weapons program). Instead, on February 25, 2005, the State Department announced that "the US will refuse North Korean leader Kim Jong-il's demand for a guarantee of 'no hostile intent' to get Pyongyang back into negotiations over its nuclear weapons programs." And on March 7, Bush nominated John Bolton to be American ambassador to the United Nations even though North Korea has refused to negotiate with him because of his insulting remarks about the country.

Japan's remilitarization worries a segment of the Japanese public and is opposed throughout East Asia by all the nations Japan victimized during World War Two, including China, both Koreas, and even Australia. As a result, the Japanese government has launched a stealth program of incremental rearmament. Since 1992, it has enacted twenty-one major pieces of security-related legislation, nine in 2004 alone. These began with the International Peace Cooperation Law of 1992, which for the first time authorized Japan to send troops to participate in UN peacekeeping operations.

Remilitarization has since taken many forms, including expanding military budgets, legitimizing and legalizing the sending of military forces abroad, a commitment to join the US missile defense "Star Wars" program—something the Canadians refused to do in February 2005—and a growing acceptance of military solutions to international problems. This gradual process was greatly accelerated in 2001 by the simultaneous coming to power of President George Bush and Prime Minister Junichiro Koizumi. Koizumi made his first visit to the United States in July of that year and, in May 2003 he received the ultimate imprimatur, an invitation to Bush's "ranch" in Crawford, Texas. Shortly thereafter, Koizumi agreed to send a contingent of 550 troops to Iraq for a year, extended their stay for another year in 2004, and on October 14, 2004, personally endorsed George Bush's reelection.

A New Nuclear Giant in the Making?

Koizumi has appointed to his various cabinets hard-line anti-Chinese, pro-Taiwanese politicians. Phil Deans, director of the Contemporary China Institute in the School of Oriental and African Studies, University of London, observes, "There has been a remarkable growth of pro-Taiwan sentiment in Japan. There is not one pro-China figure in the Koizumi Cabinet." Members of the latest Koizumi Cabinet include the Defense Agency chief Yoshinori Ono, and the Foreign Minister Nobutaka Machimura, both ardent militarists; while Foreign Minister Machimura is a member of the right-wing faction of former Prime Minister Yoshiro Mori, which supports an independent Taiwan and maintains extensive covert ties with Taiwanese leaders and businessmen.

Taiwan, it should be remembered, was a Japanese colony from 1895 to 1945. Unlike the harsh Japanese military rule over Korea from 1910 to 1945, it experienced relatively benign governance by a civilian Japanese administration. The island, while bombed by the Allies, was not a battleground during World War Two, although it was harshly occupied by the Chinese Nationalists (Chiang Kai-shek's Guomindang) immediately after the war. Today, as a result, many Taiwanese speak Japanese and have a favorable view of Japan. Taiwan is virtually the only place in East Asia where Japanese are fully welcomed and liked.

Bush and Koizumi have developed elaborate plans for military cooperation between their two countries. Crucial to such plans is the scrapping of the Japanese Constitution of 1947. If nothing gets in the way, Koizumi's ruling Liberal Democratic Party (LDP) intends to introduce a new constitution on the occasion of the party's fiftieth anniversary in November 2005. This has been deemed appropriate because the LDP's founding charter of 1955 set as a basic party goal the "establishment of Japan's own Constitution"—a reference to the fact that General Douglas MacArthur's post-World War Two occupation headquarters actually drafted the current constitution. The original LDP policy statement also called for "the eventual removal of US troops from Japanese territory," which may be one of the hidden purposes behind Japan's urge to rearm.

A major goal of the Americans is to gain Japan's active participation in their massively expensive missile defense program. The Bush administration is seeking, among other things, an end to Japan's ban on the export of military technology, since it wants Japanese engineers to help solve some of the technical problems of its so far failing Star Wars system. The United States has also been actively negotiating with Japan to relocate the Army's First Corps from Fort Lewis, Washington, to Camp Zama, southwest of Tokyo in the densely populated prefecture of Kanagawa, whose capital is Yokohama. These US forces in Japan would then be placed under the command of a four-star general, who would be on a par with regional commanders like Centcom commander John Abizaid, who lords it over Iraq and South Asia. The new command would be in charge of all Army "force projection" operations beyond East Asia and would inevitably implicate Japan in the daily military operations of the American empire. Garrisoning even a small headquarters, much less the whole First Corps made up of an estimated 40,000 soldiers, in a sophisticated and centrally located prefecture like Kanagawa is also guaranteed to generate intense public opposition as well as rapes, fights, car accidents and other incidents similar to the ones that occur daily in Okinawa.

Meanwhile, Japan intends to upgrade its Defense Agency (*Boeicho*) into a ministry and possibly develop its own nuclear weapons capability. Goading the Japanese government to assert itself militarily may well cause the country to go nuclear in order to "deter" China and North Korea, while freeing Japan from its dependency on the American "nuclear umbrella." The military analyst Richard Tanter notes that Japan already has "the undoubted capacity to satisfy all three core requirements for a usable nuclear weapon: a military nuclear device, a sufficiently accurate targeting system, and at least one adequate delivery system." Japan's combination of fully functioning fission and breeder reactors plus nuclear fuel reprocessing facilities gives it the ability to build advanced thermonuclear weapons; its H-II and H-IIA rockets, in-flight refueling capacity for fighter bombers, and military-grade surveillance satellites assure that it could deliver its weapons accurately to regional targets. What it currently lacks are the platforms (such as submarines) for a secure retaliatory force in order to dissuade a nuclear adversary from launching a preemptive first strike.

The Taiwanese Knot

Japan may talk a lot about the dangers of North Korea, but the real objective of its rearmament is China. This has become clear from the ways in which Japan has recently injected itself into the single most delicate and dangerous issue of East Asian international relations—the problem of Taiwan. Japan invaded China in 1931 and was its wartime tormentor thereafter as well as Taiwan's colonial overlord. Even then, however, Taiwan was viewed as a part of China, as the United States has long recognized. What remains to be resolved are the terms and timing of Taiwan's reintegration with the Chinese mainland. This process was deeply complicated by the fact that in 1987 Chiang Kai-shek's Nationalists, who had retreated to Taiwan in 1949 at the end of the Chinese civil war (and were protected there by the American Seventh Fleet ever after), finally ended martial law on the island. Taiwan has since matured into a vibrant democracy and the Taiwanese are now starting to display their own mixed opinions about their future.

In 2000, the Taiwanese people ended a long monopoly of power by the Nationalists and gave the Democratic Progressive Party, headed by President Chen Shui-bian, an electoral victory. A native Taiwanese (as distinct from the large contingent of mainlanders who came to Taiwan in the baggage train of Chiang's defeated armies), Chen stands for an independent Taiwan, as does his party. By contrast, the Nationalists, together with a powerful mainlander splinter party, the People First Party headed by James Soong (Song Chuyu), hope to see an eventual peaceful unification of Taiwan with China. On March 7, 2005, the Bush administration complicated these delicate relations by nominating John Bolton to be the American ambassador to the United Nations. He is an avowed advocate of Taiwanese independence and was once a paid consultant to the Taiwanese government.

In May 2004, in a very close and contested election, Chen Shui-bian was reelected, and on May 20, the notorious right-wing Japanese politician Shintaro Ishihara attended his inauguration in Taipei. (Ishihara believes that

Japan's 1937 Rape of Nanking was "a lie made up by the Chinese.") Though Chen won with only 50.1 percent of the vote, this was still a sizeable increase over his 33.9 percent in 2000, when the opposition was divided. The Taiwan Ministry of Foreign Affairs immediately appointed Koh Se-kai as its informal ambassador to Japan. Koh has lived in Japan for some thirty-three years and maintains extensive ties to senior political and academic figures there. China responded that it would "completely annihilate" any moves toward Taiwanese independence—even if it meant scuttling the 2008 Beijing Olympics and good relations with the United States.

Contrary to the machinations of American neocons and Japanese rightists, however, the Taiwanese people have revealed themselves to be open to negotiating with China over the timing and terms of reintegration. On August 23, 2004, the Legislative Yuan (Taiwan's parliament) enacted changes in its voting rules to prevent Chen from amending the constitution to favor independence, as he had promised to do in his reelection campaign. This action drastically lowered the risk of conflict with China. Probably influencing the Legislative Yuan was the warning issued on August 22 by Singapore's new prime minister, Lee Hsien-loong: "If Taiwan goes for independence, Singapore will not recognize it. In fact, no Asian country will recognize it. China will fight. Win or lose, Taiwan will be devastated."

The next important development was parliamentary elections on December 11, 2004. President Chen called his campaign a referendum on his pro-independence policy and asked for a mandate to carry out his reforms. Instead he lost decisively. The opposition Nationalists and the People First Party won 114 seats in the 225-seat parliament, while Chen's DPP and its allies took only 101. (Ten seats went to independents.) The Nationalist leader, Lien Chan, whose party won seventy-nine seats to the DPP's eighty-nine, said, "Today we saw extremely clearly that all the people want stability in this country."

Chen's failure to capture control of parliament also meant that a proposed purchase of $19.6 billion worth of arms from the United States was doomed. The deal included guided-missile destroyers, P-3 anti-submarine aircraft, diesel submarines, and advanced Patriot PAC-3 anti-missile systems. The Nationalists and James Soong's supporters regard the price as too high and mostly a financial sop to the Bush administration, which has been pushing the sale since 2001. They also believe the weapons would not improve Taiwan's security.

On December 27, 2004, mainland China issued its fifth Defense White Paper on the goals of the country's national defense efforts. As one long-time observer, Robert Bedeski, notes:

> At first glance, the Defense White Paper is a hard-line statement on territorial sovereignty and emphasizes China's determination not to tolerate any moves at secession, independence, or separation. However, the next paragraph . . . indicates a willingness to reduce tensions in the Taiwan Strait: so long as the Taiwan authorities accept the one China principle and stop their separatist activities aimed at "Taiwan independence," cross-strait talks can be held at any time on officially ending the state of hostility between the two sides.

It appears that this is also the way the Taiwanese read the message. On February 24, 2005, President Chen Shui-bian met for the first time since October 2000 with Chairman James Soong of the People First Party. The two leaders, holding diametrically opposed views on relations with the mainland, nonetheless signed a joint statement outlining ten points of consensus. They pledged to try to open full transport and commercial links across the Taiwan Strait, increase trade, and ease the ban on investments in China by many Taiwanese business sectors. The mainland reacted favorably at once. Astonishingly, this led Chen Shui-bian to say that he "would not rule out Taiwan's eventual reunion with China, provided Taiwan's 23 million people accepted it."

If the United States and Japan left China and Taiwan to their own devices, it seems possible that they would work out a *modus vivendi*. Taiwan has already invested some $150 billion in the mainland, and the two economies are becoming more closely integrated every day. There also seems to be a growing recognition in Taiwan that it would be very difficult to live as an independent Chinese-speaking nation alongside a country with 1.3 billion people, 3.7 million square miles of territory, a rapidly growing $1.4 trillion economy, and aspirations to regional leadership in East Asia. Rather than declaring its independence, Taiwan may try to seek a status somewhat like that of French Canada—a kind of looser version of a Chinese Quebec under nominal central government control but maintaining separate institutions, laws, and customs.

The mainland would be so relieved by this solution it would probably accept it, particularly if it could be achieved before the 2008 Beijing Olympics. China fears that Taiwanese radicals want to declare independence a month or two before those Olympics, betting that China would not attack then because of its huge investment in the forthcoming games. Most observers believe, however, that China would have no choice but to go to war because failure to do so would invite a domestic revolution against the Chinese Communist Party for violating the national integrity of China.

Sino–American and Sino–Japanese Relations Spiral Downward

It has long been an article of neocon faith that the US must do everything in its power to prevent the development of rival power centers, whether friendly or hostile. After the collapse of the Soviet Union, this meant they turned their attention to China as one of the US's probable next enemies. In 2001, having come to power, the neoconservatives shifted much of the US's nuclear targeting from Russia to China. They also began regular high-level military talks with Taiwan over defense of the island, ordered a shift of army personnel and supplies to the Asia-Pacific region, and worked strenuously to promote the remilitarization of Japan.

On April 1, 2001, a US Navy EP-3E Aries II electronic spy plane collided with a Chinese jet fighter off the south China coast. The American aircraft was on a mission to provoke Chinese radar defenses and then record the transmissions and procedures the Chinese used in sending up interceptors. The Chinese jet went down and the pilot lost his life, while the American plane landed safely on Hainan Island and its crew of twenty-four spies was well treated by the Chinese authorities.

It soon became clear that China was not interested in a confrontation, since many of its most important investors have their headquarters in the United States. But it could not instantly return the crew of the spy plane without risking powerful domestic criticism for obsequiousness in the face of provocation. It therefore delayed eleven days until it received a pro forma American apology for causing the death of a Chinese pilot on the edge of the country's territorial air space and for making an unauthorized landing at a Chinese military airfield. Meanwhile, the US media had labeled the crew as "hostages," encouraged their relatives to tie yellow ribbons around neighborhood trees, hailed the President for doing "a first-rate job" to free them, and endlessly criticized China for its "state-controlled media." They carefully avoided mentioning that the United States enforces around our country a 200-mile aircraft–intercept zone that stretches far beyond territorial waters.

On April 25, 2001, during an interview on national television, President Bush was asked whether he would ever use "the full force of the American military" against China for the sake of Taiwan. He responded, "Whatever it takes to help Taiwan defend herself." This was American policy until 9/11, when China enthusiastically joined the "war on terrorism" and the President and his neocons became preoccupied with their "axis of evil" and with making war on Iraq. The United States and China were also enjoying extremely close economic relations, which the big-business wing of the Republican Party did not want to jeopardize.

The Middle East thus trumped the neocons' Asia policy. While the Americans were distracted, China went about its economic business for almost four years, emerging as a powerhouse of Asia and a potential organizing node for Asian economies. Rapidly industrializing China also developed a voracious appetite for petroleum and other raw materials, which brought it into direct competition with the world's largest importers, the US and Japan.

By the summer of 2004, Bush strategists, distracted as they were by Iraq, again became alarmed over China's growing power and its potential to challenge American hegemony in East Asia. The Republican Party platform unveiled at its convention in New York in August proclaimed that "America will help Taiwan defend itself." During that summer, the navy also carried out exercises it dubbed "Operation Summer Pulse '04," which involved the simultaneous deployment at sea of seven of the US's twelve carrier strike groups. An American carrier strike group includes an aircraft carrier (usually with nine or ten squadrons of planes, a total of about eighty-five aircraft in all), a guided missile cruiser, two guided missile destroyers, an attack submarine, and a combination ammunition-oiler-supply ship. Deploying seven such armadas at the same time was unprecedented—and very expensive. Even though only three of the carrier strike groups were sent to the Pacific and no more than one was patrolling off Taiwan at a time, the Chinese became deeply alarmed that this marked the beginning of an attempted rerun of nineteenth-century gunboat diplomacy aimed at them.

This American show of force and Chen Shui-bian's polemics preceding the December elections also seemed to overstimulate the Taiwanese. On

October 26 in Beijing, Secretary of State Colin Powell tried to calm things down by declaring to the press, "Taiwan is not independent. It does not enjoy sovereignty as a nation, and that remains our policy, our firm policy. . . . We want to see both sides not take unilateral action that would prejudice an eventual outcome, a reunification that all parties are seeking."

Powell's statement seemed unequivocal enough, but significant doubts persisted about whether he had much influence within the Bush administration or whether he could speak for Vice President Cheney and Secretary of Defense Donald Rumsfeld. Early in 2005, Porter Goss, the new director of the CIA, Defense Secretary Rumsfeld, and Admiral Lowell Jacoby, head of the Defense Intelligence Agency, all told Congress that China's military modernization was going ahead much faster than previously believed. They warned that the 2005 Quadrennial Defense Review, the every-four-year formal assessment of US military policy, would take a much harsher view of the threat posed by China than the 2001 overview.

In this context, the Bush administration, perhaps influenced by the election of November 2 and the transition from Colin Powell's to Condi Rice's State Department, played its most dangerous card. On February 19, 2005, in Washington, it signed a new military agreement with Japan. For the first time, Japan joined the administration in identifying security in the Taiwan Strait as a "common strategic objective." Nothing could have been more alarming to China's leaders than the revelation that Japan had decisively ended six decades of official pacifism by claiming a right to intervene in the Taiwan Strait.

It is possible that, in the years to come, Taiwan itself may recede in importance to be replaced by even more direct Sino-Japanese confrontations. This would be an ominous development indeed, one that the United States would be responsible for having abetted but would certainly be unable to control. The kindling for a Sino-Japanese explosion has long been in place. After all, during World War Two the Japanese killed approximately 23 million Chinese throughout East Asia—higher casualties than the staggering ones suffered by Russia at the hands of the Nazis—and yet Japan refuses to atone for or even acknowledge its historical war crimes. Quite the opposite, it continues to rewrite history, portraying itself as the liberator of Asia and a victim of European and American imperialism.

In—for the Chinese—a painful act of symbolism, after becoming Japanese prime minister in 2001, Junichiro Koizumi made his first official visit to Yasukuni Shrine in Tokyo, a practice that he has repeated every year since. Koizumi likes to say to foreigners that he is merely honoring Japan's war dead. Yasukuni, however, is anything but a military cemetery or a war memorial. It was established in 1869 by Emperor Meiji as a Shinto shrine (though with its *torii* archways made of steel rather than the traditional red-painted wood) to commemorate the lives lost in campaigns to return direct imperial rule to Japan. During World War Two, Japanese militarists took over the shrine and used it to promote patriotic and nationalistic sentiments. Today, Yasukuni is said to be dedicated to the spirits of approximately 2.4 million Japanese who have died in the country's wars, both civil and foreign, since 1853.

In 1978, for reasons that have never been made clear, General Hideki Tojo and six other wartime leaders who had been hanged by the Allied Powers as war criminals were collectively enshrined at Yasukuni. The current chief priest of the shrine denies that they were war criminals, saying, "The winner passed judgment on the loser." In a museum on the shrine's grounds, there is a fully restored Mitsubishi Zero Type 52 fighter aircraft that a placard says made its combat debut in 1940 over Chongqing, then the wartime capital of the Republic of China. It was undoubtedly not an accident that, in Chongqing during the 2004 Asian Cup soccer finals, Chinese spectators booed the playing of the Japanese national anthem. Yasukuni's leaders have always claimed close ties to the imperial household, but the late Emperor Hirohito last visited the shrine in 1975 and Emperor Akihito has never been there.

The Chinese regard Yasukuni visits by the Japanese prime minister as insulting, somewhat comparable perhaps to Britain's Prince Harry dressing up as a Nazi for a costume party. Nonetheless, Beijing has tried in recent years to appease Tokyo. Chinese President Hu Jintao rolled out the red carpet for Yohei Kono, speaker of the Japanese Diet's House of Representatives, when he visited China in September 2004; he appointed Wang Yi, a senior moderate in the Chinese foreign service, as ambassador to Japan; and he proposed joint Sino-Japanese exploration of possible oil resources in the offshore seas that both sides claim. All such gestures were ignored by Koizumi who insists that he intends to go on visiting Yasukuni.

Matters came to a head in November 2004 at two important summit meetings: an Asia-Pacific Economic Cooperation (APEC) gathering in Santiago, Chile, followed immediately by an Association of Southeast Asian Nations (ASEAN) meeting with the leaders of China, Japan, and South Korea that took place in Vientiane, Laos. In Santiago, Hu Jintao directly asked Koizumi to cease his Yasukuni visits for the sake of Sino-Japanese friendship. Seemingly as a reply, in Vientiane Koizumi went out of his way to insult Chinese Premier Wen Jiabao. He said to Premier Wen, "It's about time for [China's] graduation [as a recipient of Japanese foreign aid payments]," implying that Japan intended unilaterally to end its 25-year-old financial aid program. The word "graduation" also conveyed the insulting implication that Japan saw itself as a teacher guiding China, the student.

Koizumi next gave a little speech about the history of Japanese efforts to normalize relations with China, to which Premier Wen replied, "Do you know how many Chinese people died in the Sino-Japanese war?" Wen went on to suggest that China had always regarded Japan's foreign aid, which he said China did not need, as payments in lieu of compensation for damage done by Japan in China during the war. He pointed out that China had never asked for reparations from Japan and that Japan's payments amounted to about $30 billion over twenty-five years, a fraction of the $80 billion Germany has paid to the victims of Nazi atrocities even though Japan is the more populous and richer country.

On November 10, 2004, the Japanese navy discovered a Chinese nuclear submarine in Japanese territorial waters near Okinawa. Although the Chinese apologized and called the sub's intrusion a "mistake," Defense Agency Director Ono gave it wide publicity, further inflaming Japanese public opinion against China. From that point on, relations between Beijing and Tokyo have gone steadily downhill, culminating in the Japanese–American announcement that Taiwan was of special military concern to both of them, which China denounced as an "abomination."

Over time this downward spiral in relations will probably prove damaging to the interests of both the United States and Japan, but particularly to those of Japan. China is unlikely to retaliate directly but is even less likely to forget what has happened—and it has a great deal of leverage over Japan. After all, Japanese prosperity increasingly depends on its ties to China. The reverse is not true. Contrary to what one might expect, Japanese exports to China jumped 70 percent between 2001 and 2004, providing the main impetus for a sputtering Japanese economic recovery. Some 18,000 Japanese companies have operations in China. In 2003, Japan passed the United States as the top destination for Chinese students going abroad for a university education. Nearly 70,000 Chinese students now study at Japanese universities compared to 65,000 at American academic institutions. These close and lucrative relations are at risk if the US and Japan pursue their militarization of the region.

A Multipolar World

Tony Karon of *Time* magazine has observed:

> All over the world, new bonds of trade and strategic cooperation are being forged around the US. China has not only begun to displace the US as the dominant player in the Asia Pacific Economic Cooperation organization (APEC), it is fast emerging as the major trading partner to some of Latin America's largest economies. . . . French foreign-policy think tanks have long promoted the goal of "multipolarity" in a post-Cold War world, i.e., the preference for many different, competing power centers rather than the "unipolarity" of the US as a single hyper-power. Multipolarity is no longer simply a strategic goal. It is an emerging reality.

Evidence is easily found of multipolarity and China's prominent role in promoting it. Just note China's expanding relations with Iran, the European Union, Latin America, and the Association of Southeast Asian Nations. Iran is the second-largest OPEC oil producer after Saudi Arabia and has long had friendly relations with Japan, which is its leading trading partner. (Ninety-eight percent of Japan's imports from Iran are oil.) On February 18, 2004, a consortium of Japanese companies and the Iranian government signed a memorandum of agreement to develop jointly Iran's Azadegan oil field, one of the world's largest, in a project worth $2.8 billion. The US has opposed Japan's support for Iran, causing Congressman Brad Sherman (D-CA) to charge that Bush had been bribed into accepting the Japanese–Iranian deal by Koizumi's dispatch of 550 Japanese troops to Iraq, adding a veneer of international support for the American war there.

But the long-standing Iranian–Japanese alignment began to change in late 2004. On October 28, China's oil major, the Sinopec Group, signed an agreement with Iran worth between $70 billion and $100 billion to develop the giant Yadavaran natural gas field. China agreed to buy 250 million tons of liquefied natural gas (LNG) from Iran over twenty-five years. It is the largest deal Iran has signed with a foreign country since 1996 and will include several other benefits, including China's assistance in building numerous ships to deliver the LNG to Chinese ports. Iran also committed itself to exporting 150,000 barrels of crude oil per day to China for twenty-five years at market prices.

Iran's oil minister, Bijan Zanganeh, noted on a visit to Beijing that Iran is China's biggest foreign oil supplier and said that his country wants to be China's long-term business partner. He told *China Business Weekly* that Tehran would like to replace Japan with China as the biggest customer for its oil and gas. The reason is obvious: American pressure on Iran to give up its nuclear power development program and the Bush administration's declared intention to take Iran to the UN Security Council for the imposition of sanctions (which a Chinese vote could veto). On November 6, 2004, Chinese Foreign Minister Li Zhaoxing paid a rare visit to Tehran. In meetings with Iranian President Mohammad Khatami, Li said that Beijing would indeed consider vetoing any American effort to sanction Iran at the Security Council. The US has also charged China with selling nuclear and missile technology to Iran.

China and Iran already did a record $4 billion worth of two-way business in 2003. Projects included China's building of the first stage of Tehran's Metro and a contract to build a second link worth $836 million. China will be the top contender to build four other planned lines, including a nineteen-mile track to the airport. In February 2003, Chery Automobile Company, the eighth-largest automaker in China, opened its first overseas production plant in Iran. Today, it manufactures 30,000 Chery cars annually in northeastern Iran. Beijing is also negotiating to construct a 240-mile pipeline from Iran to the northern Caspian Sea to connect with the long-distance Kazakhstan–Xinjiang pipeline that it began building in October 2004. The Kazakh pipeline has a capacity to deliver 10 million tons of oil to China per year. Despite American bluster and belligerence, Iran is anything but isolated in today's world.

The EU is China's largest trading partner and China is the EU's second-largest trading partner (after the United States). Back in 1989, to protest the suppression of pro-democracy demonstrators in Beijing's Tiananmen Square, the EU imposed a ban on military sales to China. The only other countries so treated are true international pariahs like Burma, Sudan, and Zimbabwe. Even North Korea is not subject to a formal European arms embargo. Given that the Chinese leadership has changed several times since 1989 and as a gesture of goodwill, the EU has announced its intention to lift the embargo. Jacques Chirac, the French president, is one of the strongest proponents of the idea of replacing American hegemony with a "multipolar world." On a visit to Beijing in October 2004, he said that China and France share "a common vision of the world" and that lifting the embargo will "mark a significant milestone: a moment when Europe had to make a choice between the strategic interests of America and China—and chose China."

In his trip to Western Europe in February 2005, Bush repeatedly said, "There is deep concern in our country that a transfer of weapons would be a transfer of technology to China, which would change the balance of relations between China and Taiwan." In early February, the House of Representatives voted 411 to 3 in favor of a resolution condemning the potential EU move. The Europeans and Chinese contend that the Bush administration has vastly overstated its case, that no weapons capable of changing the balance of power are involved, and that the EU is not aiming to win massive new defense contracts from China but to strengthen mutual economic relations in general. Immediately following Bush's tour of Europe, the EU Trade Commissioner, Peter Mandelson, arrived in Beijing for his first official visit. The purpose of his trip, he said, was to stress the need to create a new strategic partnership between China and Europe.

Washington has buttressed its hard-line stance with the release of many new intelligence estimates depicting China as a formidable military threat. Whether this intelligence is politicized or not, it argues that China's military modernization is aimed precisely at countering the US Navy's carrier strike groups, which would assumedly be used in the Taiwan Strait in case of war. China is certainly building a large fleet of nuclear submarines and is an active participant in the EU's Galileo Project to produce a satellite navigation system not controlled by the American military. The Defense Department worries that Beijing might adapt the Galileo technology to anti-satellite purposes.

American military analysts are also impressed by China's launch, on October 15, 2003, of a spacecraft containing a single astronaut who was successfully returned to Earth the following day. Only the former USSR and the United States had previously sent humans into outer space.

China already has 500 to 550 short-range ballistic missiles deployed opposite Taiwan and has 24 CSS-4 intercontinental ballistic missiles with a range of 13,000 kilometers to deter an American missile attack on the Chinese mainland. According to Richard Fisher, a researcher at the US-based Center for Security Policy, "The forces that China is putting in place right now will probably be more than sufficient to deal with a single American aircraft carrier battle group." Arthur Lauder, a professor of international relations at the University of Pennsylvania, concurs. He says that the Chinese military "is the only one being developed anywhere in the world today that is specifically configured to fight the United States of America."

The US obviously cannot wish away this capability, but it has no evidence that China is doing anything more than countering the threats coming from the Bush administration. It seeks to avoid war with Taiwan and the US by deterring them from separating Taiwan from China. For this reason, in March 2005, China's pro-forma legislature, the National People's Congress, passed a law making secession from China illegal and authorizing the use of force in case a territory tried to leave the country.

The Japanese government, of course, backs the American position that China constitutes a military threat to the entire region. Interestingly enough, however, the Australian government of John Howard, a loyal American ally when it comes to Iraq, has decided to defy Bush on the issue of lifting the European arms embargo. Australia places a high premium on good relations with China and is hoping to negotiate a free trade agreement between the two countries. Canberra has therefore decided to support the EU in lifting the fifteen-year-old embargo. Chirac and German Chancellor Gerhard Schröder both say, "It will happen."

The United States has long proclaimed that Latin America is part of its "sphere of influence," and because of that most foreign countries have treaded carefully in doing business there. However, in the search for fuel and minerals for its booming economy, China is openly courting many Latin American countries regardless of what Washington thinks. On November 15, 2004, President Hu Jintao ended a five-day visit to Brazil during which he signed more than a dozen accords aimed at expanding Brazil's sales to China and Chinese investment in Brazil. Under one agreement Brazil will export to China as much as $800 million annually in beef and poultry. In turn, China agreed with Brazil's state-controlled oil company to finance a $1.3 billion gas pipeline between Rio de Janeiro and Bahia once technical studies are completed. China and Brazil also entered into a "strategic partnership" with the objective of raising the value of bilateral trade from $10 billion in 2004 to $20 billion by 2007. President Hu said that this partnership symbolized "a new international political order that favored developing countries."

In the weeks that followed, China signed important investment and trade agreements with Argentina, Venezuela, Bolivia, Chile, and Cuba. Of particular interest, in December 2004 President Hugo Chávez of Venezuela visited China and agreed to give it wide-ranging access to his country's oil reserves. Venezuela is the world's fifth-largest oil exporter and normally sells about 60 percent of its output to the United States, but under the new agreements China will be allowed to operate fifteen mature oil fields in eastern Venezuela. China will invest around $350 million to extract oil and another $60 million in natural gas wells.

China is also working to integrate East Asia's smaller countries into some form of new economic and political community. Such an alignment, if it comes into being, will certainly erode American and Japanese influence in the area. In November 2004, the ten nations that make up ASEAN (Brunei, Burma, Cambodia, Indonesia, Laos, Malaysia, the Philippines, Singapore, Thailand, and Vietnam) met in the Laotian capital of Vientiane, joined by the leaders of China, Japan, and South Korea. The United States was not invited and the Japanese officials seemed uncomfortable being there. The purpose was to plan for an East Asian summit meeting to be held in November 2005 to begin creating an "East Asia Community." In December 2004, the ASEAN countries and China also agreed to create a free trade zone among themselves by 2010.

According to Edward Cody of the *Washington Post*, "Trade between China and the 10 ASEAN countries has increased about 20 percent a year since 1990, and the pace has picked up in the last several years." This trade hit $78.2 billion in 2003 and was reported to be about $100 billion by the end of 2004. As the senior Japanese political commentator Yoichi Funabashi observes, "The ratio of intra-regional trade [in East Asia] to worldwide trade was nearly 52 percent in 2002. Though this figure is lower than the 62 percent in the EU, it tops the 46 percent of NAFTA [the North American Free Trade Agreement]. East Asia is thus becoming less dependent on the US in terms of trade."

China is the primary moving force behind these efforts. According to Funabashi, China's leadership plans to use the country's explosive economic growth and its ever more powerful links to regional trading partners to marginalize the United States and isolate Japan in East Asia. He argues that the United States underestimated how deeply distrusted it had become in the region thanks to its narrow-minded and ideological response to the East Asian financial crisis of 1997, which it largely caused. On November 30, 2004, Michael Reiss, the director of policy planning in the State Department, said in Tokyo, "The US, as a power in the Western Pacific, has an interest in East Asia. We would be unhappy about any plans to exclude the US from the framework of dialogue and cooperation in this region." But it is probably already too late for the Bush administration to do much more than delay the arrival of a China-dominated East Asian community, particularly because of declining American economic and financial strength.

For Japan, the choices are more difficult still. Sino-Japanese enmity has had a long history in East Asia, always with disastrous outcomes. Before World War Two, one of Japan's most influential writers on Chinese affairs, Hotsumi Ozaki, prophetically warned that Japan, by refusing to adjust to the Chinese revolution and instead making war on it, would only radicalize the Chinese people and contribute to the coming to power of the Chinese Communist Party. He spent his life working on the question "Why should the success of the Chinese revolution be to Japan's disadvantage?" In 1944, the Japanese government hanged Ozaki as a traitor, but his question remains as relevant today as it was in the late 1930s.

Why should China's emergence as a rich, successful country be to the disadvantage of either Japan or the United States? History teaches us that the least intelligent response to this development would be to try to stop it through military force. As a Hong Kong wisecrack has it, China has just had a couple of bad centuries and now it's back. The world needs to adjust peacefully to its legitimate claims—one of which is for other nations to stop militarizing the Taiwan problem—while checking unreasonable Chinese efforts to impose its will on the region. Unfortunately, the trend of events in East Asia suggests we may yet see a repetition of the last Sino-Japanese conflict, only this time the US is unlikely to be on the winning side.

May 2006

5

THE WIDE WAR

How Donald Rumsfeld Discovered
the Wild West in Latin America

Greg Grandin

How fast has Latin America fallen from favor? Just a decade ago the Clinton administration was holding up the region as the crown jewel of globalization's promise: All is quiet on "our southern flank," reported the head of the US Southern Command, General Barry McCaffrey, in 1995, "our neighbors are allies who, in general, share similar values." "The Western Hemisphere has a lot to teach the world," said McCaffrey's boss Secretary of Defense William Cohen two years later, "as the world reaches for the kind of progress we have made."

Today, with a new generation of leaders in open rebellion against Washington's leadership, Latin America is no longer seen as a beacon unto the world but as a shadowy place where "enemies" lurk. "They watch, they probe," Donald Rumsfeld warns of terrorists in Latin America; they look for "weaknesses." According to the new head of Southcom, General Bantz Craddock, the region is held hostage by a league of extraordinary gentlemen made up of the "transnational terrorist, the narco-terrorist, the Islamic radical fundraiser and recruiter, the illicit trafficker, the money launderer, the kidnapper, [and] the gang member."

"Terrorists throughout the Southern Command area of responsibility,"

Craddock's predecessor warned, "bomb, murder, kidnap, traffic drugs, transfer arms, launder money and smuggle humans." Problems that Clinton's Pentagon presented as discrete issues—drugs, arms trafficking, intellectual property piracy, migration, and money laundering, what the editor of *Foreign Policy* Moisés Nain has described as the "five wars of globalization"—are now understood as part of a larger unified campaign against terrorism.

The Pentagon's Wide War on Everything in Latin America

Latin America, in fact, has become more dangerous of late, plagued by a rise in homicides, kidnappings, drug use, and gang violence. Yet it is not the increase in illicit activity that is causing the Pentagon to beat its alarm but rather a change in the way terrorism experts and government officials think about international security. After 9/11, much was made of al-Qaeda's virus-like ability to adapt and spread through loosely linked affinity cells even after its host government in Afghanistan had been destroyed. Defense analysts now contend that, with potential patron nations few and far between and funding sources cut off by effective policing, a new mutation has occurred. To raise money, terrorists are reportedly making common cause with gun runners, people smugglers, brand-name and intellectual property bootleggers, drug dealers, blood diamond merchants, and even old-fashioned high-seas pirates.

In other words, the real enemy facing the US in its War on Terror is not violent extremism, but that old scourge of American peacekeepers since the days of the frontier: lawlessness. "Lawlessness that breeds terrorism is also a fertile ground for the drug trafficking that supports terrorism," said former Attorney General John Ashcroft a few years ago, explaining why Congress's global counterterrorism funding bill was allocating money to support the Colombian military's fight against leftist rebels.

Counterinsurgency theorists have long argued for what they describe as "total war at the grass-roots," by which they mean a strategy not just to defeat insurgents by military force but to establish control over the social, economic, and cultural terrain in which they operate. "Drying up the sea," they call it, riffing on Mao's famous dictum, or sometimes, "draining the swamp." What this expanded definition of the terrorist threat does is take the concept of total war out of, say, the mountains of Afghanistan, and project it onto a world scale: Victory, says the Pentagon's 2006 Quadrennial

Defense Review, "requires the creation of a global environment inhospitable to terrorism."

Defining the War on Terror in such expansive terms offers a number of advantages for American security strategists. Since the United States has the world's largest military, the militarization of police work justifies the "persistent surveillance" of, well, everything and everybody, as well as the maintenance of "a long-term, low-visibility presence in many areas of the world where US forces do not traditionally operate." It justifies taking "preventive measures" in order to "quell disorder before it leads to the collapse of political and social structures" and shaping "the choices of countries at strategic crossroads" which, the Quadrennial Defense Review believes, include Russia, China, India, the Middle East, Latin America, Southeast Asia—just about every nation on the face of the earth save Britain and, maybe, France.

Since the "new threats of the 21st century recognize no borders," the Pentagon can, in the name of efficiency and flexibility, breach bureaucratic divisions separating police, military, and intelligence agencies, while at the same time demanding that they be subordinated to US command. Hawks now like to sell the War on Terror as "the Long War," but a better term would be "the Wide War," with an enemies list infinitely expandable to include everything from DVD bootleggers to peasants protesting the Bechtel Corporation. Southcom commander Craddock regularly preaches against "anti-globalization and anti-free trade demagogues," while Harvard security-studies scholar and leading ideologue of the "protean enemy" thesis Jessica Stern charges, without a shred of credible evidence, that the Venezuelan president, Hugo Chávez, is brokering an alliance between "Colombian rebels and militant Islamist groups."

A Latin American Wild West

In Latin America, the tri-border region of Paraguay, Brazil, and Argentina, centered on Paraguay's legendary city of Ciudad del Este, is ground zero for this broad view of global security. It's the place where, according to the Pentagon, "all the components of transnational lawlessness seem to converge." The region had been on the Department of Defense watch list ever since two Lebanese residents were implicated in the 1992 and 1994 Hezbollah bombings of the Israeli embassy and a Jewish community center in Buenos Aires.

Right after 9/11, Douglas Feith, Pentagon undersecretary and neocon ultra, suggested that the US hold off invading Afghanistan and instead bomb the tri-border region, just to "surprise" al-Qaeda and throw it off guard. Attention to the region increased after US troops discovered what CNN excitedly called "a giant poster of Iguaçu Falls"—Latin America's most visited tourist destination, a few miles from Ciudad del Este—hanging on the wall of an al-Qaeda operative's abandoned house in Kabul. Since then, security analysts and journalists have taken to describing the place as a "new Libya," where Hamas raises money for its operations and al-Qaeda operates training camps or sends its militants for a little R&R.

Rio may have its favelas, Mexico its Tijuana, and Colombia its jungles overrun by guerrillas, drug lords, and paramilitaries, but none of these places hold a candle to the tri-border zone. It is truly the last, or at least the most well-known, lawless territory in the Americas, the War on Terror's very own "Wild West," as one military official dubbed it.

The Pentagon's overheated definition of the terrorist threat melts away distinctions between Shias and Sunnis and between either and Marxists. Thus, we have former CIA director James Woolsey claiming that Islamic extremists and criminals in the tri-border region work together "sort of like three different Mafia families," who occasionally kill each other but more often cooperate. Jessica Stern says that there "terrorists with widely disparate ideologies—Marxist Colombian rebels, American white supremacists, Hamas, Hezbollah, and others—meet to swap tradecraft." In Ciudad del Este, "international crimes like money laundering, gunrunning, migration fraud, and drug trafficking," according to military analyst Colonel William Mendel, "recombine and metastasize." The proceeds of these various illicit trades reportedly arm Latin America's leftist guerrillas, fund Islamic terrorism, and enrich the Russian, Asian, and even Nigerian mafias—everybody, it seems, but the Corleone family. Rumors drift through the Pentagon's world that Osama bin Laden even turns a nice profit running untaxed cigarettes into Brazil.

It's difficult to assess the truth of any of these lurid allegations. The second-largest city in South America's second-poorest country, Ciudad del Este is a free-trade boomtown, home not only to roughly 30,000 Lebanese and Syrian migrants but to lots of Koreans, Chinese, and South Asians, many of them undocumented. The city is no doubt a "free zone for significant criminal activity," as former FBI director Louis Freeh once described it. Its polyglot streets are packed with money changers, armored cars, and stalls selling everything from bootlegged *War of the Worlds* DVDs and dollar-a-pop Viagra to the latest sermons by respected Shia imams. Every day, more than 40,000 people cross the International Friendship Bridge from Brazil, many looking for brand-name knockoffs either for personal use or for resale on the streets of Rio or São Paulo. Surrounded by porous borders and crisscrossed by river routes linking the continent's interior to the Atlantic, the city is certainly a trading post for Andean cocaine, Paraguayan marijuana, Brazilian weapons, and dirty money.

But security experts have found it a distinct stretch to link any of this criminal activity to al-Qaeda. A couple of years ago, for example, senior US Army analyst Graham Turbiville pointed to the purchase of 30,000 ski masks by a Ciudad del Este Lebanese businessman as evidence that terrorism was flourishing in the region. The transaction, he said, "raised many questions"—one of which was whether Turbiville was even aware that some of the world's best skiing takes place in the nearby Andes.

Newspaper accounts depicting the region as Osama's lair are inevitably based not on investigative reporting but on the word of Pentagon officials or analysts, who either recycle each other's assertions or pick up rumors circulated in the Latin American press—stories many Latin Americans insist are planted by the CIA or the Pentagon. Brazilian and Argentine intelligence and police agencies, which have done much to disperse tri-border criminal activity elsewhere, insist that no terrorist cells exist in the area.

Ciudad del Este is thick with spies from Israel, the US, various Latin American countries, and even China. "There are so many of us," an Argentine spook recently remarked, "that we are bumping into each other." If any of al-Qaeda's operatives were actually prowling the city, odds are that at least one of them would have been found by now. Yet the State Department says that no "credible information" exists confirming that the group is operating in the tri-border region, while even Southcom chief Brantz Craddock admits that the Pentagon has "not detected Islamic terrorist cells" anywhere in Latin America.

Establishing Dominion over Ungoverned Spaces

Whether or not bin Laden's deputies kick back at Iguaçu Falls with skinheads and Asian gangsters to trade war stories and sip *mate*, the specter of this unholy alliance provides plenty of cover for the Pentagon to move forward with its militarization of hemispheric relations, even as nation after nation in the region slips out of Washington's political and economic orbit.

According to the Department of Defense, the hydra-headed terrorist network now supposedly spreading across southern climes cannot be defeated if Latin American nations continue to think of criminal law enforcement and international warfare as two distinct activities. What is needed is a Herculean Army of One, a flexible fighting machine capable of waging a coordinated war against criminal terrorism on all its multiple fronts and across any border. Secretary of Defense Rumsfeld regularly tours the region urging security officials to break down bureaucratic firewalls in order to allow local police, military and intelligence services to act in an integrated manner. The goal, according to the Pentagon, is to establish "effective sovereignty" or, more biblically, "dominion" over "ungoverned spaces"—boundary areas like the tri-border region, but also poor city neighborhoods where gangs rule, rural hinterlands where civil institutions are weak, and waterways and coastlines where illegal trafficking takes place.

So far, the Pentagon has had the most success in implementing this program in Central America and Colombia. In Central America, the Bush administration has pushed the region's defense ministers to set up a multinational "rapid-response force" made up of military and police officers to counter "emerging transnational threats." Such a force, the formation of which is under way, worries human rights activists, who have worked hard since the region's fratricidal civil wars of the 1980s to strictly limit military mandates to the defense of national borders.

According to Adam Isacson, who monitors Washington's Colombia policy for the Center for International Policy, the US is "carrying out a host of activities that would have been unthinkable back in 2000." Then, the Clinton administration promised that no portion of its $4 billion counter-narcotic funding package would be used to fight leftist rebels. In 2002, however, a newly emboldened Republican Congress tucked money into its global counterterrorism funding bill to support Colombia's counterinsurgency program. Since then, the Pentagon has increasingly taken the lead in directing what is now being called a "unified campaign" against cocaine *and* guerrillas. Over the last couple of years, the number of US troops allowed in the country has doubled to 800. Some of them teach Colombian police officers light-infantry training tactics, skills usually associated with low-intensity warfare, not civilian law enforcement; but many are involved in directly executing Colombia's counterinsurgency offensive, coordinating police and military units, and providing training and intelligence support for mobile brigades and Special Forces.

Well-armed Diplomacy

In Latin America more generally, it is increasingly the Pentagon, not the State Department, which sets the course for hemispheric diplomacy. With a staff of 1,400 and a budget of $800 million, Southcom already has more money and resources devoted to Latin America than do the Departments of State, Treasury, Commerce, and Agriculture combined. And its power is growing.

For decades following the passage of the 1961 Foreign Assistance Act, it was the responsibility of the civilian diplomats over at Foggy Bottom to allocate funds and training to foreign armies and police forces. But the Pentagon has steadily usurped this authority, first to fight the War on Drugs, then the War on Terror. Out of its own budget, it now pays for about two-thirds of the security training the US gives to Latin America. In January 2006, Congress legalized this transfer of authority from State to Defense through a provision in the National Defense Authorization Act, which for the first time officially gave the Pentagon the freedom to spend millions from its own budget on aid to foreign militaries without even the formality of civilian oversight. After 9/11, total American military aid to the region jumped from roughly $400 million to more than $700 million. It has been steadily rising ever since, coming in today just shy of $1 billion.

Much of this aid consists of training Latin American soldiers—more than 15,000 every year. Washington hopes that, even while losing its grip over the region's civilian leadership, its influence will grow as each of these cadets, shaped by ideas and personal loyalties developed during his instruction period, moves up his nation's chain of command.

Training consists of lethal combat techniques in the field backed by counterinsurgency and counterterror theory and doctrine in the classroom. This doctrine, conforming as it does to the Pentagon's broad definition of the international security threat, is aimed at undermining the work civilian activists have done since the end of the Cold War to dismantle national and international intelligence agencies in the region.

Chilean General Augusto Pinochet's infamous Operation Condor in the

1970s, for example, was in effect an international consortium of state intelligence agencies that served as the central command for a continental campaign of political terror, compiling execution lists of left-wing activists, while coordinating and directing the work of police, military, and death squad units throughout Latin America. Condor was dismantled when Chile returned to civilian rule in the early 1990s. However, a similarly integrated system is exactly what the newly established Counter-Terrorism Fellowship Program, run (with no congressional supervision) out of the Pentagon's Office of Special Operations and Low Intensity Warfare Conflict, evidently hopes to restore. Every year the Program's curriculum encourages thousands of select Latin American Fellows to return to their home countries and work to increase the "cooperation among military, police, and intelligence officials" and create "an intelligence sharing network with all other governments in the region."

During the Cold War, Washington urged Latin American soldiers to police their societies for "internal enemies," which anti-Communist military regimes took as a green light to commit mass slaughter. Today, the Pentagon thinks Latin America has a new "internal enemy": Southcom's General Craddock recently told a class of Latin American cadets at the Western Hemisphere Institute for Security Cooperation (*née* School of the Americas, the alma mater of some of the region's most infamous executioners) to be on guard against anti-free-trade populists who "incite violence against their own government and their own people."

Osama at the Falls

Outside Washington's sphere of influence in Central America and Colombia, the Bush administration is finding most Latin American militaries a hard sell. Since the end of the Cold War brought sharp reductions in their budgets, the region's cash-starved armed forces eagerly take US money, training, and equipment, and regularly participate in Pentagon-led conferences, war games, and military maneuvers. Police agencies work with the FBI and the Department of Homeland Security to combat money laundering as well as gun- and drug-running operations.

But most regional security officials have snubbed Washington's attempt to rally them behind a broader ideological crusade. Two years ago at an inter-American meeting of defense ministers in Quito, Ecuador, Rumsfeld's

Latin American counterparts rejected a proposal that they coordinate their activities through Southcom. Chile's defense minister insisted that the UN is the "only forum with international legitimacy to act globally on security issues." "We are very good at taking care of our borders," sniffed Argentina's defense minister in response to Rumsfeld's claim that borders don't matter in a world of stateless terrorism. They likewise rebuffed a US plan to draw up a regional list of suspected terrorists to prevent them from obtaining visas and traveling between countries.

In contrast to the Pentagon's attempt to ratchet up a sense of ideological urgency, the region's military leaders have sounded quite a different note. "The cause of terrorism," said Brazil's José Alencar, "is not just fundamentalism, but misery and hunger." When the US delegation at the meeting pushed for "narco-terrorism" to be ranked the hemisphere's number one challenge, the Latin Americans balked, insisting that poverty was the major threat to stability. From the sidelines, the former head of Ecuador's armed forces mordantly observed that in "Latin America there are no terrorists—only hunger and unemployment and delinquents who turn to crime. What are we going to do, hit you with a banana?"

During the Cold War, Washington was able to mobilize fear of Communism—which for Latin America's political and economic leaders generally translated into fear of democracy—and so make its particular security interests seem like the region's collective security interests. Today, a majority of South Americans not only oppose the US occupation of Iraq, but refuse to get too worked up about terrorism in general. Polls have repeatedly revealed, not surprisingly, that poverty is their major concern.

Last year, a publicity foray by the Brazilian tourist town of Foz de Iguaçu, just outside of Ciudad de Este, to capitalize on its post-9/11 notoriety captures just how untroubled so many Latin Americans are by Islamic terrorism. Its city government ran full-page advertisements in leading newspapers featuring a photograph of Osama bin Laden above the caption: "When he's not busy blowing up the world, bin Laden takes a few days to relax at Iguaçu." Asked about the ads, a city spokesperson explained, "Where there is laughter, there is no terror."

In sharp contrast to the unanimity with which the hemisphere sequestered Cuba during the Cold War, the region's governments have roundly rejected the Bush administration's attempts to redefine Venezuela as a pariah state.

Brazil, in fact, signed a "strategic alliance" with Venezuelan president Hugo Chávez in 2006, promising military cooperation and economic integration, including joint projects on energy development.

The region's refusal to follow Washington's various leads on a whole range of issues reflects a broadening rift over economic issues, undercutting Washington's ability to cast the War on Terror as a common struggle. More and more Latin Americans—not just the poor and the outspoken who marched against Bush during the 2005 Summit of the Americas in Argentina, but many of the region's elites—understand that the free market orthodoxy promoted by the US over the last two decades has been the very font of their problems. In one country after another, national elections in recent years have brought to power a new Latin American left sharply critical of unbridled capitalism. Brazil, Venezuela, Argentina, and Bolivia, among other countries, are now working together to contest Washington's hemispheric authority.

A Train Wreck of a Policy

Even the Pentagon acknowledges that the "roots" of Latin America's "poor security environment" can be found in the "hopelessness and squalor of poverty." At times, it goes so far as to admit, as Southcom did in its most recent annual report, that the "free market reforms and privatization of the 1990s have not delivered on the promise of prosperity." But rather than build on this insight to trace, say, the connections between financial liberalization and money laundering or to examine how privatization and cheap imports have forced rural peasants and urban workers into the informal, often illegal, economies in areas like the tri-border region, the Department of Defense is now openly positioning itself as globalization's Praetorian Guard, making the opening up of markets across Latin America a central objective of its mission.

During the Cold War, the Pentagon had a surprisingly small physical presence in Latin America. Except for some Caribbean bases, its strategists preferred to work through local allies who shared their vision of continental security. But the failure to rally Latin America behind the War on Terror, combined with the rise of economic nationalism, has led the Pentagon to return to more historically traditional methods of flexing its muscle in the region. It has recently been establishing in the Caribbean and the Andes a chain of small but permanent military bases, known euphemistically as "cooperative security locations." The Pentagon also calls them "lily pads" and from them imagines itself leapfrogging troops and equipment, shifting its weight from one "pad" to another as crises dictate to project its power deep into Latin America.

This is where the obsession with Ciudad del Este comes in. With Argentina, Brazil, and Venezuela acting in unison to temper US ambitions, corrupt and repressive Paraguay is the new darling of the Bush administration. In 2003, Nicanor Duarte became the first Paraguayan head of state to be hosted by the White House. In August 2005, Donald Rumsfeld flew to Asunción, the first time a Secretary of Defense visited Paraguay. That trip was shortly followed by a meeting between Dick Cheney and his Paraguayan counterpart.

Even though the terrorist threat reportedly emanating from the tri-border region has yet to be substantiated, it serves as an effective stalking horse, topping the agenda not only of these high-level meetings but of every ministerial gathering sponsored by Southcom. And the drumbeat is producing some rain.

Last summer Paraguay, over the angry protests of its neighbors, invited the Pentagon to begin eighteen months of bilateral military exercises, training local troops in "domestic peacekeeping operations," small-unit maneuvers, and border control. Washington and Asunción insist that the training mission is only temporary, yet observers point to the US-built Mariscal Estigarribia air base in the northern part of the country, capable of handling large-scale military air traffic, as an indication that the Bush administration is there to stay. If so, it would give Washington its southernmost bridgehead in Latin America, within striking distance not just of the storied Ciudad del Este, but of the Guaraní Aquifer, one of the world's largest bodies of fresh water, not to speak of Bolivia's important natural gas reserves.

At the moment, it is ridiculous to say, as General Craddock recently did, that "transnational terrorism" is Latin America's "foremost" problem. Then again, Iraq was not a haven for Islamic jihadists until our national security establishment made it so.

The Pentagon today is pursuing a train wreck of a policy in the region. It continues the march of free market absolutism, which its officials insist, despite all evidence to the contrary, will generate economic opportunities and rein in crime. At the same time, as it did during the Cold War, it is going forward with the militarization of the hemisphere in order to contain the "lawlessness" that such misery generates; and, once again, it is trying to rally Latin American troops behind an ideological crusade. So far, the region's officer corps has refused to get on the bandwagon, but Washington's persuasive powers are considerable. If those in charge of the Bush administration's hemispheric diplomacy continue down these tracks, the disaster that waits may very well transform much of Latin America into the Ciudad del Este of their dreams, the Wild West of their imaginations.

April 2007

6

WHAT IF IRAN HAD INVADED MEXICO?

Noam Chomsky

Unsurprisingly, George W. Bush's announcement of a "surge" in Iraq came despite the firm opposition to any such move of Americans and the even stronger opposition of the (thoroughly irrelevant) Iraqis. It was accompanied by ominous official leaks and statements—from Washington and Baghdad— about how Iranian intervention in Iraq was aimed at disrupting our mission to gain victory, an aim which is (by definition) noble. What then followed was a solemn debate about whether serial numbers on advanced roadside bombs (IEDs) were really traceable to Iran; and, if so, to that country's Revolutionary Guards or to some even higher authority.

This "debate" is a typical illustration of a primary principle of sophisticated propaganda. In crude and brutal societies, the party line is publicly proclaimed and must be obeyed—or else. What you actually believe is your own business and of far less concern. In societies where the state has lost the capacity to control by force, the party line is simply presupposed; then, vigorous debate is encouraged within the limits imposed by unstated doctrinal orthodoxy. The cruder of the two systems leads, naturally enough, to disbelief; the sophisticated variant gives an impression of openness and freedom, and so far more effectively serves to instill the party line. It becomes beyond question, beyond thought itself, like the air we breathe.

The debate over Iranian interference in Iraq proceeds without ridicule on the assumption that the United States owns the world. We did not, for example, engage in a similar debate in the 1980s about whether the US was interfering in Soviet-occupied Afghanistan, and I doubt that *Pravda*, probably recognizing the absurdity of the situation, sank to outrage about that fact (which American officials and our media, in any case, made no effort to conceal). Perhaps the official Nazi press also featured solemn debates about whether the Allies were interfering in sovereign Vichy France, though if so, sane people would then have collapsed in ridicule.

In this case, however, even ridicule—notably absent—would not suffice, because the charges against Iran are part of a drumbeat of pronouncements meant to mobilize support for escalation in Iraq and for an attack on Iran, the "source of the problem." The world is aghast at the possibility. Even in neighboring Sunni states, no friends of Iran, majorities, when asked, favor a nuclear-armed Iran over any military action against that country. From what limited information we have, it appears that significant parts of the US military and intelligence communities are opposed to such an attack, along with almost the entire world, even more so than when the Bush administration and Tony Blair's Britain invaded Iraq, defying enormous popular opposition worldwide.

"The Iran Effect"
The results of an attack on Iran could be horrendous. After all, according to a recent March 2007 study of "the Iraq effect" by terrorism specialists Peter Bergen and Paul Cruickshank, using government and Rand Corporation data, the Iraq invasion has already led to a sevenfold increase in terror. The "Iran effect" would probably be far more severe and long-lasting. British military historian Corelli Barnett speaks for many when he warns that "an attack on Iran would effectively launch World War Three."

What are the plans of the increasingly desperate clique that narrowly holds political power in the US? We cannot know. Such state planning is, of course, kept secret in the interests of "security." Review of the declassified record reveals that there is considerable merit in that claim—though only if we understand "security" to mean the security of the Bush administration against their domestic enemy, the population in whose name they act.

Even if the White House clique is not planning war, naval deployments, support for secessionist movements and acts of terror within Iran, and other provocations could easily lead to an accidental war. Congressional resolutions would not provide much of a barrier. They invariably permit "national security" exemptions, opening holes wide enough for the several aircraft-carrier battle groups soon to be in the Persian Gulf to pass through—as long as an unscrupulous leadership issues proclamations of doom (as Condoleezza Rice did with those "mushroom clouds" over American cities back in 2002). And the concocting of the sorts of incidents that "justify" such attacks is a familiar practice. Even the worst monsters feel the need for such justification and adopt the device: Hitler's defense of innocent Germany from the "wild terror" of the Poles in 1939, after they had rejected his wise and generous proposals for peace, is but one example.

The most effective barrier to a White House decision to launch a war is the kind of organized popular opposition that frightened the political-military leadership enough in 1968 that they were reluctant to send more troops to Vietnam—fearing, we learned from *The Pentagon Papers*, that they might need them for civil-disorder control.

Doubtless Iran's government merits harsh condemnation, including for its recent actions that have inflamed the crisis. It is, however, useful to ask how we would act if Iran had invaded and occupied Canada and Mexico and was arresting US government representatives there on the grounds that they were resisting the Iranian occupation (called "liberation," of course). Imagine as well that Iran was deploying massive naval forces in the Caribbean and issuing credible threats to launch a wave of attacks against a vast range of sites—nuclear and otherwise—in the United States, if the US government did not immediately terminate all its nuclear energy programs (and, naturally, dismantle all its nuclear weapons). Suppose that all of this happened after Iran had overthrown the government of the US and installed a vicious tyrant (as the US did to Iran in 1953), then later supported a Russian invasion of the US that killed millions of people (just as the US supported Saddam Hussein's invasion of Iran in 1980, killing hundreds of thousands of Iranians, a figure comparable to millions of Americans). Would we watch quietly?

It is easy to understand an observation by one of Israel's leading military historians, Martin van Creveld. After the US invaded Iraq, knowing it to be defenseless, he noted, "Had the Iranians not tried to build nuclear weapons, they would be crazy."

Surely no sane person wants Iran (or any nation) to develop nuclear weapons. A reasonable resolution of the present crisis would permit Iran to develop nuclear energy, in accord with its rights under the Non-Proliferation Treaty, but not nuclear weapons. Is that outcome feasible? It would be, given one condition: that the US and Iran were functioning democratic societies in which public opinion had a significant impact on public policy.

As it happens, this solution has overwhelming support among Iranians and Americans, who generally are in agreement on nuclear issues. The Iranian–American consensus includes the complete elimination of nuclear weapons everywhere (82 percent of Americans); if that cannot yet be achieved because of elite opposition, then at least a "nuclear-weapons-free zone in the Middle East that would include both Islamic countries and Israel" (71 percent of Americans). Seventy-five percent of Americans prefer building better relations with Iran to threats of force. In brief, if public opinion were to have a significant influence on state policy in the US and Iran, resolution of the crisis might be at hand, along with much more far-reaching solutions to the global nuclear conundrum.

Promoting Democracy—at Home

These facts suggest a possible way to prevent the current crisis from exploding, perhaps even into some version of World War Three. That awesome threat might be averted by pursuing a familiar proposal: democracy promotion— this time at home, where it is badly needed. Democracy promotion at home is certainly feasible and, although we cannot carry out such a project directly in Iran, we could act to improve the prospects of the courageous reformers and oppositionists who are seeking to achieve just that. Among such figures who are, or should be, well known would be Saeed Hajjarian, Nobel laureate Shirin Ebadi, and Akbar Ganji, as well as those who, as usual, remain nameless, among them labor activists about whom we hear very little; those who publish the *Iranian Workers Bulletin* may be a case in point.

We can best improve the prospects for democracy promotion in Iran by sharply reversing state policy here so that it reflects popular opinion. That would entail ceasing to make the regular threats that are a gift to Iranian hardliners. These are bitterly condemned by Iranians truly concerned with democracy promotion (unlike those "supporters" who flaunt democracy slogans in the West and are lauded as grand "idealists" despite their clear record of visceral hatred for democracy).

Democracy promotion in the United States could have far broader consequences. In Iraq, for instance, a firm timetable for withdrawal would be initiated at once, or very soon, in accord with the will of the overwhelming majority of Iraqis and a significant majority of Americans. Federal budget priorities would be virtually reversed. Where spending is rising, as in military supplemental bills to conduct the wars in Iraq and Afghanistan, it would sharply decline. Where spending is steady or declining (health, education, job training, the promotion of energy conservation and renewable energy sources, veterans' benefits, funding for the UN and UN peacekeeping operations, and so on), it would sharply increase. Bush's tax cuts for people with incomes over $200,000 a year would be immediately rescinded.

The US would have adopted a national healthcare system long ago, rejecting the privatized system that sports twice the per-capita costs found in similar societies and some of the worst outcomes in the industrial world. It would have rejected what is widely regarded by those who pay attention as a "fiscal train wreck" in the making. The US would have ratified the Kyoto Protocol to reduce carbon dioxide emissions and undertaken still stronger measures to protect the environment. It would allow the UN to take the lead in international crises, including in Iraq. After all, according to opinion polls, since shortly after the 2003 invasion a large majority of Americans have wanted the UN to take charge of political transformation, economic reconstruction, and civil order in that land.

If public opinion mattered, the US would accept UN Charter restrictions on the use of force, contrary to a bipartisan consensus that this country, alone, has the right to resort to violence in response to potential threats, real or imagined, including threats to our access to markets and resources. The US (along with others) would abandon the Security Council veto and accept majority opinion even when in opposition to it. The UN would be allowed to regulate arms sales, while the US would cut back on such sales and urge other countries to do so, which would be a major contribution to reducing large-scale violence in the world. Terror would be dealt with through diplomatic and economic measures, not force, in accord with the judgment of most specialists on the topic but again in diametric opposition to present-day policy.

Furthermore, if public opinion influenced policy, the US would have diplomatic relations with Cuba, benefiting the people of both countries (and, incidentally, US agribusiness, energy corporations, and others), instead of standing virtually alone in the world in imposing an embargo (joined only by Israel, the Republic of Palau, and the Marshall Islands). Washington would join the broad international consensus on a two-state settlement of the Israel–Palestine conflict, which (with Israel) it has blocked for thirty years—with scattered and temporary exceptions—and which it still blocks in word and, more important, in deed, despite fraudulent claims of its commitment to diplomacy. The US would also equalize aid to Israel and Palestine, cutting off aid to either party that rejected the international consensus.

Evidence on these matters is reviewed in my book *Failed States* as well as in *The Foreign Policy Disconnect* by Benjamin Page (with Marshall Bouton), which also provides extensive evidence that public opinion on foreign (and probably domestic) policy issues tends to be coherent and consistent over long periods. Studies of public opinion have to be regarded with caution, but they are certainly highly suggestive.

Democracy promotion at home, while no panacea, would be a useful step towards helping our own country become a "responsible stakeholder" in the international order (to adopt the term used for adversaries), instead of being an object of fear and dislike throughout much of the world. Apart from being a value in itself, functioning democracy at home holds real promise for dealing constructively with many current problems, international and domestic, including those that literally threaten the survival of our species.

January 2006

7

"OUR INDIAN WARS ARE NOT OVER YET"

Ten Ways to Interpret the War on Terror as a Frontier Conflict

John Brown

The Global War on Terror (GWOT) is, like all historical events, unique. But both its supporters and opponents compare it to past US military conflicts. The Bush administration and the neocons have drawn parallels between GWOT and World War Two as well as GWOT and the Cold War. Joshua E. London, writing in the *National Review*, sees the War on Terror as a modern form of the struggle against the Barbary pirates. Vietnam and the Spanish-American War have been preferred analogies for other commentators. A Pulitzer Prize winning journalist, Anne Applebaum, says that the war in Iraq might be like that in Korea, because of "the ambivalence of their conclusions." For others, the War on Terror, with its loose rhetoric, brings to mind the "war on poverty" or the "war on drugs."

I'd like to suggest another way of looking at the War on Terror: as a twenty-first-century continuation of, or replication of, the American Indian wars, on a global scale. This is by no means something that has occurred to me alone, but it has received relatively little attention. Here are ten reasons why I'm making this suggestion.

1. Key supporters of the War on Terror themselves see GWOT as an Indian war. Take, for example, the right-wing intellectuals Robert Kaplan and Max Boot who, although not members of the administration, also advocate a tough military stance against terrorists. In a *Wall Street Journal*

article, "Indian Country," published on September 25, 2004, Kaplan notes that "an overlooked truth about the war on terrorism" is that "the American military is back to the days of fighting the Indians." Iraq, he notes, "is but a microcosm of the earth in this regard." Kaplan has now put his thoughts into a book, *Imperial Grunts: The American Military on the Ground*, which President Bush read over the holidays. Kaplan points out that "'Welcome to Injun Country' was the refrain I heard from troops from Colombia to the Philippines, including Afghanistan and Iraq. . . . The War on Terrorism was really about taming the frontier."

As for Max Boot, he writes, "'small wars'—fought by a small number of professional US soldiers—are much more typical of American history than are the handful of 'total' wars that receive most of the public attention. Between 1800 and 1934, US Marines staged 180 landings abroad. And that's not even counting the Indian wars the army was fighting every year until 1890." A key GWOT battlefield, Boot suggests, is Afghanistan, noting that "[i]f the past is any indication of the future, we have a lot more savage wars ahead."

2. The essential paradigm of the War of Terror—us (the attacked) against them (the attackers)—was no less essential to the mindset of white settlers regarding the Indians, starting at least from the 1622 Indian massacre of 347 people at Jamestown, Virginia. With rare exceptions, newly arrived Europeans and their descendants, as well as their leaders, saw Indians as mortal enemies who started the initial fight against them, savages with whom they could not coexist. The Declaration of Independence condemned "the inhabitants of our frontiers, the merciless Indian Savages whose known rule of warfare, is an undistinguished destruction of all ages, sexes and conditions." When governor of Virginia (1780), Thomas Jefferson stated: "If we are to wage a campaign against these Indians the end proposed should be their extermination, or their removal beyond the lakes of the Illinois River. The same world would scarcely do for them and us."

President Andrew Jackson, whose "unapologetic flexing of military might" has been compared to George W. Bush's *modus operandi*, noted in his "Case for the Removal [of Indians] Act" (December 8, 1830):

What good man would prefer a country covered with forests and ranged by a few thousand savages to our extensive Republic, studded with cities, towns, and prosperous farms, embellished with all the improvements which art can devise or industry execute, . . . and filled with all the blessings of liberty, civilization, and religion?

Us versus them is, of course, a feature of all wars, but the starkness of this dichotomy—seen by GWOT supporters as a struggle between the civilized world and a global jihad—is as strikingly apparent in the War on Terror as it was in the Indian wars.

3. GWOT is based on the principle of preventive strike, meant to put off "potential, future and, therefore, speculative attacks"—just as US Army conflicts against the Indians often were. We have to get them before they get us—such is the assumption behind both sets of wars. As Professor Jack D. Forbes wrote in a 2003 piece, "Old Indian Wars Dominate Bush Doctrines," in the *Bay Mills News*:

> Bush has declared that the US will attack first before an "enemy" has the ability to act. This could, of course, be called "The Pearl Harbor strategy" since that is precisely what the Japanese Empire did. But it also has precedents against First American nations. For example, William Henry Harrison, under pressure from Thomas Jefferson to get the American Nations out of the Illinois–Indiana region, marched an invading army to the vicinity of a Native village at Tippecanoe precisely when he knew that [Shawnee war chief and pan-tribal political leader] Tecumseh was on a tour of the south and west.

4. While US mainstream thinking about GWOT enemies is that they are total aliens—in religion, politics, economics, and social organization—there are Americans who believe that individuals in these "primitive" societies can eventually become assimilated and thus be rendered harmless through training, education, or democratization. This is similar to the view among American settlers that in savage Indian tribes hostile to civilization, there were some who could be evangelized and Christianized and brought over to the morally right, Godly side. Once "Americanized," former hostile groups, with the worst among them exterminated, can no longer pose any threat and indeed can assist in the prolongation of conflicts against remaining evildoers.

5. GWOT is fought abroad, but it's also a war at home, as the creation after 9/11 of a Department of Homeland Security illustrates. The Indian wars were domestic as well, carried out by the US military to protect

American settlers against hostile non-US citizens living on American soil. (It was not until June 2, 1924 that Congress granted citizenship to all Native Americans born in the United States.) While engaged in the Indian wars, the US fought on its own, without the help of foreign governments; such has essentially been the case with GWOT, despite the support of a few countries like Israel, the creation of a weak international "coalition" in Iraq, and NATO participation in Afghanistan operations.

6. America's close partner Israel, which over the years has taken over Arab-populated lands and welcomes US immigrants, can be considered as a kind of surrogate United States in this struggle. Expanding into the Middle East, the Israelis could be seen as following the example of the American pioneers who didn't let Indians stand in their way as they settled, with the support of the US military, an entire continent, driven by the conviction that they were supported by God, the Bible, and Western civilization. "I shall need," wrote Thomas Jefferson, "the favor of that Being in whose hands we are, who led our fathers, as Israel of old, from their native land and planted them in a country flowing with all the necessities and comforts of life." Less eloquently, Ariel Sharon put it this way: "Everything that's grabbed will be in our hands. Everything we don't grab will be in their hands."

7. As for the current states that are major battlefields of GWOT, Afghanistan and Iraq, it appears that the model for their future, far from being functional democracies, is that of Indian reservations. It is not unlikely that the fragile political structures of these states will sooner or later collapse, and the resulting tribal/ethnic entities will be controlled—assuming the US proves willing to engage in the long-term garrisoning in each area—by American forces in fortified bases, as was the case with the Indian territories in the Far West. Areas under American control will provide US occupiers with natural resources (e.g. oil), and American business—if the security situation becomes manageable—will doubtless be lured there in search of economic opportunities. Interestingly, the area outside of the Green Zone in Baghdad (where Americans have fortified themselves) is now referred to as the Red Zone—terrorist-infested territory as dangerous to non-natives as the lands inhabited by the Redskins were to whites during the Indian wars.

8. The methods employed by the US in GWOT and the Indian wars are similar in many respects: using superior technology to overwhelm the

"primitive" enemy; adapting insurgency tactics, even the most brutal ones, used by the opposing side when necessary; and collaborating with "the enemy of my enemy" in certain situations (that is, setting one tribe against another). What are considered normal rules of war have frequently been irrelevant for Americans in both conflicts, given their certainty that their enemies are evil and uncivilized. The use of torture is also a feature of these two conflicts.

9. As GWOT increasingly appears to be, the Indian wars were a very long conflict, stretching from the seventeenth century to the end of the nineteenth—the longest war in American history, starting even before the US existed as a nation. There were numerous battles of varying intensity in this conflagration with no central point of confrontation—as is the case with the War on Terror, despite its current emphasis on Iraq. And GWOT is a war being fought, like the Indian wars in the Far West, over large geographical areas—as the Heritage Foundation's Ariel Cohen puts it, almost lyrically, "in the Greater Middle East, including the Mediterranean basin, through the Fertile Crescent, and into the remote valleys and gorges of the Caucasus and Pakistan, the deserts of Central Asia, the plateaus of Afghanistan."

10. Perhaps because they are drawn-out wars with many fronts and changing commanders, the goals of GWOT and the Indian wars can be subject to many interpretations (indeed, even Secretary of Defense Rumsfeld at one point was eager to rename the War on Terror a "Global Struggle Against Violent Extremism"). For many abroad, GWOT is a brutal expression of a mad, cowboy-led country's plans to take over the world and its resources. In the United States, a large number of Americans still interpret these two wars as God-favored initiatives to protect His chosen people and allow them to flourish. But just as attitudes in the US toward Native Americans have changed in recent years (consider, for example, the saccharine 1990 film *Dances with Wolves*, which is sympathetic to an Indian tribe, in contrast to John Wayne shoot-the-Injuns movies), so suspicious views among the American public toward the still-seen-as-dangerous "them" of GWOT might evolve in a different direction. Such a change in perception, however, is unlikely to occur in the near future, especially under the current bellicose Bush regime, which manipulates voters' fear of terrorists to maintain its declining domestic support.

June 2004

8

A PSEUDOSTATE IS BORN

Adam Hochschild

Some fifteen years ago, while writing about apartheid-era South Africa, I visited one of its nominally independent black "homelands." This crazy quilt of territories was a control mechanism the white regime had come up with in a country where whites were vastly outnumbered by South Africans of other colors. For the most part rural slums, the homelands, also known as Bantustans, made up about 13 percent of the nation's land. I was driving across miles of veldt where blacks were trying to scratch a living from eroded or unyielding patches of earth that white farmers didn't want, interspersed with shantytowns of shacks constructed out of corrugated metal, discarded plasterboard, and old automobile doors. Suddenly, looming out of this desolate landscape like an ocean liner in a swamp, was a huge office building, perhaps four or five stories high and 150 yards long, with a large sign saying, in English and Afrikaans, "South African Embassy."

I remembered that building the other day when reading about the new US embassy that will open in Baghdad this week. With a staff of more than 1,700—and that may be only the beginning—it will be the largest diplomatic mission in the world. Just as our embassy will be considerably more than an embassy, so the Iraqi state that will officially come into being in its shadow next Wednesday, after the speechmaking and flag-raising are over, will be considerably less than a state.

With nearly 140,000 American troops on Iraq's soil, plus tens of thousands of additional foreign soldiers and civilian security guards armed with everything from submachine guns to helicopters, most military power will not be in Iraqi hands, nor will the power of the budget, largely set and paid for in Washington.

If the new Iraq-to-be is not a state, what is it? A half-century ago one could talk about colonies, protectorates, and spheres of influence, but in our supposedly postcolonial world, the vocabulary is poorer. We lack a word for a country where most real power is in the hands of someone else, whether that be shadowy local militias, other nations' armies, or both. Pseudostate, perhaps. From Afghanistan to the Palestinian Authority, Bosnia to Congo, pseudostates have now spread around the globe. Some of them will even be exchanging ambassadors with Iraq.

Pseudostates, in fact, are nothing new. They have a long and fascinating history, and two notable groups of them had surprising fates near the twentieth century's end.

One collection was those "homelands" of South Africa, four of which were formally granted independence. The so-called South African embassies evolved seamlessly out of the white-controlled administrations that had run these territories when they were still called "Native Reserves," just as the US embassy in Baghdad will begin life in the very same Republican Palace from which occupation administrator L. Paul Bremer III has run Iraq for the last year. The South African government invested large sums in equipping the homelands with everything from foreign ministries to luxurious, gated residential compounds for cabinet members and their families. Collaborating chiefs were made heads of state, and their territories were given flags, national anthems and coats of arms. But when a coup temporarily deposed the hand-picked president of Bophuthatswana—seven separate islands of desperately poor land and poor people spread out across hundreds of miles—it was the South African army that promptly restored him to power.

As South Africa made its miraculous transition to majority rule in the early 1990s, the homelands as separate political entities swiftly vanished. The former foreign ministries and embassies were put to other uses and the only people to whom the past trappings of homeland independence still matter today are collectors who do a lively trade in the former territories' stamps.

Another group of pseudostates, however, had a very different fate. The Soviet Union was composed of fifteen "Soviet Socialist Republics"—entities, like those in South Africa, set up on ethnic lines as mechanisms of control.

These, too, were decked out with the external symbols of sovereignty, and in the case of two Soviet pseudostates, you didn't even have to go there to see their flags. For Byelorussia and the Ukraine had something South Africa's homelands never got: seats at the United Nations, a concession Stalin wrung from the Allies at the end of World War Two.

I traveled through a number of these pseudostates in the course of reporting from the old Soviet Union, and we hardheaded journalists always knew, despite Soviet propaganda, that these so-called republics were nothing of the sort and never would be. After all, they had no armies and no independence; Russians migrated to them in large numbers, knowing that ultimate power resided in Moscow. (They could even be dissolved at Moscow's will: A short-lived sixteenth Soviet Socialist Republic along the Finnish border disappeared with little ado in 1956.) And yet, in that other great transformation of the early 1990s, unexpected by hardheaded realists and dogmatic Communists alike, it was the Soviet Union itself that evaporated. Almost overnight its fifteen pseudostates turned into real ones. Their coming to life left millions of surprised and unhappy ethnic Russians stranded outside Russia.

The Iraq that will come into being this Wednesday does not closely resemble either the South African homelands or the old Soviet republics. But their histories, however different, might suggest the same lesson to American planners: pseudostates often turn out quite differently than their inventors intend, for their very creation is an act of hubris. And the larger and more unstable the pseudostate, the greater the hubris and the more likely that imperial plans will go awry. Washington's hopes for what Iraq will be in five or ten years, or even in five or ten months, may prove as unreliable as its predictions that US invasion troops would be greeted with cheers and flowers and would be home in a year.

Clearly White House strategists have a set of hopes, already somewhat battered, for what the Iraqi pseudostate will evolve into: a willing home for the permanent military bases the Pentagon is building in the country; an oil reservoir safely under US influence; and a strategic ally against militant Islam, all with the façade, at least, of democracy. On the other hand, with its vast oil wealth and restive population, at some point Iraq could take a very different path, and embody the religious fervor of its Shia majority, demand that US forces leave, try to cancel reconstruction contracts with US firms, and reverse the privatization of state assets now under way. Of course, it's not necessarily a matter of going entirely down one path or the other. Iraq may well take on some characteristics from each—or might fracture into Sunni, Shia, and Kurdish entities, or follow a path no "expert" can now guess.

Whatever happens—whether Iraq dissolves in pieces, is seen largely as a compliant US satellite, or becomes a cheeky avatar of Arab defiance of the West—its territory seems likely to continue to be what it has rapidly become in recent months, a literal and figurative minefield for US troops and a hotbed of al-Qaeda recruitment. The volatile, unpredictable nature of pseudostates, and their role as incubators of troubles that can come back to haunt their creators, has certainly been no great historical secret. Perhaps that was why one of the candidates in the 2000 presidential election said, "I don't think our troops ought to be used for what's called nation building." The candidate was George W. Bush.

March 2004

9

TWENTY-FIRST-CENTURY GUNBOAT DIPLOMACY

Tom Engelhardt

Off the Coast

The wooden sailing ship mounted with cannons, the gunboat, the battleship, and finally the "airship"—these proved the difference between global victory and staying at home, between empire and nothing much at all. In the first couple of centuries of Europe's burst onto the world stage, the weaponry of European armies and their foes was not generally so disparate. It was those cannons on ships that decisively tipped the balance. And they continued to do so for a long, long time. Traditionally, in fact, the modern arms race is considered to have taken off at the beginning of the twentieth century with the rush of European powers to build ever larger, ever more powerful, "all-big-gun" battleships—the "dreadnoughts" (scared of nothings).

In *Exterminate All the Brutes*, a remarkable travel book that takes you into the heart of European darkness (via an actual trip through Africa), the Swede Sven Lindqvist offers the following comments on that sixteenth-century sea-borne moment when Europe was still a barbaric outcropping of Euro-Asian civilization:

> Preindustrial Europe had little that was in demand in the rest of the world. Our most important export was force. All over the rest of the world, we were regarded at the time as nomadic warriors in the style of the Mongols and the

Tatars. They reigned supreme from the backs of horses, we from the decks of ships.

Our cannons met little resistance among the peoples who were more advanced than we were. The Moguls in India had no ships able to withstand artillery fire or carry heavy guns. . . . Thus the backward and poorly resourced Europe of the sixteenth century acquired a monopoly on ocean-going ships with guns capable of spreading death and destruction across huge distances. Europeans became the gods of cannons that killed long before the weapons of their opponents could reach them.

For a while, Europeans ruled the coasts where nothing could stand up to their ship-borne cannons and then, in the mid-nineteenth century in Africa as well as on the Asian mainland, the Europeans moved inland, taking their cannons upriver with them. For those centuries, the ship was, in modern terms, a floating military base filled with the latest in high-tech equipment. And yet ships had their limits as indicated by a well-known passage about a French warship off the African coast from Joseph Conrad's novel about the Congo, *Heart of Darkness*:

In the empty immensity of earth, sky, and water, there she was, incomprehensible, firing into a continent. Pop, would go one of the six-inch guns; a small flame would dart and vanish, a little white smoke would disappear, a tiny projectile would give a feeble screech—and nothing happened. Nothing could happen. There was a touch of insanity in the proceeding, a sense of lugubrious drollery in the sight.

Well, maybe it wasn't quite so droll if you happened to be on land, but the point is made. Of course, sooner or later (sometimes, as in Latin America or India, sooner) the Europeans did make it inland with the musket, the rifle, the repeating rifle, the machine gun, artillery, and, finally by the twentieth century, the airplane filled with bombs or even, as in Iraq, poison gas. Backing up the process was often the naval vessel—as at the battle of Omdurman in the Sudan in 1898 when somewhere between 9,000 and 11,000 soldiers in the Mahdi's army were killed (with a British loss of 48), thanks to mass rifle fire, Maxim machine guns, and the batteries of the gunboats floating on the Nile.

Winston Churchill was a reporter with the British expeditionary force, and here's part of his description of the slaughter (also from Lindqvist):

> The white flags [of the Mahdi's army] were nearly over the crest. In another minute they would become visible to the batteries. Did they realize what would come to meet them? They were in a dense mass, 2,800 yards from the 32nd Field Battery and the gunboats. The ranges were known. It was a matter of machinery. . . . About twenty shells struck them in the first minute. Some burst high in the air, others exactly in their faces. Others, again, plunged into the sand, and, exploding, dashed clouds of red dust, splinters, and bullets amid the ranks. . . . It was a terrible sight, for as yet they had not hurt us at all, and it seemed an unfair advantage to strike thus cruelly when they could not reply.

And—presto!—before you knew it three-quarters of the world was a colony of Europe (or the United States or Japan). Not bad, all in all, for a few floating centuries. In the latter part of this period, the phrase "gunboat diplomacy" came into existence, an oxymoron that nonetheless expressed itself all too eloquently.

Our Little "Diplomats"

Today, "gunboat diplomacy" seems like a phrase from some antiquated imperial past (despite the thirteen US aircraft-carrier task forces that travel the world making "friendly" house calls from time to time). But if you stop thinking about literal gunboats and try to imagine how we carry out "armed diplomacy"—and, as we all know, under the Bush administration the Pentagon has taken over much that might once have been labeled "diplomacy"—then you can begin to conjure up our own twenty-first-century version of gunboat diplomacy. But first, you have to consider exactly what the "platforms" are upon which the US "exports force," upon which we mount our "cannons."

What should immediately come to mind are our military bases, liberally scattered like so many vast immobile vessels over the lands of the Earth. This has been especially true since the neocons of the Bush administration grabbed the reins of power at the Pentagon and set about reconceiving basing policy globally; set about, that is, creating more "mobile" versions of the military base, ever more stripped down for action, ever closer to what they've come to call the "arc of instability," a vast swath of lands extending from the former Yugoslavia and the former Soviet Socialist Republics (SSRs) of Eastern Europe down deep into northern Africa and all the way to the Chinese border. These are areas that represent, not surprisingly, the future energy heartland of the planet. What the Pentagon refers to as its "lily pads" strategy is meant to encircle and nail down control of this vast set of interlocking regions—the thought being that, if the occasion arises, the American frogs can leap agilely from one prepositioned pad to another, knocking off the "flies" as they go.

Thought about a certain way, the military base, particularly as reconceived in recent years, whether in Uzbekistan, Kosovo, or Qatar, is our "gunboat," a "platform" that has been ridden ever deeper into the landlocked parts of the globe—into regions like the Middle East, where our access once had some limits, or like the former Yugoslavia and the 'stans of Central Asia, where the lesser superpower of the Cold War era once blocked access entirely. Our new military bases are essentially the twenty-first-century version of the old European warships, the difference being that, once built, the base remains in place, while its parts—the modern equivalents of those sixteenth-century cannons—are capable of moving over land or water almost anywhere.

As Chalmers Johnson has calculated in his new book on American militarism *The Sorrows of Empire*, our global Baseworld consists of at least 700 military and intelligence bases, possibly—depending on how you count them up— many more. This is our true "imperial fleet" (though, of course, we have an actual imperial fleet as well, our aircraft carriers alone being like small, massively armed towns). In the last decade-plus, as the pace of our foreign wars has picked up, we've left behind, after each of them, a new set of bases like the droppings of some giant beast marking the scene with its scent. Bases were dropped into Saudi Arabia and the small Gulf emirates after our First Gulf War in 1991; into the former Yugoslavia after the Kosovo air war of 1999; into Pakistan, Afghanistan, and several of the former Central Asian SSRs after the Afghan war of 2001; and into Iraq after the 2003 invasion.

The process has speeded up under the Bush administration, but until recent weeks, if you read the US press, you would have had almost no way of knowing this. Since April 2003, for instance, when the *New York Times* front-paged Pentagon plans to build four permanent bases in Iraq, unless you wandered the Web reading the foreign press you would have been hard put to find anything at all on the subject of Iraqi bases, even though they were being built at a rapid pace. Basing is generally considered here either a topic not worth writing about or an arcane policy matter best left to the inside pages for the policy wonks and news junkies. This is in part because we Americans—and by extension our journalists—don't imagine us as garrisoning or occupying the world; and certainly don't see us as having anything faintly approaching a military empire. Generally speaking, those more than seven hundred bases, our little "diplomats" (and the rights of extraterritoriality that go with them via Status of Forces Agreements) don't even register on our media's mental map of our globe.

Only recently, however, a few basing articles have suddenly appeared and, miracle of miracles, Christine Spolar of the *Chicago Tribune* has actually written one about our permanent Iraqi bases, endearingly referred to in the military as "enduring camps." Such bases were almost certainly planned for by the Pentagon before the 2003 invasion. After all, we were also planning to withdraw most of our troops from Saudi Arabia—Osama bin Laden had complained bitterly about the occupation of Islam's holy sites—and they weren't simply going to be shipped back to the US

But the numbers of those potential enduring camps in Iraq are startling indeed. The title of Spolar's piece tells the tale: "14 'Enduring' Bases Set in Iraq"—and it begins with the line: "From the ashes of abandoned Iraqi army bases, US military engineers are overseeing the building of an enhanced system of American bases designed to last for years."

Think about fourteen bases "for years," and keep in mind that some of these bases are already comparable in size and elaborateness to the ones we built in Vietnam four decades ago. Spolar continues:

> As the US scales back its military presence in Saudi Arabia, Iraq provides an option for an administration eager to maintain a robust military presence in the Middle East and intent on a muscular approach to seeding democracy in the region. The number of US military personnel in Iraq, between 105,000 and 110,000, is expected to remain unchanged through 2006, according to military planners.
>
> "Is this a swap for the Saudi bases?" asked Army Brig. Gen. Robert Pollman, chief engineer for base construction in Iraq. "I don't know. . . . When we talk

about enduring bases here, we're talking about the present operation, not in terms of America's global strategic base. But this makes sense. It makes a lot of logical sense."

And keep in mind as well that all of this construction is being done to the tune of billions of dollars under contracts controlled by the Pentagon and, as Spolar writes, quite "separate from the State Department and its Embassy in Baghdad" (which, after June 30, is slated to be the largest embassy in the world with a "staff" of 3,000-plus).

As the Pentagon planned it, and as we knew via leaks to the press soon after the war, newly "liberated" Iraq, once "sovereignty" had been restored, was to have only a lightly armed military force of some 40,000 men and no air force. The other part of this equation, the given (if unspoken) part, was that some sort of significant long-term American military protection of the country would have to be put in place. That size Iraqi military in one of the most heavily armed regions of the planet was like an insurance policy that we would "have" to stay. And we've proceeded accordingly, emplacing our "little diplomats" right at a future hub of the global energy superhighway.

But we've made sure to cover the other on and off ramps as well. As James Sterngold of the *San Francisco Chronicle* wrote recently in a rundown of some of our post-9/11 basing policies ("After 9/11, US Policy Built on World Bases"):

> One year after US tanks rolled through Iraq and more than two years after the United States bombed the Taliban out of power in Afghanistan, the administration has instituted what some experts describe as the most militarized foreign policy machine in modern history.
>
> The policy has involved not just resorting to military action, or the threat of action, but constructing an arc of new facilities in such places as Uzbekistan, Pakistan, Qatar and Djibouti that the Pentagon calls "lily pads." They are seen not merely as a means of defending the host countries—the traditional Cold War role of such installations—but as jumping-off points for future "preventive wars" and military missions.

In fact, our particular version of military empire is perhaps unique: all "gunboats," no colonies. The combination of bases we set down in any given country is referred to in the Pentagon as our "footprint" in that country. It's a term that may once have come from the idea of "boots on the ground," but now has congealed, imagistically speaking, into a single (and assumedly singular) bootprint—as if, as it strode across the planet, the globe's only hyperpower was so vast that it could place only a single boot in any given country at any time.

Undersecretary of Defense for Policy Douglas Feith has been the main Pentagon architect of a plan to "realign" our bases so as to "forward deploy" US forces into the "arc of instability." (On a planet so thoroughly garrisoned, though, what can "forward" actually mean?) In a December 2003 speech to the Center for Strategic and International Studies ("Transforming the US Global Defense Posture"), he offered a Pentagon version of sensitivity in discussing his forward deployment plans: "Realigning the US posture will also help strengthen our alliances by tailoring the physical US 'footprint' to suit local conditions. The goal is to reduce friction with host nations, the kind that results from accidents and other problems relating to local sensitivities." (Moccasins, flip-flops, sandals anyone?)

In the meantime, to ensure that there will be no consequences if the giant foot, however enclosed, happens to stamp its print in a tad clumsily, causing the odd bit of collateral damage, he added:

> For this deployability concept to work, US forces must be able to move smoothly into, through, and out of host nations, which puts a premium on establishing legal and support arrangements with many friendly countries. We are negotiating or planning to negotiate with many countries legal protections for US personnel, through Status of Forces Agreements and agreements (known as Article 98 agreements) limiting the jurisdiction of the International Criminal Court with respect to our forces' activities.

Bradley Graham of the *Washington Post* recently offered a more precise glimpse at Feith's realignment strategy, which would move us away from our Cold War deployments, especially in Germany, Japan and Korea ("US May Halve Forces in Germany"):

> The Pentagon has drafted plans to withdraw as many as half of the 71,000 troops based in Germany as part of an extensive realignment of American military forces that moves away from large concentrations in Europe and Asia,

according to US officials. . . . US officials have said before that they intended to eliminate a number of large, full-service Cold War bases abroad and construct a network of more skeletal outposts closer to potential trouble spots in the Middle East and along the Pacific Rim.

In fact, the structure of major bases and "forward operating sites" in the arc of instability and, from Eastern Europe to the Central Asian 'stans, inside the former Soviet empire, is already in place or, as in Iraq, in the process of being built or negotiated. As Michael Kilian of the *Chicago Tribune* writes:

> [T]he United States now has bases or shares military installations in Turkey, Iraq, Saudi Arabia, Kuwait, Bahrain, Qatar, the United Arab Emirates, Oman, Ethiopia, Pakistan, Uzbekistan, Tajikistan and Kyrgyzstan, as well as on the island of Diego Garcia in the Indian Ocean.
>
> Rumsfeld and Pentagon officials are soon expected to unveil plans for a new US military "footprint" on the rest of the world. The plan is expected to include a shift of resources from the huge Cold War-era bases in Western Europe to new and smaller ones in Poland and other Eastern European nations as well as a relocation of US troops in South Korea.

In the meantime, Pentagon strategic planning for ever more aggressive future war-fighting is likely only to intensify this process. *Los Angeles Times* military analyst William Arkin recently wrote of the unveiling of Secretary of Defense Rumsfeld's plan for a new military map of the globe ("War Plans Meaner, not Leaner"):

> The Rumsfeld plan envisions what it labels a "1-4-2-1 defense strategy," in which war planners prepare to fully defend one country (the United States), maintain forces capable of "deterring aggression and coercion" in four "critical regions" (Europe, Northeast Asia, East Asia, and the Middle East and Southwest Asia), maintain the ability to defeat aggression in two of these regions simultaneously, and be able to "win decisively"—up to and including forcing regime change and occupying a country—in one of those conflicts "at a time and place of our choosing". . . . In the Clinton era, the Pentagon planned for fighting two wars simultaneously (in the Middle East and Northeast Asia). Under the new strategy, it must prepare for four. . . .

The planning model Rumsfeld and company have embraced is certainly more ambitious. It covers domestic and foreign contingencies and favors preemption over diplomacy, and military strikes over peacekeeping operations. The plan signals to the world that the United States considers nuclear weapons useful military instruments, to be employed where warranted.

Or just consider another kind of footprint—the tap dancing kind. The Pentagon's website informs us that at Lackland Air Force Base in Texas, the US Air Force has just held auditions in a "worldwide talent search" that even included a Robert de Niro impersonator. All of this was for the Tops in Blue (TIB) 2004 tour. Let me emphasize that we're not talking about an "All-American" talent contest, but a worldwide one. And, in fact, according to the Air Force press release, the winner of the "male vocalist" spot on the tour was Airman First Class Antonio Dandridge from the Thirty-fifth Civil Engineer Squadron at Misawa Air Base, Japan. A recent TIB tour managed to hit twenty-seven countries (read military bases), including Bagram Air Base in embattled Afghanistan.

We're talking a globe-girdling Baseworld here. Assumedly, the show's finale will be a rousing chorus of "We Are the World."

Twenty-second-century Gunboat Diplomacy

At least as now imagined in the Pentagon, twenty-second-century "gunboat diplomacy" will be conducted by what the Air Force's Space Command refers to as "space-based platforms" and the "cannons" will be a range of "exotic" weapons and delivery systems. In still unweaponized space (if you exclude the various spy satellites overhead), we plan for our future "ships" to travel the heavens alone, representatives of a singular heavenly version of gunboat diplomacy. Among the "five priorities for national security space efforts in 2004" set out by Peter B. Teets, undersecretary of the Air Force and director of the National Reconnaissance Office, in March 2004 in testimony before the Senate Armed Services Committee, the most striking, if also predictable, is that of "ensuring freedom of action in space"—as in freedom of action for the US, and no action at all for anyone else.

Secretary of Defense Donald Rumsfeld has long been riveted by the idea of dominating space, and in his hands space, a void, is now being re-imagined as the ocean of our imperial future, thanks to space weaponry now on the drawing boards such as the nicknamed "Rods from God." These are to be "orbiting platforms stocked with tungsten rods perhaps 20 feet long and one foot in diameter that could be satellite-guided to targets anywhere on Earth within minutes. Accurate within about 25 feet, they would strike at speeds upwards of 12,000 feet per second, enough to destroy even hardened bunkers several stories underground."

Planning among "high frontier" enthusiasts for the conquest and militarization of space began in the 1980s during the Reagan administration, but it has now reached new levels of realism (of a mad sort). Theresa Hitchens of the Center for Defense Information recently wrote in the *San Francisco Chronicle*:

> [T]he service's gloves came off with the Feb. 17 release of the new US Air Force Transformation Flight Plan. The document details a stunning array of exotic weapons to be pursued over the next decade: from an air-launched missile designed to knock satellites out of low orbit, to ground- and space-based lasers for attacking both missiles and satellites . . . Far from being aimed solely at the protection of US space capabilities, such weapons are instead intended for offensive, first-strike missions.

Ever since H. G. Wells wrote *The War of the Worlds* in 1898, we humans have been imagining scenarios in which implacable aliens with superweapons arrive from space to devastate our planet. But what if it turns out that the implacable aliens are actually us—and that, as in the sixteenth century, someday in the not-too-distant future American "ships" will "burst from space" upon the "coasts" of our planet with devastation imprinted in their programs. These are, of course, the dreams of modern Mongols.

August 2007

10

THE SOLE SUPERPOWER IN DECLINE

The Rise of a Multipolar World

Dilip Hiro

With the collapse of the Soviet Union in 1991, the United States stood tall—militarily invincible, economically unrivaled, diplomatically uncontestable, and the dominating force on information channels worldwide. The next century was to be the true "American century," with the rest of the world molding itself in the image of the sole superpower.

Yet, with not even a decade of the twenty-first century behind us, we are already witnessing the rise of a multipolar world in which new powers are challenging different aspects of American supremacy—Russia and China in the forefront, with regional powers Venezuela and Iran forming the second rank. These emergent powers are primed to erode American hegemony, not confront it, singly or jointly.

How and why has the world evolved in this way so soon? The Bush administration's debacle in Iraq is certainly a major factor in this transformation, a classic example of an imperialist power, brimming with hubris, overextending itself. To the relief of many—in the US and elsewhere—the Iraq fiasco has demonstrated the striking limitations of power for the globe's highest-tech, most destructive military machine. In Iraq, Brent Scowcroft, national security adviser to two US presidents, concedes in a recent op-ed, "We are being wrestled to a draw by opponents who are not even an organized state adversary."

The invasion and subsequent disastrous occupation of Iraq and the mismanaged military campaign in Afghanistan have crippled the credibility of the United States. The scandals at Abu Ghraib prison in Iraq and Guantánamo in Cuba, along with the widely publicized murders of Iraqi civilians in Haditha, have badly tarnished America's moral self-image. In the latest opinion poll, even in a secular state and member of NATO like Turkey, only 9 percent of Turks have a "favorable view" of the US (down from 52 percent just five years ago).

Yet there are other explanations—unrelated to Washington's glaring misadventures—for the current transformation in international affairs. These include, above all, the tightening market in oil and natural gas, which has enhanced the power of hydrocarbon-rich nations as never before; the rapid economic expansion of the mega-nations China and India; the transformation of China into the globe's leading manufacturing base; and the end of the Anglo-American duopoly in international television news.

Many Channels, Diverse Perceptions

During the 1991 Gulf War, only CNN and the BBC had correspondents in Baghdad. So the international TV audience, irrespective of its location, saw the conflict through their lenses. Twelve years later, when the Bush administration, backed by British prime minister Tony Blair, invaded Iraq, Al Jazeera Arabic broke this duopoly. It relayed images—and facts—that contradicted the Pentagon's presentation. For the first time in history, the world witnessed two versions of an ongoing war in real time. So credible was the Al Jazeera Arabic version that many television companies outside the Arabic-speaking world—in Europe, Asia and Latin America—showed its clips.

Though, in theory, the growth of cable television worldwide had raised the prospect of ending the Anglo-American duopoly in twenty-four-hour TV news, not much had happened due to the exorbitant cost of gathering and editing TV news. It was only the arrival of Al Jazeera English, funded by the hydrocarbon-rich emirate of Qatar—with its declared policy of offering a global perspective from an Arab and Muslim angle—that, in 2006, finally broke the long-established mold.

Soon France 24 came on the air, broadcasting in English and French from a French viewpoint, followed in mid-2007 by the English-language Press

TV, which aimed to provide an Iranian perspective. Russia was next in line for twenty-four-hour TV news in English for the global audience. Meanwhile, spurred by Venezuelan president Hugo Chávez, Telesur, a pan-Latin American TV channel based in Caracas, began competing with CNN in Spanish for a mass audience.

As with Qatar, so with Russia and Venezuela, the funding for these TV news ventures has come from soaring national hydrocarbon incomes—a factor draining American hegemony not just in imagery but in reality.

Russia, an Energy Superpower

Under President Vladimir Putin, Russia has more than recovered from the economic chaos that followed the collapse of the Soviet Union in 1991. After effectively renationalizing the energy industry through state-controlled corporations, he began deploying its economic clout to further Russia's foreign policy interests.

In 2005, Russia overtook the United States, becoming the second-largest oil producer in the world. Its oil income now amounts to $679 million a day. European countries dependent on imported Russian oil now include Hungary, Poland, Germany, and even Britain.

Russia is also the largest producer of natural gas on the planet, with three-fifths of its gas exports going to the twenty-seven-member European Union (EU). Bulgaria, Estonia, Finland, and Slovakia get 100 percent of their natural gas from Russia; Turkey, 66 percent; Poland, 58 percent; Germany 41 percent; and France 25 percent. Gazprom, the biggest natural gas enterprise on Earth, has established stakes in sixteen EU countries. In 2006, the Kremlin's foreign reserves stood at $315 billion, up from a paltry $12 billion in 1999. Little wonder that, in July 2006 on the eve of the G8 summit in St Petersburg, Putin rejected an energy charter proposed by the Western leaders.

Soaring foreign-exchange reserves, new ballistic missiles, and closer links with a prospering China—with which it conducted joint military exercises on China's Shandong Peninsula in August 2005—enabled Putin to deal with his American counterpart, President George W. Bush, as an equal, not mincing his words when appraising American policies.

"One country, the United States, has overstepped its national boundaries in every way," Putin told the 43rd Munich Trans-Atlantic conference on security policy in February 2007. "This is visible in the economic, political, cultural and educational policies it imposes on other nations. . . . This is very dangerous."

Condemning the concept of a "unipolar world," he added: "However one might embellish this term, at the end of the day it describes a scenario in which there is one center of authority, one center of force, one center of decision making. . . . It is a world in which there is one master, one sovereign. And this is pernicious." His views fell on receptive ears in the capitals of most Asian, African, and Latin American countries.

The changing relationship between Moscow and Washington was noted, among others, by analysts and policy makers in the hydrocarbon-rich Persian Gulf region. Commenting on the visit that Putin paid to long-time US allies Saudi Arabia and Qatar after the Munich conference, Abdel Aziz Sagar, chairman of the Gulf Research Center, wrote in the Doha-based newspaper *The Peninsula* that Russia and Gulf Arab countries, once rivals from opposite ideological camps, had found a common agenda of oil, antiterrorism, and arms sales. "The altered focus takes place in a milieu where the Gulf countries are signaling their keenness to keep all geopolitical options open, reviewing the utility of the United States as the sole security guarantor, and contemplating a collective security mechanism that involves a host of international players."

In April 2007, the Kremlin issued a major foreign policy document. "The myth about the unipolar world fell apart once and for all in Iraq," it stated. "A strong, more self-confident Russia has become an integral part of positive changes in the world."

The Kremlin's increasingly tense relations with Washington were in tune with Russian popular opinion. A poll taken during the run-up to the 2006 G8 summit revealed that 58 percent of Russians regarded America as an "unfriendly country." It has proved to be a trend. In July 2007, for instance, Major General Alexandr Vladimirov told the mass-circulation newspaper *Komsolskya Pravada* that war with the United States was a "possibility" in the next ten to fifteen years.

Chávez Rides High

Such sentiments resonated with Hugo Chávez. While visiting Moscow in June 2007, he urged Russians to return to the ideas of Vladimir Lenin, especially his anti-imperialism. "The Americans don't want Russia to keep rising," he said. "But Russia has risen again as a center of power, and we, the people of the world, need Russia to become stronger."

Chávez finalized a $1 billion deal to purchase five diesel submarines to defend Venezuela's oil-rich undersea shelf and thwart any possible future economic embargo imposed by Washington. By then, Venezuela had become the second-largest buyer of Russian weaponry. (Algeria topped the list, another indication of a growing multipolarity in world affairs.) Venezuela acquired the distinction of being the first country to receive a license from Russia to manufacture the famed AK-47 assault rifle.

By channeling some of his country's oil money to needy Venezuelans, Chávez broadened his base of support. Much to the chagrin of the Bush White House, he trounced his sole political rival, Manuel Rosales, in a December 2006 presidential contest with 61 percent of the vote. Equally humiliating to the Bush administration, Venezuela was, by then, giving more foreign aid to needy Latin American states than it was.

Following his reelection, Chávez vigorously pursued the concept of forming an anti-imperialist alliance in Latin America as well as globally. He strengthened Venezuela's ties not only with such Latin countries as Bolivia, Cuba, Ecuador, Nicaragua, and debt-ridden Argentina, but also with Iran and Belarus.

By the time he arrived in Tehran from Moscow (via Minsk) in June 2007, the 180 economic and political accords his government had signed with Tehran were already yielding tangible results. Iranian-designed cars and tractors were coming off assembly lines in Venezuela. "[The] cooperation of independent countries like Iran and Venezuela has an effective role in defeating the policies of imperialism and saving nations," Chávez declared in Tehran.

Stuck in the quagmire of Iraq and lashed by the gusty winds of rocketing oil prices, the Bush administration finds its area of maneuver woefully limited when dealing with a rising hydrocarbon power. To the insults that Chávez keeps hurling at Bush, the American response has been vapid. The reason is the crippling dependence of the United States on imported petroleum which accounts for 60 percent of its total consumed. Venezuela is the fourth-largest source of US imported oil after Canada, Mexico, and Saudi Arabia; and some refineries in the US are designed specifically to refine heavy Venezuelan oil.

In Chávez's scheme to undermine the "sole superpower," China has an important role. During an August 2006 visit to Beijing, his fourth in seven years, he announced that Venezuela would triple its oil exports to China to 500,000 barrels per day in three years, a jump that suited both sides. Chávez wants to diversify Venezuela's buyer base to reduce its reliance on exports to the US, and China's leaders are keen to diversify their hydrocarbon imports away from the Middle East, where American influence remains strong.

"The support of China is very important [to us] from the political and moral point of view," Chávez declared. Along with a joint refinery project, China agreed to build thirteen oil drilling platforms, supply eighteen oil tankers, and collaborate with the state-owned company Petroleos de Venezuela SA (PdVSA) in exploring a new oilfield in the Orinoco Basin.

China on a Stratospheric Trajectory

So dramatic has been the growth of the state-run company PetroChina that, in mid-2007, it was second only to Exxon Mobil in its market value among energy corporations. Indeed, that year three Chinese companies made it onto the list of the world's ten most highly valued corporations. Only the US had more with five. China's foreign reserves of over $1 trillion have now surpassed Japan's. With its gross domestic product soaring past Germany's, China ranks number three in the world economy.

In the diplomatic arena, Chinese leaders broke new ground in 1996 by sponsoring the Shanghai Cooperation Organization (SCO), consisting of four adjoining countries: Russia and the three former Soviet Socialist Republics of Kazakhstan, Kyrgyzstan, and Tajikistan. The SCO started as a cooperative organization with a focus on countering drug smuggling and terrorism. Later, the SCO invited Uzbekistan to join, even though it does not abut China. In 2003, the SCO broadened its scope by including regional economic cooperation in its charter. That in turn led it to grant observer status to Pakistan, India, and Mongolia—all adjoining China—and Iran which does not. When the US applied for observer status, it was rejected, an embarrassing setback for Washington, which enjoyed such status at the Association of Southeast Asian Nations (ASEAN).

In early August 2007, on the eve of an SCO summit in the Kyrgyz capital of Bishkek, the group conducted its first joint military exercises, codenamed

Peace Mission 2007, in the Russian Ural region of Chelyabinsk. "The SCO is destined to play a vital role in ensuring international security," said Ednan Karabayev, foreign minister of Kyrgyzstan.

In late 2006, as the host of a China–Africa Forum in Beijing attended by leaders of forty-eight of fifty-three African nations, China left the US woefully behind in the diplomatic race for that continent (and its hydrocarbon and other resources). In return for Africa's oil, iron ore, copper, and cotton, China sold low-priced goods to Africans, and assisted African countries in building or improving roads, railways, ports, hydroelectric dams, telecommunications systems, and schools. "The Western approach of imposing its values and political system on other countries is not acceptable to China," said Africa specialist Wang Hongyi of the China Institute of International Studies. "We focus on mutual development."

To reduce the cost of transporting petroleum from Africa and the Middle East, China began constructing a trans-Burma oil pipeline from the Bay of Bengal to its southern province of Yunan, thereby shortening the delivery distance now traveled by tankers. This undermined Washington's campaign to isolate Myanmar. (Earlier, Sudan, boycotted by Washington, had emerged as a leading supplier of African oil to China.) In addition, Chinese oil companies were competing fiercely with their Western counterparts in getting access to hydrocarbon reserves in Kazakhstan and Uzbekistan.

"China's oil diplomacy is putting the country on a collision course with the US and Western Europe, which have imposed sanctions on some of the countries where China is doing business," comments William Mellor of *Bloomberg News*. The sentiment is echoed by the other side. "I see China and the US coming into conflict over energy in the years ahead," says Jin Riguang, an oil-and-gas adviser to the Chinese government and a member of the Standing Committee of the Chinese People's Political Consultative Council.

China's industrialization and modernization have spurred the modernization of its military as well. The test-firing of the country's first anti-satellite missile, which successfully destroyed a defunct Chinese weather satellite in January 2007, dramatically demonstrated its growing technological prowess. An alarmed Washington had already noted an 18 percent increase in China's 2007 defense budget. Attributing the rise to extra spending on missiles, electronic warfare, and other high-tech items, Liao Xilong, commander of the People's Liberation Army's general logistics department, said: "The present-day world is no longer peaceful and to protect national security, stability and territorial integrity we must suitably increase spending on military modernization."

China's declared budget of $45 billion was a tiny fraction of the Pentagon's $459 billion budget. Yet, in May 2007, a Pentagon report noted China's "rapid rise as a regional and economic power with global aspirations" and claimed that it was planning to project military power farther afield from the Taiwan Straits into the Asia-Pacific region in preparation for possible conflicts over territory or resources.

The Sole Superpower in the Sweep of History

This disparate challenge to American global primacy stems as much from sharpening conflicts over natural resources, particularly oil and natural gas, as from ideological differences over democracy, American style, or human rights, as conceived and promoted by Western policy makers. Perceptions about national (and imperial) identity and history are at stake as well.

It is noteworthy that Russian officials applauding the swift rise of post-Soviet Russia refer fondly to the pre-Bolshevik Revolution era when, according to them, Tsarist Russia was a Great Power. Equally, Chinese leaders remain proud of their country's long imperial past as unique among nations.

When viewed globally and in the great stretch of history, the notion of American exceptionalism that drove the neoconservatives to proclaim the Project for the New American Century in the late twentieth century— adopted so wholeheartedly by the Bush administration in this one—is nothing new. Other superpowers have been there before and they, too, have witnessed the loss of their prime position to rising powers.

No superpower in modern times has maintained its supremacy for more than several generations. And, however exceptional its leaders may have thought themselves, the United States, already clearly past its zenith, has no chance of becoming an exception to this age-old pattern of history.

III

INVISIBLE VICTIMS OF
THE "WAR ON TERROR"

July 2005

11

THE SMASH OF CIVILIZATIONS

Chalmers Johnson

In the months before he ordered the invasion of Iraq, George Bush and his senior officials spoke of preserving Iraq's "patrimony" for the Iraqi people. At a time when talking about Iraqi oil was taboo, what he meant by patrimony was exactly that—Iraqi oil. In their "joint statement on Iraq's future" of April 8, 2003, George Bush and Tony Blair declared, "We reaffirm our commitment to protect Iraq's natural resources, as the patrimony of the people of Iraq, which should be used only for their benefit."[1] In this they were true to their word. Among the few places American soldiers actually did guard during and in the wake of their invasion were oil fields and the Oil Ministry in Baghdad. But the real Iraqi patrimony, that invaluable human inheritance of thousands of years, was another matter. At a time when American pundits were warning of a future "clash of civilizations," our occupation forces were letting perhaps the greatest of all human patrimonies be looted and smashed.

There have been many dispiriting sights on TV since George Bush launched his ill-starred war on Iraq—the pictures from Abu Ghraib, Falluja laid waste, American soldiers kicking down the doors of private homes and pointing assault rifles at women and children. But few have reverberated historically like the looting of Baghdad's museum—or been forgotten more quickly in the US.

---

1. American Embassy, London, "Visit of President Bush to Northern Ireland, April 7–8, 2003."

Teaching the Iraqis about the Untidiness of History

In archaeological circles, Iraq is known as "the cradle of civilization," with a record of culture going back more than 7,000 years. William R. Polk, the founder of the Center for Middle Eastern Studies at the University of Chicago, says, "It was there, in what the Greeks called Mesopotamia, that life as we know it today began: there people first began to speculate on philosophy and religion, developed concepts of international trade, made ideas of beauty into tangible forms, and above all developed the skill of writing."[2] No other places in the Bible except for Israel have more history and prophecy associated with them than Babylonia, Shinar (Sumer), and Mesopotamia—different names for the territory that the British around the time of World War One began to call "Iraq," using the old Arab term for the lands of the former Turkish enclave of Mesopotamia (in Greek: "between the [Tigris and Euphrates] rivers").[3] Most of the early books of Genesis are set in Iraq. (See, for instance, Genesis 10:10, 11:31; also Daniel 1–4; II Kings 24.)

The best-known of the civilizations that make up Iraq's cultural heritage are the Sumerians, Akkadians, Babylonians, Assyrians, Chaldeans, Persians, Greeks, Romans, Parthians, Sassanids, and Muslims. On April 10, 2003, in a television address, President Bush acknowledged that the Iraqi people are "the heirs of a great civilization that contributes to all humanity."[4] Only two days later, under the complacent eyes of the US army, the Iraqis would begin to lose that heritage in a swirl of looting and burning.

In September 2004, in one of the few self-critical reports to come out of Donald Rumsfeld's Department of Defense, the Defense Science Board Task Force on Strategic Communication wrote, "The larger goals of US strategy depend on separating the vast majority of non-violent Muslims from the radical-militant Islamist-Jihadists. But American efforts have not only failed in this respect: they may also have achieved the opposite of what they

---

2. William R. Polk, "Introduction," in Milbry Polk and Angela M. H. Schuster, eds., *The Looting of the Iraq Museum, Baghdad: The Lost Legacy of Ancient Mesopotamia* (New York: Harry N. Abrams, 2005), p. 5. Also see Suzanne Muchnic, "Spotlight on Iraq's Plundered Past," *Los Angeles Times*, June 20, 2005.

3. David Fromkin, *A Peace To End All Peace: The Fall of the Ottoman Empire and the Creation of the Modern Middle East* (New York: Owl Books, 1989, 2001), p. 450.

4. George Bush's address to the Iraqi people, broadcast on Towards Freedom TV, April 10, 2003.

intended."[5] Nowhere was this failure more apparent than in the indifference—even the glee—shown by Rumsfeld and his generals toward the looting on April 11 and 12, 2003, of the National Museum in Baghdad and the burning on April 14, 2003, of the National Library and Archives as well as the Library of Korans at the Ministry of Religious Endowments. These events were, according to Paul Zimansky, a Boston University archaeologist, "the greatest cultural disaster of the last 500 years." Eleanor Robson of All Souls College, Oxford, said, "You'd have to go back centuries, to the Mongol invasion of Baghdad in 1258, to find looting on this scale."[6] Yet Secretary Rumsfeld compared the looting to the aftermath of a soccer game and shrugged it off with the comment that "Freedom's untidy. . . . Free people are free to make mistakes and commit crimes."[7]

The Baghdad archaeological museum has long been regarded as perhaps the richest of all such institutions in the Middle East. It is difficult to say with precision what was lost there in those catastrophic April days in 2003 because up-to-date inventories of its holdings, many never even described in archaeological journals, were also destroyed by the looters or were incomplete thanks to conditions in Baghdad after the Gulf War of 1991. One of the best records, however partial, of its holdings is the catalog of items the museum lent in 1988 to an exhibition held in Japan's ancient capital of Nara entitled "Silk Road Civilizations." But, as one museum official said to John Burns of the *New York Times* after the looting, "All gone, all gone. All gone in two days."[8]

A single, beautifully illustrated, indispensable book edited by Milbry Polk and Angela M. H. Schuster, *The Looting of the Iraq Museum, Baghdad: The Lost Legacy of Ancient Mesopotamia* (New York: Harry N. Abrams, 2005), represents the heartbreaking attempt of over a dozen archaeological specialists on ancient Iraq to specify what was in the museum before the catastrophe, where those objects had been excavated, and the condition of those few

---

5. Office of the Under Secretary of Defense for Acquisition, Technology, and Logistics, *Report of the Defense Science Board Task Force on Strategic Communication* (Washington, DC: September 2004), pp. 39–40.

6. See Frank Rich, "And Now: 'Operation Iraqi Looting,'" *New York Times*, April 27, 2003.

7. Robert Scheer, "It's US Policy That's 'Untidy,'" *Los Angeles Times*, April 15, 2003; reprinted in "Books in Flames," *Tomdispatch*, April 15, 2003.

8. John F. Burns, "Pillagers Strip Iraqi Museum of Its Treasures," *New York Times*, April 13, 2003; Piotr Michalowski (University of Michigan), "The Ransacking of the Baghdad Museum Is a Disgrace," *History News Network*, April 14, 2003.

thousand items that have been recovered. The editors and authors have dedicated a portion of the royalties from this book to the Iraqi State Board of Antiquities and Heritage.

At a conference on art crimes held in London a year after the disaster, the British Museum's John Curtis reported that at least half of the forty most important stolen objects had not been retrieved and that of some 15,000 items looted from the Baghdad museum's showcases and storerooms about 8,000 had yet to be traced. Its entire collection of 5,800 cylinder seals and clay tablets, many containing cuneiform writing and other inscriptions some of which go back to the earliest discoveries of writing itself, was stolen.[9] Since then, as a result of an amnesty for looters, about 4,000 of the artifacts have been recovered in Iraq, and over a thousand have been confiscated in the United States.[10] Curtis noted that random checks of Western soldiers leaving Iraq had led to the discovery of several in illegal possession of ancient objects. Customs agents in the US then found more. Officials in Jordan have impounded about 2,000 pieces smuggled in from Iraq; officials in France, 500 pieces; in Italy, 300; in Syria, 300; and in Switzerland, 250. Lesser numbers have been seized in Kuwait, Saudi Arabia, Iran, and Turkey. None of these objects has as yet been sent back to Baghdad.

The 616 pieces that form the famous collection of "Nimrud gold," excavated by the Iraqis in the late 1980s from the tombs of the Assyrian queens at Nimrud, a few miles southeast of Mosul, were saved, but only because the museum had secretly moved them to the subterranean vaults of the Central Bank of Iraq at the time of the First Gulf War. By the time the Americans got around to protecting the bank in 2003, its building was a burnt-out shell filled with twisted metal beams from the collapse of the roof and all nine floors under it. Nonetheless, the underground compartments and their contents survived undamaged. On July 3, 2003, a small portion of the Nimrud holdings was put on display for a few hours, allowing a handful of Iraqi officials to see them for the first time since 1990.[11]

---

9. Polk and Schuster, pp. 209–10.

10. Mark Wilkinson, "Looting of Ancient Sites Threatens Iraqi Heritage," Reuters, June 29, 2005.

11. Polk and Schuster, pp. 23, 212–13; Louise Jury, "At Least 8,000 Treasures Looted from Iraq Museum Still Untraced," *Independent*, May 24, 2005; Stephen Fidler, "'The Looters Knew What They Wanted. It Looks Like Vandalism, but Organized Crime May Be Behind It,'" *Financial Times*, May 23, 2003; Rod Liddle, "The Day of the Jackals," *Spectator*, April 19, 2003.

The torching of books and manuscripts in the Library of Korans and the National Library was in itself a historical disaster of the first order. Most of the Ottoman imperial documents and the old royal archives concerning the creation of Iraq were reduced to ashes. According to Humberto Márquez, the Venezuelan writer and author of *Historia Universal de La Destrucción de Los Libros* (2004), about a million books and ten million documents were destroyed by the fires of April 14, 2003.[12] Robert Fisk, the veteran Middle East correspondent of the *Independent* of London, was in Baghdad the day of the fires. He rushed to the offices of the US Marines' Civil Affairs Bureau and gave the officer on duty precise map locations for the two archives and their names in Arabic and English, and pointed out that the smoke could be seen from three miles away. The officer shouted to a colleague, "This guy says some biblical library is on fire," but the Americans did nothing to try to put out the flames.[13]

The Burger King of Ur

Given the black market value of ancient art objects, US military leaders had been warned that the looting of all thirteen national museums throughout the country would be a particularly grave danger in the days after they captured Baghdad and took control of Iraq. In the chaos that followed the Gulf War of 1991, vandals had stolen about 4,000 objects from nine different regional museums. In monetary terms, the illegal trade in antiquities is the third most lucrative form of international trade globally, exceeded only by drug smuggling and arms sales.[14] Given the richness of Iraq's past, there are also over 10,000 significant archaeological sites scattered across the country, only some 1,500 of which have been studied. Following the Gulf War, a number of them were illegally excavated and their artifacts were sold to unscrupulous international collectors in Western countries and Japan. All this was known to American commanders.

In January 2003, on the eve of the invasion of Iraq, an American delegation of scholars, museum directors, art collectors, and antiquities dealers met with

---

12. Humberto Márquez, "Iraq Invasion the 'Biggest Cultural Disaster Since 1258,' " Antiwar.com, February 16, 2005.
13. Robert Fisk, "Library Books, Letters, and Priceless Documents are Set Ablaze in Final Chapter of the Sacking of Baghdad," *Independent*, April 15, 2003.
14. Polk and Schuster, p. 10.

officials at the Pentagon to discuss the forthcoming invasion. They specifically warned that Baghdad's National Museum was the single most important site in the country. McGuire Gibson of the University of Chicago's Oriental Institute said, "I thought I was given assurances that sites and museums would be protected."[15] Gibson went back to the Pentagon twice to discuss the dangers, and he and his colleagues sent several email reminders to military officers in the weeks before the war began. However, a more ominous indicator of things to come was reported in the April 14, 2003 London *Guardian*: Rich American collectors with connections to the White House were busy "persuading the Pentagon to relax legislation that protects Iraq's heritage by prevention of sales abroad." On January 24, 2003, some sixty New York-based collectors and dealers organized themselves into a new group called the American Council for Cultural Policy and met with Bush administration and Pentagon officials to argue that a post-Saddam Iraq should have relaxed antiquities laws.[16] Opening up private trade in Iraqi artifacts, they suggested, would offer such items better security than they could receive in Iraq.

The main international legal safeguard for historically and humanistically important institutions and sites is the Hague Convention for the Protection of Cultural Property in the Event of Armed Conflict, signed on May 14, 1954. The US is not a party to that convention, primarily because, during the Cold War, it feared that the treaty might restrict its freedom to engage in nuclear war; but during the 1991 Gulf War the elder Bush's administration accepted the convention's rules and abided by a "no-fire target list" of places where valuable cultural items were known to exist.[17] UNESCO and other guardians of cultural artifacts expected the younger Bush's administration to follow the same procedures in the 2003 war.

Moreover, on March 26, 2003, the Pentagon's Office of Reconstruction and Humanitarian Assistance (ORHA), headed by Lt. Gen. (ret.) Jay Garner— the civil authority the US had set up for the moment hostilities ceased—sent to all senior US commanders a list of sixteen institutions that "merit securing

---

15. Guy Gugliotta, "Pentagon Was Told of Risk to Museums; US Urged to Save Iraq's Historic Artifacts," *Washington Post*, April 14, 2003; McGuire Gibson, "Cultural Tragedy in Iraq: A Report On the Looting of Museums, Archives, and Sites," International Foundation for Art Research.

16. Liddle; Oliver Burkeman, "Ancient Archive Lost in Baghdad Blaze," *Guardian*, April 15, 2003.

17. See James A. R. Nafziger, *Art Loss in Iraq: Protection of Cultural Heritage in Time of War and Its Aftermath*, International Foundation for Art Research, www.ifar.org/heritage.htm/

as soon as possible to prevent further damage, destruction, and/or pilferage of records and assets." The five-page memo dispatched two weeks before the fall of Baghdad also said, "Coalition forces must secure these facilities in order to prevent looting and the resulting irreparable loss of cultural treasures" and that "looters should be arrested/detained." First on General Garner's list of places to protect was the Iraqi Central Bank, which is now a ruin; second was the Museum of Antiquities. Sixteenth was the Oil Ministry, the only place that US forces occupying Baghdad actually defended. Martin Sullivan, chair of the President's Advisory Committee on Cultural Property for the previous eight years, and Gary Vikan, director of the Walters Art Museum in Baltimore and a member of the committee, both resigned to protest the failure of Centcom to obey orders. Sullivan said it was "inexcusable" that the museum should not have had the same priority as the Oil Ministry.[18]

As we now know, the American forces made no effort to prevent the looting of the great cultural institutions of Iraq, its soldiers simply watching vandals enter and torch the buildings. Said Arjomand, an editor of the journal *Studies on Persianate Societies* and a professor of sociology at the State University of New York at Stony Brook, wrote, "Our troops, who have been proudly guarding the Oil Ministry, where no window is broken, deliberately condoned these horrendous events."[19] American commanders claim that, to the contrary, they were too busy fighting and had too few troops to protect the museum and libraries. However, this seems to be an unlikely explanation. During the battle for Baghdad, the US military was perfectly willing to dispatch some 2,000 troops to secure northern Iraq's oilfields, and their record on antiquities did not improve when the fighting subsided. At the 6,000-year-old Sumerian city of Ur with its massive ziggurat, or stepped temple-tower (built in the period 2112–2095 BC and restored by Nebuchadnezzar II in the sixth century BC), the Marines spray-painted their motto, "Semper Fi" (*semper fidelis*, always faithful), onto its walls.[20] The military then made the monument "off limits" to everyone in order to disguise the desecration that had occurred there,

---

18. Paul Martin, Ed Vulliamy, and Gaby Hinsliff, "US Army was Told to Protect Looted Museum," *Observer*, April 20, 2003; Rich; Paul Martin, "Troops Were Told to Guard Treasures," *Washington Times*, April 20, 2003.
19. Said Arjomand, "Under the Eyes of US Forces and This Happened?," *History News Network*, April 14, 2003.
20. Ed Vulliamy, "Troops 'Vandalize' Ancient City of Ur," *Observer*, May 18, 2003; Paul Johnson, *Art: A New History* (New York: HarperCollins, 2003), pp. 18, 35; Polk and Schuster, p. 99, fig. 25.

including the looting by US soldiers of clay bricks used in the construction of the ancient buildings.

Until April 2003, the area around Ur, in the environs of Nasiriyah, was remote and sacrosanct. However, the US military chose the land immediately adjacent to the ziggurat to build its huge Tallil Air Base with two runways measuring 12,000 and 9,700 feet respectively and four satellite camps. In the process, military engineers moved more than 9,500 truckloads of dirt in order to build 350,000 square feet of hangars and other facilities for aircraft and Predator unmanned drones. They completely ruined the area, the literal heartland of human civilization, for any further archaeological research or future tourism. On October 24, 2003, according to the Global Security Organization, the Army and Air Force built their own modern ziggurat. They "opened its second Burger King at Tallil. The new facility, co-located with [a] . . . Pizza Hut, provides another Burger King restaurant so that more service men and women serving in Iraq can, if only for a moment, forget about the task at hand in the desert and get a whiff of that familiar scent that takes them back home."[21]

The great British archaeologist Sir Max Mallowan (husband of Agatha Christie), who pioneered the excavations at Ur, Nineveh, and Nimrud, quotes some classical advice that the Americans might have been wise to heed: "There was danger in disturbing ancient monuments. . . . It was both wise and historically important to reverence the legacies of ancient times. Ur was a city infested with ghosts of the past and it was prudent to appease them."[22]

The American record elsewhere in Iraq is no better. At Babylon, American and Polish forces built a military depot, despite objections from archaeologists. John Curtis, the British Museum's authority on Iraq's many archaeological sites, reported on a visit in December 2004 that he saw "cracks and gaps where somebody had tried to gouge out the decorated bricks forming the famous dragons of the Ishtar Gate" and a "2,600-year-old brick pavement crushed by military vehicles."[23] Other observers say that the dust stirred up by US helicopters has sandblasted the fragile brick façade of the palace of

---

21. "Tallil Air Base," GlobalSecurity.org.
22. Max Mallowan, *Mallowan's Memoirs* (London: Collins, 1977), p. 61.
23. Rory McCarthy and Maev Kennedy, "Babylon Wrecked by War," *Guardian*, January 15, 2005.

Nebuchadnezzar II, king of Babylon from 605 to 562 BC.[24] The archaeologist Zainab Bahrani reports, "Between May and August 2004, the wall of the Temple of Nabu and the roof of the Temple of Ninmah, both of the sixth century BC, collapsed as a result of the movement of helicopters. Nearby, heavy machines and vehicles stand parked on the remains of a Greek theater from the era of Alexander of Macedon [Alexander the Great]."[25]

And none of this even begins to deal with the massive, ongoing looting of historical sites across Iraq by freelance grave and antiquities robbers, preparing to stock the living rooms of Western collectors. The unceasing chaos and lack of security brought to Iraq in the wake of our invasion have meant that a future peaceful Iraq may hardly have a patrimony to display. It is no small accomplishment of the Bush administration to have plunged the cradle of the human past into the same sort of chaos and lack of security as the Iraqi present. If amnesia is bliss, then the fate of Iraq's antiquities represents a kind of modern paradise.

President Bush's supporters have talked endlessly about his global war on terrorism as a "clash of civilizations." But the civilization we are in the process of destroying in Iraq is part of our own heritage. It is also part of the world's patrimony. Before our invasion of Afghanistan, we condemned the Taliban for their dynamiting of the monumental third century AD Buddhist statues at Bamiyan in March 2001. Those were two gigantic statues of remarkable historical value, and the barbarism involved in their destruction blazed in headlines and horrified commentaries in the US. Today, our own government is guilty of far greater crimes when it comes to the destruction of a whole universe of antiquity, and few here, when they consider Iraqi attitudes toward the American occupation, even take that into consideration. But what we do not care to remember, others may recall all too well.

---

24. Owen Bowcott, "Archaeologists Fight to Save Iraqi Sites," *Guardian*, June 20, 2005.
25. Zainab Bahrani, "The Fall of Babylon," in Polk and Schuster, p. 214.

July 2005

1 2

UNNAMED AND UNNOTICED

Iraqi Casualties

Judith Coburn

How many Iraqis have died in our war in their country? Is there a better symbol of how the war for Iraq has already been lost than our ignorance about the cost of the war to Iraqis?

"Cost of the war": a cliché to normalize the carnage, like the anaesthetizing term "collateral damage" and that new semantic horror, "torture lite." And yet the "cost of the war" report, by now a hackneyed convention of American journalism, includes only American casualties—no Iraqis—itself a violation of the American mainstream media's own professed commitment to "objectivity." Three years of "anniversary" articles in the American media adding up the so-called "cost of the war" in Iraq have focused exclusively on Americans killed, American dollars spent, American hardware destroyed, with barely a mention of the Iraqi dead as part of that "cost."

The dead are counted. But they are Americans. The names are named. But they are Americans. The names and numbers of the dead are intoned aloud or their photographs papered on media "walls" and they are always only American.

Publishing or pronouncing the names of the American dead every day without ever mentioning the names of the Iraqi dead offers a powerful message that only American dying matters. In Indochina, during the years

I covered that war, we counted but didn't name Americans. That wasn't done until after the war was over. We never counted and never named the Vietnamese, Cambodian, and Lao dead. Still today, though the estimates run into the millions, there is no reliable count of how many Indochinese died or were hurt in our war there. Not to mention El Salvador, Nicaragua, Panama, Haiti, and the First Gulf War.

But there's no way to count, protest American journalists. What they mean is that the Pentagon doesn't count for them—"We don't do body counts," was the way General Tommy Franks put the matter during our Afghan war. But Iraq Body Count (IBC) counts as does the Brookings Institution among others. As of July 13, IBC estimated Iraqi civilian casualties to be between 22,838 and 25,869, an extremely conservative number. (The range between the two figures represents occasional discrepancies in the number of civilian casualties reported by different media sources about the same incident.) So what journalists really mean is that only Pentagon counting counts and that the prosecutor of the war is the only "reliable" source on the magnitude of its own killing. Pentagon casualty figures are rarely questioned. When anyone else counts, these figures are given short shrift.

Who Counts?

The alternative media, bloggers included, have seized on General Franks's words with outrage. But the fact is the Pentagon does count. It just doesn't care to add those dead bodies up, let alone tell the American public or the rest of the world how many dead Iraqis there have been or how many more are being killed at this very moment. In Iraq, as in Vietnam and the First Gulf War, every unit of the American military must file "after action" reports about any "contact" with the enemy. Most of these include injuries and deaths to civilians (even if these are often counted as enemy-soldier deaths to cover them up, a practice the media eventually exposed in Vietnam, but has not yet explored in Iraq). Also, any injury or death of a suspected civilian is supposed to be reported in a separate "incident" report. "We do keep records of innocent civilians who are killed accidentally by coalition force soldiers," Brigadier General Mark Hertling, assistant commander for the First Armored Division, told *New York Times* reporter Jeffrey Gettleman in March 2004. "And, in fact, in every one of those innocent death situations, we conduct internal investigations to determine what happened."

The military also has a compensation program for victims injured or killed by American soldiers under the Foreign Claims Act. The bar for qualifying for this program is absurdly high—the victim must know and be able to prove which specific military unit injured or killed her or his relative, have a claim form filled out by that unit admitting its responsibility, have two witnesses and produce copies of medical reports, not to mention being willing in the first place to approach the very forces who inflicted the suffering. Compensation is apparently approved for only 50 percent of those who get up the nerve to file for it. But the military does at least have figures on how many Iraqis have been compensated, which it has refused to release, even to Vermont Senator Patrick Leahy, who requested them. CNN, *Newsday*, the Associated Press, and the *Christian Science Monitor* have managed to ferret out a partial count: the Pentagon doled out $2.2 million to Iraqis between May 2003 and February 2004 with 5,700 out of 11,300 cases approved. (But since such compensation includes damage to property and people wounded as well as killed, this figure doesn't translate into numbers of civilian casualties.)

Under another American government program, the Iraqi War Victims Fund, mandated by Congress and renamed for young aid worker Marla Ruzicka after her death in a car-bomb attack in Baghdad, $2.4 billion in relief and reconstruction funds will include compensation for Iraqi civilian casualties. Once details are worked out of how the victims will be found, there might be figures of some sort, should the Bush administration deign to release them.

As for Iraq Body Count's methods, if it is to be added to their count of civilians killed, each civilian death must be reported by two separate media sources from IBC's approved list of media websites and then cross-checked by two different IBC staffers from the original compiler. More important, IBC counts only civilian deaths inflicted by US-led coalition forces, so civilians killed by suicide bombers, insurgent attacks, or the increasing number of assassinations and kidnappings by insurgents and others are not reflected in their totals. As a result, the IBC figures certainly now greatly underestimate the actual toll of the ongoing war on Iraqi civilians—by far the highest "cost" of the war.

Human Rights Watch reports that while coalition forces killed more Iraqi civilians than the insurgents did in the early months of the war, now insurgents are killing many more civilians than coalition forces. The Education for Peace in Iraq project, a nonprofit group of antiwar Gulf War veterans, Iraqis, and others, reports that insurgents are now killing fifteen times the number of civilians killed by coalition forces and that the number of civilians killed by insurgents has doubled since the first six months of 2004. Just last week, in its July 14, 2005 issue, the *New York Times* front-paged rare Iraqi Interior Ministry figures showing insurgents are now killing an average of 800 Iraqi policemen and civilians a month.

It's hardly surprising that the Pentagon is loath to tell us how many innocent Iraqis it has killed. It's a political issue. Early in the war, the Iraqi Health Ministry ordered morgues and hospitals to count the number of war dead and wounded coming in. They reported 1,764 civilians killed in the summer of 2003. But the American occupation's Coalition Provisional Authority (CPA) ordered them to stop counting. After the interim Iraqi government took over, the Health Ministry tried again to count but was ordered in October 2004 by the new government of Prime Minister Iyad Allawi to stop releasing the figures. Last week's Interior Ministry figures, given to the *Times* at its request, are the first official Iraqi counts to be released since then.

The lack of "official" figures, however, shouldn't absolve the media—or Americans—from their blindness to Iraqi suffering, since available figures, incomplete as they are, are staggering for a guerrilla war. Reliable sources have certainly done their best to count, sources like IBC, Brookings, and the Iraqi and American epidemiologists who estimated in a study published in October 2004, in the British medical journal the *Lancet* that 100,000 Iraqis might have died in the war by September 2004.

These sources are admittedly critical of the war. But as such, are they less "objective" than the Pentagon? The American media apparently thinks so. Yet Iraq Body Count's figures are clearly conservative exactly because they depend on media reports. Because it is now so dangerous for journalists to travel outside Baghdad or even the capital's "Green Zone" where Westerners huddle, many Iraqi deaths go unreported and are thus uncounted by IBC. (Using hospital or morgue records also results in an undercount since Iraqis often don't bring their dead, or near-dead, to chronically overwhelmed, understaffed hospitals and morgues.) Ironically, IBC, once heralded as a brilliantly conceived breakthrough in monitoring war casualties—impossible without the Internet—is now an object of some dismay among antiwar activists because its methodology inevitably leads to a casualty undercount.

"Collateral Damage" as a Collateral Story

Most of the American media have now had their one dutiful piece on IBC. But is it such a radical idea for, say, the *New York Times* to have a box next to its daily listing of Americans killed in Iraq with IBC's or Brookings's Iraq Index count of how many Iraqis have been killed by coalition forces? A header could explain the source, just as one now cites the Pentagon as the source for Americans killed. Why, when Ted Koppel read the names of the American dead on *Nightline* on the anniversary of the war, couldn't he have added at least a few Iraqi names to the list?

The politics of counting got thick the week before the American presidential election when the *Lancet*, the British medical journal, put on line a study by American and Iraqi epidemiologists comparing death rates before and after the March 2003 invasion. The study estimated that at least 100,000 Iraqis (and possibly many more) had died in the eighteen months that followed the invasion of Iraq who would not have died had the war not happened. Coalition air strikes were the largest cause of violent death. The international media has generally misreported the 100,000 as estimated civilian deaths. But the study actually makes clear that the 100,000 estimate includes all Iraqi dead—police, soldiers and insurgents as well as civilians. Last week, Swiss researchers announced at a UN press conference that, using the data from the *Lancet* study, they estimated that, out of the estimated 100,000 dead Iraqis, 39,000 were civilians who had been killed since the war began.

The *Lancet* study was based on interviews by a team of Iraqi scientists. It made headlines in Europe but dropped like a stone in the US (as did the recent Swiss report). The study's lead American author Johns Hopkins Professor of Public Health Les Roberts may have shot himself in the foot by rushing the study out in the midst of 24/7 election coverage in the US. He admitted to Lila Guterman of the *Chronicle of Higher Education* that he was anti-Bush and hoped to swing votes away from the President. Had the study been released after the election, however, in a more sober, scientific way, the American media might still have buried it, as it has the whole issue of civilian casualties. Only the *Washington Post* took much notice. But the *Post* got Human Rights Watch military expert Mark Garlasco on the record opining that the figure was way too high (even though he hadn't read the report). Without the respected HRW imprimatur, there was even more reason than election mania for the rest of the American media to spike the report. Ironically, it may have been the American media's own longstanding blindness to the suffering of Iraqi civilians that made the 100,000 estimate *seem* too shockingly high to be credible to American reporters and their editors.

Only the enterprising Lila Guterman followed up, interviewing other epidemiologists around the US, who found the methodology and the study itself to be sound. Guterman also underlined the incredible bravery of the Iraqi scientists who risked their lives traveling throughout Iraq—even to radical Sunni strongholds like Falluja—to interview Iraqis about how many of their families had been killed or injured in the war. (What does it say about the mainstream media that—except for the Associated Press and recently the *New York Times*—crucial stories about Iraqi civilian casualties are being broken here by publications like *Editor and Publisher* and the *Chronicle of Higher Education?*)

Granted, it's impossible for any individual journalist in Iraq to count how many Iraqi civilians have been hurt in the war. You'd have to visit every battle site, every morgue, and every hospital every day—in a country where, for reporters, it's dangerous just to leave your hotel. Then there is the problem of distinguishing who is a civilian and who is an insurgent in a guerrilla war where combatants don't wear uniforms. But a few American journalists haven't taken that as an excuse not to try to count as best they can. The Associated Press, under New York editor Richard Pyle (AP's longtime Saigon bureau chief during the Vietnam War), was the first and only news organization to ask its reporters in Iraq, soon after the invasion, to try to count the civilian dead. On June 11, 2003, AP reported that 3,240 Iraqis civilians had been killed up to that moment in the war, based on a survey of sixty of Iraq's largest hospitals. AP reporters, especially Niko Price, have stayed on the civilian casualty story, continuing to monitor civilian casualties regularly, reporting soaring casualties in hard-fought battles like the one for Hilla or the siege of Falluja last November where approximately six hundred civilians reportedly died.

AP broke the story of the CPA suppression of the Health Ministry's count of civilian deaths, reported the huge increase in car bombs after the handover of sovereignty and—alone in the mainstream American media—included Iraqi casualty figures as well as American ones in their "anniversary" pieces about "the cost of the war." The *New York Times*—especially reporter Sabrina Tavernise—has recently stepped up coverage of civilian casualties. One ingenious survey effort for the *Times*, written by Norimitsu Onishi with reporting by the paper's Iraqi staff (unnamed, perhaps for their safety), reported that in one week—October 11–17, 2004—208 Iraqis died, including policemen, civilians, journalists, politicians, and soldiers. (It did not include deaths in Kurdish areas.) The story pulled together sources from hospitals, the Iraqi and American military, news sources, and reporting by Iraqi reporters for the *Times*.

But stories highlighting the magnitude of Iraqi suffering have been rare indeed. A study by George Washington University researchers found that American television coverage of the invasion of Iraq itself was remarkably sanitized. Only 13.5 percent of the 1,710 TV news stories they reviewed from the start of the war to the fall of Baghdad on April 9, 2003 included shots of wounded or dead Americans or Iraqis. Only 4 percent showed any dead. One reason the war may seem so inconsequential to so many Americans is that the casualties, as reported in the American media, are almost exclusively American and so are relatively modest (though hardly inconsequential, of course, to those who knew and cared for the dead). "Collateral damage" has lived up to its name. Iraqi casualties have been collateral to the story of the war told by most American journalists—just as they have been to the warmakers in Washington and London.

War in Another Galaxy

Counting the dead, however, may not finally be the point. Numbers seldom convey human suffering in a way that moves the distant onlooker. Most coverage of Iraqi civilian casualties is anecdotal—the daily carnage of yet more suicide bombs, the daily photo of ripped-up cars and ripped-apart bodies. Unnamed victims, and all of them—except rarely—Iraqi.

While there has been some fine reporting out of Iraq by journalists like the *Washington Post*'s Anthony Shadid, there is no one in Iraq like Gloria Emerson, the *New York Times*'s prize-winning reporter in Vietnam, with her boundless outrage against the war and her novelist's eye. Emerson's war wasn't the "bang bang" (as she called it). She covered war from the graveyards where Vietnamese mourned their dead and from the streets where homeless kids hustled GIs, and lepers held out their babies for alms. Her story was how the Vietnamese got by, day by day, in the war, simply how they could stand it. So far in Iraq there has been no Gloria Emerson listening, as she did one night in Saigon to her Vietnamese interpreter Nguyen Ngoc Luong and his office-mates recite from memory verses from *The Tale of Kieu*, Vietnam's great epic poem, their psychic bulwark against the mayhem that was devouring their country. But that kind of passionate identification with the people of a war-torn country, that kind of—dare we call it personal— journalism which might help summon American empathy for the Iraqi victims of our war machine, isn't in fashion these days. Media cool and caution rule in our culture of fear.

There are photographs, even a few great war photographs, coming out of Iraq. Peter Turnley's photo essay in *Harper's*, "The Bereaved," which matched images of Iraqis and Americans mourning their dead is magnificent. But this isn't Vietnam—the first "television war," as Michael Arlen so aptly named it. East Timor, Somalia, the First Gulf War, Bosnia, Rwanda, Chechnya, Darfur, Congo . . . The list goes on and on. By now, there have been so many TV wars, so many grisly scenes, that they all blur together. *Star Wars* is so much more exciting anyway, closer to home in the cineplex or on DVD, and it's all happening far away in another galaxy. There's no military draft to concentrate kids' and parents' attention. And it isn't the sixties—cynicism reigns rather than the reach for freedom that led so many Americans then to take on the powers that be. Should the war intrude? Follow the advice of Brigadier General Mark Kimmitt, who, when asked about images of Iraqi civilians killed by Americans, recommended: "Change the channel."

Patterns of Brutality

Another part of the civilian casualty story neglected by our media involves American military tactics that have inflicted unnecessary suffering on civilians. The indispensable Human Rights Watch, which has staff specialists in military affairs, has done two detailed research reports on some of these patterns. The October 2003 report *Hearts and Minds* charged that American soldiers often used "indiscriminate force," especially at checkpoints after insurgent bombings, and also in raids on civilian houses, causing many civilian casualties. Few of these injuries to civilians are investigated by the military, HRW found. The report pointed out that many checkpoints were manned and that house searches were conducted by soldiers who had been trained for combat, not policing, and it called for more training in police techniques.

Although a December 2003 HRW report, *Off Target*, found that "US-led coalition forces took precautions to spare civilians," it decried the use of cluster munitions (launched both from the air and the ground) by the American military. These particularly vicious weapons, which pepper victims with shrapnel so small that the shards shred flesh and are impossible to remove, are being used in Iraqi cities. They can maim long after their original use. The unexploded bomblets remain live and often go off in the hands of children. "Tens of thousands of duds" litter Iraq—as they still do Vietnam, Cambodia, and many other war-torn countries—the report charges. HRW reported that cluster bombs had caused "at least hundreds of civilian casualties" by June 2003.

Besides cluster munitions, a new and improved version of napalm—the Vietnam War's other most grisly weapon—and its chemical cousin white phosphorus have been used by American forces in Iraq, a fact known to few Americans because our media has barely reported on the subject. The Pentagon has admitted that it used napalm near the Kuwaiti border during the invasion, though the use seems to have been more widespread than the Pentagon said. For instance, the Bush administration reportedly lied to its British allies about its use. (In Europe, the evident use of napalm by the US in its assault on the Iraqi city of Falluja in November 2004 sparked headlines and furious opposition in the British Parliament.)

Almost nothing has been reported in the American media about bombing operations in Iraq and especially the use of bunker-buster bombs to target what the US military calls "high value targets" or insurgent leaders, who are often dug deep in heavily populated urban neighborhoods. HRW's *Off Target* examined four such attacks and charged that they caused "dozens of civilian casualties" while failing to kill the targeted leaders. Six months after *Off Target* was released, a front-page piece in the *New York Times* on such targeted attacks actually quoted Human Rights Watch. But the piece focused on the spectacular "zero success rate" of the leadership raids, not on civilian casualties caused by the bombing.

Such Human Rights Watch reports usually receive dutiful but cursory one-time coverage in the American media. A few hundred words on page 14, a few seconds on the evening news: hardly the kind of media spotlight that could turn Iraqi suffering into a burning issue for most Americans. So far, these laudable reports haven't been able to change the nature of the Iraq War story in the United States. "The Faces of the Fallen," as the *Washington Post* calls its daily count, remain American.

Still, a few million Americans in today's antiwar movement care how many Iraqis are dying and are committed to honoring them. When the American Friends Service Committee put its exhibit "Eyes Wide Open" on the road with a pair of boots for every American soldier who has died in Iraq, it also had a "Wall of Remembrance" with the names of more than 11,000 Iraqis who have died in the war. The Iraqis' names, as well as the American ones, were read at ceremonies at the AFSC wall, the way veterans read the names of the American—but not the Indochinese—dead at the Vietnam Veterans' Memorial in Washington.

While in the Capitol these days there may be no Senator William Fulbright (whose hearings on the Vietnam War galvanized official Washington), there is some eloquence and even some action about Iraqi suffering from a few politicians like West Virginia Senator Robert Byrd, Massachusetts Senator Edward Kennedy, who also campaigned vigorously to help Vietnamese war victims forty years ago, and Vermont's Senator Patrick Leahy. As Leahy reminded his colleagues in a speech on the Senate floor on May 10, 2005: "More than 90 percent of the casualties in World War One were soldiers. That changed in World War Two and since then, it is overwhelmingly civilians who suffer the casualties. Yet while rosters are kept of the fallen soldiers, no official record is kept of the civilians. This is wrong. It denies those victims the dignity of being counted, the respect of being honored, and it prevents their families from receiving the help they need."

July 2006

13

THE HIDDEN WAR ON WOMEN IN IRAQ

Ruth Rosen

Abu Ghraib. Haditha. Guantánamo. These are words that shame our country. Now, add to them Mahmudiya, a town twenty miles south of Baghdad. There, this March, a group of five American soldiers allegedly were involved in the rape and murder of Abeer Qassim Hamza, a young Iraqi girl. Her body was then set on fire to cover up their crimes; her father, mother, and sister were murdered. The rape of this one girl, if proven true, is probably not simply an isolated incident. But how would we know? In Iraq, rape is a taboo subject. Shamed by the rape, relatives of this girl wouldn't even hold a public funeral and were reluctant to reveal where she is buried.

Like women everywhere, Iraqi women have always been vulnerable to rape. But since the American invasion of their country, the reported incidence of sexual terrorism has accelerated markedly—and this despite the fact that few Iraqi women are willing to report rapes either to Iraqi officials or to occupation forces, fearing to bring dishonor upon their families. In rural areas, female rape victims may also be vulnerable to "honor killings" in which male relatives murder them in order to restore the family's honor. "For women in Iraq," Amnesty International concluded in a 2005 report, "the stigma frequently attached to the victims instead of the perpetrators of sexual crimes makes reporting such abuses especially daunting."

This specific rape of one Iraqi girl, however, is now becoming symbolic of the way the Bush administration has violated Iraq's honor; Prime Minister Nouri al-Maliki has already launched an inquest into the crime. In an administration that normally doesn't know the meaning of an apology, the American ambassador, Zalmay Khalilzad, and the top American commander in Iraq, General George W. Casey, Jr., both publicly apologized. In a fierce condemnation, the Muslim Scholars Association in Iraq denounced the crime: "This act, committed by the occupying soldiers, from raping the girl to mutilating her body and killing her family, should make all humanity feel ashamed."

Shame, yes, but that is hardly sufficient. After all, rape is now considered a war crime by the International Criminal Court.

It wasn't always that way. Soldiers have long viewed women as spoils of war, even when civilian or military leaders condemned such behavior, but in the early 1990s, a new international consensus began to emerge on the act of rape. Prodded by an energized global women's movement, the General Assembly of the United Nations passed a Declaration on the Elimination of Violence Against Women in 1993. Subsequent statutes in the International Criminal Tribunals for the Former Yugoslavia and for Rwanda, as well as the Rome Statute for the International Criminal Court in July 2002, all defined rape as a crime against humanity or a war crime.

No one accuses American soldiers of running through the streets of Iraq, raping women as an instrument of war against the insurgents (though such acts are what caused three Bosnian soldiers, for the first time in history, to be indicted in 2001 for the war crime of rape).

Still, the invasion and occupation of Iraq have had the effect of humiliating, endangering, and repressing Iraqi women in ways that have not been widely publicized in the mainstream media. As detainees in prisons run by Americans, they have been sexually abused and raped; as civilians, they have been kidnapped, raped, and then sometimes sold for prostitution; and as women—and, in particular, as among the more liberated women in the Arab world—they have increasingly disappeared from public life, many becoming shut-ins in their own homes.

Rape and Sexual Humiliation in Prisons

The scandal of prisoner abuse at Abu Ghraib focused on the torture, sexual abuse, and humiliation of Iraqi men. A variety of sources suggest that female prisoners suffered similar treatment, including rape.

Few Americans probably realize that the American-run prison at Abu

Ghraib also held female detainees. Some of them were arrested by Americans for political reasons—because they were relatives of Baathist leaders or because the occupying forces thought they could use them as bargaining chips to force male relatives to inform on insurgents or give themselves up.

According to a July 2003 Human Rights Watch report, the secrecy surrounding female detentions "resulted from a collusion of the families and the occupying forces." Families feared social stigma; the occupying forces feared condemnation by human rights groups and anger from Iraqis who saw such treatment of women by foreigners as a special act of violation.

On the condition of anonymity and in great fear, some female detainees nevertheless did speak with human rights workers after being released from detention. They have described beatings, torture, and isolation. Like their male counterparts, they reserve their greatest bitterness for sexual humiliations suffered in American custody. Nearly all female detainees reported being threatened with rape. Some women were interrogated naked and subjected to derision and humiliating remarks by soldiers.

On May 20, 2004, the British *Guardian* reported that one female prisoner managed to smuggle a note out of Abu Ghraib. She claimed that American guards were raping the few female detainees held in the prison and that some of them were now pregnant. In desperation, she urged the Iraqi resistance to bomb the jail in order to spare the women further shame.

Amal Kadham Swadi, one of seven Iraqi female attorneys attempting to represent imprisoned women, told the *Guardian* that only one woman she met with was willing to speak about rape. "She was crying. She told us she had been raped. Several American soldiers had raped her. She had tried to fight them off, and they had hurt her arm. She showed us the stitches. She told us, 'We have daughters and husbands. For God's sake don't tell anyone about this.'"

Professor Huda Shaker, a political scientist at Baghdad University, also told the *Guardian* that women in Abu Ghraib have been sexually abused and raped. She identified one woman, in particular, who was raped by an American military policeman, became pregnant, and later disappeared.

Professor Shaker added, "A female colleague of mine was arrested and taken there. When I asked her after she was released what happened at Abu Ghraib, she started crying. Ladies here are afraid and shy of talking about such subjects. They say everything is OK. Even in a very advanced society in the west it is very difficult to talk about rape."

Shaker herself encountered a milder form of sexual abuse at the hands of one American soldier. At a checkpoint, she said, an American soldier "pointed the laser sight [of his gun] directly in the middle of my chest. . . . Then he pointed to his penis. He told me, 'Come here, bitch, I'm going to fuck you.' "

Writing from Baghdad, Luke Hardin of the *Guardian* reported that at Abu Ghraib journalists have been forbidden from talking to female detainees, who are cloistered in tiny windowless cells. Senior US military officers who have escorted journalists around Abu Ghraib, however, have admitted that rapes of women took place in the cellblock where nineteen "high-value" male detainees were also being held. Asked how such abuse could have happened, Colonel Dave Quantock, now in charge of the prison's detention facilities, responded, "I don't know. It's all about leadership. Apparently it wasn't there."

No one should be surprised that women detainees, like male ones, were subjected to sexual abuse at Abu Ghraib. Think of the photographs we've already seen from that prison. If acts of ritual humiliation could be used to "soften up" men, then the rape of female detainees is hardly unimaginable.

But how can we be sure? In January 2004, Lieutenant General Ricardo Sanchez, the senior US military official in Iraq, ordered Major General Antonio M. Taguba to investigate persistent allegations of human rights abuses at Abu Ghraib. The March 2004 Taguba Report confirmed that in at least one instance a US military policeman had raped at least one female prisoner and that guards had videotaped and photographed naked female detainees. Seymour Hersh reported in the May 17, 2004, issue of the *New Yorker* magazine that these secret photos and videos, most of which still are held under wraps by the Pentagon, show American soldiers "having sex with a female Iraqi prisoner." Additional photos have made their way to the websites of Afterdowningstreet.org and Salon.com. In one photograph, a woman is raising her shirt, baring her breasts, presumably as she was ordered to do.

The full range of pictures and videotapes are likely to show a great deal more. Members of Congress who viewed all the pictures and videotapes from Abu Ghraib seemed genuinely shaken and sickened by what they saw. Senate Majority Leader Bill Frist (R-TN) called them "appalling"; the then

Senate Minority Leader Tom Daschle described them as "horrific." Ever since the scandal broke in April 2004, human rights and civil liberties groups have been engaged in a legal battle with the Department of Defense, demanding that it release the rest of the visual documents. Only when all those documents are available to the general public will we have a clearer— and undoubtedly more ghastly—record of the sexual acts forced upon both female and male detainees.

Sexual Terrorism on the Streets

Meanwhile, the chaos of the war has also led to a rash of kidnappings and rapes of women outside of prison walls. After interviewing rape and abduction victims, as well as eyewitnesses, Iraqi police and health professionals, and US military police and civil affairs officers, Human Rights Watch released a report in July 2003 titled *Climate of Fear: Sexual Violence and Abduction of Women and Girls in Baghdad.* Only months after Baghdad fell to US forces, they had already learned of twenty-five credible allegations of rape and/or abduction of Iraqi women. Not surprisingly, the report found that "police officers gave low priority to allegations of sexual violence and abduction, that the police were under-resourced, and that victims of sexual violence confronted indifference and sexism from Iraqi law enforcement personnel." Since then, as chaos, violence, and bloodletting have descended on Iraq, matters have only gotten worse.

After the American invasion, local gangs began roaming Baghdad, snatching girls and women from the street. Interviews with human rights investigators have produced some horrifying stories. Typical was nine-year-old "Saba A." who was abducted from the stairs of the building where she lives, taken to an abandoned building nearby, and raped. A family friend who saw Saba A. immediately following the rape told Human Rights Watch: "She was sitting on the stairs, here, at 4:00 p.m. It seems to me that probably he hit her on the back of the head with a gun and then took her to [a neighboring] building. She came back fifteen minutes later, bleeding [from the vaginal area]. [She was still bleeding two days later, so] we took her to the hospital." The medical report by the US military doctor who treated Saba A. "documented bruising in the vaginal area, a posterior vaginal tear, and a broken hymen."

In 2005, Amnesty International also interviewed abducted women. The story of "Asma," a young engineer, was representative. She was shopping with her mother, sister, and a male relative when six armed men forced her into a car and drove her to a farmhouse outside the city. They repeatedly raped her. A day later, the men drove her to her neighborhood and pushed her out of the car.

As recently as June 2006, Mayada Zhaair, spokeswoman for the Women's Rights Association, a local NGO, reported, "We've observed an increase in the number of women being sexually abused and raped in the past four months, especially in the capital."

No one knows how many abducted women have never returned. As one Iraqi police inspector testified, "Some gangs specialize in kidnapping girls, they sell them to Gulf countries. This happened before the war too, but now it is worse, they can get in and out without passports." Others interviewed by Human Rights Watch argued that such trafficking in women had not occurred before the invasion.

The US State Department's June 2005 report on the trafficking of women suggested that the extent of the problem in Iraq is "difficult to appropriately gauge" under current chaotic circumstances, but cited an unknown number of Iraqi women and girls being sent to Yemen, Syria, Jordan, and Persian Gulf countries for sexual exploitation.

In May 2006, Brian Bennett wrote in *Time* magazine that a visit to

the Khadamiyah Women's Prison in the northern part of Baghdad immediately produces several tales of abduction and abandonment. A stunning 18-year-old nicknamed Amna, her black hair pulled back in a ponytail, says she was taken from an orphanage by an armed gang just after the US invasion and sent to brothels in Samarra, al-Qaim on the border with Syria, and Mosul in the north before she was taken back to Baghdad, drugged with pills, dressed in a suicide belt and sent to bomb a cleric's office in Khadamiyah, where she turned herself in to the police. A judge gave her a seven-year jail sentence "for her sake" to protect her from the gang, according to the prison director.

"Families and courts," Bennett reported, "are usually so shamed by the disappearance [and presumed rape] of a daughter that they do not report these kidnappings. And the resulting stigma of compromised chastity is such that even if the girl should resurface, she may never be taken back by her relations."

Disappearing Women

To avoid such dangers, countless Iraqi women have become shut-ins in their own homes. Historian Marjorie Lasky has described this situation in *Iraqi Women Under Siege*, a 2006 report for Codepink, an antiwar women's organization. Before the war, she points out, many educated Iraqi women participated fully in the workforce and in public life. Now, many of them rarely go out. They fear kidnap and rape; they are terrified of getting caught in the crossfire between Americans and insurgents; they are frightened by sectarian reprisals; and they are scared of Islamic militants who intimidate or beat them if they are not "properly covered."

Terri Judd reported thus in the British *Independent* of June 8, 2006:

> In the British-occupied south, where Muqtada al-Sadr's Mehdi Army retains a stranglehold, women insist the situation is at its worst. Here they are forced to live behind closed doors only to emerge, concealed behind scarves, hidden behind husbands and fathers. Even wearing a pair of trousers is considered an act of defiance, punishable by death.

Invisible women—for some Iraqi fundamentalist Islamic leaders, this is a dream come true. The Ministry of the Interior, for example, recently issued notices warning women not to go out on their own. "This is a Muslim country and any attack on a woman's modesty is also an attack on our religious beliefs," said Salah Ali, a senior ministry official. Religious leaders in both Sunni and Shia mosques have used their sermons to persuade their largely male congregations to keep working women at home. "These incidents of abuse just prove what we have been saying for so long," said Sheikh Salah Muzidin, an imam at a mosque in Baghdad. "That it is the Islamic duty of women to stay in their homes, looking after their children and husbands rather than searching for work—especially with the current lack of security in the country."

In the early 1970s, American feminists redefined rape and argued that it was an act driven not by sexual lust, but by a desire to exercise power over another person. Rape, they argued, was an act of terrorism that kept all women from claiming their right to public space. That is precisely what has happened to Iraqi women since the American invasion of Iraq. Sexual terrorism coupled with religious zealotry has stolen their right to claim their place in public life.

This, then, is a hidden part of the unnecessary suffering loosed by the reckless invasion of Iraq. Amid the daily explosions and gunfire that make the papers is a wave of sexual terrorism, whose exact dimensions we have no way of knowing, and that no one here notices, unleashed by the Bush administration in the name of exporting "democracy" and fighting "the war on terror."

February 2007

14

NOT THE SAME AS BEING EQUAL

Women in Afghanistan

Ann Jones

Born in Afghanistan but raised in the United States, like many in the world-wide Afghan diaspora, Manizha Naderi is devoted to helping her homeland. For years she worked with Women for Afghan Women, a New York-based organization serving Afghan women wherever they may be. Last fall, she returned to Kabul, the capital, to try to create a family guidance center. Its goal was to rescue women—and their families—from homemade violence. It's tough work. After three decades of almost constant warfare, most citizens are programmed to answer the slightest challenge with violence. In Afghanistan it's the default response.

Manizha Naderi has been sizing up the problem in the capital and last week she sent me a copy of her report. A key passage went like this:

> During the past year, a rash of reports on the situation of women in Afghanistan has been issued by Afghan governmental agencies and by foreign and local nongovernmental organizations (NGOs) that claim a particular interest in women's rights or in Afghanistan or both. More reports are in the offing. What has sparked them is the dire situation of women in the country, the systematic violations of their human rights, and the failure of concerned parties to achieve significant improvements by providing women with legal protections

rooted in a capable, honest, and stable judiciary system, education and employment opportunities, safety from violence, much of it savage, and protection from hidebound customs originating in the conviction that women are the property of men.

I'd hoped for better news. Instead, her report brought back so many things I'd seen for myself during the last five years spent, off and on, in her country.

Last year in Herat, as I was walking with an Afghan colleague to a meeting on women's rights, I spotted an ice cream vendor in the hot, dusty street. I rushed ahead and returned with two cones of lemony ice. I held one out to my friend. "Forgive me," she said. "I can't." She was wearing a burqa.

It was a stupid mistake. I'd been in Afghanistan a long time, in the company every day of women encased from head to toe in pleated polyester body bags. Occasionally I put one on myself, just to get the feel of being stifled in the sweaty sack, blind behind the mesh eye mask. I'd watched women trip on their burqas and fall. I'd watched women collide with cars they couldn't see. I knew a woman badly burned when her burqa caught fire. I knew another who suffered a near-fatal skull fracture when her burqa snagged in a taxi door and slammed her to the pavement as the vehicle sped away. But I'd never before noted this fact: it is not possible for a woman wearing a burqa to eat an ice cream cone.

We gave the cones away to passing children and laughed about it, but to me it was the saddest thing.

Ever since the United States invaded Afghanistan in 2001, George W. Bush has boasted of "liberating" Afghan women from the Taliban and the burqa. His wife Laura, after a publicity junket to Afghanistan in 2005, appeared on Jay Leno's show to say that she hadn't seen a single woman wearing a burqa.

But these are the sorts of wildly optimistic self-delusions that have made Bush notorious. His wife, whose visit to Afghanistan lasted almost six hours, spent much of that time at the American air base and none of it in the Afghan streets where most women, to this day, go about in big blue bags.

It's true that after the fall of the Taliban lots of women in the capital went back to work in schools, hospitals, and government ministries, while others found better-paying jobs with international humanitarian agencies. In

2005, thanks to a quota system imposed by the international community, women took 27 percent of the seats in the lower house of the new parliament, a greater percentage than women enjoy in most Western legislatures, including that of the United States. Yet these hopeful developments are misleading.

The fact is that the "liberation" of Afghan women is mostly theoretical. The Afghan Constitution adopted in 2004 declares: "The Citizens of Afghanistan—whether man or woman—have equal Rights and Duties before the Law." But what law? The judicial system—ultra-conservative, inadequate, incompetent, and notoriously corrupt—usually bases decisions on idiosyncratic interpretations of Islamic Sharia, tribal customary codes, or simple bribery. And legal "scholars" instruct women that having "equal Rights and Duties" is not the same as *being* equal to men.

Post-Taliban Afghanistan, under President Hamid Karzai, ratified key international agreements on human rights: the Universal Declaration of Human Rights, the International Treaty of Civil and Political Rights, and CEDAW: the Convention on the Elimination of All Forms of Discrimination Against Women. Like the Constitution, these essential documents provide a foundation for realizing the human rights of women.

But building on that paper foundation—amid poverty, illiteracy, misogyny, and ongoing warfare—is something else again. That's why, for the great majority of Afghan women, life has scarcely changed at all. That's why even an educated and informed leader like my colleague, on her way to a UN agency to work on women's rights, is still unable to eat an ice cream cone.

For most Afghan women the burqa is the least of their problems.

Afghanistan is just about the poorest country in the world. Only Burkina Faso and Niger sometimes get worse ratings. After nearly three decades of warfare and another of drought, millions of Afghans are without safe water or sanitation or electricity, even in the capital city. Millions are without adequate food and nutrition. Millions have access only to the most rudimentary healthcare, or none at all.

Diseases such as tuberculosis and polio, long eradicated in most of the world, flourish here. They hit women and children hard. One in four children die before the age of five, mostly from preventable illnesses such as cholera and diarrhea. Half of all women of childbearing age who die do so in childbirth, giving Afghanistan one of the highest maternal death rates in the world. The average life expectancy of an Afghan woman hovers around forty-two years.

Notice that we're still talking women's rights here: the fundamental economic and social rights that belong to all human beings.

There are other grim statistics. About 85 percent of Afghan women are illiterate. About 95 percent are routinely subjected to violence in the home. And the home is where most Afghan women in rural areas, and many in cities, are still customarily confined. Public space and public life belong almost exclusively to men. President Karzai heads the country while his wife, a qualified gynecologist with needed skills, stays at home.

These facts are well known. During more than five years of Western occupation, they haven't changed.

Afghan women and girls are, by custom and practice, the property of men. They may be traded and sold like any commodity. Although Afghan law sets the minimum marriageable age for girls at sixteen, girls as young as eight or nine are commonly sold into marriage. Women doctors in Kabul maternity hospitals describe terrible life-threatening "wedding night" injuries that husbands inflict on child brides. In the countryside, far from medical help, such girls die.

Under the tribal code of the Pashtuns, the dominant ethnic group, men customarily hand over women and girls—surplus sisters or widows, daughters or nieces—to other men to make amends for some offense or to pay off some indebtedness, often to a druglord. To Pashtuns the trade-off is a means of maintaining "justice" and social harmony, but international human rights observers define what happens to the women and girls used in such "conflict resolution" as "slavery."

Given the rigid confinement of women, a surprising number try to escape. But any woman on her own outside the home is assumed to be guilty of the crime of *zina*—engaging in sexual activity. That's why "running away" is itself a crime. One crime presupposes the other.

When she is caught, as most runaways are, she may be taken to jail for an indefinite term or returned to her husband or father or brothers who may then murder her to restore the family honor.

The same thing happens to a rape victim, force being no excuse for sexual contact—unless she is married to the man who raped her. In that case, she can be raped as often as he likes.

In Kabul, where women and girls move about more freely, many are snatched by traffickers and sold into sexual slavery. The traffickers are seldom pursued or punished because once a girl is abducted she is as good as dead anyway, even to loving parents, who are bound by the code of honor. The weeping mother of a kidnapped teenage girl once told me, "I pray she does not come back because my husband will have to kill her."

Many a girl kills herself. To escape beatings or sexual abuse or forced marriage. To escape prison or honor killing, if she's been seduced or raped or falsely accused. To escape life, if she's been forbidden to marry the man she would choose for herself.

Suicide also brings dishonor, so families cover it up. Only when city girls try to kill themselves by setting themselves on fire do their cases become known, for if they do not die at once, they may be taken to hospital. In 2003, scores of cases of self-immolation were reported in the city of Herat; the following year, as many were recorded in Kabul. Although such incidents are notoriously underreported, during the past year 150 cases were noted in western Afghanistan, 197 in Herat, and at least 34 in the south.

The customary codes and traditional practices that made life unbearable for these burned girls predate the Taliban, and they remain in force today, side by side with the new constitution and international documents that speak of women's rights.

Tune in a Kabul television station and you'll see evidence that Afghan women are poised at a particularly schizophrenic moment in their history. Watching televised parliamentary sessions, you'll see women who not only sit side by side with men—a dangerous, generally forbidden proximity—but actually rise to argue with them. Yet who can forget poor murdered Shaima, the lively, youthful presenter of a popular TV chat show for young people? Her father and brother killed her, or so men and women say approvingly, because they found her job shameful. Mullahs and public officials issue edicts from time to time condemning women on television, or television itself.

Many people believe the key to improving life for women, and all Afghans, is education, particularly because so many among Afghanistan's educated elite left the country during its decades of wars. So the international community invests in education projects—building schools, printing textbooks, teaching teachers, organizing literacy classes for women—and the

Bush administration in particular boasts that five million children now go to school.

But that's fewer than half the kids of school age, and less than one-third of the girls. The highest enrollments are in cities—85 percent of children in Kabul—while, in the Pashtun south, enrollments drop below 20 percent overall and near zero for girls. More than half the students enrolled in school live in Kabul and its environs, yet even there an estimated 60,000 children are not in school but in the streets, working as vendors, trash-pickers, beggars, or thieves.

None of this is new. For a century, Afghan rulers—from kings to communists—have tried to unveil women and advance education. In the 1970s and 1980s, many women in the capital went about freely, without veils. They worked in offices, schools, hospitals. They went to university and became doctors, nurses, teachers, judges, engineers. They drove their own cars. They wore Western fashions and traveled abroad. But when Kabul's communists called for universal education throughout the country, provincial conservatives opposed to educating women rebelled.

Afghan women of the Kabul elite haven't yet caught up to where they were thirty-five years ago. But once again ultra-conservatives are up in arms. This time it's the Taliban, back in force throughout the southern half of the country. Among their tactics: blowing up or burning schools (150 in 2005, 198 in 2006) and murdering teachers, especially women who teach girls. UNICEF estimates that in four southern provinces more than half the schools—380 out of 748—no longer provide any education at all. In September 2006 the Taliban shot down the middle-aged woman who headed the provincial office for women's affairs in Kandahar. A few brave colleagues went back to the office in body armor, knowing it would not save them. Now, in the southern provinces—more than half the country—women and girls stay home.

I blame George W. Bush, the "liberator" who looked the other way. In 2001, the United States military claimed responsibility for these provinces, the heart of Taliban country; but diverted to adventures in the oil fields of Iraq, it failed for five years to provide the security international humanitarians needed to do the promised work of reconstruction. Afghans grew discouraged. In the summer of 2006, when the US handed the job to NATO, British and Canadian "peacekeepers" walked right into war with the resurgent

Taliban. By year's end, more than 4,000 Afghans were dead—Taliban, "suspected" insurgents, and civilians. Speaking recently of dead women and children—trapped between US bombers and NATO troops on the one hand and Taliban forces backed (unofficially) by Pakistan on the other—President Karzai began to weep.

It's winter in Afghanistan now. No time to make war. But come spring, the Taliban promise a new offensive to throw out Karzai and foreign invaders. The British commander of NATO forces has already warned: "We could actually fail here."

He also advised a British reporter that Westerners shouldn't even mention women's rights when more important things are at stake. As if security is not a woman's right. And peace.

Come spring, Afghan women could lose it all.

March 2007

15

GUANTÁNAMO IS NOT A PRISON

Eleven Ways to Report on Gitmo without Upsetting the Pentagon

Karen J. Greenberg

Several weeks ago, I took the infamous media tour of the facilities at Guantánamo. From the moment I arrived on a dilapidated Air Sunshine plane to the time I boarded it heading home, I had no doubt that I was on a foreign planet or, at the very least, visiting an impeccably constructed movie set. Along with two European colleagues, I was treated to two-days-plus of a military-tour schedule packed with site visits and interviews (none with actual prisoners) designed to "make transparent" the base, its facilities, and its manifold contributions to the national security of the United States.

The multi-storied, maximum-security complexes, rimmed in concertina wire, set off from the road by high wire-mesh fences, and the armed tower guards at Camp Delta, present a daunting sight. Even the less restrictive quarters for "compliant" inmates belied any notion that Guantánamo is merely a holding facility for those awaiting charges or possessing useful information.

In the course of my brief stay, thanks to my military handlers I learned a great deal about Gitmo decorum, as the military would like us to practice it. My escorts told me how best to describe the goings-on at Guantánamo, regardless of what my own eyes and prior knowledge told me.

Here, in a nutshell, is what I picked up. Consider this a guide of sorts to what the officially sanctioned report on Guantánamo would look like, wrapped in the proper decorum and befitting the jewel-in-the-crown of American offshore prisons . . . or, to be Pentagon-accurate, "detention facilities."

1. *Guantánamo is not a prison.* According to the military handlers who accompanied us everywhere, Guantánamo is officially a "detention facility." Although the two most recently built complexes, Camps Five and Six, were actually modeled on maximum and medium security prisons in Indiana and Michigan respectively, and although the use of feeding tubes and the handling of prisoners now take into account the guidelines of the American Corrections Association (and increasingly those of the Bureau of Prisons as well), it is not acceptable to use the word "prison" while at Gitmo.

2. *Consistent with not being a prison, Guantánamo has no prisoners, only enemies,* specifically, "unlawful enemy combatants." One of my colleagues was even chastised for using the word "detainee." "Detained enemy combatants" or "unlawful enemy combatants," we learned, were the proper terms.

3. *Guantánamo is not about guilt and innocence—or, once an enemy combatant, always an enemy combatant.* "Today, it is not about guilt or innocence. It's about unlawful enemy combatants," Rear Admiral Harry B. Harris, Jr., the Commanding Officer of Guantánamo, tells us. "And they are all unlawful enemy combatants." This, despite the existence of the official category "No Longer an Enemy Combatant," which does not come up in our discussions. Nor was the possibility that any of the detainees at Guantánamo might have been mistakenly detained ever discussed. As the administrator for the tribunals that are to determine the status of each detainee explained to us, the US government takes "a risk when we transfer" detainees out of Guantánamo.

4. *No trustworthy lawyers come to Guantánamo.* Our handlers use the term "habeas lawyers" as a seemingly derogatory catch-all for lawyers in general, both defense attorneys—those who are defending their clients before the military commissions—and *habeas* attorneys, those who seek to challenge in US courts the government's right to detain their clients. The US military and its Public Affairs Officers are convinced that the terrorists are transmitting

information to their colleagues in the outside world via their lawyers. According to our escorts, "habeas lawyers" may be the unwitting pawns of terrorists. As a PowerPoint presentation at the outset of our formal tour (and subsequent remarks) make clear to us, it is the belief of the American authorities that the detainees are using their lawyers in accordance with the directives outlined in the al-Qaeda training manual that was discovered in Manchester, England, in 2000. This manual, they assure us, encourages terrorists to "take advantage of visits with habeas lawyers to communicate and exchange information with those outside."

5. *Recently, at least, few if any reliable journalists have been reporting on Guantánamo;* only potential betrayers are writing about it. "The media" arrive with ostensibly open eyes. Yet these guests, graciously hosted from morning to night, go home perversely refusing to be complimentary to their hosts. They suffer from "the chameleon effect," as I was told more than once by military public information office personnel, and "we just don't understand it." For our part, we visitors didn't understand why we were forbidden to walk anywhere—even to the bathroom—by ourselves, talk to anyone other than those we were introduced to (none actual prisoners), or even take a morning run up and down the street we were lodged on, although there was not a prisoner in sight.

6. *After years of isolation, the detainees still possess valuable information—especially today.* When asked what kind of useful information the detainees could possibly have for interrogators, many having already been locked away in Gitmo for over five years, the answer was: "I believe that we are, in fact, getting good and useful and interesting intelligence—even after five years." Right now, they are especially useful. This is because, Admiral Harris told us, "We have up-and-coming leadership in al-Qaeda and in the Taliban in Afghanistan [and] we don't know what they look like. There's never been a photograph taken of them or there's never been a photograph that US forces have of them. But their contemporaries . . . are quite often the same individuals that are in the camps here today. So we will work with law enforcement . . . and their sketch artists will work with these detainees, the compliant and cooperative detainees. . . . And those pictures will be sent out to the forward fighting area." No one asked just

how reliable our own memories would be after five years of isolated detention.

7. *Guantánamo contains no individuals—inside the wire or out.* The prisoners are referred to not by name, but by number. The guards and others, even outside the confines of the prison camp, remove the Velcroed names which are on their uniforms, leaving blank strips on their chests where their identity would normally be, or they replace their names with their ranks. Either way, they strive to remain anonymous. They tell us that they fear retaliation against themselves and their families from a presumably all-seeing, all-reaching *jihadi* network. With the media, most follow the same rules. We, too, could evidently land them in trouble with al-Qaeda. Thus, many refuse to tell us their names, warning those we greet to be careful not to mistakenly call them by name in front of us.

8. *Guantánamo's deep respect for Islam is unappreciated.* All the food served in the prison is *halal*, prepared in a separate kitchen constructed solely for the detainees. All cells, and outdoor areas, and even the detainee waiting room in the courthouse where the Military Commissions will be held, have arrows pointing to Mecca. All compliant detainees have prayer rugs and prayer beads. All detainees, no matter how they behave, have Korans. The library includes books on Islamic history, on Islamic philosophy, and on Mohammed and his followers. Our escorts are armored against our protests about the denial of legal rights to prisoners. The right to challenge their detention in court, actually being charged with a crime, or adhering to the basic rules of procedure and evidence that undergird American law—none of this is important. They do not see that what's at stake is not building a mosque at Gitmo, any more than it is about serving gourmet food, or about the cushy, leather interrogation chairs we are shown. It is about extending the most basic of legal rights, including the presumption of innocence, to those detained here.

9. *At Guantánamo, hard facts are scarce.* This, we are told, is a security measure. "As the 342nd media group to come through here, you'll notice that we speak vaguely. We can't be specific. You will notice that we talk in approximate terms and estimates only. Those are operational security

measures. We don't want to take away position"—a phrase which I took as shorthand for revealing actual numbers, names, locations, dates, et cetera.

Typical examples of preserving Gitmo security through a refusal to give out specific facts:

"What is that building?" [I am referring to one directly in our view.]
"Which building?"
"How long has the lieutenant been here?"
"Since she got here."
"Where is Radio Range?" [This is the area on which the camps are built.]
"I never heard of it."

10. *Guantánamo houses no contradictions.* And if you notice any—and they're hard to miss—it's best to keep quiet about them, unless you want a sergeant without a name chastising you about the dangers posed by enemy combatants, or one of the officers without a name reprimanding your lower-ranking escort for giving out "misinformation." Stories are regularly presented to portray a policy as particularly generous to the detainees; only later does someone mention that it might have been an answer to the needs of the guards themselves. A typical example:

"We allow two hours of recreation a day in order to comply with the Geneva Conventions," they tell us. But a guide at another moment leads us to believe that there is actually a more pressing reason for allowing the recreation. "We need them to go outside so that we can search their cells for weapons and contraband."

These sorts of contradictions leave me ultimately feeling sorry for our escorts. It is not their fault that they know so little about the place they are charged with explaining to us. Most of them arrived roughly eight months ago and were handed a defensive script. They are often quite sincere when they tell us that they don't know answers to our questions.

They actually don't know what went on before their arrival, or where things were located in earlier days, or if perchance abuses or outbursts, not to speak of torture, might have occurred at Gitmo, or even who was in charge as little as a year ago. Few, if any, from the old days are there to instruct or correct them.

Of course, if they wanted to, they could learn the details that many of us have picked up over the years simply by reading or by talking to those who spent time there. But this is not their task; they are but mouthpieces, nothing more, as they try to tell us time and again when we ask our questions. And, anyway, they themselves expect to leave relatively unscathed sometime this spring.

Finally, for those of us who want to write about Guantánamo and who are grateful for having been shown around and had the myths and realities of the Bush administration's most notorious detention facility laid out so clearly, a final lesson:

11. *Those who fail to reproduce the official narrative are not welcome back.* "Tell it the wrong way and you won't be back," one of our escorts warns me over lunch.

Only time will tell if I got it right.

April 2007

16

"I AM NOW A REFUGEE"

The Iraqi Crisis that Has No Name

Dahr Jamail

Since the shock-and-awe invasion of Iraq began in March 2003, that country's explosive unraveling has never left the news or long been off the front page. Yet the fallout beyond its borders from the destruction, disintegration, and ethnic mayhem in Iraq has almost avoided notice. And yet with—according to United Nations estimates—approximately 50,000 Iraqis fleeing their country each month (and untold numbers of others being displaced internally), Iraq is producing one of the—if not the—most severe refugee crises on the planet, a crisis without a name and without significant attention.

For the last two weeks, I've been in Syria, visiting refugee centers and camps, the offices and employees of the United Nations High Commissioner for Refugees (UNHCR), and poor neighborhoods in Damascus that are filling up with desperate, almost penniless Iraqi refugees, sometimes living fifteen to a room. In statistical and human terms, these few days offered a small window into the magnitude of a catastrophe that is still unfolding and shows no sign of abating in any immediately imaginable future.

Let's start with the numbers, inadequate as they are. The latest UN figures concerning the refugee crisis in Iraq indicate that between 1 million and 1.2 million Iraqis have fled across the border into Syria; about 750,000 have crossed into Jordan (increasing its modest population of 5.5 million by 14 percent); at least another 150,000 have made it to Lebanon; over 150,000 have emigrated to Egypt; and—these figures are the trickiest of all—over 1.9 million are now estimated to have been internally displaced by civil war and sectarian cleansing within Iraq.

These numbers are staggering in a population estimated in the pre-invasion years at only 26 million. At a bare minimum, in other words, at least one out of every seven Iraqis has had to flee his or her home due to the violence and chaos set off by the Bush administration's invasion and occupation of Iraq.

Yet, as even the UN officials on the scene admit, these are undoubtedly low-end estimates. "We rely heavily on the official numbers given to us by the Syrian government concerning the Iraqi refugees coming here," Sybella Wilkes, the regional public information officer for the UNHCR, told me while we talked recently at the main refugee processing center in Douma, a city on the outskirts of the Syrian capital. Even the high-end UNHCR estimate of 1.2 million Iraqi refugees in Syria (a country of only 17 million people) was, she told me, probably too low.

According to Wilkes, the Syrian government, using tallies taken from its southern border posts, privately estimates the number to be closer to 1.4–1.5 million Iraqis in Syria. The UNHCR operation here, desperately underfunded and short of staff, does not have people on the border tallying numbers and has no way to check on the real magnitude of the disaster under way.

Yet in their work they can feel its oppressive weight daily. Erdogan Kalkan, a 35-year-old Turkish UNHCR employee of fifteen years, told me that the overworked staff have already scheduled a total of 35,000 appointments with refugees seeking aid in Syria; only 25,000 of those refugees have actually had their cases addressed—and that barely scratches the surface of the problem. "We have been increasing our processing capacity from the beginning," he said, while puffing on a cigarette. We were speaking in a newly converted warehouse where Iraqi families now can meet with UNHCR workers in cramped white cubicles and be interviewed about why they left Iraq and what their most immediate needs are.

UNHCR's budget for Iraqis in Syria in 2006 was a bare $700,000, less than one dollar per refugee crossing the border. UNHCR needs far greater financial resources even to begin to help the mass of Iraqi refugees in the country, as well as food, medicine, and aid from other UN agencies. At the moment, it is essentially the only UN agency assisting Iraqis in Syria, Lebanon, and Jordan. UNICEF and other UN agencies have voiced interest, but as yet have provided little support in Syria, according to Kalkan.

Adham Mardini, the public information assistant for UNHCR in Damascus, told me their budget in Syria has risen precipitously to $16 million for 2007, although that, too, remains far below what would be necessary simply to fulfill the most basic needs of the most desperate of the refugees. It adds up to a little over $13 per Iraqi refugee per year—if you don't include the refugees in Syria from Somalia, Palestine, Afghanistan, and other war-torn areas for whom UNHCR is also responsible (along with UNHCR overhead). Iraqi refugees receive food supplements from UNICEF, but only in the most severe cases of need, and cash is simply unavailable for distribution.

Back in late 2006, UNHCR in Damascus started out as the most modest of operations—with two processing clerks, each seeing between five and seven cases daily. Now, there are twenty-five clerks processing more than 200 cases daily, not to mention guards, drivers, new computers, a Red Crescent aid station at the center, a new bathroom, and plans for adding a child center, psychological counseling services, and a community center before the Secretary General of the UN visits later this month.

Yet all of this is still nowhere near enough to keep up with the implacable flood of Iraqis entering Syria every month. Iraqis, who now comprise a little over 8 percent of the population of this small country, tell stories about why they left their land and what they are dealing with today, which these numbers, staggering as they are, do not.

More Than Numbers

"I left everything behind," Salim Hamad, a former railroad worker from Baghdad, told me. "My house was empty when I left, and I have no idea what became of it." We met in a small teashop in the sprawling Yarmouk refugee camp in Damascus. It is perhaps not inappropriate that Yarmouk is primarily a Palestinian refugee camp, since the Iraqi diaspora represents the largest exodus of refugees in the Middle East since the state of Israel was created in 1948. The camp is an uninspiring mass of high, gray apartment buildings through which snake crowded roads. According to locals, tens of thousands of Iraqis have already joined their ranks, with the numbers increasing daily, and Salim Hamad is not atypical of the new arrivals.

Five months ago, Salim had to sell his car, his furniture, and most of his other belongings simply to raise enough money to bring his wife and three children to Syria. They had grown tired and fearful, he told me, of seeing corpses in their streets every day.

Because Jordan's pro-US King Abdullah had long since clamped down on Iraqi entry to his country, for Salim and countless others Syria has been the only available destination. Yarmouk, with electricity and running water, is in fact one of the better areas for refugees. The two other main refugee camps into which Iraqis are now flooding, Jaramana and Sayada Zainab, present far grimmer living conditions, including more than ten people sleeping in rooms without beds, lacking potable drinking water and in some cases heat, and with intermittent electricity.

Other Iraqis are living in poorer city neighborhoods, eating up their savings, sometimes relying on the goodwill of Syrian friends or relatives. Given visa restrictions, which prohibit Iraqis from working here (except, of course, in the black market economy), when often meager savings run out, the crisis is sure to worsen exponentially.

UNHCR recently offered the following staggering projection: according to its best estimates about 12 percent of Iraq's population, now assumed to be about 24 million people, will be displaced by the end of 2007. We're talking about nearly 3 million ever more destitute Salim Hamads by the New Year. (Add to that Iraq's growing population of internal refugees and its spiraling civilian death tolls and you have the kind of decimation of a nation rarely seen—with, undoubtedly, more to come.)

A report released on March 22, 2007 by the NGO Refugees International calls the flight of Iraqis from war-torn Iraq "the world's fastest growing displacement crisis."

"The situation now is pushing Syria and Jordan to the maximum," the UNCHR's Wilkes told me. "Syria's 'open door' policy is extraordinary, but economically and socially we wonder how long it can be maintained. We're very aware of the impact on these governments this crisis is having. We're hoping the international community will help share the burden."

The primary trigger for this crisis was the 2003 invasion and occupation of Iraq, and yet President Bush and his top officials have taken no significant steps whatsoever to share in the resulting refugee burden. To date, the administration has issued only 466 visas to Iraqis. Under recent pressure from the UN, it has said that it would offer an additional 7,000 visas—but without either announcing the criteria for accepting such refugees or even when the visas might be issued. Upon hearing this paltry number, an Iraqi refugee said to me in disbelief: "Seven thousand out of over four million Iraqis who have either fled their country or are internally displaced? . . . I don't know if he could insult us more if he tried."

"I ask all nations, particularly the United States, to do all that they can to help us," was the way Qasim Jubouri, a banker who fled Baghdad with his family in order to keep them alive, put the matter to me. "Since the US government caused all of this, shouldn't they also be responsible for helping us now?"

Like Salim, he too left for Syria with nothing more than some clothing and his meager savings. Now, the money he brought is running out and he has no idea how he will feed his family when it's gone.

32-year-old Ali Ahmed has a similar tale to tell. "I was a financial manager of seven companies in Baghdad, but I had to leave my house, my car, and just about everything." After militiamen fired on his car in the once upscale Mansoor district of Baghdad, Ali fled to Jordan. He returned to Iraq to try again, but once more faced death in an attack in which six employees from his management firm were killed.

And even that wasn't the end of it. "We had eleven engineers from one company detained by the Mehdi Army [the militia of Shia cleric Muqtada al-Sadr]. We never heard from them again. I knew then that I had to drop everything and run for my life."

Ali does not see himself returning soon. "I don't expect to go back for at least fifteen to twenty years. I have left everything behind, and now I have nothing but a small food store I run here. But it is not enough. Not the UN, nor any government, least of all the Iraqi government, is doing enough to help us." (The Syrian government, thus far, maintains a policy of looking the other way when it comes to modest or menial jobs Iraqis find that don't put Syrians out of work.)

Another Iraqi refugee told me of being detained by Mehdi Army militia members and having a rod forced down his throat as part of his "interrogation." He was lucky to come out of the experience alive. Many, on either side of the worsening sectarian struggle, do not. The slaughter of Sunnis by the Medhi Army and the slaughter of Shias by Sunni extremist groups have become commonplace.

Despite the fact that Sadr recently ordered his militia to focus all its attacks on occupation forces, scores of dead bodies turning up on Baghdad's streets each day prove otherwise.

Iraqis who worked with, or have been in any way associated with, the American military or occupation authorities are faring at least as badly, if not worse. Everyone collaborating in any way with US forces in Iraq is now targeted—along with their families.

"I used to work with the Americans near Kut," Sa'ad Hussein, a 34-year-old electrical engineer told me. "I worked for Kellogg, Brown, and Root [then a subsidiary of oil services giant Halliburton] to construct an Iraqi base there until I got my death threat on a piece of paper slipped under my door on my return to Baghdad. I had no choice but to flee."

"Things are getting so much worse in Iraq," was the way Salim Hamad, who fled five months ago, summed up life in his former homeland as our interview was ending. "There is a big difference between those who left four years ago and those who left four days ago. Everything in Iraq is based on sectarianism now and there is no protection—neither from the Americans, nor the Iraqi government."

Fleeing "Freedom and Democracy"

Sa'ad Hussein, who arrived in Damascus only three months ago, described the Baghdad he left as a "city of ghosts" where the black banners of death announcements hang on most streets. There is, he claimed (and this was verified by others we spoke to among the more recent refugees), normally only one hour of electricity a day and no jobs to be found.

"I was an ex-captain in the Iraqi Army, and I think that's why I was threatened, in addition to working with the occupation authorities," he explained. When asked how many of his former Sunni army colleagues had also received death threats, he replied, "All of them." It was not safe, he told me, for him to go back to the now largely Shia Iraqi Army because, "I may be killed. This is the new freedom and democracy we have."

On all measurable levels, life in Baghdad, now well into the fifth year of

US occupation, has become hellish for Iraqis who have attempted to remain, which, of course, only adds to the burgeoning numbers who daily become part of the exodus to neighboring lands. It is generally agreed that the delivery of security, electricity, potable water, health care, and jobs—that is, the essentials of modern urban life—are all significantly worse than during the last years of the reign of Saddam Hussein.

"The Americans are detaining so many people," Ali Hassan, a 41-year-old from the Hay Jihad area of Baghdad said as we spoke in front of the central UNHCR office in downtown Damascus. "And my brother was killed by Shia militiamen after he refused to give them the keys to empty Sunni houses we were looking after."

As scores of other refugees crowded around photographer Jeff Pflueger and me, wanting to tell their stories, Hassan, a Shia who also fled Baghdad just three months ago, added, "Now I can't go back. I am a refugee and I still don't feel secure because I still fear the Mehdi Army."

"So many Iraqis never leave their homes now because they are too afraid to go out due to the militias," Abdul Abdulla, a 68-year-old who fled Baghdad with his family, insisted, having literally grabbed the microphone I was using to tape my interview with Hassan.

From the volatile Yarmouk area of Baghdad, Abdulla, a Sunni, said Shia militia members waited on the outskirts of his neighborhood in order to detain anyone trying to leave. "We stayed in our homes, but even then some people were being detained from their own houses. These death squads started coming after [former US ambassador John] Negroponte arrived. And the Iraqi government is definitely involved because they depend on [the militias]."

While talking with Abdulla, I noticed a woman in a black *abaya* or gown covering her entire body, one of her arms in a cast, standing nearby.

When I approached Eman Abdul Rahid, a 46-year-old mother from Baghdad, she willingly told me her sad story, all too typical of civilian life in the Iraqi capital today. "I was injured," she said, "because I was near a car bomb, which killed my daughter . . . There is killing, and threats of more killing, and explosions daily in Baghdad.

"America is the reason why Iraq was invaded, so we would like the American administration to give aid to us refugees," she added. "I would like people to read this and tell Bush to help us."

Six Months and Counting

Sundays and Mondays at the UNHCR refugee processing center in Douma are mob scenes. Refugees, some of whom have been waiting several months for their first interview at the center, an event crucial to finding aid, arrive in taxis, minibuses, on foot, or on buses specially hired by UNHCR. They line up outside a freshly painted white and blue gate, manned by security guards, and slowly trickle into the converted warehouse to wait eagerly for their names and numbers to be called.

On one of my Monday visits, as my friend Jeff and I approached the warehouse-turned-processing-center there were more than a thousand Iraqis crowded around the entrance hoping to get in. Taxis honked their way through the gathering crowds of refugees, each of whom held a number representing his or her place in line, along with passports and other required papers.

As we were being escorted inside the center by UNHCR public information assistant Adham Mardini, he told us that the previous day between 6,000 and 7,000 Iraqi refugees had descended on the place. On that day alone, 2,179 future appointments had been scheduled, each representing an average of 3.6 people, since many of them are set by the heads of families. "Sundays and Mondays are always crazy here because these are the days we set their appointments," he commented. "And these people now have to wait up to six months just for their interview."

Some Iraqis showing up are, however, in need of emergency care. Refugees often arrive without medicines, and with serious heart problems, kidney failure, sizeable burns across their bodies, or ill-healed wounds—and that's not even to speak of the psychological problems they face from violence seen or experienced or from lives completely uprooted. All of this, the UNHCR center must try to face. A surprising number of arrivals are simply put in ambulances to be either taken to local hospitals or treated by the Syrian Red Crescent.

Under a makeshift roof outside the warehouse but inside the outer gate, families lucky enough to have their numbers come up on this day are filling out forms. Men stand writing on sheets of paper pressed against walls; women hold crying babies amid the cacophony and chaos. Periodically, a UNHCR volunteer appears at the door of the building with a bullhorn to announce

154

the names of those who should prepare to be interviewed. Most of them have been waiting at least four months for this day.

Iraqis continue to crowd through the door from the road as I talk with Mardini. "As you can see, the Baghdad security plan is working very well," he says with a wry smile. From hundreds of miles away, it's his organization that is providing what "security" is available, and it can't hope to keep up with the steadily increasing numbers of desperate Iraqis.

To make matters worse, UNHCR officials have been noticing an increase in Kurdish refugees from the previously more peaceable northern regions of Iraq. "Over 50 percent of all newcomers in the last two weeks are Kurds," Kalkan, the UNHCR veteran of fifteen years whom I'd spoken with before, says as he joins Mardini and me at the door. The two of them express a modest mix of frustration and discouragement, given the circumstances. After all, just as UNHCR in Damascus begins to ramp up to accommodate the massive numbers of refugees they have to deal with, the flow increases confoundingly.

Perhaps an hour later, when we make our way back to the street, the hoard of refugees has miraculously dwindled to only a few dozen forlorn Iraqis outside the now-closed door. We can't understand what made them all disappear so quickly.

"I came here three times to get this appointment because it was so crowded," an Iraqi doctor tells me, as he holds number 525, showing his place in line. "I arrived today at 5 A.M. with my family of eleven for this appointment and now they have postponed it!" He had been one away in line when the door was closed for the day. Due to the burgeoning number of refugees, half the UNHCR interviewers had to be shifted to the task of scheduling future appointments for newcomers. Thus, half of the interviews for this day had been canceled.

"Now I have to wait another two months," the doctor told me, as I stared into his tired eyes. He's still holding his number in his hand as a small crowd begins to build around us and others start to pour out similar stories of frustration and despair. As voices rise in frustration, Jeff flashes me a look of concern and we decide to thank them for their time and move on. Other than writing their collective tale of woe and taking their photos to show the world the faces of this growing crisis, there is little else we can do.

Abu Talat

Abu Talat, a 58-year-old father of four, was my primary interpreter during my eight months in Iraq. Six months ago he finally gave up hope of remaining in his home in Baghdad, took his family, and like hundreds of thousands of other Iraqis fled to Syria. One of the luckier refugees, he had enough savings to rent a humble two-room apartment in Damascus.

He has always been, and remains, a proud man. Having served in the Iraqi Army until 1990, he holds military traits like dignity, honesty, and honor in the highest regard. While I've always offered to help him in any way I could as his life disintegrated, only once did he ever accept a meager sum of money from me.

Upon my arrival in Syria, he invited me to his home to share dinner with his family. After the meal, while we were drinking strong tea, he asked his daughter to show me the certificate from the UNHCR which proves that they are officially refugees. He handed me the paper and watched me as I read it.

The document lists him as the head of the family. A black-and-white photo of him is at the top of the page, and the names and ages of his family members are at the bottom. Just above them is the following text:

> This is to certify that the above named person has been recognized as a refugee by [the United Nations High Commissioner for Refugees] pursuant to its extended mandate. As a refugee, [he/she] is a person of concern to the office of the United High Commissioner for Refugees, and should, in particular, be protected from forcible return to a country where [he/she] would face threats to his or her life or freedom. Any assistance accorded to above named individual would be most appreciated.

I glanced at him, not knowing what to say, then handed the paper back. He looked it over himself, as if in disbelief, then let his gaze focus on nothing in particular, while his chest heaved as he visibly struggled to master the urge to weep. Finally, he said to no one in particular, "I am now a refugee."

IV

UNDER THE BOMBS

July 2006

17

DEGRADING BEHAVIOR

The Middle East and the Barbarism of War from the Air

Tom Engelhardt

Barbarism seems an obvious enough category. Ordinarily in our world, the barbarians are *them*. *They* act in ways that seem unimaginably primitive and brutal to us. For instance, they kidnap or capture someone, American or Iraqi, and cut off his head. Now, isn't that the definition of barbaric? Who does that anymore? The eighth century, or maybe the word "medieval"—anyway, some brutal past time—comes to mind immediately, and to the mass mind of our media even faster.

Similarly, to jump a little closer to modernity, *they* strap on grenades, plastic explosives, bombs of various ingenious sorts fashioned in home labs, with nails or other bits of sharp metal added to create instant shrapnel meant to rend human flesh, to maim and kill. Then they approach a target—an Israeli bus filled with civilians and perhaps some soldiers, a pizza parlor in Jerusalem, a gathering of Shia or Sunni worshippers at or near a mosque in Iraq or Pakistan, or of unemployed potential police or army recruits in Ramadi or Baghdad, or of shoppers in an Iraqi market somewhere in that country, or perhaps a foreigner on the streets of Kabul—and they blow themselves up. Or they arm backpacks or bags and step onto trains in London, Madrid, Mumbai, and set the bags off.

Or, to up the technology and modernity a bit, they wire a car to explode, put a jihadist in the driver's seat, and drive it into—well, this is now common enough that you can pick your target. Or perhaps they audaciously hijack four just-fuelled jets filled with passengers and run two of them into the World Trade Center, one into the Pentagon, and another into a field in Pennsylvania. This is, of course, the very definition of barbaric.

Now, let's jump a step further into our age of technological destruction, becoming less face-to-face, more impersonal, without, in the end, changing things that much. *They* send rockets from southern Lebanon (or even cruder ones from the Gaza Strip) against Israeli towns and cities. These rockets can only vaguely be aimed. Some can be brought into the general vicinity of an inhabited area; others, more advanced, into specific urban neighborhoods many tens of miles away—and then they detonate, killing whoever is in the vicinity, which normally means civilians just living their lives, even, in one recent Hezbollah volley aimed at Nazareth, two Israeli Arab children. In this process, thousands of Israelis have been temporarily driven from their homes.

In the case of rockets by the hundreds lofted into Israel by an armed, organized militia, meant to terrorize and harm civilian populations, these are undoubtedly war crimes. Above all, they represent a kind of barbarism that—with the possible exception of some of those advanced Hezbollah rockets—feels primitive to us. Despite the explosives, cars, planes, all so basic to our modern way of life, such acts still seem redolent of ancient, less civilized times when people did especially cruel things to each other face to face.

The Religion of Air Power

That's *them*. But what about us? On our we/they planet, most groups don't consider themselves barbarians. Nonetheless, we have largely achieved nonbarbaric status in an interesting way—by removing the most essential aspect of the American (and, right now, Israeli) way of war from the category of the barbaric. I'm talking, of course, about air power, about raining destruction down on the earth from the skies, and about the belief—so common, so long-lasting, so deep-seated—that bombing others, including civilian populations, is a "strategic" thing to do; that air power can, in relatively swift measure, break the "will" not just of the enemy, but of that enemy's society; and that such a way of war is the royal path to victory.

This set of beliefs was common to air-power advocates even before modern air war had been tested, and repeated unsuccessful attempts to put these convictions into practice have never really shaken—not for long anyway—what is essentially a war-making religion. The result has been the development of the most barbaric style of warfare imaginable, one that has seldom succeeded in breaking *any* societal will, though it has destroyed innumerable bodies, lives, stretches of countryside, villages, towns, and cities.

Even today, we find Israeli military strategists saying things that could have been put in the mouths of their air-power-loving predecessors endless decades ago. The *New York Times's* Steven Erlanger, for instance, recently quoted an unnamed "senior Israeli commander" this way: "He predicted that Israel would stick largely to air power for now. . . . 'A ground maneuver won't solve the problem of the long-range missiles,' he said. 'The problem is the will to launch. We have to break the will of Hezbollah . . .' " Don't hold your breath is the first lesson history teaches on this particular assessment of the powers of air war; the second is that, a decade from now, some other "senior commander" in some other country will be saying the same thing, word for word.

When it comes to brutality, the fact is that ancient times have gotten a bad rap. Nothing in history was more brutal than the twentieth century's style of war-making—than those two world wars with their air armadas, backed by the most advanced industrial systems on the planet. Powerful countries then bent every elbow, every brain, to support the destruction of other human beings *en masse*, not to speak of the Holocaust (which was assembly-line warfare in another form), and the various colonial and Cold War campaigns that went on in the Third World from the 1940s on; which, in places like Korea and Vietnam, Laos and Cambodia, substituted the devastation of air power locally for a war between the two superpowers which might have employed the mightiest air weaponry of all to scour the Earth.

It may be that the human capacity for brutality, for barbarism, hasn't changed much since the eighth century, but the industrial revolution—and in particular the rise of the airplane—opened up new landscapes to brutality, while the view from behind the gun-sight, then the bomb-sight, and finally the missile-sight slowly widened until all of humanity was taken in. From the lofty, godlike vantage point of the strategic (as well as the literal) heavens, the military and the civilian began to blur on the ground. Soldiers and citizens, conscripts and refugees alike, became nothing but tiny, indistinguishable hordes of ants, or nothing at all but the structures that housed them, or even just concepts, indistinguishable one from the other.

One Plane, One Bomb

As far as anyone knows, the first bomb was dropped—by hand—over the Italian colony of Libya. According to Sven Lindqvist's *A History of Bombing*, one Lieutenant Giulio Cavotti "leaned out of his delicate monoplane and dropped the bomb—a Danish Haasen hand grenade—on the North African oasis Tagiura, near Tripoli. Several moments later, he attacked the oasis Ain Zara. Four bombs in total, each weighing two kilos, were dropped during this first air attack."

That was 1911 and the damage was minimal. Only thirty-four years later, vast armadas of B-17s and B-29s were taking off, up to a thousand planes at a time, to bomb Germany and Japan. In the case of Tokyo—then constructed almost totally out of highly flammable materials—a single raid carrying incendiary bombs and napalm that began just after midnight on March 10, 1945 proved capable of incinerating or killing at least 90,000 people, possibly many more, from such a height that the dead could not be seen (though the stench of burning flesh carried up to the planes). The first American planes to arrive over the city, wrote historian Michael Sherry in his book *The Rise of American Air Power*, "carved out an X of flames across one of the world's most densely packed residential districts; followers fed and broadened it for some three hours thereafter."

What descended from the skies, as James Carroll puts it in *House of War*, was "1,665 tons of pure fire . . . the most efficient and deliberate act of arson in history. The consequent firestorm obliterated fifteen square miles, which included both residential and industrial areas. Fires raged for four days." It was the bonfire of bonfires and not a single American plane was shot down.

On August 6, 1945, all the power of that vast air armada was again reduced to a single plane, the *Enola Gay*, and a single bomb, Little Boy, dropped near a single bridge in a single city, Hiroshima, which in a single moment of a sort never before experienced on the planet did what it had taken 300 B-29s and many hours to do to Tokyo. In those two cities—as well as Dresden and other German and Japanese cities subjected to "strategic bombing"—the dead (perhaps 900,000 in Japan and 600,000 in Germany) were invariably preponderantly civilian, and far too distant to be seen by plane crews often dropping their bombloads in the dark of night, giving the scene below the look of Hell on Earth.

So 1911: one plane, one bomb. 1945: one plane, one bomb—but this time at least 120,000 dead, possibly many more. Two bookmarks less than four decades apart in the first chapter of a history of the invention of a new kind of warfare, a new kind of barbarism that, by now, is the way we expect war to be made, a way that no longer strikes us as barbaric at all. This wasn't always the case.

The Shock of the New
When military air power was in its infancy and silent films still ruled the movie theaters, the first air-war films presented pilots as knights of the heavens, engaging in courageous, chivalric, one-on-one combat in the skies. As that image reflects, in the wake of the meat-grinder of trench warfare in World War One, the medieval actually seemed far less brutal, a time much preferable to those years in which young men had died by their hundreds of thousands, anonymously, from machine guns, artillery, poison gas, all the lovely inventions of industrial civilization, ground into the mud of no-man's-land, often without managing to move their lines or the enemy's more than a few hundred yards.

The image of chivalric knights in planes jousting in the skies slowly disappeared from American screens, as after the 1950s would, by and large, air power itself even as the war film went on (and on and on). It can last be found perhaps in the film *Top Gun*; in old Peanuts comics in which Snoopy remains forever the Red Baron; and of course, post-*Star Wars*, in the fantasy realm of outer space where Jedi Knights took up lethal sky-jousting in the late 1970s, X-wing fighter to X-wing fighter, and in zillions of video games to follow. In the meantime, the one-way air slaughter in South Vietnam would be largely left out of the burst of Vietnam films that would start hitting the screen from the late 1970s on.

In the real, off-screen world, that courtly medieval image of air power disappeared fast indeed. As World War Two came ever closer and it became more apparent what air power was best at—what would now be called "collateral damage"—the shock set in. When civilians were first purposely targeted and bombed in the industrializing world rather than in colonies like Iraq, the act was initially widely condemned as inhuman by a startled world.

People were horrified when, during the Spanish Civil War in 1937, Hitler's Condor Legion and planes from fascist Italy repeatedly bombed the Basque town of Guernica, engulfing most of its buildings in a firestorm that killed hundreds, if not thousands, of civilians. If you want to get a sense of the power of that act to shock then, view Picasso's famous painting of protest done almost immediately in response. (When Secretary of State Colin Powell went to the UN in February 2003 to deliver his now infamous speech explaining what we supposedly knew about Saddam Hussein's weapons of mass destruction, UN officials—possibly at the request of the Bush administration—covered over a tapestry of the painting that happened to be positioned where Powell would have to pass on his way to deliver his speech and where press comments would be offered afterwards.)

Later in 1937, as the Japanese began their campaign to conquer China, they bombed a number of Chinese cities. A single shot of a Chinese baby wailing amid the ruins, published in *Life* magazine, was enough to horrify Americans (even though the actual photo may have been doctored). Air power was then seen as nothing but a new kind of barbarism. According to historian Sherry, "In 1937 and 1938, [President Roosevelt] had the State Department condemn Japanese bombing of civilians in China as 'barbarous' violations of the 'elementary principles' of modern morality." Meanwhile, observers checking out what effect the bombing of civilians had on the "will" of society offered nothing but bad news to the strategists of air power. As Sherry writes:

> In the *Saturday Evening Post*, an American army officer observed that bombing had proven "disappointing to the theorists of peacetime." When Franco's rebels bombed Madrid, did the Madrilenos sue for peace? No, they shook futile fists at the murderers in the sky and muttered, "Swine." His conclusion: "Terrorism from the air has been tried and found wanting. Bombing, far from softening the civil will, hardens it."

Already similar things are being written about the Lebanese, though, in our media, terms like "barbarism" and "terrorism" are unlikely to be applied to Israel's war from the heavens. *New York Times* correspondent Sabrina

Tavernise, for instance, reported the following from the site of a destroyed apartment building in the bomb-shocked southern Lebanese port of Tyre:

> Whatever the target, the result was an emotional outpouring in support of Hezbollah. Standing near a cluster of dangling electrical wires, a group of men began to chant. "By our blood and our soul, we'll fight for you, Nasrallah!" they said, referring to Hezbollah's leader, Sheik Hassan Nasrallah. In a foggy double image, another small group chanted the same thing, as if answering, on the other side of the smoke.

World War Two began with the German bombing of Warsaw. On September 9, 1939, according to Carroll, President Roosevelt "beseeched the war leaders on both sides to 'under no circumstances undertake the bombardment from the air of civilian populations of unfortified cities.' " Then came, the terror bombing of Rotterdam and Hitler's Blitz against England in which tens of thousands of British civilians died and many more were displaced, each event proving but another systemic shock to what was left of global opinion, another unimaginable act by the planet's reigning barbarians.

British civilians, of course, still retain a deserved reputation for the stiff-upper-lip-style bravery with which they comported themselves in the face of a merciless German air offensive against their cities that knew no bounds. No wills were broken there, nor would they be in Russia (where, in 1942, perhaps 40,000 were killed in German air attacks on the city of Stalingrad alone)—any more than they would be in Germany by the far more massive Allied air offensive against the German population.

All of this, of course, came before it was clear that the United States could design and churn out planes faster, in greater numbers, and with more firepower than any country on the planet and then wield air power far more massively and brutally than anyone had previously been capable of doing. That was before the US and Britain decided to fight fire with fire by blitz- and terror-bombing Germany and Japan. (The US moved more slowly and awkwardly than the British from "precision bombing" against targets like factories producing military equipment or oil storage depots— campaigns that largely failed—to "area bombing" that was simply meant to annihilate vast numbers of civilians and destroy cities. But move American strategists did.) That was before Dresden and Hiroshima; before Pyongyang, along with much of the Korean peninsula, was reduced to rubble from the air in the Korean War; before the Plaine des Jarres was bombed back to the Stone Age in Laos in the late 1960s and early 1970s, before the B-52s were sent against the cities of Hanoi and Haiphong in the terror bombing of Christmas 1972 to wring concessions out of the North Vietnamese at the peace table in Paris; before the first President Bush ended the First Gulf War with a "turkey shoot" on the "highway of death" as Saddam Hussein's largely conscript military fled Kuwait City in whatever vehicles were at hand; before we bombed the rubble in Afghanistan into further rubble in 2001; and before we shock-and-awed Baghdad in 2003.

Taking the Sting out of Air War

Somewhere in this process, a new language to describe air war began to develop—after, in the Vietnam era, the first "smart bombs" and "precision-guided weapons" came on line. From then on, air attacks would, for instance, be termed "surgical," and civilian casualties would be dismissed as but "collateral damage." All of this helped removed the sting of barbarity from the form of war we had chosen to make our own (unless, of course, you happened to be one of those "collateral" people under those "surgical" strikes). Just consider, for a moment, that, with the advent of the First Gulf War, air power—as it was being applied—essentially became entertainment, a Disney-style, *son-et-lumière* spectacular over Baghdad to be watched in real time on television by a population of noncombatants from thousands of miles away.

With that same war, the Pentagon started calling press briefings and screening nose-cone photography, essentially little Iraqi snuff films, in which you actually looked through the precision-guided bomb- or missile-sights yourself, found your target, and followed that missile or smart bomb right down to its explosive impact. If you were lucky, the Pentagon even let you check out the after-mission damage assessments. These films were so nifty, so like the high-tech video-game experience just then coming into being, that they were used by the Pentagon as reputation enhancers. From then on, Pentagon officials not only described their air weaponry as "surgical" in its abilities, but showed you the "surgery" (just as the Israelis have been doing with their footage of "precision" attacks in Lebanon). What you didn't see, of course, was the "collateral damage" which, when the Iraqis put it on screen, was promptly dismissed as so much propaganda.

And yet this new form of air war had managed to move far indeed from the image of the knightly joust, from the sense, in fact, of battle at all. In those years, except over the far north of Korea during the Korean War or over North Vietnam and some parts of South Vietnam, American pilots, unless in helicopters, went into action (as Israeli ones do today) knowing that the dangers to them were usually minimal—or, as over that Iraqi highway of death, nonexistent. War from the air was in the process of becoming a one-way street of destruction.

At an extreme, with the arrival of fleets of Hellfire-missile-armed unmanned Predator drones over Iraq, the "warrior" would suddenly find himself seven thousand miles away at Nellis Air Force Base near Las Vegas, delivering "precision" strikes that almost always, somehow, managed to kill collaterally. In such cases, war and screen war have indeed merged.

This kind of war has the allure, from a military point of view, of ever fewer casualties on one end in return for ever more on the other. It must also instill a feeling of bloodless, godlike control over those enemy "ants" (until, of course, things begin to go wrong, as they always do), as well as a sense that the world can truly be "remade" from the air, by remote control, and at a great remove. This has to be a powerful, even a transporting fantasy for strategists, however regularly it may be denied by history.

Despite the cleansed language of air war, and no matter how good the targeting intelligence or smart the bomb (neither of which can be counted on), civilians who make the mistake of simply being alive and going about their daily business die in profusion whenever war descends from the heavens. This is the deepest reality of war today.

Afghanistan, Iraq, Lebanon . . . [Fill in the Blank]

In fact, the process of removing air power from the ranks of the barbaric, of making it, if not glorious (as in those visually startling moments when Baghdad was shock-and-awed), then completely humdrum, and so of no note whatsoever, has been remarkably successful in our world. In fact, we have loosed our air power regularly on the countryside of Afghanistan, and especially on rebellious urban areas of Iraq in "targeted" and "precise" attacks on insurgent concentrations and "al-Qaeda safe houses" (as well as in more wholesale assaults on the old city of Najaf and on the city of Falluja) largely without comment or criticism. In the process, significant parts of two cities in a country we occupied and supposedly "liberated" were reduced to rubble and everywhere civilians, not to speak of whole wedding parties, were blown away without our media paying much attention at all.

Our various air campaigns—our signature way of war—have hardly been noticed, and almost never focused on, by the large numbers of journalists embedded with US forces or in one way or another on the ground in Iraq and Afghanistan. Remember, we're talking here about the dropping of up to 2,000-pound bombs regularly, over years, often in urban areas. Just imagine, if you live in a reasonably densely populated area, what it might mean collaterally to have such bombs or missiles hit your block or neighborhood, no matter how "accurate" their aim.

Until Seymour Hersh wrote a piece from Washington for the December 5, 2005 *New Yorker*, entitled "Up in the Air," our reporters had, with rare exceptions, simply refused to look up; and despite a flurry of attention then, to this day, our continuing air campaigns are largely ignored. Yet here is a US Air Force summary of just a single, nondescript day of operations in Iraq, one of hundreds and hundreds of such days, some far more intense, since we invaded that country: "In total, coalition aircraft flew 46 close-air support missions for Operation Iraqi Freedom. These missions included support to coalition troops, infrastructure protection, reconstruction activities and operations to deter and disrupt terrorist activities."

And here's the summary of the same day in Afghanistan: "In total, coalition aircraft flew 32 close-air support missions in support of Operation Enduring Freedom. These missions included support to coalition and Afghan troops, reconstruction activities and route patrols." Note that, in Afghanistan, as the situation has worsened militarily and politically, the old Vietnam-era B-52s, the carpet-bombers of that war, have been called back into action, again without significant attention here.

Now, with the fervent backing of the Bush administration, another country is being "remade" from the air—in this case, Lebanon. With the highest-tech American precision-guided and bunker-busting bombs, the Israelis have been launching air strike after air strike, thousands of them, in that country. They have hit an international airport; the nation's largest milk factories; a major food factory; aid convoys; Red Cross ambulances; a UN observer post; a power plant; apartment complexes; villages because they house or support the enemy; branches of banks because they might facilitate Hezbollah finances;

the telecommunications system because of the messages that might pass along it; highways because they might transport weapons to the enemy; bridges because they might be crossed by those transporting weapons; a lighthouse in Beirut harbor for reasons unknown; trucks because they might be transporting those weapons (though they might also be transporting vegetables); families who just happen to be jammed into cars or minivans fleeing at the urging of the attackers who have turned at least 20 percent of all Lebanese (and probably many more) into refugees, while creating a "landscape of death" (in the phrase of the superb *Washington Post* reporter Anthony Shadid) in the southern part of the country. In this process, civilian casualties have mounted steadily—assumedly far beyond the figure of just over 400 now regularly being cited in our press, because Lebanon has no way to search the rubble of its bombed buildings for the dead; nor, right now, the time and ability to do an accurate count of those who died more or less in the open.

And yet, of course, the "will" of the enemy is not broken and, among Israel's leaders and its citizens, frustration mounts; so threats of more and worse are made and worse weapons are brought into play; and wider targeting fields are opened up; and what might faintly pass for "precision bombing" is increasingly abandoned for the equivalent of "area bombing." And the full support system—which is simply society—for the movement in question becomes the "will" that must be broken; and in this process, what we call "collateral damage" is moved, by the essential barbaric logic of air power, front and center, directly into the crosshairs.

Already Israeli Prime Minister Olmert is "vowing" to use the "most severe measures" to end Hezbollah rocket attacks—and in the context of the present air assault that is a frightening threat. All this because, as in Iraq, as elsewhere, air power has once again run up against another kind of power, a fierce people power (quite capable of its own barbarities) that, over the decades, the bomb and missile have proved frustratingly incapable of dismantling or wiping out. Already, as the *Guardian*'s Ian Black points out, "The original objective of 'breaking Hizbullah' has been quietly watered down to 'weakening Hizbullah.' "

In such a war, with such an enemy, the normal statistics of military victory may add up only to defeat, a further frustration that only tends to ratchet the destruction higher over time. Adam Shatz put this well recently in the *Nation* when he wrote:

[Hezbollah leader] Nasrallah is under no illusions that his small guerrilla movement can defeat the Israeli Army. But he can lose militarily and still score a political victory, particularly if the Israelis continue visiting suffering on Lebanon, whose government, as they well know, is powerless to control Hezbollah. Nasrallah, whom the Israelis attempted to assassinate on July 19 with a twenty-three-ton bomb attack on an alleged Hezbollah bunker, is doubtless aware that he may share the fate of his predecessor, Abbas Musawi, who was killed in an Israeli helicopter gunship attack in 1992. But Hezbollah outlived Musawi and grew exponentially, thanks in part to its followers' passion for martyrdom. To some, Nasrallah's raid may look like a death wish. But it is almost impossible to defeat someone who has no fear of death.

As the Israelis are rediscovering—though, by now, you'd think that military planners with half a brain wouldn't have to destroy a country to do so—it is impossible from the air to "surgically" separate a movement and its supporters. When you try, you invariably do the opposite: fusing them ever more closely, while creating an even larger, ever angrier base for the movement whose essence is, in any case, never literal geography, never simply a set of villages or bunkers or military supplies to be taken and destroyed.

Degrading Behavior

Someday someone will take up the grim study of the cleansing language of air power. Every air war, it seems, now has its new words meant to take the sting out of its essential barbarism. In the case of the Israeli air assault on Lebanon, the term—old in the military world but never before so widely adopted in such a commonplace way—is "degrading," not as at Abu Ghraib, but as in "to impair in physical structure or function." It was once a technical military term; in this round of air war, however, it is being used to cover a range of sins.

Try Googling the term. It turns out to be almost literally everywhere. It can be found in just about any article on Israel's air war, used in this fashion: "CBS News senior White House correspondent Bill Plante reports that around the world the US opposition to a cease-fire is viewed as the US giving Israel a 'green-light' to degrade the military capability of Hezbollah." Or in a lead in a *New York Times* piece this way: "The outlines of an

American-Israeli consensus began to emerge Tuesday in which Israel would continue to bombard Lebanon for about another week to degrade Hezbollah's capabilities, officials of the two countries said." Or more generally, as in a *Washington Post* piece, in this fashion: "In the administration's view, the new conflict is not just a crisis to be managed. It is also an opportunity to seriously degrade a big threat in the region, just as Bush believes he is doing in Iraq." Or as Henry A. Crumpton, the State Department's coordinator for counterterrorism, wielded it: "It's not just about the missiles and launchers. . . . [I]t's about the roads and transport, the ability to command and control. All that is being degraded. But it's going to take a long time. I don't believe this is going to be over in the next couple of days." Or as an Israeli general at a Washington think tank told the *Washington Times*: "Israel has taken it upon itself to degrade Hezbollah's military capabilities." Sometimes degradation of this sort can be quantified: "A senior Israeli official said Friday that the attacks to date had degraded Hezbollah's military strength by roughly half, but that the campaign could go on for two more weeks or longer." More often, it's a useful term exactly because it's wonderfully vague, quite resistant to quantification, the very opposite of "precision" in its ambiguity, and capable of taking some of the sting out of what is actually happening. It turns the barbarity of air war into something close to a natural process— of, perhaps, erosion, of wearing down over time.

As air wars go, the one in Lebanon may seem strikingly directed against the civilian infrastructure and against society; in that, however, it is historically anything but unique. It might even be said that war from the air, since first launched in Europe's colonies early in the twentieth century, has always been essentially directed against civilians. As in World War Two, air power— no matter its stated targets—almost invariably turns out to be worst for civilians and, in the end, to be aimed at society itself. In that way, its damage is anything but "collateral," never truly "surgical," and never in its overall effect "precise." Even when it doesn't start that way, the frustration of not working as planned, of not breaking the "will," invariably leads, as with the Israelis, to ever wider, ever fiercer versions of the same, which, if allowed to proceed to their logical conclusion, will bring down not society's will, but society itself.

For the Lebanese prime minister what Israel has been doing to his country may be "barbaric destruction"; but, in our world, air power has long been robbed of its barbarism (suicide air missions excepted). For us, air war involves dumb hits by smart bombs, collateral damage, and surgery that may do in the patient, but is not barbaric. For that you need personally to cut off a head.

August 2006

18

SIEGE NOTES

Rasha Salti

1

I am writing now from a café, in west Beirut's Hamra district. It is filled with people who are trying to escape the pull of twenty-four-hour news reporting. Like me. The electricity has been cut off for a while now, and the city has been surviving on generators. The old system that was so familiar at the time of the war, where generators were allowed a lull to rest, is back. The café is dark, hot, and humid. Espresso machines and blenders are silenced. Conversations, rumors, frustrations waft through the room.

I am better off here than at home, following the news, live, on-the-spot documentation of our plight in sound bites.

The sound of Israeli warplanes overwhelms the air on occasion. They drop leaflets to conduct a "psychological" war. Yesterday, their sensitivity training urged them to advise inhabitants of the southern suburbs to flee because the night promised to be "hot." Today, the leaflets warn that they plan to bomb all other bridges and tunnels in Beirut. People are flocking to supermarkets to stock up on food.

This morning, I wrote in my emails to people inquiring about my well-being that I was safe, and that the targets seem to be strictly Hezbollah sites and their constituencies. Now, I regret typing that. They will escalate.

Until a few hours ago, they had only bombed the runways of the airport, as if to "limit" the damage. A few hours ago, four shells were dropped on the buildings of our brand-new, shining airport.

The night was harrowing. The southern suburbs and the airport were bombed from air and sea. The apartment where I am living has a magnificent view of the bay of Beirut. I could see the Israeli warships firing at their leisure.

2

It is now nighttime in Beirut. The day was heavy, busy with shelling from the air and sea, but so far the night has been quiet in Beirut. We are advised to brace ourselves for a bad night, although at this stage most analysis is reading tea leaves.

In the present conflict, a secular, egalitarian democrat such as me has no real place for representation or maneuver. Neither have I and my ilk succeeded in carving a space for ourselves, nor have the prevailing forces (the two poles) agreed to make allocations for us. That is our defeat and our failure. In Lebanon, we are caught in the stampede and the crossfire. I am not a supporter of Hezbollah, but this has become a war with Israel. In the war with Israel, there is no force in the world that will have me stand side by side with the IDF [Israel Defense Forces] or the Israeli state.

The "showcase" last night began with Israeli shells targeting [Hezbollah leader] Hassan Nasrallah's home in the southern suburbs. As soon as the shells exploded, the media reported them and waited to confirm that he and his family had survived. About half an hour later, the newscaster announced that Hassan Nasrallah planned to address the nation and the Arab world by phone.

I never thought he was charismatic. A huge majority of people do. He's very young to hold the position of leadership that he does. He's a straight talker, not particularly eloquent, but he speaks in an idiom that appeals to his immediate constituency in Lebanon but is also compelling to a constituency in the Arab world that harbors disillusionment, despondency, and powerlessness with the failed promises of Arab nationalism to defeat Israel and restore dignity. He is not corrupt, he lives simply, and displays a bent for Spartan asceticism.

He began by declaring an open war in response to Israel's assault. He reiterated that Hezbollah did not fear an open war. That they have long been prepared for this confrontation. Interestingly, he claimed that they possessed missiles that could reach Haifa, and "far beyond Haifa, beyond, beyond Haifa," thereby admitting that it was Hezbollah that fired the missiles at Haifa (until then they denied having fired them). It is not clear what he meant by "far beyond Haifa." Did he mean Tel Aviv?

3

Today was a bad day. The shelling started from the morning countrywide and has not let up until now. Tonight the shelling is again focused on the southern suburbs, Haret Hreyk and Bir el-Abed. The first neighborhood is where the headquarters of Hezbollah are located. They have been targeted several times and there is extensive damage. The leadership has not been harmed. A great number of the inhabitants have been evacuated, but the afternoon shelling targeted residential areas. I am up, anxious, writing. As if it served a purpose of sorts.

Foreign diplomatic missions are making plans to evacuate their nationals. They had planned to evacuate people by sea, but after today's shelling of the ports, they may have to rethink their strategy. Should I evacuate? Does one turn one's back on a "historic" station in the Arab-Israeli conflict? I was shamed this morning for having these thoughts . . . And now, at 1:30 a.m., as the Israeli airplanes fill up my sky, I am writing them again.

4

Things seem to be heating up. Missiles hit Haifa and the shelling on the south and southern suburbs [of Beirut] is unrelenting.

[Israeli Prime Minister] Ehud Olmert promised scorched earth in south Lebanon after missiles hit Haifa. Warnings have been sent to inhabitants of the south to evacuate their villages, because the Israeli response to Hezbollah will be "scorched earth." As major roads are destroyed and the south has been remapped into enclaves, it is not clear how these people are supposed to evacuate. And where to.

So Hezbollah dragged us without asking our opinion into this hell. We are in this hell, caught in this crossfire together. We need to survive and save as many lives as possible. The Israelis are now betting on the implosion of Lebanon. It will not happen. There is UNANIMITY that Israel's response is entirely, entirely, UNJUSTIFIED. We will show the Arab leadership that it is possible to have internal dissent and national unity, pluralism, divergence of opinion and face this new sinister chapter of the Arab–Israeli conflict.

5

We live now from "breaking news" to "breaking news." I have been in the café for one hour now. This is what I have heard so far:

1. A text message traveled to my friend's cell phone: a breaking news item from the Israeli military command. If Hezbollah does not stop shelling Galilee and northern towns, Israel will hit the entire electricity network of Lebanon.
2. Hezbollah shells Haifa, Safad, and colonies in south Golan.
3. A text message traveled to my other friend's cell phone, from an expat who left for Damascus and is catching a flight back to London. "All flights out of Damascus are cancelled. Do you know anything?"
4. An Israeli shell fell near the house of the bartender. His family is stranded in the middle of rubble in Hadath. He leaps out of the café and frantically calls to secure passage for them to the mountains.
5. Hezbollah downed an F-16 Israeli plane into Kfarshima (near Hadath). Slight jubilation in a café that thrives on denial.

"Breaking news" becomes the clock that marks the passage of time. You find yourself engaging in the strangest of activities: You catch a piece of breaking news, you leap to another room to announce it to family although they heard it too, and then you text-message it to others. At some point in the line-up, you become yourself the messenger of "breaking news." Along the way you collect other pieces of "breaking news" which you deliver back. Between the two sets of breaking news, you gather up facts and try to add them up to fit a scenario. Then you recall previously mapped scenarios. Then you realize none works. Then you exhale. And zap. Until the next piece of breaking news comes. It just gets uglier. You fear nighttime. For some reason, you believe the shelling will get worse at night. When vision is impaired, when darkness envelops everything. But it's not true. Shelling is as intense during the day as it is during the night.

There has been "intense" diplomatic activity between yesterday and today. UN envoys, ambassadors, EU [European Union] envoys, all kinds of men and women coming and going carrying messages to the Lebanese government from the "international community" and the "Israeli counterpart." Officially they have led to nothing.

I started writing these diary notes to friends outside Lebanon to remain sane and give them my news. I was candid and transparent with all my emotions. The ones I had and the ones I did not have. By the third diary note, I was getting replies, applause and rebuke from people I did not know who had read them.

A journalist from Israel's Channel Two contacted me by email and asked for an interview. I was uncomfortable with the idea at first, for fear that my words be distorted and my genuine, candid sentiments quoted to serve arguments I do not endorse. That journalist seems like a nice person, but I have no reason to trust her and she understands my misgivings. She sent me the set of questions below for me to answer so she can air them on TV or use them for some report. I decided to share them with you all.

1. How your day looks like from the morning. What you did today. Did you have coffee? How do you get the news—television? Radio? Internet?
The routine of our days is totally changed. We now live under a regimen of survival under siege. Those of us still not wounded and not stranded do whatever needs to be done to survive until the next day. Coffee, yes, I have coffee in the morning, and at noon, and in the afternoon. Perhaps I have too much coffee. The passage of time is all about monitoring news, checking that everyone's OK, and figuring out what has to be done to help those in distress. News is on all the time.

I am at home now, listening to the radio on one side, writing emails on the other side. Air-conditioning is on. I live in the center of the city. Later I will go to the office. I think life in my city continues but in a lower volume. Life as it were, or as previously understood, in my city has stopped. No gym classes, and I am accumulating cellulite, hence chances of finding second husband are lessened. (Can I make the IDF pay for that?) Air-conditioning is dependent on electricity or generator working. Power cuts are the rule now and the generator works only on a schedule. So yes, without air-conditioning and with power cuts, my "semitic" curls produce unruly coif and I have to admit, I am enduring the siege with bad hair.

2. Can you describe the neighborhood you live in?
So it will be bombed? No thank you. I live in a very privileged neighborhood, far from the southern suburbs. After the evacuation of foreign nationals (and bi-nationals) is complete, everyone is expecting doom and if Israelis decide to give us a dose of tough love as they did in the southern suburbs my life will probably be in serious danger as my family's and everyone who has decided to stay here.

3. Can you say something about yourself—like what you do for living?
I organize cultural events and I am a freelance writer. I used to live in New York City and moved to Beirut Tuesday, July 11. I have no life at the present moment. I try to do a few things over the Internet, but that's increasingly difficult.

4. In Israel our leaders think that targeting Hezbollah and other places in Lebanon will make the rest of the local population turn against Hezbollah. Is this true?
It is pure folly, but even if it were true it is a terrible strategy, an imploded Lebanon is a nightmare to all, not only the Lebanese but to everyone. Does Israel want an Iraq at its doorstep? There seems to be consensus now in Israel over the military campaign. It is because Israelis are not yet pressing their leadership and military with the smart questions. Do you actually believe it would be possible to eliminate the Shia sect from Lebanon, and that it would go down easy in the region? If the Americans are advising you, duck for cover or move. Need I list their record of wisdom and foresight recently? Vietnam, Central America, Somalia, Afghanistan, Iraq. If you need to listen to imperialists, find less idiotic ones, at least who have a sense of history. God help us all if Rumsfeld is also in charge of your well-being. This war will bring doom to all. Stop, cut everybody's losses. Wars can be stopped before the body count is "intolerable" or an entire country has been reduced to rubble.

5. What is the atmosphere in the streets of Beirut, if you can tell?
Beirut is quiet, dormant, huddled. We are caged, but there is tenacious solidarity. You have to understand that we see ourselves under an unwarranted attack from Israel. The capture of two soldiers DOES NOT justify Israel's response.

6. What is the atmosphere among your friends?
The consensus is solidarity. Our country is under attack. Otherwise, we are an exceedingly plural society, everyone has a theory and a point of view, and we coexist. Humoring one another.

I hope you will wake up to the nightmare you have dragged us into. I hope you will want to have fire ceased as soon as possible. I hope you will deem our humanity as valuable as your own.

Best, Rasha.

6

11:30 p.m. I have about half an hour before the generator shuts down. Most of Beirut is in the dark. I dare not imagine what the country is like.

Today was a particularly strange day for me because I was granted an opportunity to leave tomorrow morning, by car to Syria, then to Jordan, and from there by plane to wherever I am supposed to be right now. For days I have been itching to leave because I want to pursue my professional commitments, meet deadlines, and continue with my life. For days I have been battling ambivalence towards this war, estranged from the passions it has roused around me and from engagement in a cause. And yet when the phone call came informing me that I had to be ready at 7:00 a.m. the next morning, I asked for a pause to think. I was torn. The landscape of the human and physical, the depth of destruction, the toll of nearly 250 deaths, more than 800 injured and 400,000 displaced, had bound me to a sense of duty. It was not even patriotism, it was actually the will to defy Israel. They cannot do this and drive me away. They will not drive me away.

I decided to stay. I don't know when I will have another opportunity to leave.

7

One of my closest friends, my beloved sister really, Maria left two days ago. Up until a few hours before she was supposed to follow instructions from the British embassy for evacuation, she could not get herself to leave. She has two boys aged nine and five. Maria and her husband lived in London for a long while and earned citizenship there. Everyone who matters in her life called and urged her to evacuate with the Britons. She had moved from Beirut to the mountains on the second day of the siege. Our phone conversations had the rare virtue of being "constitutional," they charged our respective systems and reminded us of the people we once were, the lives we once lived. We asked the same question over and over, "Should I leave?", "Should you leave?" . . . She did not want to but felt she ought to for the boys.

She caved in two days ago. I called as she waited on the docks with her two sons. Her husband did not want to leave. "It's awful, it's awful . . .," she kept saying. "It's awful, it's awful . . .," I echoed her. "Have I done the right thing?" she pleaded. "Absolutely," I replied without a hint of hesitation. I could not help telling her that I would miss her. It felt selfish, childishly needy in the way children can be self-centered and dependent. In truth I was terrified of living through this siege without her. I felt like a good part of my heart, at least a good part of what I love about being in Beirut, was standing at the docks waiting with her two sons.

8

I accompanied journalists to Haret Hreyk two days ago. I suspect I am still shell-shocked from the sight of the destruction. I have never, ever seen destruction in that fashion. Western journalists kept talking about a "post-apocalyptic" landscape. The American journalists were reminded of Ground Zero. There are no gaping holes in the ground, just an entire neighborhood flattened into rubble. Mounds and mounds of smoldering rubble. Blocks of concrete, metal rods, mixed with furnishings, and the stuff that made up the lives of residents: photographs, clothes, dishes, CD-ROMs, computer monitors, knives and forks, books, notebooks, tapes, alarm clocks. The contents of hundreds of families stacked amidst smoking rubble. A couple of buildings had been hit earlier that morning and were still smoking, buildings were still collapsing slowly.

I was frightened to death. I stopped in front of one of the buildings that housed clinics and offices that provide social services. There seemed to be a sea of CD-ROMs and DVDs all over. I picked up one, expecting to find something that had to do with the Hezbollah propaganda machine (and it is pretty awesome). The first one read "*Sahh el-Nom* 1", the second "*Sahh el-Nom* 17". *Sahh el-Nom* was a very popular sitcom produced by Syrian TV in the 1960s.

Haret Hreyk is also where Hezbollah had a number of their offices. Al-Manar TV station is located in the block that has come to be known as the "security compound" (or "security square"), the office of their research and policy studies center, and other institutions attached to the party. It is said that in that heavily inhabited square of blocks, more than thirty-five buildings were destroyed entirely.

One of the buildings was still burning. It had been shelled earlier that day at dawn. Clouds of smoke were exhaling from amidst the ravages. The rubble was very warm; as I stepped on concrete and metal, my feet felt the heat.

9

My siege notes are beginning to disperse. I write disjointed paragraphs but I cannot discipline myself to write every day. I miss the world. I miss life. I miss myself.

People around me also go through these ups and downs, but I find them generally to be more resilient, more steadfast, more courageous than I. I am consumed by other people's despair. It's not very smart—I mean for a strategy of survival.

I am haunted by the nameless and faceless caught under rubble. In the undergrounds of destroyed buildings or simply in the midst of its ravages. Awaiting to be given a proper burial.

10

I have tried to the best of my abilities to keep up to date with professional commitments from my former life. It's almost impossible, but if I stop I know I will fall apart entirely. It is surreal to write emails following up with work. The world outside is decidedly distant. The mental image of my apartment in New York is practically impossible to summon. Avenue A, the deli at the corner and the Yemenis who own it, all lapsed. This is what happens when you are under siege. My friend Christine said to me yesterday that she forces herself to go to the office to keep from going insane, but she cannot remember anything about her work before the siege started. The sound of Israeli air raids comes every so often just low enough to spread chills of horror and fright. But the droves of displaced who arrive here every day have transformed the space of the city. Their wretchedness is the poignant marker of the war.

I spent the afternoon yesterday in Karm el-Zeytoon, a neighborhood in Ashrafieh [a Christian area of east Beirut] (that translates literally to "olive grove") where some schools have been opened to house some of the displaced from the south and from Beirut's southern suburb. I played cards with a six-year-old with one elbow in a cast and eyes sparkling with humor. An elderly overweight woman came over and asked R. to find her and her sister a room. She could not tolerate the heat or the mosquitoes in her old age and health conditions. She begged her. She wanted to die in dignity, not like that, on a mattress in a school. She could barely hold back her tears.

I left them reluctantly.

11

Throughout the war, shelling, siege, grief, and sorrow, the bougainvilleas have been in full, glorious bloom. Their colors are dizzying in their intensity: purplish red, boastful fuchsia, glaring white, and sometimes canary yellow. Most of the time, their bloom, which is the objective outcome of "natural" factors, namely, access to water, sun, heat, and even perhaps wind, has irritated me. Everything has changed in this time of war, except the full glorious bloom of the bougainvilleas. Other flowering trees have wilted, or died, as their franchised gardeners or patrons no longer operate on the same schedule or have evacuated on the ships of the bi-nationals.

On the road to Saida, I was struck, irked, and even upset at the bougainvilleas' full bloom. Between their abundant leaves and flowers, vignettes of the ravages appeared. Bridges torn in their midst are framed by the purple and fuchsia bloom of the bougainvilleas.

We drove along the old road. It had not survived unscathed. There were small holes in its middle, and pieces of rocks, cement, and debris. From within the winding inner roads, the new highway was visible and the big craters from the shelling.

The coastal road would have been bustling at this time in the summer. Expats, bi-nationals, students on summer vacation, and tourists. This is the stretch of the south's most-visited beaches. They range from the very fancy to the modest. At this time in the summer, the roads would have been busy with the town's handsome beach boys, tanned, strutting in swim trunks and a claim to some local fame. Everything was eerily deserted. Even army soldiers, posted in spots with seemingly no rhyme or reason, walked cautiously, expecting to duck for cover at any moment. Life all around had folded and packed.

We drove by closed homes, doors locked, windows shut, shutters sealed. The last gaze of their dwellers still lingering on the front porches, the gaze of a hesitant farewell that quickly ran a checklist to make sure all was safely tucked away and hoped for the best, maybe even whispered a prayer or invoked God or Christ's clemency and then hurried into the car and sped away for a temporary safer haven.

The bay of Saida appeared, and the coastal highway leading to its seaside *corniche* was entirely deserted. The bridge that unloads traffic from the highway onto the *corniche* had been pounded. Carcasses of cars lined its sides, some buried under blocks of concrete. We drove around and turned and entered Saida from roads tucked behind. The orange groves were dizzyingly fragrant. Car traffic inside the city was heavy. Pedestrian traffic was heavy.

Saida had received more than 100,000 displaced until two days ago.

I was told people were renting entrances of buildings to sleep at night, or the garages of cars. So far more than eighty-five schools were housing all these displaced, in addition to an old prison and the building of the court of justice.

The building stood on a hill overlooking old Saida and the fort. There was a soft gentle breeze and all was quieter up on that hill.

We were guided by one of the administrators. The floor was inundated with natural light. Even the corridor was well-lit. The rooms were spacious and fit with four beds. The floor was not at full capacity.

In the next room lay two women. One was of an advanced age. Her son sat next to her and was caring for her. Across from her was an elderly woman who had physical disabilities and could not walk. She was from Abbassiyeh. She had been left behind. The mayor of that village had dropped her off and left. She did not speak. No one knew anything about her. She carried no identity papers. She lay in bed and stared into the garden. Her gaze was not unfocused. In fact it was intent. I have rarely seen such sharp, pure, and focused sorrow. We moved around her room and she did not budge. The hospital administrator greeted her, to no reply.

Ahmad and I drove back the same way. My heart had never felt as heavy. There was a lot to hang onto. I looked forward to the fragrance of orange blossoms and was now forgiving to the full glorious bloom of the bougainvilleas.

April 2007

19

WILL AMERICAN BOMBS KILL MY DREAMS?

Behzad Yaghmaian

I am a child of the *coup d'état*, born in Iran a few days after the CIA helped overthrow the popular, democratic government of Prime Minister Mohammad Mossadegh in 1953.

Not long before my birth, facing nationwide protests, the Shah of Iran was forced to abdicate his power and flee the country. My mother used to tell me how men and women celebrated in the streets, how strangers gave flowers and sweets to each other. "The Shah left," they cried with joy. However, the celebration did not last long. In just a few more days, the political landscape changed again. Men paid by the US government began to roam the streets of Tehran, armed with truncheons and chains, assaulting Mossadegh's supporters. Soon the Shah returned and Mossadegh was put under house arrest. That was when I was born.

A witch-hunt for the followers of Mossadegh, communists, anyone who opposed the Shah and the *coup d'état* now began. Many were jailed—and tortured. Some opposition figures went underground or left the country; the rest lived in fear of the Shah and, within a few years, the Savak, his brutal secret police (also set up with CIA help).

Even as a child, I knew about the Savak. I remember adults whispering about it at family gatherings. The fear was palpable. I drew the obvious conclusion: the Savak was more powerful and far more horrible than *Zahhak*, a legendary Iranian monster with snakes growing out of his shoulders that I feared as a child.

My family did not respect the Shah or America; they *feared* them. My father forbade us to mention them at family gatherings. "Politics is not any of our business," he would say. It was his mantra. He feared being spied on by the Savak, our neighbors, or strangers. Later, I learned how the Americans helped create the Savak, trained the Shah's torturers, advised the Shah, and closed their eyes to everything that happened in his political prisons. I was told how young men and women were tortured in these jails and I came to agree with my father; politics was not any of my business.

When I was in the fifth grade, I first saw tanks, soldiers, and angry protesters—at the intersection by my home. Sticks in their hands, and throwing stones, these men broke the windows of our local phone booth and of the stores around the intersection. They were shouting, "Death to the Shah," "Death to America." I heard the gunshots—many of them. Scared, yet curious, I went to the rooftop of my house to watch the chanting men. "Come downstairs," my father shouted. "This isn't any of our business."

My home was near the main army barracks in Tehran, the elementary school I attended only a short walk away from the scene of serious street riots. The school was somehow an extension of my family: my uncle was the principal, my mother and aunt were teachers. I understood the seriousness of what was happening on the streets only when, in the middle of taking an arithmetic exam, I noticed the vice principal and my aunt in our classroom, whispering to my teacher and glancing at me. I was only half-done when the teacher walked over, examined my test papers, and whispered the remaining answers to me.

Joining my aunt, I raced home through the tense, half-deserted streets of my neighborhood, leaving the other students struggling with the exam. "Too dangerous to be out. Everyone was worried for you," my aunt said. I did not leave home again that day or the next.

In the streets in those days—it was 1963—people talked about a man they called Ayatollah Khomeini. Some liked him; others did not. I was too young to understand any of the adult discussions around me, but I could grasp the meaning of the tanks on our streets. Later, I learned that they were in my neighborhood to quell a rebellion by Khomeini's supporters. As a result, he was exiled to Iraq.

In high school, I would see police officers in helmets, swinging their truncheons outside the campus of Tehran University; sometimes I even saw them beating protesting students. But I would walk away, staying out of trouble just as my elders had advised me.

Onto the Streets

Then, one day in February 1970, I didn't walk away.

At six in the morning, my mother woke me and sent off on the chore I hated most, buying fresh bread for breakfast. In the neighborhood bakery, I was dawdling, enjoying the heat of the fire from the glowing oven, the intoxicating aroma of fresh bread, when a young man in black trousers, a suit jacket that didn't match, and a brown, hand-knitted V-neck sweater pulled over a shirt of a different color approached me. Short and unassuming, he had an instantly forgettable face that I remember vividly to this day.

"Sorry for intruding," he said politely, introducing himself as a student from Tehran University. I can't claim to recall the details of our conversation, only his question, the one that intrigued me, but left me uncomfortable and scared.

"Do you know about the student strike over the bus-fare hike?" he asked. I did not, I told him, but I certainly knew about the Shah's recently announced plan to increase fares by 150 percent. Everyone did. This threatened to make my life far more difficult. I was born to a lower-middle-class family and the fare hike would have meant taking the bus to school, but walking forty-five minutes to get home. Like many in my school, I was, until that moment, prepared to do exactly that. End of story.

Quietly but passionately, the young man told me of the student decision to force the government to retract its new policy. "Will you come out and join us?" he asked, encouraging me to boycott my high-school classes that day and do just what I had always feared: protest. Although there were no other customers in the bakery, the pervasive fear of being watched by the Savak left me feeling uncomfortable. As soon as my bread had been slipped out of the oven, I paid the baker, shook the young man's hand, and rushed home—not, of course, mentioning a word about my unexpected encounter.

I took the bus to school that morning and was attending a lecture in physics when a sudden uproar in the hallway disrupted my peace. Stamping feet, banging on doors, hundreds of students were marching through the corridors, shouting, inviting everyone to join them in the school courtyard.

The teacher, hoping to maintain order, continued his lecture, but his students simply packed up their books and stormed from the classroom. Following them without hesitation, I joined the protest. For a brief moment, my fears, it seemed, had vanished.

From that courtyard, we poured into the streets—against the Shah, against America, against everything that had once terrified me—disrupting traffic, joining others from nearby schools. Rumors circulated in the crowd. Arrests had been made at Tehran University. Students had attacked the Iran–America Society Cultural Center, breaking windows and chanting anti-American slogans. Later that day, we rode the bus home—free. The next day, the government announced a policy reversal: the bus fares would be left unchanged.

A World of Silences

In college in the early 1970s, some of my classmates would disappear for weeks or months at a time. No one asked why. Everyone knew they had been taken away by the Savak. When they returned, we still did not ask questions.

This happened to a classmate I respected. Like the young university student I met at that bakery, he was provincial. Most of the other students in the school wore jeans or more stylish Western outfits; he wore trousers and suit jackets, the typical outfit of provincial folks. Different as we were, he often engaged me in conversations about life and our studies.

One day, he stopped coming to school. A week passed, then another and another; still, his seat remained empty. There were whispers about his whereabouts, but no one discussed his absence openly. Soon, other students began disappearing: a petite woman, a tall, bearded fellow, and a youth from a far-away province.

Three months passed . . . and then, one morning, I saw him sitting alone on a bench in the main lobby of our school, thin and frail. I embraced him, said a few words, and departed. I wanted to ask questions; I did not. He wanted to tell me stories; he did not. And life went on in that silence.

"No Gas for Iranians"

I left Iran for graduate studies in the United States in 1976. On February 9, 1979, an Islamic government replaced the Shah's regime. From New York I watched the mass protests and shootings in Tehran on television.

Once again, there were those tanks in the streets and people chanting "Death to the Shah," "Death to America." Once again, they were joyously shouting "Long live Khomeini." The Shah fled the country. I was happy to see him go, happy Iran was free of America.

I read how students and ordinary citizens stormed the Shah's prisons, unlocking every cell, freeing all political prisoners. Some had been in jail since the 1953 *coup d'état*. Those opening the prisons fancied turning them into museums, which would educate future generations in the wrongdoings of the Shah and his American supporters. No longer, they dreamed, would Iranians be tortured for opposing them.

Such hopes, unfortunately, did not last. By the time I returned to Iran in the summer of 1979, the country was already facing life under a repressive theocratic state, albeit an anti-American one. Iranians who had taken part in the mass movement in the streets that, miraculously, overthrew the Shah were now dealing with a government that wished to control every aspect of their lives. It promptly banned all music, foreign movies, and theater; subjected women to what it considered an Islamic *hijab*, forcing them to cover their hair and wear baggy robes in dark colors; it had no hesitation about shutting down newspapers and magazines that questioned its policies. Government militias and paid thugs raided the headquarters of oppositional political organizations, attacked bookstores, and burnt books.

By that fall, the Shah's political prisons were once again being used to jail and torture Iranians. Many of the freed political prisoners had been returned to their cells. Ironically, this time around they were charged with being *friends* of America, aka "the Great Satan." Anyone who challenged the government was accused of helping the United States to undermine the Islamic Republic; the cold war with the Great Satan was now a convenient pretext for imprisoning journalists, writers, and student activists—anyone, in fact, who dared to disagree with the reigning theocrats. They were labeled "enemies of the state," "agents of America." It was the beginning of a new era.

And yet much remained eerily the same. With many still being jailed and tortured, this time for liking America or being considered its voice in Iran, we Iranians remained hostages to the strange, entangled, never-ending relationship between the two countries.

In the US, Iran now underwent a similar transformation from ally to enemy after a group of student backers of Khomeini seized the US embassy in Tehran, holding fifty of its residents hostage for 444 days. I was back in the Bronx, attending Fordham University, when, during that crisis, Ronald Reagan termed Iranians "barbarians." If I was hurt by the label, the Iranian government welcomed it as the best proof of America's "animosity towards the Islamic Revolution."

The hostage crisis opened a new chapter in the Iranian–American relationship, evoking anger among some of my fellow students at Fordham. A long banner, for instance, hanging from a wall of one of the dormitories read: "Save oil, burn Iranians." Hoping to offer a sense of the Iranian grievances against the US that lay behind these events, I agreed to be interviewed by the student paper. I explained the way the effects of the CIA's covert action in the 1953 coup had rippled down to our moment, how Iranian democracy had been a victim of American support for the Shah.

A few days after the interview was published, in a letter to the paper's editor, a group of students wrote, "The Iranian student must watch his back when he walks home alone late at night." Similar threats continued, along with occasional physical harassment. Meanwhile, Iranian students in Southern states were reportedly denied service at restaurants and gas stations—"No gas for Iranians," was a gas station sign of the times; some Iranians were even beaten up.

The Reagan administration only increased its rhetoric against Iran in this period, matched phrase for phrase by the Iranians, as the war of words between the two countries became ever more intense. Action replaced words after Iraqi dictator Saddam Hussein invaded Iran in 1980, starting an eight-year bloodletting between the two countries that would leave hundreds of thousands dead and wounded.

Hoping to weaken, or perhaps topple, the Islamic Republic, the US and its regional allies—Saudi Arabia and the Arab Emirates—aided the Iraqi war effort, providing Saddam with large grants and credit. Later in the conflict, the Pentagon provided Iraq with invaluable operational and planning intelligence as well as satellite information about the movements of Iranian forces, even when it knew that Saddam would use nerve gas against them. Meanwhile, the besieged Iranian government continued to persecute its domestic critics, accusing them of being the agents of the "Great Satan."

Loving the Great Satan

Like many Iranians studying in universities in the West, I stayed away from Iran, later applying for US citizenship and making the US my new home. In May 1995, after sixteen years, I returned as a visiting university lecturer, part of a special United Nations program. The Iran of my childhood was all but gone. Large murals of the "fallen martyrs" of the Iran–Iraq War, and anti-American posters were everywhere. The security forces and the *bassij*—the "moral police"—patrolled the streets in their jeeps and station wagons. The war with Iraq had long ended, but Tehran remained visibly under its shadow— a city of martyrs and anti-American warriors, the authorities proclaimed.

Even the street names had changed; many were now named after the martyrs of that brutal war. There was nothing left of my old neighborhood. My home, the bakery, my elementary school, everything had been razed. In their place were a freeway and new residential projects. I recognized only four homes at the far end of the alley where I grew up. On a discolored and bent plaque nailed to a wall was the name of one of my childhood playmates: "Martyr Ali Sharbatoghli."

Inside Tehran homes, behind closed doors, lay another Iran, startlingly unlike the façade so carefully constructed by the government. In the streets, women covered their hair and wore long, baggy robes to disguise their curves; inside they wore Western clothes—jeans and revealing dresses. They lived two lives.

A version of America, as filtered through Hollywood (and Iranian exiles in southern California), was in every home. Through bootlegged music from LA, or the songs of Pink Floyd, Metallica, Guns N' Roses, and other Western rock icons of the time, Tehranis embraced what the government called "the infidel." They danced to his music and imitated the lifestyle they absorbed from satellite TV and pirated Hollywood films. Tapes of American movies sometimes made it to the Iranian capital before they were commercially released in the US. Even those who opposed the US politically and could not forgive or forget its role in the 1953 coup and the Shah's prison state found joy in American pop culture. In private conversations, relatives, friends, even absolute strangers inquired about my life in the States or the possibility of somehow escaping to America.

It appeared that Iranians could not live without America. Even the government needed the Great Satan to repress its opponents, while Tehranis took refuge in American pop culture to escape the life created for them by that very government.

In 1997, two years after my visit, a smiling reformist cleric, Mohammad Khatami, became president. Iranians were energized. Hope returned. And when I visited in July 1998, it seemed that a new Iran was truly emerging. Khatami was but one of many of the original architects of the Islamic Republic who were now calling for a change in direction: a reversal of foreign policy, a freer press, and the expansion of civil liberties.

Khatami himself championed a radical change in Iran's foreign policy, advocating what was called a "dialogue of civilizations." He set a new tone, calling for a rapprochement between Iran and the West, especially the United States. Khatami's presidency helped bring into the open deep divisions inside the country: between the government and the people as well as within that government itself. It also highlighted the touchstone role the US continued to play in Iranian politics and society.

Now, however, for the first time in a quarter-century, many believed an opportunity existed to end the hostility that had only hurt the Iranian people. Young and old, Iranians seemed to welcome this chance. Even some among the former Embassy hostage-takers expressed regrets and became a part of the growing reform movement, while advocating rapprochement with America. Four years after Khatami was elected president, a poll administered by Abbas Abdi, one of the student leaders of the hostage taking, revealed that 75 percent of Iranians favored dialogue with the American people. Abdi was subsequently jailed.

Despite resistance from conservatives, an independent press was emerging; old taboos were being questioned. There were political rallies that not long before would have led directly to jail; there were informal meetings, debates, protests, art exhibits, theater openings, and a burst of other forms of political and artistic expression. The fear and anxiety I had sensed everywhere two years earlier seemed to have abated. Young men and women openly defied the government through their body politics, their recurring protests, their fearless confrontations with the police. They broke taboos, expressed their feelings openly, and risked beatings and arrest. I encountered a small group of such young Iranians during my overnight detention in Tehran—a vision of what a new Iranian society might have felt like and a painful reminder that the forces of the old order were still alive and all too well.

My Night in Jail

It was a mild evening in February 1999. I was sitting on a park bench with a female friend when two members of the security forces walked toward me. By the time the thought of escaping crossed my mind, it was already too late. I imagined the worst. There I was in the park in the dark with a woman not related to me by blood or marriage. That was still a crime in the Islamic Republic of Iran.

"Get up, get up, let's go," one guard demanded.

I asked for an explanation.

"Shut up. Let's go," he insisted, demanding my identification card. All I had was my faculty ID from Ramapo College in New Jersey. Uneducated, the guards could not read the card.

"What is this?"

I responded that I was a professor from America visiting my ailing father in Tehran.

"America . . ." the guard repeated the word, still holding my card, but now staring at me. Had I thought about it, I would have realized that an American ID card would be used against me, and my appearance—I was wearing a fashionable winter coat and a long scarf—would be a cause of envy and anger.

My friend and I now had no choice but to follow the guards to a building on the north end of the park. We were ushered into a room where there were other arrested young men and women, a few uniformed officers, and a middle-aged man in plain clothes behind a desk.

"Against the wall! Stay right there!" shouted the arresting guard.

The man in plain clothes asked about us, and the guard showed him our identification cards. "A professor from the United States," said the guard.

"Get over here!" the man shouted.

Approaching his desk, I began, "Why am I . . .?" but his heavy hand crashing into my face cut my question short. I hit the wall behind me.

"What's that fuzz under your lips?" the interrogator asked, pointing to the small patch of hair. "Did your mommy tell you to grow this?" Laughter erupted.

"I'll break you into pieces before I let you go," said the man. "Do you think this is Los Angeles? We'll show you where you are. This is Iran not America. We'll show you!" And he struck my face again with that heavy hand. Having nearly lost my balance, I leaned against the wall.

"I'll show you where you are," he kept repeating, staring at my faculty ID card, then turning and hitting me. By now he was smiling triumphantly, while armed, uniformed men kept wandering into the room to stare at me, inspect me from head to toe. "American," they would say, with a mixture of wonderment and contempt, looking at each other, laughing. My face was throbbing, my ears literally ringing from the repeated strikes. I remained silent, wishing this were a bad dream.

Two hours of insults and beatings followed before the interrogation ended. I was then handcuffed and two soldiers took me to a nearby temporary jail for those committing "moral deviance." A metal door opened. I entered. "Take off your belt and shoelaces," said the prison guard. I handed him my keys and other sharp objects. The metal door closed behind me. I was officially jailed.

"This is your home for the night," the guard said, opening the door to a small, stuffy, windowless cell. It was packed with young men, sitting on the dirty carpet, leaning against the wall. "Welcome," a number of them said.

"Please, here . . ." a thin man in his early twenties squeezed aside to open a space for me.

"What are *you* doing here? You don't seem to belong," said another man. Without hesitation, I told my story. Intrigued and excited by the presence of a visitor from America, they seized the moment. In no time, I was flooded with questions about life, music, girls, about all that was officially forbidden in Iran.

"Have you been to Los Angeles?" a talkative young man inquired. "I would do anything to go there!" Others floated the names of Iranian singers living in Los Angeles—the exiled singers of the Shah's time and new pop stars. "Have you ever seen Sandy in person?" a very young inmate asked about a singer I had never heard of. "How many times have you gone to Dariush's concerts?" he asked about the most popular singer among the young before the Islamic Revolution. "How does he look in person? Give him my regards."

Another young inmate quietly inquired about Pink Floyd and Santana. "Have you ever gone to a Pink Floyd concert?" he asked in an awed whisper. I remembered my own youth, those long hours listening to Pink Floyd and Dariush, that same longing for a chance to see them in person. A generation later, in an Islamic Republic, what had changed?

"How can I emigrate to America?" a man who hadn't said a word asked from across the room.

Suddenly, an older inmate began singing a popular song associated with Hayedeh, an icon from the Shah's time. She had died in exile in Los Angeles five years earlier. The cell fell into silence.

My night in prison ended and I was taken to court the next morning. As I left the cell, the inmates embraced me one by one, promising to remain in touch. "Say hello to Los Angeles," an inmate said jauntily. "Write about us in the newspapers. Tell people about our conditions. Don't forget us."

I was handcuffed, put in a van, and driven away to court. Later that day, I was released on bail; many of the men in my cell undoubtedly didn't have the same luck, remaining behind closed doors, dreaming of their favorite singers in America. My moment among them was a reminder of the gulf that separated our worlds. Soon enough—far sooner than I wanted—I would return to the US; they would remain in embattled Iran, only dreaming about America.

How I Left

My departure was unexpected. It came after a week of nationwide protests against the government. On July 8, 1999—just as in my youth—a small contingent of students left the housing compound of Tehran University, marching in protest this time against the closure of the reformist newspaper *Salam*. It was a peaceful demonstration which ended without a confrontation with the authorities as the protesting students returned to their rooms that evening. In the early morning hours of July 9, however, the anti-riot police and plain-clothes thugs burst into the housing compound, assaulting sleeping students with chains and batons, even setting rooms on fire. One student was killed; many were injured and taken away to jail.

By midday, news of the attack had reached university campuses all across the city; hundreds now joined the embattled students of Tehran University, setting up barricades, occupying the housing compound. By the time I arrived, ordinary citizens had already joined in, while the student protest had moved out of the university and been transformed into a full-blown street riot.

On July 10, thousands of students and youths gathered at the entrance of Tehran University, chanting slogans against the Supreme Religious Leader,

Ayatollah Ali Khamenei, shouting "Death to the Dictator" and "Freedom Now." In the streets around the university's historic entrance, scenes reminiscent of the 1979 revolution were taking place. Stores were shut down for fear of violence.

On July 12, Ayatollah Khamenei responded by calling the protesters "agents of America" and ordering a clampdown. "Our main enemies in spying networks are the designers of these plots," he declared. "Where do you think the money that is allocated by the US Congress to campaign against the Islamic Republic of Iran is being spent? No doubt that that budget and a sum several times larger are spent on such schemes against Iran."

Two days later, swinging their truncheons and thick chains, anti-riot police and bearded men in slippers attacked the demonstrators. More than two thousand of them were jailed. The student uprising was put down. Soon after, I received a call from a journalist friend.

"Do you have an exit visa on your passport? Leave Iran quietly and soon," he said.

A cell within the Ministry of Intelligence, he informed me, had compiled a "thick file" about my activities in Iran. The government was now looking for scapegoats, people they could blame for the student protests. My profile fit the bill perfectly for the Islamic Republic. After all, I was an American citizen, gave lectures on political economy, wrote weekly columns for reformist papers, traveled in and out of Iran, and had close ties with the students. "Spying for America" was a common charge against people like me in those days. I was to be framed and displayed to the public as an enemy of the state.

Fearing for my life, I went into hiding and, on July 19, flew to Dubai. A week later, I was back in New York. My short rendezvous with even a limited democracy in Iran had ended.

Dreams of War, Dreams of Peace

Many things have changed in Iran since 1999. The reformists have largely been pushed out of the government. The new president, Mahmoud Ahmadinejad, and the people around him have been working hard to reverse whatever progress was made in the areas of foreign policy and civil liberties during Khatami's presidency.

Changes no less important occurred in the United States which, of course, got its own fundamentalist government in 2000. In 2002, President George W. Bush declared Iran an official member of his "Axis of Evil," and in the past few years the anti-Iranian rhetoric has only escalated. Iran is now viewed by the current administration as the main threat to American interests in the Middle East, the premier rogue state in the region, a supporter of international terrorism, and enough of a menace to warrant war planning on a major scale. Officials in Iran have been using similar rhetoric about America. The war of words has reached dangerous levels. A real war seems conceivable.

For two years now, respected investigative journalists like the *New Yorker*'s Seymour Hersh have been reporting on the existence of elaborate Bush administration preparations for a full-scale air campaign on Iran, possibly including the "nuclear option." The administration's obsession with Iran's nuclear ambitions, its rhetoric about the danger of a nuclear Iran to Israel and to world security, and its orchestrated efforts (and relative success) in referring Iran's case to the Security Council all seem like the prelude to a war against Iran. Adding to this impression are the administration's drumbeat of claims about Iranian "interference" in Iraq, about its contribution to American casualties by supposedly supplying advanced elements for the making of roadside bombs to the Iraqi insurgency, as well as about its support for terrorist movements in Lebanon and Palestine (as Mr Bush repeated in his 2006 State of the Union address). In addition, the dispatching of more aircraft-carrier task forces to the Persian Gulf and the arrest of Iranian diplomats in Iraq only increase my fears of war. Is it truly possible that this administration could launch such a war against my childhood home, creating a new, more horrific version of 1953, another half-century-plus of bitterness, another half-century-plus of an Iranian obsession with America?

The specter of war is haunting me now. Recurring nightmares interrupt my sleep. I see those last houses in my old neighborhood reduced to rubble and dust, bridges destroyed, homes burned to the ground. In my solitude, I wonder how my neighbors in New York will treat me if a war breaks out. Will they display American flag decals on their windows? Will they tie yellow ribbons to trees? I think of my students, and wonder whether they will see me as an enemy the day the United States begins bombing Iran or will they think to console me, to ask how my family is coping with the war? Will they sooner or later be dispatched to Iran to aim their guns at my loved ones?

I wish to tell my students and neighbors of the dream I have been carrying with me for years. I dream, someday, of returning to the place I've kept so close to my heart, of breathing the fresh air in the mountains surrounding Tehran, of drinking tea in the humble teahouses on the bank of the narrow stream that gives life to those barren hills. I dream of buying fresh parsley and tomatoes from the old man on the street corner next to my mother's home, greeting the baker with a smile.

Will American bombs kill my dream?

V

THE PETRO-INDUSTRIAL COMPLEX
AND ITS DISCONTENTS

May 2007

20

THE PRIZE OF IRAQI OIL

Michael Schwartz

The struggle over Iraqi oil has been going on for a long, long time. One could date it back to 1980 when President Jimmy Carter—before his Habitat for Humanity days—declared that Persian Gulf oil was "vital" to American national interests. So vital was it, he announced, that the US would use "any means necessary, including military force" to sustain access to it. Soon afterwards, he announced the creation of a Rapid Deployment Joint Task Force, a new military command structure that would eventually develop into the United States Central Command (Centcom) and give future presidents the ability to intervene relatively quickly and massively in the region.

Or we could date it all the way back to World War Two, when British officials declared Middle Eastern oil "a vital prize for any power interested in world influence or domination," and US officials seconded the thought, calling it "a stupendous source of strategic power and one of the greatest material prizes in world history."

The date when the struggle for Iraqi oil began is less critical than our ability to trace the ever-growing willingness to use "any means necessary" to control such a "vital prize" into the present. We know, for example, that, before and after he ascended to the vice-presidency, Dick Cheney has had his eye squarely on the prize. In 1999, for example, he told the Institute of Petroleum Engineers that, when it came to satisfying the exploding demand for oil, "the Middle East, with two-thirds of the world's oil and the lowest cost, is still where the prize ultimately lies." The mysterious Energy Task Force he headed on taking office in 2001 eschewed conservation or developing alternative sources as the main response to any impending energy crisis, preferring instead to make the Middle East "a primary focus of US international energy policy." As part of this focus, the Energy Task Force recommended that the administration put its energy, so to speak, into convincing Middle Eastern countries "to open up areas of their energy sectors to foreign investment"—in other words, into a policy of reversing twenty-five years of state control over the petroleum industry in the region.

The Energy Task Force set about planning how to accomplish this historic reversal. We know, for instance, that it scrutinized a detailed map of Iraq's oil fields, together with the (non-American) oil companies scheduled to develop them (once the UN sanctions still in place on Saddam Hussein's regime were lifted). It then worked jointly with the administration's national security team to find a compatible combination of military and economic policies that might inject American power into this equation. According to Jane Mayer of the *New Yorker*, the National Security Council directed its staff "to cooperate fully with the Energy Task Force as it considered the 'melding' of two seemingly unrelated areas of policy: 'the review of operational policies towards rogue states,' such as Iraq, and 'actions regarding the capture of new and existing oil and gas fields.' "

While we cannot be sure that this planning itself was instrumental in setting the US on a course toward invading Iraq, we can be sure that plenty of energy was being expended in Washington planning for the disposition of Iraq's massive oil reserves once that invasion was successfully executed. In 2002, just a year after Cheney's Energy Task Force completed its work, and before the US had officially decided to invade Iraq, the State Department "established a working group on oil and energy" as part of its Future of Iraq project. It brought together influential Iraqi exiles, US government officials, and international consultants. Later, several Iraqi members of the group became part of the Iraqi government. The result of the project's work was a "draft framework for Iraq's oil policy" that would form the foundation for the energy policy now being considered by the Iraqi Parliament.

The Prize

The specific prize in Iraq is certainly worthy of almost any kind of preoccupation. Indeed, Iraq could someday become the most important source of petrochemical energy on the planet.

According to the US Energy Information Administration, Iraq possesses 115 billion barrels of proven oil reserves, the third-largest in the world (after Saudi Arabia and Iran). About two-thirds of its known oil reserves are located in Shia southern Iraq, and the final third in Kurdish northern Iraq. However, in energy terms, only about 10 percent of the country has actually been explored and there is good reason to believe that modern methods—which have not been applied since the beginning of the Iraq–Iran War in 1980—might well uncover magnitudes more oil. Estimates of the possible new finds offered by officials of various interested governments range from 45 billion to 214 billion additional barrels, depending on the source; but some nongovernmental experts see the final treasure exceeding 400 billion barrels. If the latter figure is correct, then Iraq would likely become the world's largest source of oil.

For the most part, Iraq's petroleum has "attractive chemical properties"; that is, its oil is considered to be of very high quality. Moreover, both its current fields and many of the potential new discoveries would be extremely cheap to access, if security weren't such a problem today in Iraq. James Paul, of the international policy monitoring group the Global Policy Forum, offers this positive view: "According to *Oil and Gas Journal*, Western oil companies estimate that they can produce a barrel of Iraqi oil for less than $1.50 and possibly as little as $1. . . . This is similar to production costs in Saudi Arabia and lower than virtually any other country."

With the price of a barrel of crude oil today above $64 a barrel, the potential for profits is stupendous and the only question is: Who will pocket them—the oil companies or the Iraqi government—and, if the former, which oil companies will those be? It is not inconceivable that any major oil companies able to claim a large portion of the Iraqi oil spoils could double, triple, or even quintuple their already gigantic global profits.

Under Saddam Hussein, Iraqi oil never fulfilled the potential of even its proven oil fields. A modest goal for the country's oil industry would have been producing 3.5 million barrels per day, but the temporary disruptions caused by the Iraq–Iran War and the more permanent ones caused by UN sanctions imposed after the Gulf War in 1991 severely limited production. From the late 1990s until the American invasion in 2003, Iraq averaged around 2.5 million barrels per day.

Knowledge of this level of underproduction was certainly one factor in Deputy Secretary of Defense Paul Wolfowitz's pre-war prediction that the administration's invasion and occupation of Iraq would pay for itself; he hoped for a quick postwar increase in production to 3.5 million barrels per day or, at the $30 per barrel price of oil at that time, close to $40 billion per year in revenues. An expected expansion in production levels (once the oil giants were brought into the mix) to perhaps 6.5 million barrels, through the development of new oil fields or more efficient exploitation of existing fields, had the potential to more than cover the expected American short-term military costs *and* leave the new Iraqi government flush as well.

This, then, was the allure of melding energy policy and military policy, as Cheney's energy group and allied administration officials envisioned it.

The Initial Campaign to Capture Iraqi Oil
With all this history, the particular way the US sprang into action as soon as its forces arrived in Baghdad was hardly surprising. While American troops simply stood by as unrestrained looting severely damaged the dawn-of-civilization treasures in the National Museum, compromised the ability of hospitals to deliver health care, and destroyed many government offices, large numbers of American soldiers were deployed to protect the Oil Ministry and its associated holdings. This effort was certainly emblematic of the newly established occupation's priorities.

Not long after President Bush declared "major combat operations in Iraq have ended" under a "Mission Accomplished" banner on the deck of the aircraft carrier the USS *Abraham Lincoln*, Paul Bremer, the new head of the American occupation, promulgated a series of laws designed, among other things, to kick-start the development of Iraqi oil. In addition to attempting to transfer management of existing oil facilities (well heads, refineries, pipelines, and shipping) to multinational corporations, he also set about creating an oil policy framework, unique in the region, that would allow the major companies to develop the country's proven reserves and even to begin drilling new wells.

All these plans were, however, quickly frustrated, both by the growing

Sunni insurgency and by civil resistance. Iraq's oil workers quickly unionized—even though Bremer extended Saddam's prohibition on unions in state-owned companies—and effectively resisted the transfer of management duties to foreign companies. In one noteworthy moment, the oil workers actually refused to take orders from Bechtel officials in the oil hub of Basra, thus preserving their own jobs as well as the right of the Iraqi state-owned Southern Oil Company to continue to control the operation in that region. Bechtel's management contract was subsequently voided.

At the same time the growing insurgency, acting on a general Iraqi understanding that a major goal of the occupation was to "steal" Iraqi oil, systematically began to attack the oil pipelines that traveled through the Sunni areas of the country. Within a few months, all oil exports in the northern part of Iraq were interrupted—and the northern export pipelines have remained generally unusable ever since.

To resistance of various sorts must be added the "contribution" of the major American corporations involved in "reconstructing" Iraq, notably Halliburton and Bechtel. These crony corporations, with close ties to the Bush administration, accepted huge fees to rehabilitate dilapidated or damaged oil facilities. Almost without fail, they chose not to repair existing plants locally or to employ the raft of skilled Iraqi technicians who had used remarkable ingenuity in maintaining these facilities during a dozen years of UN sanctions. Working under cost-plus agreements that guaranteed a fixed profit rate no matter how much an operation ultimately cost, they preferred instead to install expensive new proprietary equipment. Then, in the absence of any outside oversight, they ran up huge expenses and frequently failed to complete their contracts, leaving the oil facilities they were servicing in states of disrepair or partial repair—and equipped with technology that local technicians could not service.

Meanwhile, the major oil companies refused Bremer's invitation to invest their own money in Iraqi projects, pointing out the obvious—that the insurgency and the spreading chaos made such investments unwise. In addition, they were well aware that Bremer's regime in Baghdad lacked clear authority to sign contracts with them. This, in turn, meant that their investments might be in jeopardy once a legitimate government took power. When technical sovereignty was finally handed over to an appointed Iraqi government headed by the CIA's favorite Iraqi exile, Iyad Allawi, in June

2004, the new premier embraced Bremer's policy, but to no avail. The international oil companies were no more impressed with his future than they had been with Bremer's. Like Wolfowitz, they knew that Iraq "floats on a sea of oil"; unlike him, they were no dreamers. They weren't willing to risk their capital in the dangerous and legally ambiguous circumstances then prevailing.

As a result, the first two years of Bush administration efforts to "access" Iraqi oil failed—and dismally so at that. Average production never exceeded the bottom-of-the-barrel 2.5 million barrels Saddam's regime managed to extract on its worst days. By 2006, production had slipped below 2 million barrels per day.

Dealing with the Iraqi Government

It is difficult to judge how much Bremer's inability to implement the pre-planned oil policy contributed to the Bush administration decision to reverse its plans for Iraqi "democracy"—which, as Juan Cole has pointed out, involved council-based elections, an electorate restricted to a small elite, and Bremer as "a MacArthur in Baghdad for years"—and push for an elected Iraqi government. It certainly is true, however, that this change triggered a campaign aimed at the "capture of new and existing oil and gas fields."

As soon as the first elections for a temporary Iraqi government were completed in January 2005, American officials in Iraq began lobbying forcefully for adoption of the very policy that the State Department's pre-invasion Future of Iraq project had drafted. The State Department planners had concluded that Production Sharing Agreements (PSAs)—a method that granted multinational oil companies effective control of oil fields without transferring permanent ownership to them—would be the basic instrument through which a future "independent" Iraq would develop new oil fields. Wary by now of being seen as the chief advocate of this policy, which it so desperately wanted in place, the Bush administration concocted a strategy that would enlist the international community in pressuring Iraq to adopt its program.

This was done by making the International Monetary Fund (IMF), a key player in Iraqi oil policy. Through loans in the 1980s and reparations imposed for his invasion of Kuwait in 1990, Saddam had accumulated $120 billion in external debt, the largest per capita debt in the world and a potentially insurmountable obstacle to economic recovery, even in oil-rich Iraq. One option available to the new government was to declare this debt "odious," a technical term in international law referring to debt accumulated by authoritarian rulers for their own personal or political aggrandizement.

Saddam's expansionist war against Iran, his use of public funds to build ostentatious monuments and palaces, his transfer of billions to his personal accounts, and his failure to maintain the infrastructure of the country all were excellent evidence that the debt was indeed odious; and the US claimed as much for almost $40 billion of it, held by nineteen industrialized countries known as the Paris Club. Instead of seeking to cancel this debt (and the remaining $80 billion) entirely, however, the Bush administration sent James Baker, former secretary of state under George H. W. Bush, to the Paris Club to negotiate conditional forgiveness. The resulting agreement immediately forgave $12 billion, but left $28 billion on the books. A second $12 billion would be abrogated when the Iraqi government signed onto "a standard International Monetary Fund program," and a further $8 billion three years later, after the IMF confirmed Iraqi compliance. Even if "successful," almost $8 billion would still be outstanding to the Paris Club— together with $80 billion not covered by the agreement.

The "standard International Monetary Fund program," not surprisingly, included the now familiar American policies regarding Iraqi oil, as well as the use of Production Sharing Agreements and a host of other provisions that would open the Iraqi economy as a whole, and the oil sector in particular, to investment by multinational corporations. Among the most punitive of the provisions was a demand for an end to the economic breadbasket that guaranteed all Iraqi families low prices for fuel and food staples. In a country with, by 2005, somewhere between 30 percent and 70 percent unemployment, average wage levels under $100 per month, and escalating inflation, these Saddam-era subsidies meant the difference between basic subsistence and disaster for a large proportion of Iraqis.

Independent journalists Basav Sen and Hope Chu summarized the new agreement thus: "A move that appears on the surface to be beneficial for Iraq—debt cancellation—is being used as a tool of control by the World Bank, the IMF and the wealthy creditor countries. What is more, it is a tool of control that will last long after the withdrawal of US combat forces." Zaid Al-Ali, an international lawyer working on development issues in Iraq, described the agreement as a "perfect illustration of how the industrialized world has used debt as a tool to force developing nations to surrender sovereignty over their economies." The newly elected Iraqi National Assembly promptly denounced the agreement as "a new crime committed by the creditors who financed Saddam's oppression." This forceful expression reflected the opinions of the Assembly's constituents. After all, 76 percent of Iraqis believed that the main reason for the Bush administration's invasion was "to control Iraqi oil."

As it happened, the protest did not prevent the Iraqi government from endorsing the deal. Otherwise, it faced the prospect of the US—which still had operational control over Iraqi finances—simply appropriating most of its revenues for debt service. When the agreement was announced, interim oil minister Thamir Ghadbhan, a British-trained technocrat, publicly protested the provisions eliminating fuel and food subsidies. He was subsequently pushed out.

The US then began pressuring the Iraqi government to draft a definitive petrochemical law that would conform to the IMF guidelines. Given the levels of resistance to the very idea, this work was conducted in secret and took until the end of 2006 to complete. As independent journalist Joshua Holland described the process:

> Just months after the Iraqis elected their first constitutional government, USAID sent a BearingPoint adviser to provide the Iraqi Oil Ministry "legal and regulatory advice in drafting the framework of petroleum and other energy-related legislation, including foreign investment". . . . The Iraqi Parliament had not yet seen a draft of the oil law as of July [2006], but by that time . . . it had already been reviewed and commented on by US Energy Secretary Sam Bodman, who also "arranged for Dr Al-Shahristani to meet with nine major oil companies—including Shell, BP, ExxonMobil, ChevronTexaco and ConocoPhillips—for them to comment on the draft."

Even the Iraqi Study Group, James Baker's Commission, got into the act at the end of 2006, devoting three pages of its proposal for a partial redeployment of American forces from Iraq to exhorting the Iraqis to enact a petrochemical bill that would place its oil reserves in the hands of the major oil companies.

The Proposed Petrochemical Bill

When the Draft Hydrocarbon Law was finally delivered to the Iraqi Parliament on February 18, 2007, key provisions had already been leaked and immediately denounced by the full spectrum of the Iraqi opposition. Taking turns registering dismay were the majority of the Parliament, a wide range of government officials, the leadership of the major Sunni political parties, the union of oil workers, the Sadrists—the most powerful Shia grouping—and the visible leadership of the insurgency.

All this led to many changes in the law, including the removal of all mention of either privatization or Production Sharing Agreements, which would have given multinational oil companies fifteen to twenty-five years of basically unregulated operational control over Iraqi oil facilities. The amended version in no way excluded the use of PSAs, but it removed the explosive designation from the actual wording of the law.

It is worth reviewing the logic of PSAs to understand why the US was so determined to make them a part of the law, and why many Iraqis were so ferociously opposed.

Production Sharing Agreements are generally applied in circumstances where there is a strong possibility that oil exploration will be extremely costly or even fail, and/or where extraction is likely to prove prohibitively expensive. To offset huge and risky investments, the contracting company is guaranteed a proportion of the profits, if and when oil is extracted and sold. In the most common of these agreements, the proportion remains very high until all development costs are amortized, allowing the investing company to recoup its investment expenditures (if oil is found), and then to be rewarded with a larger-than-normal profit margin for the remainder of the contract which, in the Iraqi case, could extend for up to twenty-five years.

This is perhaps a reasonably fair, or at least necessary, bargain for a country that cannot generate sufficient investment capital on its own, where exploration is difficult (perhaps underwater or deep underground), where the actual reserves may prove small, and/or where ongoing costs of extraction are very high.

None of these conditions apply in Iraq: huge reservoirs of easily accessible oil are already proven to exist, with more equally accessible fields likely to be discovered with little expense. This is why none of Iraq's neighbors utilize

PSAs. Saudi Arabia, Kuwait, Iran, and the United Arab Emirates all pay the multinationals a fixed rate to explore and develop their fields; and all of the profits become state revenues.

The advocates of PSAs in Iraq justify their use by arguing that $20 billion would be needed to develop the Iraqi fields fully and that favorable PSAs are the only way to attract such heavy doses of finance capital under the current highly dangerous circumstances. This assertion seems, however, to be little more than a smokescreen. No major oil companies are willing to invest in Iraq now, no matter how sweet the deal. If order is restored, on the other hand, Iraq would have no trouble attracting vast amounts of finance capital to develop reserves that could well be worth in excess of $10 trillion, and hence would have no need whatsoever for PSAs.

Based on leaked information, journalists reported that the PSAs envisioned by the Iraqi petrochemical law contained extremely favorable provisions for the oil companies, in which they would be entitled to 70 percent of profits until development expenses were amortized and 20 percent afterwards. This would have guaranteed them at least twice the typical profit margin over the long run, and many times that figure during the initial years.

There are other elements in the law (and the possible PSA contracts) that have also roused resistance inside Iraq. Among the most controversial are the following:

1. Insofar as PSAs or their legal equivalent were enacted, Iraq would lose control over what levels of oil the country produced with the potential to substantially weaken the grip of OPEC on the oil market.
2. The law would allow the oil companies to fully repatriate all profits from oil sales, almost insuring that the proceeds would not be reinvested in the Iraqi economy.
3. The Iraqi government would not have control over oil company operations inside Iraq. Any disputes would be referred instead to pro-industry international arbitration panels.
4. No contracts would be public documents.
5. Contracting companies would not be obliged to hire Iraqi workers, and could pursue the current policy of employing American technicians and South Asian manual laborers.

Several African countries with vast mineral riches have been subjected to these sorts of conditions, with large multinational companies extracting both minerals and profits while returning only a tiny fraction of the proceeds to the local population. As the resources are taken out of the ground and the country, the local population actually becomes poorer, while the potential for future prosperity is drained.

The draft petrochemical law, if enacted and implemented, could ensure that Iraq would remain in a state of neoliberal poverty in perpetuity, even if order did return to the country.

The Resistance

The petrochemical law is hardly assured of successful passage, and—even if passed—is in no way assured of successful implementation. Resistance to it, spread as it is throughout Iraqi society, has already shown itself to be a formidable opponent to the dwindling power of the American occupation.

The Parliament itself may be the first line of defense. It challenged the original IMF agreement and has refused to consider the bill for two months, already missing a March deadline for passage that American politicians of both parties had pronounced an important "benchmark" by which to judge the viability of Prime Minister Nouri al-Maliki's government.

In addition, the government officials responsible for administering the oil industry could prove formidable opponents. Rafiq Latta, a London-based oil analyst, told *Nation* reporter Christian Parenti, "The whole culture of the ministry opposes [the law]. . . . Those guys ran the industry very well all through the years of sanctions. It was an impressive job, and they take pride in 'their' oil."

Perhaps most formidable of all is the Federation of Oil Unions, with 26,000 members and allies throughout organized labor. The oil workers overturned contracts in 2003 and 2004 that would have placed substantial oil facilities under multinational corporate control; and they initiated a vigorous campaign against the US-sponsored oil program as early as June 2005—calling a conference to oppose privatization attended by "workers, academics, and international civil-society groups." In January 2006, they convened a convention composed of all major Iraqi union groups in Amman, Jordan, which issued a manifesto opposing the entire neoliberal US program for Iraq, including any compromise on national control of oil production.

At a second Amman labor meeting in December 2006, the Federation of Oil Unions announced its opposition to the pending law even before it was released. Iraq's trade unions, speaking in a single voice, declared that:

> Iraqi public opinion strongly opposes the handing of authority and control over the oil to foreign companies, that aim to make big profits at the expense of the people. They aim to rob Iraq's national wealth by virtue of unfair, long-term oil contracts that undermine the sovereignty of the State and the dignity of the Iraqi people.

When the bill was made public, oil union president Hassan Jumaa denounced it before yet another protest meeting, stating; "History will not forgive those who play recklessly with our wealth. . . . We consider the new law unbalanced and incoherent with the hopes of those who work in the oil industry. It has been drafted in a great rush in harsh circumstances." He then called on the government to consult Iraqi oil experts (who had not participated in drafting the law) and "ask their opinion before sinking Iraq into an ocean of dark injustice."

If the oil workers and their union allies decide to organize protests or strikes, they are likely to have the Iraqi public on their side. As three-quarters of Iraqis believe that the United States invaded in order to gain control of Iraqi oil, most observers believe they will surely agree with the oil workers that this law is a vehicle for that control. Even Iyad Allawi has now publicly taken a stand opposing it, perhaps the best indication that opposition will be virtually unanimous.

Finally—and no small matter—the armed resistance is also against the oil law. The Sunni insurgency underscored its opposition by assassinating Vice President Adel Abdul Mahdi, a major advocate of the pending law, on the day the bill was made public. The significance of the opposition of the Sunni insurgency is amplified by the stance of the Sadrists, the most rebellious segment of the Shia majority. Sadr spokesman Sheikh Gahaith Al Temimi warned journalist Christian Parenti that while the Sadrists would "welcome" foreign investment in oil, they would do so only "under certain conditions. We want our oil to be developed, not stolen. If a bad law were to be passed, all people of Iraq would resist it."

It seems clear that what the oil law has the power to do is substantially escalate the already unmanageable conflict in Iraq. Active opposition by the Parliament alone, or by the unions alone, or by the Sunni insurgency alone, or by the Sadrists alone might be sufficient to defeat or disable the law. The possibility that such disparate groups might find unity around this issue, mobilizing both the government bureaucracy and overwhelming public opinion to their cause, holds a much greater threat: the possibility of creating a unified force that might push beyond the oil law to a more general opposition to the American occupation.

Like so many American initiatives in Iraq, the oil law, even if passed, might never be worth more than the paper it will be printed on. The likelihood that any future Iraqi government that takes on a nationalist mantle will consider such an agreement in any way binding is nil. One day in perhaps the not so distant future, that "law," even if briefly the law of the land, is likely to find itself in the dustbin of history, along with Saddam's various oil deals. As a result, the Bush administration's "capture of new and existing oil and gas fields" is likely to end as a predictable fiasco.

June 2007

2 1

THE PENTAGON VS PEAK OIL

How Wars of the Future May Be Fought Just to Run the Machines That Fight Them

Michael T. Klare

Sixteen gallons of oil. That's how much the average American soldier in Iraq and Afghanistan consumes on a daily basis—either directly, through the use of Humvees, tanks, trucks, and helicopters, or indirectly, by calling in air strikes. Multiply this figure by 162,000 soldiers in Iraq, 24,000 in Afghanistan, and 30,000 in the surrounding region (including sailors aboard US warships in the Persian Gulf) and you arrive at approximately 3.5 million gallons of oil: the daily petroleum tab for US combat operations in the Middle East war zone.

Multiply that daily tab by 365 and you get 1.3 billion gallons: the estimated annual oil expenditure for US combat operations in Southwest Asia. That's greater than the total annual oil usage of Bangladesh, population 150 million— and yet it's a gross underestimate of the Pentagon's wartime consumption.

Such numbers cannot do full justice to the extraordinary gas-guzzling expense of the wars in Iraq and Afghanistan. After all, for every soldier stationed "in theater," there are two more in transit, in training, or otherwise in line for eventual deployment to the war zone—soldiers who also consume enormous amounts of oil, even if less than their compatriots overseas. Moreover, to sustain an "expeditionary" army located halfway around the world, the Department of Defense (DoD) must move millions of tons of arms, ammunition, food, fuel, and equipment every year by plane or ship, consuming additional tankerloads of petroleum. Add this to the tally and the Pentagon's war-related oil budget jumps appreciably, though exactly how much we have no real way of knowing.

And foreign wars, sad to say, account for but a small fraction of the Pentagon's total petroleum consumption. Possessing the world's largest fleet of modern aircraft, helicopters, ships, tanks, armored vehicles, and support systems—virtually all powered by oil—the DoD is, in fact, the world's leading consumer of petroleum. It can be difficult to obtain precise details on the DoD's daily oil hit, but an April 2007 report by a defense contractor, LMI Government Consulting, suggests that the Pentagon might consume as much as 340,000 barrels (14 million gallons) every day. This is greater than the total national consumption of Sweden or Switzerland.

Not "Guns *versus* Butter," but "Guns *versus* Oil"

For anyone who drives a motor vehicle these days, this has ominous implications. With the price of gasoline now 75 cents to a dollar more a gallon than it was just six months ago, it's obvious that the Pentagon is facing a potentially serious budgetary crunch. Just like any ordinary American family, the DoD has to make some hard choices: it can use its normal amount of petroleum and pay more at the Pentagon's equivalent of the pump, while cutting back on other basic expenses; or it can cut back on its gas use in order to protect favored weapons systems under development. Of course, the DoD has a third option: it can go before Congress and plead for yet another supplemental budget hike, but this is sure to provoke renewed calls for a timetable for an American troop withdrawal from Iraq, and so is an unlikely prospect at this time.

Nor is this destined to prove a temporary issue. As recently as two years ago, the US Department of Energy (DoE) was confidently predicting that the price of crude oil would hover in the $30 per barrel range for another quarter-century or so, leading to gasoline prices of about $2 per gallon. But then came Hurricane Katrina, the crisis in Iran, the insurgency in southern Nigeria, and a host of other problems that tightened the oil market, prompting the DoE to raise its long-range price projection into the $50 per barrel range. This is the amount that figures in many current governmental budgetary forecasts—including, presumably, those of the Department of Defense. But just how realistic is this? The price of a barrel of crude oil today is hovering in the $66 range. Many energy analysts now say that a price range of $70–$80 per barrel (or possibly even significantly more) is far more likely to be our fate for the foreseeable future.

A price rise of this magnitude, when translated into the cost of gasoline, aviation fuel, diesel fuel, home heating oil, and petrochemicals, will play havoc with the budgets of families, farms, businesses, and local governments. Sooner or later, it will force people to make profound changes in their daily lives—as benign as purchasing a hybrid vehicle in place of an SUV or as painful as cutting back on home heating or health care simply to make an unavoidable drive to work. It will have an equally severe effect on the Pentagon budget. As the world's number one consumer of petroleum products, the DoD will obviously be disproportionately affected by a doubling in the price of crude oil. If it can't turn to Congress for redress, it will have to reduce its profligate consumption of oil and/or cut back on other expenses, including weapons purchases.

The rising price of oil is producing what Pentagon contractor LMI calls a "fiscal disconnect" between the military's long-range objectives and the realities of the energy marketplace. "The need to recapitalize obsolete and damaged equipment [from the wars in Iraq and Afghanistan] and to develop high-technology systems to implement future operational concepts is growing," it explained in an April 2007 report. However, an inability "to control increased energy costs from fuel and supporting infrastructure diverts resources that would otherwise be available to procure new capabilities."

And this is likely to be the least of the Pentagon's worries. The Department of Defense is, after all, the world's richest military organization, and so can be expected to tap into hidden accounts of one sort or another in order to pay its oil bills *and* finance its many pet weapons projects. However, this assumes that sufficient petroleum will be available on world markets to meet the Pentagon's ever-growing needs—by no means a foregone conclusion. Like every other large consumer, the DoD must now confront the looming—but hard to assess—reality of "Peak Oil"; the very real possibility that global oil production is at or near its maximum sustainable ("peak") output and will soon commence an irreversible decline.

That global oil output will eventually reach a peak and then decline is no longer a matter of debate; all major energy organizations have now embraced this view. What remains open for argument is precisely *when* this moment will arrive. Some experts place it comfortably in the future— meaning two or three decades down the pike—while others put it in this very decade. If there is a consensus emerging, it is that peak oil output will occur somewhere around 2015. Whatever the timing of this momentous event, it is apparent that the world faces a profound shift in the global availability of energy, as we move from a situation of relative abundance to one of relative scarcity. It should be noted, moreover, that this shift will apply, above all, to the form of energy most in demand by the Pentagon: the petroleum liquids used to power planes, ships, and armored vehicles.

The Bush Doctrine Faces Peak Oil

Peak oil is not one of the global threats the Department of Defense has ever had to face before; and, like other US government agencies, it tended to avoid the issue, viewing it until recently as a peripheral matter. As intimations of peak oil's imminent arrival increased, however, it has been forced to sit up and take notice. Spurred perhaps by rising fuel prices, or by the growing attention being devoted to "energy security" by academic strategists, the DoD has suddenly taken an interest in the problem. To guide its exploration of the issue, the Office of Force Transformation within the Office of the Under Secretary of Defense for Policy commissioned LMI to conduct a study on the implications of future energy scarcity for Pentagon strategic planning.

The resulting study, "Transforming the Way the DoD Looks at Energy," was a bombshell. Determining that the Pentagon's favored strategy of global military engagement is incompatible with a world of declining oil output, LMI concluded that "current planning presents a situation in which the aggregate operational capability of the force may be unsustainable in the long term."

LMI arrived at this conclusion from a careful analysis of current US military doctrine. At the heart of the national military strategy imposed by the Bush administration—the Bush Doctrine—are two core principles: *transformation*, or the conversion of America's stodgy, tank-heavy Cold War military apparatus into an agile, continent-hopping, high-tech, futuristic war machine; and *preemption*, or the initiation of hostilities against "rogue states" like Iraq and Iran, thought to be pursuing weapons of mass destruction. What both principles entail is a substantial increase in the Pentagon's consumption of petroleum products—either because such plans rely, to an increased extent, on air and sea power or because they imply an accelerated tempo of military operations.

As summarized by LMI, implementation of the Bush Doctrine requires that "our forces must expand geographically and be more mobile and expeditionary so that they can be engaged in more theaters and prepared for expedient deployment anywhere in the world"; at the same time, they "must transition from a reactive to a proactive force posture to deter enemy forces from organizing for and conducting potentially catastrophic attacks." It follows that, "to carry out these activities, the US military will have to be even more energy intense. . . . Considering the trend in operational fuel consumption and future capability needs, this 'new' force employment construct will likely demand more energy/fuel in the deployed setting."

The resulting increase in petroleum consumption is likely to prove dramatic. During Operation Desert Storm in 1991, the average American soldier consumed only four gallons of oil per day; as a result of George W. Bush's initiatives, a US soldier in Iraq is now using four times as much. If this rate of increase continues unabated, the next major war could entail an expenditure of 64 gallons per soldier per day.

It was the unassailable logic of this situation that led LMI to conclude that there is a severe "operational disconnect" between the Bush administration's principles for future war fighting and the global energy situation. The administration has, the company notes, "tethered operational capability to high-technology solutions that require continued growth in energy sources"— and done so at the worst possible moment historically. After all, the likelihood is that the global energy supply is about to begin diminishing rather than expanding. Clearly, writes LMI in its April 2007 report, "it may not be possible to execute operational concepts and capabilities to achieve our security strategy if the energy implications are not considered." And when those energy implications are considered, the strategy appears "unsustainable."

The Pentagon as a Global Oil Protection Service

How will the military respond to this unexpected challenge? One approach, favored by some within the DoD, is to go "green"—that is, to emphasize the accelerated development and acquisition of fuel-efficient weapons systems so that the Pentagon can retain its commitment to the Bush Doctrine, but consume less oil while doing so. This approach, if feasible, would have the obvious attraction of allowing the Pentagon to assume an environmentally friendly façade while maintaining and developing its existing, interventionist force structure.

But there is also a more sinister approach that may be far more highly favored by senior officials. To ensure itself a "reliable" source of oil in perpetuity, the Pentagon will increase its efforts to maintain control over foreign sources of supply, notably oil fields and refineries in the Persian Gulf region, especially in Iraq, Kuwait, Qatar, Saudi Arabia, and the United Arab Emirates. This would help explain the recent talk of US plans to retain "enduring" bases in Iraq, along with its already impressive and elaborate basing infrastructure in these other countries.

The US military first began procuring petroleum products from Persian Gulf suppliers to sustain combat operations in the Middle East and Asia during World War Two, and has been doing so ever since. It was, in part, to protect this vital source of petroleum for military purposes that, in 1945, President Roosevelt first proposed the deployment of an American military presence in the Persian Gulf region. Later, the protection of Persian Gulf oil became more important for the economic well-being of the United States, as articulated in President Jimmy Carter's "Carter Doctrine" speech of January 23, 1980, as well as in President George H. W. Bush's August 1990 decision to stop Saddam Hussein's invasion of Kuwait, which led to the First Gulf War—and, many would argue, the decision of the younger Bush to invade Iraq over a decade later.

Along the way, the American military has been transformed into a "global oil protection service" for the benefit of US corporations and consumers, fighting overseas battles and establishing its bases to ensure that we get our daily fuel fix. It would be both sad and ironic if the military now began fighting wars mainly so that it could be guaranteed the fuel to run its own planes, ships, and tanks—consuming hundreds of billions of dollars a year that could instead be spent on the development of petroleum alternatives.

March 2006

22

MY SAUDI ARABIAN BREAKFAST

Chad Heeter

Please join me for breakfast. It's time to fuel up again.

On the table in my small Berkeley apartment this particular morning is a healthy-looking little meal—a bowl of imported McCann's Irish oatmeal topped with Cascadian Farms organic frozen raspberries, and a cup of Peet's Fair Trade Blend coffee. Like most of us, I prepare my breakfast at home and the ingredients for this one probably cost me about $1.25. (If I went to a café in downtown Berkeley, I'd likely have to add another $6.00, plus tip, for the same.)

My breakfast fuels me up with about 400 calories, and it satisfies me. So, for just over a buck and half an hour spent reading the morning paper in my own kitchen, I'm energized for the next few hours. But before I put spoon to cereal, what if I consider this bowl of oatmeal porridge (to which I've just added a little butter, milk, and a shake of salt) from a different perspective. Say, a Saudi Arabian one.

Then, what you'd be likely to see—what's really there, just hidden from our view (not to say our taste buds)—is about four ounces of crude oil. Throw in those luscious red raspberries and that cup of java (another three ounces of crude), and don't forget those modest additions of butter, milk, and salt (another ounce), and you've got a tiny bit of the Middle East right here in my kitchen.

Now, let's drill a little deeper into this breakfast. Just where does this tiny gusher of oil actually come from? (We'll let this oil represent all fossil fuels in my breakfast, including natural gas and coal.)

Nearly 20 percent of this oil went into growing my raspberries on Chilean farms many thousands of miles away, those oats in the fields of County Kildare, Ireland, and that specially raised coffee in Guatemala—think tractors as well as petroleum-based fertilizers and pesticides.

The next 40 percent of my breakfast fossil-fuel equation is burned up between the fields and the grocery store in processing, packaging, and shipping.

Take that box of McCann's oatmeal. On it is an inviting image of pure, healthy goodness—a bowl of porridge, topped by two peach slices. Scattered around the bowl are a handful of raw oats, what look to be four acorns, and three fresh raspberries. Those raw oats are actually a reminder that the flakes require a few steps twixt field and box. In fact, a visit to McCann's website illustrates each step in the cleaning, steaming, hulling, cutting, and rolling that turns the raw oats into edible flakes. Those five essential steps require significant energy costs.

Next, my oat flakes go into a plastic bag (made from oil), which is in turn inserted into an energy-intensive, pressed wood-pulp, printed paper box. Only then does my "breakfast" leave Ireland and travel over 5,000 fuel-gorging, CO_2-emitting miles by ship and truck to my grocery store in California.

Coming from another hemisphere, my raspberries take an even longer fossil-fueled journey to my neighborhood. Though packaged in a plastic bag labeled Cascadian Farms (which perhaps hints at a birthplace in the good old Cascade mountains of northwest Washington), the small print on the back, stamped "A Product of Chile," tells all—and what it speaks of is a 5,800-mile journey to northern California.

If you've been adding up percentages along the way, perhaps you've noticed that a few tablespoons of crude oil in my bowl have not been accounted for. That final 40 percent of the fossil fuel in my breakfast is used up by the simple acts of keeping food fresh and then preparing it. In home kitchens and restaurants, the chilling in refrigerators and the cooking on stoves using electricity or natural gas gobbles up more energy than you might imagine.

For decades, scientists have calculated how much fossil fuel goes into our food by measuring the amount of energy consumed in growing, packing, shipping, consuming, and finally disposing of it. The "caloric input" of fossil fuel is then compared to the energy available in the edible product, the "caloric output."

What they've discovered is astonishing. According to researchers at the University of Michigan's Center for Sustainable Agriculture, an average of over seven calories of fossil fuel is burned up for every calorie of energy we get from our food. This means that in eating my 400-calorie breakfast, I will in effect have "consumed" 2,800 calories of fossil fuel energy. (Some researchers claim the ratio to be as high as ten to one.)

But this is only an average. My cup of coffee gives me only a few calories of energy, but to process just one pound of coffee requires over 8,000 calories of fossil fuel energy—the equivalent energy found in nearly a quart of crude oil, 30 cubic feet of natural gas, or around two and a half pounds of coal.

So how do you gauge how much oil went into your food?

First check out how far it traveled. The further it traveled, the more oil it required. Next, gauge how much processing went into the food. A fresh apple is not processed, but Kellogg's Apple Jacks cereal requires enormous amounts of energy to process. The more processed the food, the more oil it required. Then consider how much packaging is wrapped around your food. Buy fresh vegetables instead of canned, and buy bulk beans, grains, and flour if you want to reduce that packaging.

By now, you're thinking that you're in the clear, because you eat strictly organically grown foods. When it comes to fossil fuel calculations though, the manner in which food's grown is where differences stop. Whether conventionally grown or organically grown, a raspberry is shipped, packed, and chilled the same way.

Yes, there are some savings from growing organically, but possibly only of a slight nature. According to a study by David Pimentel at Cornell University, 30 percent of fossil fuel expenditure on farms growing conventional (nonorganic) crops is found in chemical fertilizer. This 30 percent is not consumed on organic farms, but only if the manure used as fertilizer is produced in very close proximity to the farm. Manure is a heavy, bulky product. If farms have to truck bulk manure for any distance over a few miles, the savings are eaten up in diesel fuel consumption, according to

Pimentel. One source of manure for organic farmers in California is the chicken producer Foster Farms. Organic farmers in Monterey County, for example, will have to truck tons of Foster's manure from their main plant in Livingston to fields over one hundred miles away.

So the next time we're at the grocer, do we now have to ask not only where and how this product was grown, but how far its manure was shipped?

Well, if you're in New York City picking out a California-grown tomato that was fertilized with organic compost made from kelp shipped from Nova Scotia, maybe it's not such a bad question. But should we give up on organic? If you're buying organic raspberries from Chile each week, then yes. The fuel cost is too great, as is the production of the greenhouse gases along with it. Buying locally grown foods should be the first priority when it comes to saving fossil fuel.

But if there were really truth in packaging, on the back of my oatmeal box where it now tells me how many calories I get from each serving, it would also tell me how many calories of fossil fuels went into this product. On a scale from one to five—with one being nonprocessed, locally grown products and five being processed, packaged imports—we could quickly average the numbers in our shopping cart to get a sense of the ecological footprint of our diet. From this we would gain a truer sense of the miles-per-gallon in our food.

What appeared to be a simple, healthy meal of oatmeal, berries, and coffee looks different now. I thought I was essentially driving a Toyota Prius hybrid by having a very fuel-efficient breakfast, but by the end of the week I've still eaten the equivalent of over two quarts of Valvoline. From the perspective of fossil fuel consumption, I now look at my breakfast as a waste of precious resources. And what about the mornings that I head to Denny's for a Grand Slam breakfast: eggs, pancakes, bacon, sausage? On those mornings—forget about fuel efficiency—I'm driving a Hummer.

What I eat for breakfast connects me to the planet, deep into its past with the fossilized remains of plants and animals which are now fuel, as well as into its future, when these nonrenewable resources will likely be in scant supply. Maybe these thoughts are too grand to be having over breakfast, but I'm not the only one on the planet eating this morning. My meal traveled thousands of miles around the world to reach my plate. But then there's the rise of perhaps 600 million middle-class Indians and Chinese. They're already demanding the convenience of packaged meals and the taste of foreign flavors. What happens when middle-class families in India or China decide they want their Irish oats for breakfast, topped by organic raspberries from Chile? They'll dip more and more into the planet's communal oil well. And someday soon, we'll all suck it dry.

October 2005

23

THE OTHER HURRICANE

Has the Age of Chaos Begun?

Mike Davis

The genesis of two Category Five hurricanes (Katrina and Rita) in a row over the Gulf of Mexico is an unprecedented and troubling occurrence. But for most tropical meteorologists the truly astonishing "storm of the decade" took place in March 2004. Hurricane Catarina—so named because it made landfall in the southern Brazilian state of Santa Catarina—was the first recorded South Atlantic hurricane in history.

Textbook orthodoxy had long excluded the possibility of such an event; sea temperatures, experts claimed, were too low and wind shear too powerful to allow tropical depressions to evolve into cyclones south of the Atlantic Equator. Indeed, forecasters rubbed their eyes in disbelief as weather satellites down-linked the first images of a classical whirling disc with a well-formed eye in these forbidden latitudes.

In a series of recent meetings and publications, researchers have debated the origin and significance of Catarina. A crucial question is this: Was Catarina simply a rare event at the outlying edge of the normal bell curve of South Atlantic weather—just as, for example, Joe DiMaggio's incredible fifty-six-game hitting streak in 1941 represented an extreme probability in baseball (an analogy made famous by Stephen Jay Gould)—or was Catarina a "threshold" event, signaling some fundamental and abrupt change of state in the planet's climate system?

Scientific discussions of environmental change and global warming have long been haunted by the specter of nonlinearity. Climate models, like econometric models, are easiest to build and understand when they are simple linear extrapolations of well-quantified past behavior, when causes maintain a consistent proportionality to their effects.

But all the major components of global climate—air, water, ice, and vegetation—are actually nonlinear: at certain thresholds they can switch from one state of organization to another, with catastrophic consequences for species too finely tuned to the old norms. Until the early 1990s, however, it was generally believed that these major climate transitions took centuries, if not millennia, to accomplish. Now, thanks to the decoding of subtle signatures in ice cores and sea-bottom sediments, we know that global temperatures and ocean circulation can, under the right circumstances, change abruptly—in a decade or even less.

The paradigmatic example is the so-called "Younger Dryas" event, 12,800 years ago, when an ice dam collapsed, releasing an immense volume of meltwater from the shrinking Laurentian ice sheet into the Atlantic Ocean via the instantly created St Lawrence River. This "freshening" of the North Atlantic suppressed the northward conveyance of warm water by the Gulf Stream and plunged Europe back into a thousand-year ice age.

Abrupt switching mechanisms in the climate system—such as relatively small changes in ocean salinity—are augmented by causal loops that act as amplifiers. Perhaps the most famous example is sea-ice albedo: the vast expanses of white, frozen Arctic Ocean ice reflect heat back into space, thus providing positive feedback for cooling trends; alternatively, shrinking sea ice increases heat absorption, accelerating both its own further melting and planetary warming.

Thresholds, switches, amplifiers, chaos—contemporary geophysics assumes that Earth history is inherently revolutionary. This is why many prominent researchers—especially those who study topics like ice sheet stability and North Atlantic circulation—have always had qualms about the consensus projections of the Intergovernmental Panel on Climate Change (IPCC), the world authority on global warming.

In contrast to Bushite flat-Earthers and shills for the oil industry, their skepticism has been founded on fears that the IPCC models fail to allow adequately for catastrophic nonlinearities like the Younger Dryas. Where other researchers model the late-twenty-first-century climate that our children will live with upon the precedents of the Altithermal (the hottest phase of the current Holocene period, 8,000 years ago) or the Eemian (the previous, even warmer interglacial episode, 120,000 years ago), growing numbers of geophysicists toy with the possibilities of runaway warming returning the Earth to the torrid chaos of the Paleocene-Eocene Thermal Maximum (PETM: 55 million years ago) when the extreme and rapid heating of the oceans led to massive extinctions.

Dramatic new evidence has emerged recently that we may be headed, if not back to the dread, almost inconceivable PETM, then to a much harder landing than envisioned by the IPCC.

As I flew toward Louisiana and the carnage of Katrina three weeks ago, I found myself reading the August 23 issue of *EOS*, the newsletter of the American Geophysical Union. I was poleaxed by an article entitled "Arctic System on Trajectory to New, Seasonally Ice-Free State," co-authored by twenty-one scientists from almost as many universities and research institutes. Even two days later, walking among the ruins of the Lower Ninth Ward, I found myself worrying more about the *EOS* article than the disaster surrounding me.

The article begins with a recounting of trends familiar to any reader of the Tuesday science section of the *New York Times*: for almost thirty years, Arctic sea ice has been thinning and shrinking so dramatically that "a summer ice-free Arctic Ocean within a century is a real possibility." The scientists, however, add a new observation—that this process is probably irreversible. "Surprisingly, it is difficult to identify a single feedback mechanism within the Arctic that has the potency or speed to alter the system's present course."

An ice-free Arctic Ocean has not existed for at least one million years and the authors warn that the Earth is inexorably headed toward a "super-interglacial" state "outside the envelope of glacial–interglacial fluctuations that prevailed during recent Earth history." They emphasize that within a century global warming will probably exceed the Eemian temperature maximum and thus obviate all the models that have made this their essential scenario. The scientists also suggest that the total or partial collapse of the

Greenland Ice Sheet is a real possibility—an event that would definitely throw a Younger Dryas wrench into the Gulf Stream.

If they are right, then we are living on the climate equivalent of a runaway train that is picking up speed as it passes the stations marked "Altithermal" and "Eemian." "Outside the envelope," moreover, means that we are leaving behind not only the serendipitous climatic parameters of the Holocene— the last 10,000 years of mild, warm weather that have favored the explosive growth of agriculture and urban civilization—but also those of the late Pleistocene that fostered the evolution of *Homo sapiens* in eastern Africa.

Other researchers undoubtedly will contest the extraordinary conclusions of the *EOS* article and—we must hope—suggest the existence of countervailing forces to this scenario of an Arctic albedo catastrophe. But for the time being, at least, research on global change is pointing toward worst-case scenarios.

All of this, of course, is a perverse tribute to industrial capitalism and extractive imperialism as geological forces so formidable that they have succeeded in scarcely more than two centuries—indeed, mainly in the past fifty years—in knocking the Earth off its climatic pedestal and propelling it toward the nonlinear unknown.

The demon in me wants to say: Party and make merry. No need now to worry about Kyoto, recycling your aluminum cans, or using too much toilet paper, when, soon enough, we'll be debating how many hunter-gatherers can survive in the scorching deserts of New England or the tropical forests of the Yukon.

The good parent in me, however, screams: How is it possible that we can now contemplate with scientific seriousness whether our children's children will themselves have children? Let Exxon answer that in one of their sanctimonious ads.

September 2005

24

SUCKER'S BETS FOR THE NEW CENTURY

The US after Katrina

Bill McKibben

If the images of skyscrapers collapsed in heaps of ash were the end of one story—the US safe on its isolated continent from the turmoil of the world—then the picture of the sodden Superdome with its peeling roof marks the beginning of the next story, the one that will dominate our politics in the coming decades of this century: America befuddled about how to cope with a planet suddenly turned unstable and unpredictable.

Over and over last week, people said that the scenes from the convention center, the highway overpasses, and the other, suddenly infamous Crescent City venues didn't "look like America," that they seemed instead to be straight from the Third World. That was almost literally accurate, for poor, black New Orleans (whose life had never previously been of any interest to the larger public) is not so different from other poor and black parts of the world: its infant mortality and life expectancy rates, its educational achievement statistics mirroring scores of African and Latin American enclaves.

But it was accurate in another way, too, one full of portent for the future. A decade ago, environmental researcher Norman Myers began trying to add up the number of humans at risk of losing their homes from global warming. He looked at all the obvious places—coastal China, India, Bangladesh, the tiny island states of the Pacific and Indian oceans, the Nile delta, Mozambique, on and on—and predicted that by 2050 it was entirely possible that 150 million people could be "environmental refugees," forced from their homes by rising waters. That's more than the number of political refugees sent scurrying by the bloody century we've just endured.

Try to imagine, that is, the chaos that attends busing 15,000 people from one football stadium to another in the richest nation on Earth, and then multiply it by four orders of magnitude and resituate your thoughts in the poorest nations on earth.

And then try to imagine doing it over and over again—probably without the buses.

Because so far, even as blogs and websites all over the Internet fill with accusations about the scandalous lack of planning that led to the collapse of the levees in New Orleans, almost no one is addressing the much larger problems: the scandalous lack of planning that has kept us from even beginning to address climate change, and the sad fact that global warming means the future will be full of just this kind of horror.

Consider the first of these larger problems for just a minute. No single hurricane is "the result" of global warming. But a month before Katrina hit, MIT hurricane specialist Kerry Emmanuel published a landmark paper in the British science magazine *Nature* showing that tropical storms were now lasting half again as long and spinning winds were 50 percent more powerful than just a few decades before. The only plausible cause: the ever-warmer tropical seas on which these storms thrive. Katrina, a Category One storm when it crossed Florida, roared to full life in the abnormally hot water of the Gulf of Mexico. It then punched its way into Louisiana and Mississippi—the latter a state now governed by Haley Barbour, who in an earlier incarnation as a Republican power broker and energy lobbyist helped persuade President Bush to renege on his promise to treat carbon dioxide as a pollutant.

So far the US has done exactly nothing even to try to slow the progress of climate change: we're emitting far more carbon than we were in 1988, when scientists issued their first prescient global-warming warnings. Even if, at that moment, we'd started doing all that we could to overhaul our energy economy, we'd probably still be stuck with the one degree Fahrenheit increase in global average temperature that's already driving our current disruptions. Now scientists predict that without truly dramatic change in the very near future, we're likely to see the planet's mercury rise five degrees before this century is out. That is, five times more than we've seen so far.

Which leads us to the second problem. For the ten thousand years of human civilization, we've relied on the planet's basic physical stability. Sure, there have been hurricanes and droughts and volcanoes and tsunamis, but averaged out across the Earth, it's been a remarkably stable run. If your grandparents inhabited a particular island, chances were that you could too. If you could grow corn in your field, you could pretty much count on your grandkids being able to do likewise. Those are now sucker's bets—that's what those predictions about environmental refugees really mean.

Here's another way of saying it. In the twentieth century, we've seen change in human societies speed up to an almost unimaginable level, one that has stressed every part of our civilization. In this century, we're going to see the natural world change at the same kind of rate. That's what happens when you increase the amount of heat trapped in the atmosphere. That extra energy expresses itself in every way you can imagine: more wind, more evaporation, more rain, more melt, more . . . more . . . more.

And there is no reason to think we can cope. Take New Orleans as an example. It is currently pro forma for politicians to announce that it will be rebuilt, and doubtless it will be. Once. But if hurricanes like Katrina go from once-in-a-century storms to once-in-a-decade-or-two storms, how many times are you going to rebuild it? Even in America there's not that kind of money—especially if you're also having to cope with, say, the effects on agriculture of more frequent and severe heat waves, and the effects on human health of the spread of mosquito-borne diseases like dengue fever and malaria, and so on ad infinitum. Not to mention the costs of converting our energy system to something less suicidal than fossil fuel, a task that becomes more expensive with every year that passes.

Our rulers have insisted by both word and deed that the laws of physics and chemistry do not apply to us. That delusion will now start to vanish. Katrina marks Year One of our new calendar, the start of an age in which the physical world has flipped from sure and secure to volatile and unhinged. New Orleans doesn't look like the America we've lived in. But it very much resembles the planet we will inhabit the rest of our lives.

VI

NAME THAT WAR

October 2006

25

GEORGE BUSH'S WAR OF THE WORDS

Tom Engelhardt

For Homer, those epithets attached to his heroes and gods were undoubt-edly mnemonic devices—the fleet-footed Achilles, Poseidon the Earth-shaker, the wily Odysseus, the ox-eyed Hera. But isn't it strange how many similar, if somewhat less heroic, catchwords and phrases have adhered to key officials of the Bush administration these last years. Here's my own partial list:

President George ("Brownie, you're doing a heck of a job") Bush, Vice President Dick ("last throes") Cheney, Secretary of Defense Donald ("stuff happens") Rumsfeld, then National Security Adviser now Secretary of State Condoleezza ("mushroom cloud") Rice, CIA Director George ("slam dunk") Tenet, Deputy Secretary of Defense Paul ("[Iraq] floats on a sea of oil") Wolfowitz, Centcom Commander General Tommy ("We don't do body counts") Franks, then White House Counsel now Attorney General Alberto ("quaint") Gonzales, and withdrawn Supreme Court nominee and White House Counsel Harriet ("You are the best governor ever") Miers.

You know a person by the company he or she keeps—so the saying goes. You could also say that you know an administration by the linguistic company it keeps; and though George Bush is usually presented as an inarticulate stumbler of a speech and news-conference giver, it's nothing short of remarkable how many new words and phrases (or redefined old ones) this president and his administration have managed to lodge in our lives and our heads.

Since September 11, 2001, the United States has been not so much the planet's lone "hyperpower" as its gunslinger in that great Western ("dead or alive") tradition that George and Dick learned about in the movies of their childhood. But fast as they've reached for their guns, over the last years they've reached for one thing faster: their dictionaries.

And of all the words that came to their minds post-9/11, the first and fastest was an old one—"war." Within hours of the 9/11 attacks, it was already on the scene and being redefined by administration officials and supporters. We would not, for instance, actually declare war. After all, who was war to be declared on? We were simply "at war" and that was that. Since then, according to George Bush and his associates, we have been fighting either "the Global War on Terror" (aka GWOT), "the long war," "the millennium war," "World War Three," or "World War Four." We not only entered an immediate state of war, but one meant to last generations, and with it we got a commander-in-chief presidency secretly redefined in such a way as to place it outside any legal boundaries.

We were, then, at war. But the first war we were "at" was a war of the words and at its heart from the beginning was the status of the people we were capturing on or near various battlefields, or even kidnapping off the streets of European cities, and exactly what we could do to them. If John F. Kennedy is remembered for saying, "Ich bin ein Berliner," perhaps when history shrinks George W. Bush to a sound bite it will be, "We abide by the law of the United States; we do not torture." To say those words—repeatedly—he has had to mount not a soapbox, nor even the TV or radio version of a bully pulpit, but a pile of torn, trampled dictionaries.

If you don't believe me, go back and read, for instance, the infamous "torture memo" of 2002 in which the top legal minds of the Justice Department and the White House Counsel's office labored over how to define "severe" and "pain" in such a way that almost no pain inflicted during a prisoner's interrogation would ever prove too "severe." Whole sections of that document sound like they were cobbled together by a learned panel for a new edition of some devil's dictionary. ("The word 'profound' has a number of meanings, all of which convey a significant depth. Webster's *New International Dictionary 1977* [2nd edn 1935] defines profound as . . .")

In the end, these experts defined "torture" to suit administration needs in the following pretzeled fashion: "Must be equivalent in intensity to the pain accompanying serious physical injury, such as organ failure, impairment of bodily function, or even death." And though, under pressure, the "torture memo" was finally disavowed, the President has been able to claim that "we do not torture" only by adhering to its ludicrous definitions. (Even then, this administration's interrogators *have* tortured prisoners.) This was in fact a typical Bush-era document of shame, symbolic of the bureaucratic lawlessness let loose at the heart of government by officials intent on creating a pseudo-legal basis for replacing the rule of law with the rule of a commander-in-chief.

Never has an administration rolled up its sleeves and redefined our terms more systematically or unnervingly with less attention to reality.

When a dynasty fell in ancient China, it was believed that part of the explanation for its demise lay in the increasing gap between words and reality. The emperor of whatever new dynasty had taken power would then perform a ceremony called "the rectification of names" to bring language and what it was meant to describe back into sync. We Americans need to lose the emperor part of the equation, but adopt such a ceremony. Never have our realities and our words for them been quite so out of whack.

Between August 2005, when, armed with two cheap tape recorders and a scribbled list of questions, I first met historian and activist Howard Zinn in a coffee shop, and last summer, I had a chance to hang out with and interview eleven iconoclastic thinkers and activists, all of whom were concerned with how to describe the realities of our imperial world as well as with the fate of our country. Recently, these interviews were gathered into a book, *Mission Unaccomplished: Tomdispatch Interviews with American Iconoclasts and Dissenters.* What follows are apt quotes from each of the interviewees—and my own brief discussions of Bush-redefined words. Think of it as a kind of call-and-response essay as well as my own modest bow to eleven engaged souls whom I admire.

Howard Zinn: "I came to the conclusion that, given the technology of modern warfare, war is inevitably a war against children, against civilians. When you look at the ratio of civilian to military dead, it changes from 50–50 in World War Two to 80–20 in Vietnam, maybe as high as 90–10 today. . . . When you face that fact, war is now always a war against civilians, and so against children. No political goal can justify it, and so the great challenge before the human race in our time is to solve the problems of tyranny and aggression, and do it without war."

Collateral Damage: It's been all collateral damage all the time from official Pentagon lips since George W. Bush launched our Afghan war just weeks after September 11, 2001, and followed it relatively quickly with an invasion of Iraq. Wedding parties wiped out; children killed by accident; civilians murdered at places like Haditha and Ishaqi; scores of Iraqi civilians dead in the first air strikes on Baghdad (and not a single Iraqi leader killed); thousands of innocent Iraqi civilians swept up in US raids and tossed into Abu Ghraib prison for endless months without charges; "terrorist safe houses" hit from the air in crowded urban neighborhoods where nearby residents simply died.

Since March 2003, over 2,700 American soldiers, over 200 troops from allied forces, and several hundred private contractors or mercenaries have died in Iraq. (Another 340 Americans have died in Afghanistan.) We have no idea how many Iraqi soldiers, insurgents, and militia members have died in that same period along with many tens of thousands of Iraqi civilians, all "collateral damage." But we do know one thing. In modern wars, especially those conducted in part from the air (as both the Iraq and Afghan ones have been), there's nothing "collateral" about civilian deaths. If anything, the "collateral deaths" are those of the combatants on any side. Civilian deaths are now the central fact, the very essence of modern imperial warfare. Not seeing that means not seeing war.

James Carroll: "The good things of the Roman Empire are what we remember about it—the roads, the language, the laws, the buildings, the classics . . . But we pay very little attention to what the Roman Empire was to the people at its bottom—the slaves who built those roads . . . the oppressed and occupied peoples who were brought into the empire if they submitted, but radically and completely smashed if they resisted at all . . . We Americans are full of our sense of ourselves as having benign imperial impulses. That's why the idea of the American Empire was celebrated as a benign phenomenon. We were going to bring order to the world. Well, yes . . . as long as you didn't resist us. And that's where we really have something terrible in common with the Roman Empire. . . . We must reckon with imperial power as it is felt by people at the bottom. Rome's power. America's."

The New Rome: In neocon Washington, there was an early burst of pride in empire. The US wasn't just, as in the 1990s, the planet's "global sheriff," it was now the mightiest power in history, an imperial goliath that put the old British empire and possibly even the Roman one in the shade. Right-wing pundit Charles Krauthammer wrote in *Time* magazine even before the attacks of 9/11: "America is no mere international citizen. It is the dominant power in the world, more dominant than any since Rome. Accordingly, America is in a position to reshape norms, alter expectations, and create new realities. How? By unapologetic and implacable demonstrations of will." Between the first of those "implacable demonstrations of will" in the fall of 2001 and Bush's "Mission Accomplished" moment in May 2003, many other pundits weighed in, embracing the idea of empire in a way that had once been taboo in the US. Fareed Zacaria of *Newsweek* was typical in speaking of "'a comprehensive uni-polarity' that nobody has seen since Rome dominated the world." Max Boot in *USA Today* wrote a piece headlined, "American Imperialism? No Need to Run Away from Label." ("[O]n the whole, US imperialism has been the greatest force for good in the world during the past century.") For the liberal and squeamish, there was Michael Ignatieff in the *New York Times* magazine urging us not to "embrace" imperialism, but merely to do our duty and pick up "the burden" of Empire Lite.

Five years later with the sack of Rome looking more applicable to our world than a Pax Romana, perhaps another old word should be making its reappearance: "Tyranny" ("A government in which a single ruler is invested with absolute power.") Outside the United States, the Bush administration has already set itself up as a tyranny with its private network of prisons, its secret airlines for kidnapping anyone it chooses, and its power to wage war on the say-so of no one but itself anywhere it cares to. Domestically, the picture is still mixed, but the danger signals are obvious.

Juan Cole: "[Iraq] is one of the great foreign policy debacles of American history. There's an enormous amount at stake in the oil Gulf and Bush is throwing grenades around in the cockpit of the world economy. So I think he has dug his own grave with regard to Iraq policy."

Regime Change, Shock and Awe, Decapitation, Cakewalk: Ah, Iraq. What a field of linguistic fantasy play for Bush administration officials. "Regime change" was the global order of the day, if that "axis of evil" (and perhaps sixty other nations rumored to harbor terrorists) didn't attend to us. "Shock and awe" was what we would bring to Iraq, thereby humbling the whole "axis of evil" in a single awesome rain of destruction from the skies. As the planet's most dazzling military power, we would then go on a "cakewalk" (a high-strutting dance) to Baghdad and beyond, reorganizing the whole Middle East to our taste. "Decapitation" would be what would happen to Saddam's regime.

Behind such words lay inside-the-Beltway dreams of absolute global domination, of imposing a planetary Pax Americana by force of arms. It was the sort of scheme that once would have been the property of some "evil empire" we stood against. Behind it all, for an administration deeply linked to the energy business, lay control over the oil heartlands of the planet, known to this administration as "the arc of instability." Oil, or what George Bush referred to (before launching his invasion) as "Iraq's patrimony," was of such interest that just about the only places our troops guarded in those first "post-war" days of looting were oil fields and the Oil Ministry building in Baghdad. Of course, what Bush and his friends succeeded in visiting on the region was ever-spreading chaos. Since 2001, in its own version of the rectification of names, the Bush administration has actually been creating a genuine "arc of instability" stretching from Central Asia to the Horn of Africa. The grenades are indeed now in the cockpit.

Cindy Sheehan: "Katrina was a natural disaster that nobody could help, but the man-made disaster afterwards was just horrible. I mean, number one, all our resources are in Iraq. Number two, what little resources we did have were deployed far too late. George Bush was golfing and eating birthday cake with John McCain while people were hanging off their houses praying to be rescued. He's so disconnected from this country—and from reality. I heard a line yesterday that I thought was perfect. This man said he thinks Katrina will be Bush's Monica."

Homeland: It may be an ugly word, with overtones of Nazi Germany (and perhaps the World War Two-era Soviet Union as well), but now it's ours, a truly un-American replacement for "nation" or "country." Like a number of Bush-era terms, it was lurking in the shadows before 9/11. Now, we have a homeland as well as "homeland security," and even a Department of Homeland Security, a giant and, as Katrina demonstrated, remarkably ineffective new bureaucracy. By its very name, the "Defense" Department should, of course, be our Department of Homeland Security. But its focus is now on dominating the rest of the planet (and space), so instead we have two Defense Departments, both quagmires of civilian bureaucratic ineptitude, both lucrative as anything, neither going anywhere soon. If this isn't an attempt not just to redefine American reality, but to bankrupt it, I can't imagine what is. George Bush has been our Katrina.

Chalmers Johnson: "Part of empire is the way it's penetrated our society, the way we've become dependent on it. . . . The military budget is starting to bankrupt the country. It's got so much in it that's well beyond any rational military purpose. It equals just less than half of total global military spending. And yet here we are, stymied by two of the smallest, poorest countries on Earth. Iraq before we invaded had a GDP the size of the state of Louisiana, and Afghanistan was certainly one of the poorest places on the planet. And yet these two places have stopped us."

Footprint, Enduring Camp, Lily Pad: Call this a sampler of the euphemistic language that goes with garrisoning the planet. In the Bush years, the Pentagon has not only grown ever more gargantuan, but has come to occupy the heartlands of foreign (and increasingly domestic) policy. It has essentially displaced the State Department from diplomacy and is now in the process of displacing the CIA from covert intelligence operations. In these years, Pentagon strategists, discussing the US's 700-plus military bases around the world, began speaking of our military "footprint" on the planet— in the singular. As an imperial colossus, it seems, only one military boot at a time could even fit on the planet.

By the time American troops entered Baghdad in April 2003, the Pentagon already had plans on the drawing boards for four massive permanent military bases in Iraq, but the phrase "permanent base" was not to be used. For a while, these were referred to, charmingly enough, as "enduring camps" (like so many summer establishments for children who had overstayed their leave). In the same way, the strategic-basing posture of this era, meant to bring deployable US troops ever closer to locking down that "arc of instability," involved "lily pad" bases—the thought being that, if the occasion arose, American "frogs," armed to the teeth with pre-positioned munitions, would be able to hop agilely from one pre-positioned "pad" to another, knocking off the "flies" as they went. This is part of the strange, defanged language with which American leaders meant to create a Pax Americana planet.

Ann Wright: "Thirty-five years in the government between my military service and the State Department, under seven administrations. It was hard. I liked representing America. I kept hoping the administration would go back to the Security Council for its authorization to go to war. . . . I was hoping against hope that our government would not go into what really is an illegal war of aggression that meets no criteria of international law. When it was finally evident we were going to do so, I said to myself: It ain't going to be on my watch."

Service: And what about missing words? "Service to country," such an honorable concept, was swept with "sacrifice" into Bush's dustbin of history. In response to 9/11, the President famously told Americans to sacrifice for his coming wars by leading normal lives, going shopping as usual, and visiting Disney World. The only ones capable of truly "serving" their country, as this President seems to see it, are CIA kidnappers, the illegal eavesdroppers of the National Security Agency, and the interrogators who perform the tough acts of torture that have been redefined by administration lawyers as something else entirely. And yet, in these years, the ideal of service has not died. Retired colonel and State Department official Ann Wright—at present, an antiwar activist—was one of three diplomats who resigned to protest the onrushing invasion of Iraq in 2003. They have since been joined by a veritable fallen legion of government employees, who were honorable or steadfast enough in their duties or actually believed too fully in our Constitution, and so found themselves forced to resign in protest, quit, or simply be pushed off the cliff by cronies of this administration.

Someone needs to redefine the "checks and balances" of the American system. The only operative check-and-balance for most of the past five years has been one the Founding Fathers never dreamed of (because they couldn't imagine a government structure like ours) and that's been the angry, leaking, protesting members of the federal government, the intelligence community, the military, and the bureaucracy. (On the other side of that equation, no one has yet come fully to grips with, or reported decently on, the depth of the Bush purge of the government, the replacement of officials down to the lowest levels with administration pals, cronies, and ideologues.)

Mark Danner: "When you look at the record, the phrase I come back to, not only about interrogation but the many other steps that constitute the Bush state of exception, state of emergency, since 9/11 is 'take the gloves off.'"

Extraordinary Rendition, Secret Prisons, Torture: Donald Rumsfeld's "office" was calling for interrogators to take off those "gloves" in the case of the "American Taliban," John Walker Lindh, soon after he was captured in late 2001. It became a commonplace phrase inside the government (and even among the military in Iraq). Given the image, you wonder what exactly was under those gloves. In Langley, Virginia, according to Ron Suskind in his new book *The One Percent Doctrine*, CIA director George Tenet was using a far blunter image. He was talking about "taking off the shackles" (that supposedly had been put on the CIA in the Vietnam/Watergate era).

Rendition—as in "render unto Caesar"—gained that "extraordinary" quickly indeed as the CIA began kidnapping terror "suspects" around the world and no longer rendering them to the American court system (as in the Clinton years) but to various Third World allies willing to torture them or to American "secret prisons"—a phrase that, in the previous century, would have been reserved for the Gestapo or Stalin's NKVD.

In the meantime, administration lawyers began redefining "torture," a word not normally considered terribly difficult to grasp, more or less out of existence. By the time they were done, mock drowning, an interrogation "technique" called (as if it were surfing) "waterboarding," ceased for a while to be what even medieval Europe knew it to be: "the water torture." In no other single area did Bush administration officials (and their legal camp followers) reach more quickly for their dictionaries to pretzel and torture the language. This represented a very specific kind of reach for power. After all, if you could kidnap or capture a man anywhere on Earth, transport him to a secret prison (or at least, as with Guantánamo, one beyond the purview of any court), and then torture him, and if it could all be redefined as within the bounds of legality and propriety, then you had captured a previously unknown kind of power for the presidency that was as un-American as the word "homeland." Think of it this way: those who can torture openly, can do anything.

Mike Davis: "It's clear that the future of guerrilla warfare, insurrection against the world system, has moved into the city. Nobody has realized this with as much clarity as the Pentagon. . . . Its strategists are way ahead of geopoliticians and traditional foreign-relations types in understanding the significance of a world of slums. . . . There's really quite an extraordinary military literature trying to address what the Pentagon sees as the most novel terrain of this century, which it now models in the slums of Karachi, Port au Prince, and Baghdad."

Preventive War: From the militarized heavens to the slum cities of the Third World, the Pentagon is doing all the R&D. It already has its advanced weaponry for 2020, 2030, 2040 on the drawing boards. It's planning for and dreaming about the future in a way inconceivable for any other part of the government. It not only has a space command, but, for the first time, a separate command for our own continent (US Northcom) that is preparing for future hurricanes, future pandemics, future domestic disasters of every sort, now that our civil government, growing ever larger, handles things ever less well.

The Bush administration has elevated not just the Pentagon, but the principle of, and a belief in the efficacy of, force to the level of an idol to be worshiped. In 2002, the President suggested a new term—preventive war—which was then embedded in the National Security Strategy of the United States, a key planning document. At the time, Condoleezza Rice put the thinking behind the term this way: "As a matter of common sense, the United States must be prepared to take action, when necessary, before threats have fully materialized." This was, in fact, a recipe for waging war any time an administration cared to. No longer would the United States wait until the eve of an attack to strike "preemptively." Now, if it even occured to the President or Vice President that there was a "one percent" chance some country might someday somehow endanger us, we were free to launch our forces; and "preventive" sounded so much better than the previous term, "war of aggression." For this administration, and so for Americans, a war of aggression had preemptively been moved into the same category with preventive medicine.

Katrina vanden Heuvel: "Sometimes, though, frustration lies in the feeling that you just can't convey the enormity of, say, the Bush administration's unitary executive theory. How do you convey that no previous administration I know of has so openly, so brazenly, on so many fronts tried to subvert the Constitution, that what we're living through is a crisis that may bode the death knell of our democracy. Why aren't people jumping up and down?"

Unitary Executive Theory: This isn't a theory, but a long-planned grab for tyrannical control under the President's "commander-in-chief" powers in a carefully redefined "wartime" situation that will not stop being so in our lifetimes. This "theory" was meant to give a gloss of Constitutional legality to any conceivable presidential act. What the "unitary" meant was "no room for you" when it came to Congress and the courts. The "executive" was, as former Secretary of State Colin Powell's Chief of Staff Larry Wilkinson put it, rule by a "cabal," a cult of true believers inside the presidential bubble, impermeable to outside opinion or pressure. They were eager—when it came to torture, unlimited forms of surveillance, and the ability to define reality—to invest individuals secretly with something like the powers of gods.

Andrew Bacevich: "[W]e are in deep, deep trouble. An important manifestation of that trouble is this shortsighted infatuation with military power. . . . There's such an unwillingness to confront the dilemmas we face as a people that I find deeply troubling. I know we're a democracy. We have elections. But it's become a procedural democracy. Our politics are not really meaningful. In a meaningful politics, you and I could argue about important differences, and out of that argument might come not resolution or reconciliation, but at least an awareness of the consequences of going your way as opposed to mine. We don't even have that argument. That's what's so dismaying."

Democracy: Since September 11, 2001, George W. Bush and his top officials have aggressively advanced into the world under the banner of spreading not stability, but democracy (at cruise missile point). But they defined the freedom to vote (as the recent Palestinian elections showed) only as the freedom to vote as they wished the vote to go—and it generally didn't. Meanwhile, at home, the Republican Party was practicing an advanced form of gerrymandering, election financing, smear advertising, and voter suppression tactics that made a mockery of the electoral process. Everyone was to vote gloriously, but matters were to be prepared—geographically, financially, and in terms of public opinion—so that the vote would be nothing but a confirmation of what already was. What, after all, do you call it when, in what is considered the most wide-open election for the House of Representatives in more than a decade, only perhaps 40 to 50 of 435 seats are actually competitive (and that's considered extraordinary). Since 1998, 98 percent of House incumbents have won reelection, while in the last "open" election in 1994, when a Republican "revolution" took the House in what the *New York Times* calls "a seismic realignment," 91 percent of incumbents were nonetheless reelected.

Barbara Ehrenreich: "Today, we have this even larger federal government, more and more of it being war-related, surveillance-related. I mean it's gone beyond our wildest Clinton administration dreams. I think progressives can't just be seen as pro-big-government when big government has gotten so nasty. Katrina's a perfect example of how militarized the government has gotten even when it's supposedly trying to help people. The initial response of the government was a military one. When they finally got people down there, it was armed guards to protect the fancy stores and keep people in that convention center—at gunpoint."

"Brownie, you're doing a heck of a job!": And it has been a heck-of-a-job! In both the United States and Iraq, government has become ever less effective and meaningful; the plunderers have been let loose to "reconstruct" each country; the deepest fears have been released and deep divisions exacerbated.

We all know what a failed state is—one of those marginal lands where anarchy is the rule and government not the norm. To offer but two examples:

Afghanistan is a failed state, a narco-warlord-insurrectionary land where the government barely controls the capital, Kabul; Iraq is now a failed state, a civil-war-torn, insurrectionary land where the government does not even control the capital, Baghdad. But here's a term that isn't in our language: "Failed empire." It might be worth using in any ceremonies meant to bring words and reality closer together.

August 2007

26

PITCHING THE IMPERIAL REPUBLIC

Bonaparte and Bush on Deck

Juan Cole

French Egypt and American Iraq can be considered bookends on the history of modern imperialism in the Middle East. The Bush administration's already failed version of the conquest of Iraq is, of course, on everyone's mind; while the French conquest of Egypt, now more than two centuries past, is all too little remembered, despite having been led by Napoleon Bonaparte, whose career has otherwise hardly languished in obscurity. There are many eerily familiar resonances between the two misadventures, not least among them that both began with supreme arrogance and ended as fiascoes. Above all, the leaders of both occupations employed the same basic political vocabulary and rhetorical flimflammery, invoking the spirit of liberty, security, and democracy while largely ignoring the substance of these concepts.

The French general and the American president do not much resemble one another—except perhaps in the way the prospect of conquest in the Middle East appears to have put fire in their veins and in their unappealing tendency to believe their own propaganda (or at least to keep repeating it long after it became completely implausible). Both leaders invaded and occupied a major Arabic-speaking Muslim country; both harbored dreams of a "Greater Middle East"; both were surprised to find themselves enmeshed in long, bitter, debilitating guerrilla wars. Neither genuinely cared about grassroots democracy, but both found its symbols easy to invoke for gullible domestic publics. Substantial numbers of their new subjects quickly saw, however, that they faced occupations, not liberations.

My own work on Bonaparte's lost year in Egypt began in the mid-1990s, and I had completed about half of *Napoleon's Egypt: Invading the Middle East* before September 11, 2001. I had no way of knowing then that a book on such a distant, scholarly subject would prove an allegory for Bush's Iraq War. Nor did I guess that the United States would give old-style colonialism in the Middle East one last try, despite clear signs that the formerly colonized would no longer put up with such acts and had, in the years since World War Two, gained the means to resist them.

The Republic Militant Goes to War

In June 1798, as his enormous flotilla—36,000 soldiers, thousands of sailors, and hundreds of scientists on twelve ships of the line—swept inexorably toward the Egyptian coast, the young General Napoleon Bonaparte issued a grandiose communiqué to the bewildered and seasick troops he was about to march into the desert without canteens or reasonable supplies of water. He declared, "Soldiers! You are about to undertake a conquest, the effects of which on civilization and commerce are incalculable."

The prediction was as tragically inaccurate in its own way as the pronouncement George W. Bush issued some two centuries later, on May 1, 2003, also from the deck of a great ship of the line, the aircraft carrier USS *Abraham Lincoln*. "Today," he said, "we have the greater power to free a nation by breaking a dangerous and aggressive regime. With new tactics and precision weapons, we can achieve military objectives without directing violence against civilians."

Both men were convinced that their invasions were announcing new epochs in human history. Of the military vassals of the Ottoman empire who then ruled Egypt, Bonaparte predicted: "The Mameluke Beys who favor exclusively English commerce, whose extortions oppress our merchants, and who tyrannize over the unfortunate inhabitants of the Nile, a few days after our arrival will no longer exist."

Bonaparte's laundry list of grievances about them consisted of three charges. First, the beys were, in essence, enablers of France's primary enemy at that time, the British monarchy which sought to strangle the young

249

French republic in its cradle. Second, the rulers of Egypt were damaging France's own commerce by extorting taxes and bribes from its merchants in Cairo and Alexandria. Third, the Mamluks ruled tyrannically, having never been elected, and oppressed their subjects whom Bonaparte intended to liberate.

This holy trinity of justifications for imperialism—that the targeted state is collaborating with an enemy of the republic, is endangering the positive interests of the nation, and lacks legitimacy because its rule is despotic—would all be trotted out over the subsequent two centuries by a succession of European and American leaders whenever they wanted to go on the attack. One implication of these familiar rhetorical turns of phrase has all along been that democracies have a license to invade any country they please, assuming it has the misfortune to have an authoritarian regime.

George W. Bush, of course, hit the same highlights in his "mission accomplished" speech, while announcing on the *Abraham Lincoln* that "major combat operations" in Iraq "had ended." "The liberation of Iraq," he proclaimed, "is a crucial advance in the campaign against terror. We've removed an ally of al-Qaeda, and cut off a source of terrorist funding." He put Saddam Hussein's secular, Arab nationalist Baath regime and the radical Muslim terrorists of al-Qaeda under the sign of September 11th, insinuating that Iraq was allied with the primary enemy of the United States and so posed an urgent menace to its security. (In fact, captured Baath Party documents show that Saddam's fretting security forces, on hearing that Abu Musab al-Zarqawi had entered Iraq, put out an all points bulletin on him, imagining—not entirely correctly—that he had al-Qaeda links.) Likewise, Bush promised that Iraq's alleged "weapons of mass destruction" (which existed only in his own fevered imagination) would be tracked down, again implying that Iraq posed a threat to the interests and security of the US, just as Bonaparte had claimed that the Mamluks menaced France.

According to the President, Saddam's overthrown government had lacked legitimacy, while the new Iraqi government, to be established by a foreign power, would truly represent the conquered population. "We're helping to rebuild Iraq, where the dictator built palaces for himself, instead of hospitals and schools. And we will stand with the new leaders of Iraq," Bush pledged, "as they establish a government of, by, and for the Iraqi people." Bonaparte, too, established governing councils at the provincial and national levels, staffing them primarily with Sunni clergymen, declaring them more representative of the Egyptian people than the beys and emirs of the slave soldiery who had formerly ruled that province of the Ottoman empire.

Liberty as Tyranny

For a democracy to conduct a brutal military occupation against another country in the name of liberty seems, on the face of it, too contradictory to elicit more than hoots of derision at the hypocrisy of it all. Yet the militant republic, ready to launch aggressive war in the name of "democracy," is everywhere in modern history, despite the myth that democracies do not typically wage wars of aggression. Ironically, some absolutist regimes, like those of modern Iran, were remarkably peaceable, if left alone by their neighbors. In contrast, republican France invaded Belgium, Holland, Spain, Germany, Italy, and Egypt in its first decade (though it went on the offensive in part in response to Austrian and Prussian moves to invade France). The United States attacked Mexico, the Seminoles and other Native polities, Hawaii, the Spanish empire, the Philippines, Haiti, and the Dominican Republic in just the seven-plus decades from 1845 to the eve of the US entry into World War One.

Freedom and authoritarianism are nowadays taken to be stark antonyms, the provinces of heroes and monsters. Those closer to the birth of modern republics were comforted by no such moral clarity. In *Danton's Death*, the young Romantic playwright Georg Büchner depicted the radical French revolutionary and proponent of executing enemies of the Republic, Maximilien Robespierre, whipping up a Parisian crowd with the phrase "The revolutionary regime is the despotism of liberty against tyranny." And nowhere has liberty proved more oppressive than when deployed against a dictatorship abroad; for, as Büchner also had that famed "incorruptible" devotee of state terror observe, "In a Republic only republicans are citizens; Royalists and foreigners are enemies."

That sunlit May afternoon on the USS *Abraham Lincoln*, President Bush seconded Büchner's Robespierre. "Because of you," he exhorted the listening sailors of an aircraft carrier whose planes had just dropped 1.6 million pounds of ordnance on Iraq, "our nation is more secure. Because of you, the tyrant has fallen, and Iraq is free."

Security for the republic had already proved ample justification to launch a war the previous March, even though Iraq was a poor, weak, ramshackle Third World country, debilitated by a decade of sanctions imposed by the United Nations and the United States, without so much as potable drinking water or an air force. Similarly, the Mamluks of Egypt—despite the sky-high taxes and bribes they demanded of some French merchants—hardly constituted a threat to French security.

The overthrow of a tyrannical regime and the liberation of an oppressed people were constant refrains in the shipboard addresses of both the General and the President, who felt that the liberated owed them a debt of gratitude. Bonaparte lamented that the beys "tyrannize over the unfortunate inhabitants of the Nile," or, as one of his officers, Captain Horace Say, opined, "The people of Egypt were most wretched. How will they not cherish the liberty we are bringing them?" Similarly, Bush insisted, "Men and women in every culture need liberty like they need food and water and air. Everywhere that freedom arrives, humanity rejoices; and everywhere that freedom stirs, let tyrants fear."

Not surprisingly, expectations that the newly conquered would exhibit gratitude to their foreign occupiers cropped up repeatedly in the dispatches and letters of men on the spot who advocated a colonial forward policy. President Bush put this dramatically in January 2007, long after matters had not proceeded as expected: "We liberated that country from a tyrant. I think the Iraqi people owe the American people a huge debt of gratitude. That's the problem here in America: they wonder whether or not there is a gratitude level that's significant enough in Iraq."

Liberty in this two-century-old rhetorical tradition, moreover, was more than just a matter of rights and the rule of law. Proponents of various forms of liberal imperialism saw tyranny as a source of poverty, since arbitrary rulers could just usurp property at will and so make economic activity risky, as well as opening the public to crushing and arbitrary taxes that held back commerce. The French quartermaster François Bernoyer wrote of the Egyptian peasantry: "Their dwellings are adobe huts, which prosperity, the daughter of liberty, will now allow them to abandon." Bush took up the same theme on the *Abraham Lincoln*: "Where freedom takes hold, hatred gives way to hope. When freedom takes hold, men and women turn to the peaceful pursuit of a better life."

"Heads Must Roll"

In both eighteenth-century Egypt and twenty-first-century Iraq, the dreary reality on the ground stood as a reproach to, if not a wicked satire upon, these high-minded pronouncements. The French landed at the port of Alexandria on July 1, 1798. Two and a half weeks later, as the French army advanced along the Nile toward Cairo, a unit of General Jean Reynier's division met opposition from 1,800 villagers, many armed with muskets. Sergeant Charles François recalled a typical scene. After scaling the village walls and "firing into those crowds," killing "about 900 men," the French confiscated the villagers' livestock—"camels, donkeys, horses, eggs, cows, sheep"—then "finished burning the rest of the houses, or rather the huts, so as to provide a terrible object lesson to these half-savage and barbarous people."

On July 24, Bonaparte's Army of the Orient entered Cairo and he began reorganizing his new subjects. He grandiosely established an Egyptian Institute for the advancement of science and gave thought to reforming police, courts, and law. But terror lurked behind everything he did. He wrote General Jacques Menou, who commanded the garrison at the Mediterranean port of Rosetta, saying, "The Turks [Egyptians] can only be led by the greatest severity. Every day I cut off five or six heads in the streets of Cairo. . . . [T]o obey, for them, is to fear." (Mounting severed heads on poles for viewing by terrified passers-by was another method the French used in Egypt.)

That August, the Delta city of Mansura rose up against a small French garrison of about 120 men, chasing the Bluecoats into the countryside, tracking them down, and methodically killing all but two of them. In early September, the Delta village of Sonbat, inhabited in part by Bedouin of the western Dirn tribe, also rose up against the Europeans. Bonaparte instructed one of his generals, "Burn that village! Make a terrifying example of it." After the French army had indeed crushed the rebellious peasants and chased away the Bedouin, General Jean-Antoine Verdier reported back to Bonaparte with regard to Sonbat, "You ordered me to destroy this lair. Very well, it no longer exists."

The most dangerous uprisings confronting the French were, however, in Cairo. In October, much of the city mobilized to attack the more than 20,000 French troops occupying the capital. The revolt was especially fierce in the al-Husayn district, where the ancient al-Azhar madrassa (or seminary) trained 14,000 students, where the city's most sacred mosque stood, and where wealth was concentrated in the merchants and guilds of the Khan al-Khalili bazaar. At the same time, the peasants and Bedouin of the countryside around Cairo rose in rebellion, attacking the small garrisons that had been deployed to pacify them.

Bonaparte put down this Egyptian "revolution" with the utmost brutality, subjecting urban crowds to artillery barrages. He may have had as many rebels executed in the aftermath as were killed in the fighting. In the countryside, his officers launched concerted campaigns to decimate insurgent villages. At one point, the French are said to have brought nine hundred heads of slain insurgents to Cairo in bags and ostentatiously dumped them out before a crowd in one of that city's major squares to instill Cairenes with terror. (Two centuries later, the American public would come to associate decapitations by Muslim terrorists in Iraq with the ultimate in barbarism, but even then hundreds of such beheadings were not carried out at once.)

The American deployment of terror against the Iraqi population has, of course, dwarfed anything the French accomplished in Egypt by orders of magnitude. After four mercenaries, one a South African, were killed in Falluja in March 2004 and their bodies were desecrated, President Bush is alleged to have said "heads must roll" in retribution.

An initial attack on the city faltered when much of the Iraqi government threatened to resign and it was clear major civilian casualties would result. The crushing of the city was, however, simply put off until after the American presidential election in November 2004. When the assault, involving air power and artillery, came, it was devastating, damaging two-thirds of the city's buildings and turning much of its population into refugees. (As a result, thousands of Fallujans still live in the desert in tent villages with no access to clean water.)

Bush must have been satisfied. Heads had rolled. More often, faced with opposition, the US Air Force simply bombed already-occupied cities, a technology Bonaparte (mercifully) lacked. The strategy of ruling by terror and of swift, draconian punishment for acts of resistance was, however, the same in both cases.

The British sank much of the French fleet on August 1, 1798, marooning Bonaparte and his troops in their newly conquered land. In the spring of

1799, the French army tried—and failed—to break out through Syria, after which Bonaparte himself chose the better part of valor. He slipped out of Egypt late that summer, returning to France. There, he would swiftly stage a coup and come to power as First Consul, which would give him the opportunity to hone his practice of bringing freedom to other countries— this time in Europe. By 1801, joint British and Ottoman forces had defeated the French in Egypt; the French troops were transported back to their country on British vessels. This first Western invasion of the Middle East in modern times had ended in serial disasters that Bonaparte would misrepresent to the French public as a series of glorious triumphs.

Ending the Era of Liberal Imperialism

Between 1801 and 2003 stretched endless decades in which colonialism proved a plausible strategy for European powers in the Middle East, including the French enterprise in Algeria (1830–1962) and the British veiled protectorate over Egypt (1882–1922). In these years, European militaries and their weaponry were so advanced, and the means of resistance to which Arab peasants had access were so limited, that colonial governments could be imposed.

That imperial moment passed with celerity after World War Two, in part because the masses of the Third World joined political parties, learned to read, and—with how-to-do-it examples all around them—began to mount political resistance to foreign occupations of every sort. While the twenty-first-century American arsenal has many fancy, exceedingly destructive toys in it, nothing has changed with regard to the ability of colonized peoples to network socially and, sooner or later, push any foreign occupying force out.

Bonaparte and Bush failed because both launched their operations at moments when Western military and technological superiority was not assured. While Bonaparte's army had better artillery and muskets, the Egyptians had a superb cavalry and their old muskets were serviceable enough for purposes of sniping at the enemy. They also had an ally with advanced weaponry and the desire to use it—the British navy.

In 2007, the high-tech US military—as had been true in Vietnam in the 1960s and 1970s, as was true for the Soviets in Afghanistan in the 1980s— is still vulnerable to guerrilla tactics and effective low-tech weapons of resistance such as roadside bombs. Even more effective has been the guerrillas' social warfare, their success in making Iraq ungovernable through the promotion of clan and sectarian feuds, through targeted bombings and other attacks, and through sabotage of the Iraqi infrastructure.

From the time of Bonaparte to that of Bush, the use of the rhetoric of liberty versus tyranny, of uplift versus decadence, appears to have been a constant among imperialists from republics—and has remained domestically effective in rallying support for colonial wars. The despotism (but also the weakness) of the Mamluks and of Saddam Hussein proved sirens practically calling out for Western interventions. According to the rhetoric of liberal imperialism, tyrannical regimes are always at least potentially threats to the Republic, and so can always be fruitfully overthrown in favor of rule by a Western military. After all, that military is invariably imagined as closer to liberty since it serves an elected government. (Intervention is even easier to justify if the despots can be portrayed, however implausibly, as allied with an enemy of the republic.)

For both Bush and Bonaparte, the genteel diction of liberation, rights, and prosperity served to obscure or justify a major invasion and occupation of a Middle Eastern land, involving the unleashing of slaughter and terror against its people. Military action would leave towns destroyed, families displaced, and countless dead. Given the ongoing carnage in Iraq, President Bush's boast that, with "new tactics and precision weapons, we can achieve military objectives without directing violence against civilians," now seems not just hollow but macabre. The equation of a foreign military occupation with liberty and prosperity is, in the cold light of day, no less bizarre than the promise of war with virtually no civilian casualties.

It is no accident that many of the rhetorical strategies employed by George W. Bush originated with Napoleon Bonaparte, a notorious spinmeister and confidence man. At least Bonaparte looked to the future, seeing clearly the coming breakup of the Ottoman empire and the likelihood that European powers would be able to colonize its provinces. Bonaparte's failure in Egypt did not forestall decades of French colonial success in Algeria and Indochina, even if that era of imperial triumph could not, in the end, be sustained in the face of the political and social awakening of the colonized. Bush's neocolonialism, on the other hand, swam against the tide of history, and its failure is all the more criminal for having been so predictable.

May 2007

27

WORDS IN A TIME OF WAR

Taking the Measure of the First Rhetoric-Major President

Mark Danner*

When my assistant greeted me, a number of weeks ago, with the news that I had been invited to deliver the commencement address to the Department of Rhetoric, I thought it was a bad joke. There is a sense, I'm afraid, that being invited to deliver The Speech to students of rhetoric is akin to being asked out for a romantic evening by a porn star: whatever prospect you might have of pleasure is inevitably dampened by performance anxiety—the suspicion that your efforts, however enthusiastic, will inevitably be judged according to stern professional standards. A daunting prospect.

The only course, in both cases, is surely to plunge boldly ahead. And that means, first of all, saluting the family members gathered here, and in particular you, the parents.

Dear parents, I welcome you today to your moment of triumph. For if a higher education is about acquiring the skills and knowledge that allow one to comprehend and thereby get on in the world—and I use "get on in the world" in the very broadest sense—well then, oh esteemed parents, it is your children, not those boringly practical business majors and pre-meds

* This was originally a commencement address given to graduates of the Department of Rhetoric at Zellerbach Hall, University of California, Berkeley, on May 10, 2007.

your sanctimonious friends have sired, who have chosen with unerring grace and wisdom the course of study that will best guide them in this very strange polity of ours. For our age, ladies and gentlemen, is truly the Age of Rhetoric.

Now I turn to you, my proper audience, the graduating students of the Department of Rhetoric of 2007, and I salute you most heartily. In making the choice you have, you confirmed that you understand something intrinsic, something indeed . . . intimate about this age we live in. Perhaps that should not surprise us. After all, you have spent your entire undergraduate years during time of war—and what a very strange wartime it has been.

When most of you arrived on this campus, in September 2003, the rhetorical construction known as the War on Terror was already two years old and that very real war to which it gave painful birth, the war in Iraq, was just hitting its half-year mark. Indeed, the Iraq War had already ended once, in that great victory scene on the USS *Abraham Lincoln* off the coast of San Diego, where the President, clad jauntily in a flight suit, had swaggered across the flight deck and, beneath a banner famously marked "Mission Accomplished," had declared: "Major combat operations in Iraq have ended. In the battle of Iraq, the United States and our allies have prevailed."

Of the great body of rich material encompassed by my theme today— "Words in a Time of War"—surely those words of George W. Bush must stand as among the era's most famous, and most rhetorically unstable. For whatever they may have meant when the President uttered them on that sunny afternoon of May 1, 2003, they mean something quite different today, almost exactly four years later. The President has lost control of those words, as of so much else.

At first glance, the grand spectacle of May 1, 2003 fits handily into the history of the pageantries of power. Indeed, with its banners and ranks of cheering, uniformed extras gathered on the stage of that vast aircraft carrier— a stage, by the way, that had to be turned in a complicated maneuver so that the skyline of San Diego, a few miles off, would not be glimpsed by the television audience—the event and its staging would have been quite familiar to, and no doubt envied by, the late Leni Riefenstahl (who, as filmmaker to the Nazis, had no giant aircraft carriers to play with). Though vast and impressive, the May 1 extravaganza was a propaganda event of a traditional sort, intended to bind the country together in a second precise image of victory—the first being the pulling down of Saddam's statue in

Baghdad, also staged—an image that would fit neatly into campaign ads for the 2004 election. The President was the star, the sailors and airmen and their enormous dreadnought were props in his extravaganza.

However ambitiously conceived, these were all very traditional techniques, familiar to any fan of Riefenstahl's famous film spectacular of the 1934 Nuremberg rally, *Triumph of the Will*. As trained rhetoricians, however, you may well have noticed something different here, a slightly familiar flavor just beneath the surface. If ever there was a need for a "disciplined grasp" of the "symbolic and institutional dimensions of discourse"—as your Rhetoric Department's website puts it—surely it is now. For we have today an administration that not only is radical—unprecedentedly so—in its attitudes toward rhetoric and reality, toward words and things, but is willing, to our great benefit, to state this attitude clearly.

I give you my favorite quotation from the Bush administration, put forward by the proverbial "unnamed administration official" and published in the *New York Times* magazine by the fine journalist Ron Suskind in October 2004. Here, in Suskind's recounting, is what that "unnamed administration official" told him:

> The aide said that guys like me were "in what we call the reality-based community," which he defined as people who "believe that solutions emerge from your judicious study of discernible reality." I nodded and murmured something about Enlightenment principles and empiricism. He cut me off. "That's not the way the world really works anymore," he continued. "We're an empire now, and when we act, we create our own reality. And while you're studying that reality—judiciously, as you will—we'll act again, creating other new realities, which you can study too, and that's how things will sort out. We're history's actors . . . . and you, all of you, will be left to just study what we do."

I must admit to you that I love that quotation; indeed, with your permission, I would like hereby to nominate it for inscription over the door of the Rhetoric Department, akin to Dante's welcome above the gates of Hell: "Abandon hope, all ye who enter here."

Both admonitions have an admirable bluntness. These words from "Bush's Brain"—for the unnamed official speaking to Suskind seems to have been none other than the selfsame architect of the aircraft carrier moment, Karl Rove, who bears that pungent nickname—these words sketch out with breathtaking frankness a radical view in which power frankly determines reality, and rhetoric, the science of flounces and folderols, follows meekly and subserviently in its train. Those in the "reality-based community"— those such as we—are figures a mite pathetic, for we have failed to realize the singular new principle of the new age: Power has made reality its bitch.

Given such sweeping claims for power, it is hard to expect much respect for truth, or perhaps it should be "truth"—in quotation marks—for when you can alter reality at will, why pay much attention to the idea of fidelity in describing it? What faith, after all, is owed to the bitch that is wholly in your power, a creature of your own creation?

Of course I should not say "those such as we" here, for you, dear graduates of the Rhetoric Department of 2007, you are somewhere else altogether. This is, after all, old hat to you; the line of thinking you imbibe with your daily study, for it is present in striking fashion in Foucault and many other intellectual titans of these last decades—though even they might have been nonplussed to find it so crisply expressed by a finely tailored man sitting in the White House. Though we in the "reality-based community" may just now be discovering it, you have known for years the presiding truth of our age, which is that the object has become subject and we have a fanatical follower of Foucault in the Oval Office. Graduates, let me say it plainly and incontrovertibly: George W. Bush is the first rhetoric-major president.

The Dirtied Face of Power

I overstate perhaps, but only for a bit of—I hope—permitted rhetorical pleasure. Let us gaze a moment at the signposts of the history of the present age. In January 2001, the Rhetoric-Major President came to power after a savage and unprecedented electoral battle that was decided not by the ballots of American voters—for of these he had 540,000 fewer than his Democrat rival—but by the votes of Supreme Court Justices, where Republicans prevailed 5 to 4, making George W. Bush the first president in more than a century to come to the White House with fewer votes than those of his opponent.

In this singular condition, and with a Senate precisely divided between parties, President Bush proceeded to behave as if he had won an overwhelming electoral victory, demanding tax cuts greater and more regressive than those he had outlined in the campaign. And despite what would seem to have been debilitating political weakness, the President shortly achieved this first success in "creating his own reality." To act as if he had overwhelming political power would mean he *had* overwhelming political power.

This, however, was only the overture of the vast symphonic work to come, a work heralded by the huge, clanging, echoing cacophony of 9/11. We are so embedded in its age that it is easy to forget the stark, overwhelming shock of it: nineteen young men with box cutters seized enormous transcontinental airliners and *brought those towers down*. In an age in which we have become accustomed to two, three, four, five suicide attacks in a single day—often these multiple attacks in Baghdad don't even make the front pages of our papers—it is easy to forget the blunt, scathing shock of it, the impossible image of the second airliner disappearing into the great office tower, almost weirdly absorbed by it, and emerging, transformed into a great yellow and red blossom of flame, on the other side; and then, half an hour later, the astonishing flowering collapse of the hundred-story structure, transforming itself, in a dozen seconds, from mighty tower to great plume of heaven-reaching white smoke.

The image remains, will always remain, with us; for truly the weapon that day was not box cutters in the hands of nineteen young men, nor airliners at their command. The weapon that day was the television set. It was the television set that made the image possible, and inextinguishable. If terror is first of all a way of talking—the propaganda of the deed, indeed—then that day the television was the indispensable conveyer of the conversation: the recruitment poster for fundamentalism, the only symbolic arena in which America's weakness and vulnerability could be dramatized on an adequate scale. Terror—as Menachem Begin, the late Israeli prime minister and the successful terrorist who drove the British from Mandate Palestine, remarked in his memoirs—terror is about destroying the prestige of the imperial regime; terror is about "dirtying the face of power."

President Bush and his lieutenants surely realized this and it is in that knowledge, I believe, that we can find the beginning of the answer to one of the more intriguing puzzles of these last few years: What exactly lay at the root of the almost fanatical determination of administration officials to attack and occupy Iraq? It was, obviously, the classic "overdetermined" decision, a tangle of fear, in the form of those infamous weapons of mass destruction; of imperial ambition, in the form of the neoconservative project to "remake the Middle East"; and of realpolitik, in the form of the "vital interest" of securing the industrial world's oil supplies.

In the beginning, though, was the felt need on the part of our nation's leaders—men and women so worshipful of the idea of power and its ability to remake reality itself—to restore the nation's prestige, to wipe clean that dirtied face. Henry Kissinger, a confidant of the President, when asked by Bush's speechwriter why he had supported the Iraq War, responded: "Because Afghanistan was not enough." The radical Islamists, he said, want to humiliate us. "And we need to humiliate them." In other words, the presiding image of the War on Terror—the burning towers collapsing on the television screen—had to be supplanted by another, the image of American tanks rumbling proudly through a vanquished Arab capital. It is no accident that Secretary of Defense Donald Rumsfeld, at the first "war cabinet" meeting at Camp David the Saturday after the 9/11 attacks, fretted over the "lack of targets" in Afghanistan and wondered whether we "shouldn't do Iraq first." He wanted to see those advancing tanks marching across our television screens, and soon.

In the end, of course, the enemy preferred not to fight with tanks, though they were perfectly happy to have us do so, the better to destroy these multi-million-dollar anachronisms with so-called IEDs (improvised explosive devices), worth a few hundred bucks apiece. This is called asymmetrical warfare, and one should note here with some astonishment how successful it has been these last half-dozen years. In the post-Cold War world, after all, as one neoconservative theorist explained shortly after 9/11, the United States was enjoying a rare "uni-polar moment." It deployed the greatest military and economic power the world has ever seen. It spent more on its weapons, its army, navy, and air force, than the rest of the world combined.

It was the assumption of this so-called preponderance that lay behind the philosophy of power enunciated by Bush's Brain and that led to an attitude toward international law and alliances that is, in my view, quite unprecedented in American history. That radical attitude is brilliantly encapsulated in a single sentence drawn from the National Security Strategy of the United States of 2003: "Our strength as a nation-state will continue to be challenged by those who employ a strategy of the weak using international *fora*, judicial processes and terrorism." Let me repeat that little troika of "weapons of the weak": international *fora* (meaning the United Nations and like institutions), judicial processes (meaning courts, domestic and international), and . . . terrorism. This strange gathering, put forward by the government of the United States, stems from the idea that power is, in fact, everything. In such a world, courts—indeed, law itself—can only limit the power of the most powerful state. Wielding preponderant power, what need has it for law? The latter must be, by definition, a weapon of the weak. The most powerful state, after all, *makes* reality.

Asymmetric Warfare and Dumb Luck

Now, here's an astonishing fact: fewer than half a dozen years into this "unipolar moment," the greatest military power in the history of the world stands on the brink of defeat in Iraq. Its vastly expensive and all-powerful military has been humbled by a congeries of secret organizations fighting mainly by means of suicide vests, car bombs and improvised explosive devices—all of them cheap, simple, and effective, indeed so effective that these techniques now comprise a kind of ready-made insurgency kit freely available on the Internet and spreading in popularity around the world, most obviously to Afghanistan, that land of few targets.

As I stand here, one of our two major political parties advocates the withdrawal—gradual, or otherwise—of American combat forces from Iraq, and many in the other party are feeling the increasing urge to go along. As for the Bush administration's broader War on Terror, as the State Department detailed recently in its annual report on the subject, the number of terrorist attacks worldwide has never been higher, nor have such attacks ever been more effective. True, al-Qaeda has not attacked again within the United States. They do not need to. They are alive and flourishing. Indeed, it might even be said that they are winning. For their goal, despite the rhetoric of the Bush administration, was not simply to kill Americans but, by challenging the United States in this spectacular fashion, to recruit great numbers to their cause and to move their insurgency into the heart of the Middle East. And all these things they have done.

How could such a thing have happened? In their choice of enemy, one might say that the terrorists of al-Qaeda had a great deal of dumb luck, for they attacked a country run by an administration that had a radical conception of the potency of power. At the heart of the principle of asymmetric warfare—

al-Qaeda's kind of warfare—is the notion of using your opponent's power against him. How does a small group of insurgents without an army, or even heavy weapons, defeat the greatest conventional military force the world has ever known? How do you defeat such an army if you don't have an army? Well, you borrow your enemy's. And this is precisely what al-Qaeda did. Using the classic strategy of provocation, the group tried to tempt the superpower into its adopted homeland. The original strategy behind the 9/11 attacks—apart from humbling the superpower and creating the greatest recruiting poster the world had ever seen—was to lure the United States into a ground war in Afghanistan, where the one remaining superpower (like the Soviet Union before it) was to be trapped, stranded, and destroyed. It was to prepare for this war that Osama bin Laden arranged for the assassination, two days before 9/11—via bombs secreted in the video cameras of two terrorists posing as reporters—of the Afghan Northern Alliance leader, Ahmed Shah Massood, who would have been the United States's most powerful ally.

Well aware of the Soviets' Afghanistan debacle—after all, the US had supplied most of the weapons that defeated the Soviets there—the Bush administration tried to avoid a quagmire by sending plenty of air support, lots of cash, and, most important, very few troops, relying instead on its Afghan allies. But if bin Laden was disappointed in this, he would soon have a far more valuable gift: the invasion of Iraq, a country that, unlike Afghanistan, was at the heart of the Middle East and central to Arab concerns, and, what's more, a nation that sat squarely on the critical Sunni–Shia divide, a potential ignition switch for al-Qaeda's great dream of a regional civil war. It is on that precipice that we find ourselves teetering today.

Critical to this strange and unlikely history were the administration's peculiar ideas about power and its relation to reality—and beneath that a familiar imperial attitude, if put forward in a strikingly crude and harsh form: "We're an empire now and when we act we create our own reality." Power, untrammeled by law or custom; power, unlimited by the so-called weapons of the weak, be they international institutions, courts, or terrorism—power can remake reality. It is no accident that one of Karl Rove's heroes is President William McKinley, who stood at the apex of America's first imperial moment, and led the country into a glorious colonial adventure in the Philippines that was also meant to be the military equivalent of a stroll in the park and that, in the event, led to several years of bloody insurgency—an insurgency, it bears noticing, that was only finally put down with the help of the extensive use of torture, most notably waterboarding, which has made its reappearance in the imperial battles of our own times.

If we are an empire now, as Mr Rove says, perhaps we should add, as he might not, that we are also a democracy, and therein, rhetoric graduates of 2007, lies the rub. A democratic empire, as even the Athenians discovered, is an odd beast, like one of those mythological creatures born equally of lion and bird, or man and horse. If one longs to invade Iraq to restore the empire's prestige, one must convince the democracy's people of the necessity of such a step. Herein lies the pathos of the famous weapons-of-mass-destruction issue, which has become a kind of synecdoche for the entire lying mess of the past few years. The center stage of our public life is now dominated by a simple melodrama: Bush wanted to invade Iraq; Bush told Americans that Iraq had weapons of mass destruction; Iraq did not have such weapons. Therefore Bush lied, and the war was born of lies and deception.

I hesitate to use that most overused of rhetorical terms—irony—to describe the emergence of this narrative at the center of our national life, but nonetheless, and with apologies: It is ironic. The fact is that officials of the Bush administration *did* believe there were weapons of mass destruction in Iraq, though they vastly exaggerated the evidence they had to prove it and, even more, the threat that those weapons might have posed, had they been there. In doing this, the officials believed themselves to be "framing a guilty man"; that is, like cops planting a bit of evidence in the murderer's car, they believed their underlying case was true; they just needed to dramatize it a bit to make it clear and convincing to the public. What matter, once the tanks were rumbling through Baghdad and the war was won? Weapons would be found, surely; and if only a few were found, who would care? By then, the United States military would have created a new reality.

I have often had a daydream about this. I see a solitary Army private—a cook perhaps, or a quartermaster—breaking the padlock on some forgotten warehouse on an Iraqi military base, poking about and finding a few hundred, even a few thousand, old artillery shells, leaking chemicals. These shells—forgotten, unusable—might have dated from the time of the First Gulf War, when Iraq unquestionably possessed chemical munitions. (Indeed, in the 1980s, the United States had supplied targeting intelligence that helped the

Iraqis use them effectively against the Iranians.) And though now they had been forgotten, leaking, unusable, still they would indeed be weapons of mass destruction—to use the misleading and absurd construction that has headlined our age—and my solitary cook or quartermaster would be a hero, for he would have, all unwittingly, "proved" the case.

My daydream could easily have come to pass. Why not? It is nigh unto miraculous that the Iraqi regime, even with the help of the United Nations, managed so thoroughly to destroy or remove its once-existing stockpile. And if my private had found those leaky old shells what would have been changed thereby? Yes, the administration could have pointed to them in triumph and trumpeted the proven character of Saddam's threat. So much less embarrassing than the "weapons of mass destruction program related activities" that the administration still doggedly asserts were "discovered." But, in fact, the underlying calculus would have remained: that, in the months leading up to the war, the administration relentlessly exaggerated the threat Saddam posed to the United States and relentlessly understated the risk the United States would run in invading and occupying Iraq. And it would have remained true and incontestable that—as the quaintly fact-bound British foreign secretary put it eight months before the war, in a secret British cabinet meeting made famous by the so-called Downing Street Memo—"the case [for attacking Iraq] was thin. Saddam was not threatening his neighbors and his WMD capability was less than that of Libya, North Korea or Iran."

Which is to say, the weapons were a rhetorical prop and, satisfying as it has been to see the administration beaten about the head with that prop, we forget this underlying fact at our peril. The issue was never whether the weapons were there or not; indeed, had the weapons really been the issue, why could the administration not have let the UN inspectors take the time to find them (as, of course, they never would have)? The administration needed, wanted, had to have, the Iraq war. The weapons were but a symbol, the necessary *casus belli*, what Hitchcock called the MacGuffin—that glowing mysterious object in the suitcase in Quentin Tarantino's *Pulp Fiction*: that is, a satisfyingly concrete object on which to fasten a rhetorical or narrative end, in this case a war to restore American prestige, project its power, remake the Middle East.

The famous weapons were chosen to play this leading role for "bureaucratic reasons," as Paul Wolfowitz, then Deputy Secretary of Defense and until quite recently the unhappy president of the World Bank, once remarked to a lucky journalist. Had a handful of those weapons been found, the underlying truth would have remained: Saddam posed nowhere remotely near the threat to the United States that would have justified running the enormous metaphysical risk that a war of choice with Iraq posed. Of course, when you are focused on magical phrases like "preponderant power" and "the uni-polar moment," matters like numbers of troops at your disposal—and the simple fact that the United States had too few to sustain a long-term occupation of a country the size of Iraq—must seem mundane indeed.

Imperial Words and the Reality-based Universe

I must apologize to you, Rhetoric Class of 2007. Ineluctably, uncontrollably, I find myself slipping back into the dull and unimaginative language of the reality-based community. It must grate a bit on your ears. After all, we live in a world in which the presumption that we were misled into war, that the Bush officials knew there were no weapons and touted them anyway, has supplanted the glowing, magical image of the weapons themselves. It is a presumption of great use to those regretful souls who once backed the war so fervently, not least a number of Democratic politicians we all could name, as well as many of my friends in the so-called liberal punditocracy who now need a suitable excuse for their own rashness, gullibility, and stupidity. For this, Bush's mendacity seems perfectly sized and ready to hand.

There is, however, full enough of that mendacity, without artificially adding to the stockpile. Indeed, all around us we've been hearing these last many months the sound of ice breaking, as the accumulated frozen scandals of this administration slowly crack open to reveal their queasy secrets. And yet the problem, of course, is that they are not secrets at all. One of the most painful principles of our age is that scandals are doomed to be revealed— and to remain stinking there before us, unexcised, unpunished, unfinished.

If this Age of Rhetoric has a tragic symbol, then surely this is it: the frozen scandal, doomed to be revealed, and revealed, and revealed, in a never-ending torture familiar to the rock-bound Prometheus and his poor half-eaten liver. A full three years ago, the photographs from Abu Ghraib were broadcast by CBS on *Sixty Minutes II* and published by Seymour Hersh in the *New Yorker*; nearly as far back I wrote a book entitled *Torture and*

Truth, made up largely of Bush administration documents that detailed the decision to use "extreme interrogation techniques" or—in the First President of Rhetoric's phrase—"an alternative set of procedures" on prisoners in the War on Terror.

He used this phrase in September 2006 in a White House speech kicking off the midterm election campaign, at a time when accusing the Democrats of evidencing a continued softness on terror—and a lamentable unwillingness to show the needed harshness in "interrogating terrorists"—seemed a winning electoral strategy. And indeed Democrats seemed fully to agree, for they warily elected not to filibuster the Military Commissions Act of October 2006, which arguably made many elements of the "alternative sets of procedures" explicitly legal. And Democrats did win both houses of Congress, a victory perhaps owed in part to their refusal to block Bush's interrogation law. Who can say? What we can say is that if torture today remains a "scandal," a "crisis," it is a crisis in that same peculiar way that crime or AIDS or global warming are crises: that is, they are all things we have learned to live with.

Perhaps the commencement address to the Department of Rhetoric at the University of California at Berkeley is not the worst of places to call for a halt to this spinning merry-go-round. I know it will brand me forever a member of the reality-based community if I suggest that the one invaluable service the new Democratic Congress can provide all Americans is a clear accounting of how we came to find ourselves in this present time of war: an authorized version, as it were, which is, I know, the most pathetically retrograde of ideas.

This would require that people like Mr Wolfowitz, Mr Rumsfeld, and many others be called before a select, bipartisan committee of Congress to tell us what, in their view, really happened. I squirm with embarrassment putting forward such a pathetically unsophisticated notion, but failing at least the minimally authorized version that Congress could provide, we will find ourselves forever striving—by chasing down byways like the revelation of the identity of Valerie Plame, or the question of whether or not George Tenet bolstered his "slam dunk" exclamation in the Oval Office with an accompanying Michael Jordan-like leap—to understand how precisely decisions were made between September 11, 2001 and the invasion of Iraq eighteen months later.

Don't worry, though, rhetoric graduates: such a proposal has about it the dusty feel of past decades; it is as "reality-based" as can be and we are unlikely to see it in our time. What we are likely to see is the ongoing collapse of our first Rhetoric-Major President, who, with fewer than one American in three now willing to say they approve of the job he is doing, is seeing his power ebb by the day. Tempting as it is, I will urge you not to draw too many overarching conclusions from his fate. He has had, after all, a very long run—and I say this with the wonder that perhaps can only come from having covered both the 2000 and 2004 election campaigns from Florida, and the Iraq War.

I last visited that war in December 2006, when Baghdad was cold and gray and I spent a good deal of time drawing black Xs through the sources listed in my address book, finding them, one after another, either departed or dead. Baghdad seemed a sad and empty place, with even its customary traffic jams gone, and the periodic, resonating explosions barely attracting glances from those few Iraqis to be found on the streets.

How, in these "words in a time of war," can I convey to you the reality of that place at this time? Let me read to you a bit of an account from a young Iraqi woman of how that war has touched her and her family, drawn from a newsroom blog. The words may be terrible and hard to bear, but—for those of you who have made such a determined effort to learn to read and understand—this is the most reality I could find to tell you. This is what lies behind the headlines and the news reports and it is as it is.

We were asked to send the next of kin to whom the remains of my nephew, killed on Monday in a horrific explosion downtown, can be handed over . . . So we went, his mum, his other aunt and I . . .

When we got there, we were given his remains. And remains they were. From the waist down was all they could give us. "We identified him by the cell phone in his pants pocket. If you want the rest, you will just have to look for yourselves. We don't know what he looks like."

. . . We were led away, and before long a foul stench clogged my nose and I retched. With no more warning we came to a clearing that was probably an inside garden at one time; all round it were patios and rooms with large-pane windows to catch the evening breeze Baghdad is renowned for. But now it had become a slaughterhouse, only instead of cattle, all around were human bodies. On this side, complete bodies; on that side, halves, and everywhere body parts.

We were asked what we were looking for; "upper half" replied my companion, for I was rendered speechless. "Over there." We looked for our boy's broken body between tens of other boys' remains; with our bare hands sifting them and turning them.

Millennia later we found him, took both parts home, and began the mourning ceremony.

The foregoing were words from an Iraqi family, who find themselves as far as they can possibly be from the idea that, when they act, they create their own reality—that they are, as Bush's Brain put it, "history's actors." The voices you heard come from history's objects, and we must ponder who the subjects are, who exactly is acting upon them.

The car bomb that so changed their lives was not set by Americans; indeed, young Americans even now are dying to prevent such things. I have known a few of these young Americans. Perhaps you have as well, perhaps they are in the circles of your family or of your friends. I remember one of them, a young lieutenant, a beautiful young man with a puffy, sleepy face, looking at me when I asked whether or not he was scared when he went out on patrol—this was October 2003, as the insurgency was exploding. I remember him smiling a moment and then saying, with evident pity for a reporter's lack of understanding, "This is war. We shoot, they shoot. We shoot, they shoot. Some days they shoot better than we do." He was patient in his answer, smiling sleepily in his young beauty, and I could tell he regarded me as from another world, a man who could never understand the world in which he lived. Three days after our interview, an explosion near Falluja killed him.

Contingency, accidents, the metaphysical ironies that seem to stitch history together like a lopsided quilt—all these have no place in the imperial vision. A perception of one's self as "history's actor" leaves no place for them. But they exist and it is invariably others, closer to the ground, who see them, know them, and suffer their consequences.

You have chosen a path that will let you look beyond the rhetoric that you have studied and into the heart of those consequences. Of all people you have chosen to learn how to see the gaps and the loose stitches and the remnant threads. Ours is a grim age, this Age of Rhetoric, still infused with the remnant perfume of imperial dreams. You have made your study in a propitious time, oh graduates, and that bold choice may well bring you pain, for you have devoted yourselves to seeing what it is that stands before you. If clear sight were not so painful, many more would elect to have it. Today, you do not conclude but begin: today you commence. My blessings upon you, and my gratitude to you for training yourself to see. Reality, it seems, has caught up with you.

VII

BRINGING IT ALL BACK HOME

September 2005

28

CORPORATIONS OF THE WHIRLWIND

The Reconstruction of New Oraq

Nick Turse and Tom Engelhardt

At times it is hard to ignore the comparisons between Baghdad (where I was less than a month ago and have spent more of the last two years) and New Orleans: the anarchy, the looting, some of it purely for survival, some of it purely opportunistic. We watched a flatbed truck drive by, a man on the back with an M-16 looking up on the roofs for snipers, as is common in Iraq. Private security contractors were stationed outside the Royal St Charles Hotel; when asked if things were getting pretty wild around the area, one of them replied, "Nope. It's pretty Green Zone here."

David Enders, "Surviving New Orleans," *Mother Jones* online

In the decade before September 11, 2001, "globalization," a word now largely missing-in-action, was on everyone's lips and we constantly heard about what a small, small world this really was. In the aftermath of Hurricane Katrina, that global smallness has grown positively claustrophobic and particularly predatory. Iraq and New Orleans now seem to be morphing into a single entity, New Oraq, to be devoured by the same limited set of corporations, let loose and overseen by the same small set of Bush administration officials. In George Bush's new world of globalization, first comes the destruction and only then does one sit down at the planetary table to sup.

In recent weeks, news has been seeping out of Iraq that the "reconstruction" of that country is petering out, because the money is largely gone. According to American officials, reported T. Christian Miller of the *Los Angeles Times* last week, "The US will halt construction work on some water and power plants in Iraq because it is running out of money for projects." A variety of such reconstruction projects crucial to the everyday lives of Iraqis, the British *Guardian* informs us, are now "grinding to a halt" as "plans to overhaul the country's infrastructure have been downsized, postponed or abandoned because the $24bn budget approved by Congress has been dwarfed by the scale of the task."

Water and sanitation projects have been particularly hard hit, while staggering sums, once earmarked for reconstruction, are being shunted to private security firms whose hired guns are assigned to guard the projects that can't be done. With funds growing scarce, various corporations closely connected to the Bush administration, having worked the Iraqi disaster for all it was worth (largely under no-bid, cost-plus contracts), are now looking New Orleans–ward.

Ground Zero Iraq

The American occupation of Iraq began in April 2003 with a prolonged moment of chaos that set the stage for everything to follow. In the first days after Baghdad fell, the occupying army stood by idly (guarding only the Oil Ministry and the intelligence services) while Iraqi looters swept away the institutional, administrative, and cultural underpinnings of the country. The newly installed Coalition Provisional Authority (CPA), soon to be led by American viceroy L. Paul Bremer, followed up by promptly disbanding the only institution that remained half-standing, the Iraqi military. At the same time, a new American administration was set up inside the increasingly well-fortified and isolated Green Zone in Baghdad, staffed largely by Bush cronies. ("Neocon kindergarten" was the way some insiders derisively referred to the young Bush supporters sent out from Washington to staff the lower levels of the CPA for months at a time.)

The CPA then instituted a flat tax, abolished tariffs, swept away laws that might have prevented the foreign ownership of Iraqi companies, allowed the full repatriation of profits abroad, and threatened to reduce state-sponsored food and fuel subsidies. For Iraqis, this was more than just "shock and awe";

it was to be caught in the whirlwind. Call it Year Zero for Iraq or Ground Zero for the new Bush order. Iraq, stripped for action, was ready to be strip-mined—and it was then that Washington called in its crony corporations to "reconstruct" the land.

Leading the list was Kellogg, Brown & Root (KBR), a subsidiary of the energy firm Halliburton, the mega-corporation Vice President Dick Cheney once presided over. From providing fuel to building bases, doing kitchen duty to supplying laundry soap, it supported the newly privatized, stripped-down American military—and for that it "received more money from the US involvement in Iraq than any other contractor," a sum that has already crested ten billion dollars with no end in sight. The Bechtel Corporation, the San Francisco-based engineering firm, known at home for its staggering cost overruns on Boston's "Big Dig" and its especially close ties to the Republican Party, raked in almost $3 billion in Iraq reconstruction contracts just in the nine months after the fall of Saddam Hussein. Fluor Corporation, an Orange County, California-based firm that inked a joint $1.1 billion deal with a London company in 2004 for "construction services for water distribution and treatment systems in Iraq," was a winner; so was the Shaw Group Inc. which, in early 2004, opened a Baghdad office to support "an approximately $47 million task order in Iraq for facility upgrades, installation of utilities and other infrastructure improvements" and was also awarded a separate $88.7 million construction deal, among other contracts. Another successful bidder in the Iraq lottery was CH2M Hill, a Colorado-based company that, in a joint venture, took in a $28.5 million reconstruction contract in 2004 and teamed up with other contractors for a $12.7 million electrical power generation deal. These firms were joined at the table by other heavy-hitters and a dizzying array of smaller-fry American subcontractors, from the KBR-connected food service company Event Source to Bechtel's marine survey subcontractor Titan Maritime.

Over two years after the American superpower occupied Iraq and called in its reconstructors, however, the scorecard for "reconstruction" looked remarkably like one for deconstruction. The country was essentially looted and no one was left on guard, not even at the Oil Ministry. Money was spent profligately, and sometimes evidently simply pilfered. L. Paul Bremer himself reputedly had a slush fund of $600 million dollars in cash for which, according to Ed Harriman (who in the *London Review of Books* did a superb study of the various reports by US auditors on the ensuing mayhem), there was "no paperwork."

When Bremer left Baghdad in June 2004, the CPA had already run through $20 billion dollars in Iraqi funds, mostly generated by oil revenues and earmarked for "the benefit of the Iraqi people" (though only $300 million in US funds). Much of it seems to have gone to American companies for their various reconstruction tasks. US auditors, Harriman reports, "have so far referred more than a hundred contracts, involving billions of dollars paid to American personnel and corporations, for investigation and possible criminal prosecution." It was evidently a field day of malfeasance and—a particular signature of the Bush administration—lack of accountability. In the meantime, KBR was massively overcharging the Pentagon for all those privatized tasks the military no longer cared to do, while its officials were living the good life. (Typically, KBR's "tiger team" of accountants, sent out to Kuwait to check on company overcharges, stayed in a five-star hotel to the tune of $1 million in taxpayer money.)

The results we now know well. Electricity and oil production, for instance, still remain at or below the figures for the worst days of Saddam Hussein's embattled regime; and on that cleared land at Ground Zero Iraq, a fierce resistance movement rages, while, from Basra to Mosul, disappointment with and disapproval of the American occupiers only grows.

Now, these same corporations are being loosed on the southeastern United States on the same no–bid, cost-plus basis. Like Baghdad and much of Iraq, New Orleans and the Mississippi coast have just experienced "shock and awe"—Katrina's winds and waters, not US cruise missiles. With troops occupying New Orleans, the Bush administration-allied corporations of the whirlwind that feed off chaos and destruction are already moving in. In this sense, the next wave of chaos has, from their point of view, arrived like the proverbial cavalry, just in the nick of time.

Bringing the Post-war Home

As Reuters recently reported:

A slowing of reconstruction work in Iraq has freed up people for Fluor Corp. to begin rebuilding in the US Gulf Coast region after Hurricane Katrina, the big engineering and construction company's chairman and chief executive said on Friday. "Our rebuilding work in Iraq is slowing down and this has made some people available to respond to our work in Louisiana," Fluor chief Alan Boeckmann said in a telephone interview.

And Fluor responded in a thoroughly reasonable way—they put an experienced man on the job, sending their "senior project manager" in Iraq to Louisiana.

In fact, with Congress already making a $62 billion initial down payment on post-Katrina reconstruction work, the Bush administration has just given out its first six reconstruction contracts, five of them—could anyone be surprised?—to Iraqi reconstructors, including Fluor. Small world indeed. The Bush version of crony capitalism should perhaps be termed predatory capitalism, following as it does so closely in the wake of war and natural disaster much as camp followers used to trail armies, ready, in case of victory, to loot the baggage train of the enemy.

But let's pull back for a moment and try to reconstruct, however briefly, at least a modest picture of the massively interconnected world of the reconstructors. A good place to start is with George Bush's pal Joseph Allbaugh, a member of his "so-called iron triangle of trusted Texas cohorts." Allbaugh seems to display in his recent biography just about every linkage that makes New Oraq what it is clearly becoming. He ran the Bush presidential campaign of 2000; subsequently he was installed as the director of FEMA (which, in congressional testimony, he characterized as "an oversized entitlement program"), counseling (as Harold Meyerson of the *American Prospect* [September 8, 2005] pointed out recently) "states and cities to rely instead on 'faith-based organizations . . . like the Salvation Army and the Mennonite Disaster Service.' "

As at the Coalition Provisional Authority in Baghdad, so at FEMA in Washington, the larder of administrators would soon be stocked with second- and third-rate Bush supporters and cronies. Five of FEMA's top eight managers would, according to Spencer S. Hsu of the *Washington Post* (September 9, 2005), arrive with "virtually no experience in handling disasters," three of them "with ties to President Bush's 2000 campaign or to the White House advance operation." A "brain drain" of competent administrators followed as, like the Pentagon's, FEMA's focus turned to the war on terror, money was drained from natural-disaster work, and the agency was "privatized" with previously crucial activities outsourced to Bush-friendly corporations.

In March 2003, Allbaugh departed FEMA, putting the increasingly starved and downsized operation in the hands of Michael Brown, an old college buddy whose previous job had been overseeing the International Arabian Horse Association. Allbaugh then made his faith-based career choice; no, not to join the Salvation Army or the Mennonite Disaster Service. Instead he opted for what the Bush administration really believed in—both in Iraq and at home. He became a high-priced consultant/lobbyist, founding in the ensuing years three consulting firms. At Blackwell Fairbanks, LLC, he teamed up with Andrew Lundquist, who led the Dick Cheney task force that produced the administration's National Energy Policy, to "successfully represen[t] clients before the executive and legislative branches of the United States government." Then there was the Allbaugh Company through which he represents Halliburton's KBR as well as military-industrial powerhouse Northrop Grumman. Finally, there was New Bridge Strategies, LLC, where he serves as chairman and director. New Bridge Strategies bills itself as "a unique company that was created specifically with the aim of assisting clients to evaluate and take advantage of business opportunities in the Middle East following the conclusion of the US-led war in Iraq."

Not surprisingly, the firm's vice chairman and director, Ed Rogers (who, during the "2004 campaign cycle . . . made over 150 live TV news appearances defending and promoting the Bush administration"), also serves as vice chairman of the consulting firm Barbour, Griffith & Rogers, Inc. (which he founded with Haley Barbour, now the governor of storm-battered Mississippi); New Bridge's director, Lanny Griffith, who serves as the CEO of Barbour, Griffith & Rogers, "was national chairman for the Bush/Cheney Entertainment Task Force and coordinated entertainment for the 2001 Bush Inaugural." He was, typically enough, one of the 2004 Bush campaign's Rangers—an elite group of fundraisers, each of whom was responsible for gathering up over $200,000 for the President; New Bridge Strategies' Advisory Board member Jamal Daniel is "a Principal with Crest Investment Company," a firm co-chaired by the President's younger brother Neil.

In answer to critics who claimed that he and others were cashing in on their service to Bush and Cheney, Allbaugh responded, "I don't buy the 'revolving door' argument. This is America. We all have a right to make a living."

As president and CEO at Allbaugh Co. and assumedly as a former head of FEMA, not to say as close friend and mentor to FEMA's (now departed) head and as a presidential pal, Allbaugh found himself at the front of the Katrina disaster line, apparently pushing hard (although he denied it) for such companies as—you guessed it—KBR and the Shaw Group. By September 7, 2005 at the latest, unlike the administration, he was down in Louisiana surveying the damage along the Gulf Coast and the wreckage of the agency he once presided over, while directing his clients to the lucrative world of American disaster, now that the lucrative world of Iraqi disaster had been sucked reasonably dry.

Ground Zero New Orleans

On September 12, 2005, the *Wall Street Journal* reported, "FEMA and the Army Corps of Engineers have awarded six contracts, most for as much as $100 million, for recovery and rebuilding work." It should be of little surprise that the Shaw Group landed two of these $100 million deals (a FEMA contract to refurbish existing buildings and for other emergency housing tasks as well as an Army Corps of Engineers contract to aid recovery efforts, including pumping water from New Orleans). Others on the list included a who's who of favorite Bush administration contractors from Iraq: Bechtel, Fluor, and CH2M Hill (all signed on to construct temporary housing). In fact, of the companies on the *Journal*'s list, only one (Dewberry, LLC) was not, apparently, involved in Iraq. Halliburton, of course, was not left out in the cold. In the immediate aftermath of the hurricane, its KBR subsidiary reaped "$29.8 million in Pentagon contracts to begin rebuilding Navy bases in Louisiana and Mississippi."

These companies, however, aren't the only ones returning from Iraq, like so many predator drones, to pick up lucrative deals. In the wake of Katrina, Intelsat, a global satellite services provider that, in Iraq, had teamed up with Bechtel on a big USAID reconstruction program, agreed to new post-Katrina contracts with the Defense Department and FEMA. Similarly, just two days after Katrina ravaged the Gulf Coast, the Air National Guard contracted with another satellite services provider, Segovia, which, according to a 2004 company press release, had "emerged as a key telecommunications provider for the Iraqi reconstruction efforts."

Along with their service in Iraq, the Katrina reconstruction companies are tied together in another important way. They tend to be particularly well linked to the Bush administration and the Republican Party. As former Oklahoma Republican Governor Frank Keating said of Allbaugh, "Joe . . . knows how elected officials and appointed officials like me think and work, and that culture is a fraternity." Halliburton, for instance, picked off "another high-level Bush appointee, Kirk Van Tine, early in 2005 to work as a lobbyist. Similarly, in 2001, Bush appointed Robert G. Card, then a senior vice president at CH2M Hill, undersecretary at the Department of Energy, a position he held until 2004. Today, Card is the president and group chief executive of the International Group at CH2M Hill.

Not surprisingly, during the 2004 election season CH2M Hill was the top "construction services" contributor to political campaigns, sending nearly 70 percent of its $476,800 in contributions to Republican candidates. In fact, fourteen people on the CH2M payroll contributed to Bush's 2004 campaign, including the company's chairman and CEO, president, senior vice president, and president of regional operations, each of whom gave between $1,000 and $2,000. Meanwhile, Bechtel's political action committee contributed 68 percent of its funds to Republican candidates and causes; Halliburton, which ranks among the top twenty "oil and gas" contributors to political campaigns, handed out 87 percent of its money to Republicans.

Theoretically, there should be nothing more glorious than the job of healing the war-torn or rebuilding the lives of those devastated by natural disaster, nor anything more relevant to government. Unfortunately, in the case of KBR World, there's nothing glorious about it, except the five-star hotels for the reconstructors. Prediction is usually a dismal science for any writer. In this case, however, it's already easy to imagine—as some Democrats in Congress are beginning to do—the consequences of Bush-style "reconstruction" in the United States.

Those no-bid, cost-plus contracts already being dealt out to the usual suspects tell you what you need to know about future cost overruns, klepto-reconstruction activities, and the like which are practically guaranteed to deconstruct the bulk of the Gulf Coast and leave New Orleans, the destroyed parts of Mississippi, and the hundreds of thousands of evacuees, not to speak of Congress, gasping for breath amid a landscape largely sucked dry, not of water, but of cash and sustenance.

George Bush's version of capitalism is of a predatory, parasitical kind. It feeds on death, eats money, goes home when the cash stops flowing, and leaves further devastation in its wake. New Orleans, like a rotting corpse, naturally attracts all sorts of flies. Reports have been trickling in that the private security firms—call them mercenary corporations—like Blackwater USA, which have flooded Iraq with an estimated twenty to twenty-five thousand hired guns (some paid up to $1,000 a day), have been taking the same route back to New Orleans and the Mississippi coast as KBR, Bechtel, and the Shaw Group.

They first arrived in the employ of private corporations and local millionaires who wanted their property protected. A week or so into September, however, Jeremy Scahill and Daniela Crespo of *Democracy Now!* found the hired guns of Blackwater cruising the streets of New Orleans, carrying assault weapons, claiming to have been deputized, insisting that they were working for the Homeland Security Department and that they were sleeping in camps the Department had organized. ("'When they told me New Orleans, I said, "What country is that in?"' said one of the Blackwater men.") Then, on September 13, the *Washington Post* reported that "Blackwater USA, known for its work supporting military operations in Iraq, said it would provide 164 armed guards to help provide security at FEMA sites in Louisiana."

Today, New Orleans's streets are under military occupation; its property is guarded by hired guns; and the corporations of the whirlwind are pouring into town. All that's missing is the insurgency.

June 2005

29

THE CHAUFFEUR'S DILEMMA

Arlie Hochschild

Let's consider our political moment through a story. Suppose a chauffeur drives a sleek limousine through the streets of New York, a millionaire in the back seat. Through the window, the millionaire spots a homeless woman and her two children huddling in the cold, sharing a loaf of bread. He orders the chauffeur to stop the car. The chauffeur opens the passenger door for the millionaire, who walks over to the mother and snatches the loaf. He slips back into the car and they drive on, leaving behind an even poorer family and a baffled crowd of sidewalk witnesses. For his part, the chauffeur feels real qualms about what his master has done, because unlike his employer, he has recently known hard times himself. But he drives on nonetheless. Let's call this the Chauffeur's Dilemma.

Absurd as it seems, we are actually witnessing this scene right now. At first blush, we might imagine that this story exaggerates our situation, but let us take a moment to count the loaves of bread that have recently changed hands and those that soon will. Then, let's ask why so many people are letting this happen.

1. On average, the 2003 tax cut has already given $93,500 to every millionaire. It is estimated that 52 percent of the benefits of George W. Bush's 2001–03 tax cuts have enriched the wealthiest 1 percent of Americans (those with an average annual income of $1,491,000).

2. On average, the 2003 tax cut gave $217 to every middle-income person. By 2010, it is estimated that just 1 percent of the benefits of the tax cut will go to the bottom 20 percent of Americans (those with an average annual income of $12,200).

3. During at least one year since 2000, 82 of the largest American corporations—including General Motors, El Paso Energy, and, before the scandal broke, Enron—paid no income tax.

In the meantime, the poor are being bled. Long-term unemployment has risen while the Bush administration has cut long-term unemployment benefits. Most American cities are looking at 15 percent cuts in already bare-boned budgets, which will close more libraries, cancel more after-school and ESL (English as a second language) programs, and limit access to health clinics.

Proposed budget cuts beginning in 2006 are threatening the funding given to low-income programs. According to the Center on Budget and Policy Priorities, with these cuts in place, low-income programs will be significantly reduced over the next five years. By 2010, elementary and secondary education funding will be cut by $4.6 billion, or 12 percent; 670,000 fewer women and children will receive assistance through the Women, Infants, and Children Supplemental Nutrition Program; Head Start, which currently serves about 906,000 children, will serve 100,000 fewer children; and 370,000 fewer low-income families, elderly people, and people with disabilities will receive rental assistance with rental vouchers. Bush proposes to cut housing and community-development aid by more than 30 percent in 2006 alone.

It's not hard to understand why the millionaire, with the power to satisfy so many desires, might want to claim another's bread. But why does the chauffeur open the door? Why do about half of lower- and middle-income Americans approve of tax cuts that favor the rich and budget cuts that deprive the poor?

We often hear two explanations for this. First, George W. Bush has deflected public attention from the bread transfer at home to political enemies abroad. Second, Americans have been repeatedly told over the past three decades that the government—military spending aside—is grossly wasteful and hopelessly inefficient. So why not pocket a little money yourself, no matter who gets the lion's share, if it's being wasted anyway?

But by itself can anti-government propaganda—added to war fever—explain why so many Americans are rolling over in the face of such an extraordinary transfer from poor to rich? Most Americans used to believe, after all, that the government could help people achieve the American dream. In 1970, when America had far fewer homeless children and millionaires, it helped people more, and taxpayers begrudged it less. Most people were proud that the United States was a middle-class society, without much in the way of an overclass or an underclass. They credited their government for fostering this ideal. Many Christians among them thought taxes on the rich and programs for the poor expressed a vital Christian ideal: sharing.

But three things have changed since 1970: attitudes toward governmental redistribution, economic times, and the shape of empathy. Attitudes toward redistribution are different—even among those who would stand to benefit the most. When asked in a 2003 Hart and Teeter poll, "Do you think this (Bush) tax plan benefits mainly the rich or benefits everyone?" 56 percent of blue-collar men (those without a college degree) who answered "yes" (the plan favors the rich) still favored the plan. For blue-collar men living on annual family incomes of $30,000 or less, half supported it. Apart from the super-rich, who overwhelmingly vote Republican, an interesting pattern emerges: even many of those with a fragile grip on the American dream go along with taking bread from the poor and giving it to the rich.

What is being forged, then, is a strange, covert moral deal between the millionaire and the hard-pressed chauffeur, sealed by the right-wing church. It is a deal that says, in essence, "Let's ignore the needy at home, exacerbate the class divide, wage war after war abroad, and sustain the idea that all this is morally good."

The Empathy Squeeze

What is happening in the heart of the chauffeur? He has himself known hard times, and is as capable as anyone else of compassion. What about his circumstances, his religious beliefs, and Bush's manipulation of these might lead him to harden his heart?

For some time now, many families have felt squeezed between high hopes and declining prospects. Most Americans strongly believe in working hard and moving up the ladder of success. They "identify up" with people more rich, famous, and lucky than they, rather than "identifying down" with people more poor, obscure, and unlucky. However underpaid, our chauffeur dreams of becoming a millionaire more than he dreads lying homeless in the street. If others can rise to the top, he figures, why can't he?

And in decades past, he had good reason to aim high. For every decade in the 150 years before 1970—including the decade of the Great Depression—real earnings rose. As University of Massachusetts economist Rick Wolff points out, however tough a man's job or long his hours, he could usually look forward to a bigger paycheck.

But after 1970, the real earning power of male wages—and I focus here on men, for they are the closer fit to the profile of the chauffeur—stopped rising. Their dream was linked, it turned out, to jobs in an industrial sector that had been automated out or outsourced abroad. Their old union-protected, high-wage, blue-collar jobs began to disappear as new nonunion, low-wage, service-sector jobs appeared. Indeed, the man with a high-school diploma or a few years of college found few new high-opportunity jobs in the much-touted new economy, while the vast majority ended up in low-opportunity jobs near the bottom. As jobs in the middle have become harder to find, his earning power has fallen, his benefits have shrunk, and his job security has been reduced.

As a result, Wolff argues, two things happened. First, life at home became tougher. Wives took paid jobs—and this in a society that had given little thought to paid parental leave or family-friendly policies. For men as well as women, hours of work have increased. From 1973 to 1996, average hours per worker went up 19 percent. Since the 1970s, increases have occurred in involuntary job loss, in work absences due to illness or disability, and in debt and bankruptcy. The proportion of single-mother families rose from 12 percent in 1970 to 26 percent in 2003.

Tougher times have led, in turn, to an "empathy squeeze." That is, many people responded to this crisis by withdrawing into their own communities, their own families, themselves. If a man gets fired or demoted, if he can't make his house payments, if his wife is leaving him, or if his son is failing in school, he feels like he's got enough on his hands. He can't afford to feel sorry for so many other people. He's trying to be a good father, a helpful neighbor, and friend to people he knows who themselves need more help. He localizes empathy. He narrows his circle of empathy in a way that coincides with George W. Bush's hourglass America. Pay a tax to help a homeless mother in another city? Forget it. Charity begins at home.

Despite this, many people who voted for Bush may feel real qualms about the homeless mother and her hungry children. They experience the chauffeur's dilemma. In his heart of hearts, the chauffeur feels bad that he has put such space between himself and the homeless woman's plight. If he goes to a Christian church, he wants to be a good, giving, sharing Christian.

And here is where Bush and his social-issues team make a stealthy empathy grab. How? They "privatize" the chauffeur's morality, and in two ways. They do it first by redefining "good" as a matter not of giving or of sharing but of judging. The chauffeur is offered the chance to feel good by disapproving of homosexuals and of economic failures while quietly setting aside the idea of helping the poor, the disabled, the mentally ill, and the unemployed. Second and more important, Bush proposes the idea of giving through private, religious channels, and thus offers moral cover for the idea of giving less. We will stop giving to the less fortunate as citizens through our government and start giving as parishioners through our churches. But, quite apart from this as a bid to expand the fold, it is a way of offering a moral free pass to the act of replacing a lake with a drop of water.

Rather than fixing the problems that make people anxious, Bush takes advantage of the very feelings of anxiety, frustration, and fear that insecurity creates—and that his policies exacerbate—while deflecting hopes away from government help. He makes life quietly harder at home while pointing a finger of blame at one enemy after another abroad. He is, I think, deregulating American capitalism with one hand while regulating the resulting anxiety with the other. And to do this, he has enlisted powerful allies on the corporate and religious right.

The Chauffeur and the Rapture

This leads me to a second effect of economic distress that Wolff notes: rising membership in nontraditional Protestant churches. Among these are some churches that promote the belief that the world is coming to an end, and that, following this, Christians will ascend to heaven in a Rapture while all others will suffer in hell. Those who hold to these beliefs are not a minor group. According to a recent Gallup poll, 36 percent of Americans believe that the world is coming to an end. The twelve-volume *Left Behind* series of Christian novels has sold more than 62 million copies.

We can understand the appeal of the idea of a Rapture, though not, or not only, in the believer's terms. There *is* a world literally coming to an end—the industrial world of the well-paid blue-collar worker. It is a world to which the working man and woman have already sacrificed much time and from which the promised rewards are disappearing. Belief in the Rapture provides, I would speculate, an escape from real anxiety over this very great earthly loss. Internet images of the Rapture often portray thin, well-dressed white people rising up into heaven to join awaiting others. The excluded are welcomed. The rejected are accepted. The downwardly mobile become upwardly mobile. The Rapture creates a celestial split between haves and have-nots, with no one in the middle. And in this vision, those caught in a social class squeeze are at last securely on top. The Rapture absorbs the sting of being hardworking losers in the harsh and rigged winner's culture of the radical right.

In a just society, of course, there need be no permanent economic losers. It is well within the capacity of a wisely led American government to restore a living wage to every worker. The power of the people once pointed in that direction. Popular uprisings in the 1930s led to massive demonstrations, strikes, and eventually Works Progress Administration projects, unemployment insurance, and our Social Security system.

But today's impulse to protest goes into blockading abortion clinics and writing Darwin out of school textbooks. The inner-city homeless, children in overcrowded public schools, unemployed in need of job retraining, and the 18 percent of American children who don't get enough to eat each day become part of the glimpsed world the chauffeur passes by, and his church can only do so much for them.

Like many others, I felt moved by the Christians who knelt in prayer for the family of the late Terri Schiavo, the comatose patient on life support in Florida. But it made me wonder why we don't see similar vigils drawing attention to near-comatose victims of winter living on city sidewalks. They've been taken off life support, too.

The chauffeur knows this and wants to do the moral thing. But he's worse off himself. He feels he has less to give. Bush offers him a way to feel good about giving less—make a general ethic of giving less. He can downsize his conscience and still feel good. This deal, first struck between right-wing anti-tax interests and evangelicals back in the 1970s, offers a way to satisfy the chauffeur's better angel while getting his OK to take the bread. If right-wing ministers have talked our chauffeur into believing in the Rapture, this belief, too, can become just another reason to drive on.

In a sense, Bush is exploiting the common man twice over—once by ignoring his own plight and that of the poor, and twice by covering it over with military drums and tin-man morality. We really need to turn both things around. But to do that, we need to remind the chauffeur, wherever he is, that it's within his power to stop the car—tax the millionaire, help the homeless, and offer new hope to those in between. Otherwise, the deal Bush is brokering between millionaire and chauffeur will impoverish the chauffeur—in his pocketbook and in his soul.

July 2007

3 0

DEMOCRATIC DOUBLESPEAK ON IRAQ

Questions Unasked, Answers Never Volunteered

Ira Chernus

Pity the poor Democratic candidates for president, caught between Iraq and a hard place. Every day, more and more voters decide that we must end the war and set a date to start withdrawing our troops from Iraq. Most who will vote in the Democratic primaries concluded long ago that we must leave Iraq, and they are unlikely to let anyone who disagrees with them have the party's nomination in 2008.

But what does it mean to "leave Iraq"? Here's where most of the Democratic candidates come smack up against that hard place. There is a longstanding bipartisan consensus in the foreign-policy establishment that the US must control every strategically valuable region of the world—and none more so than the oil heartlands of the planet. That's been a hard-and-fast rule of the elite for some six decades now. No matter how hard the task may be, they demand that presidents be rock-hard enough to get the job done.

So whatever "leave Iraq" might mean, no candidate of either party likely to enter the White House on January 20, 2009 can think it means letting Iraqis determine their own national policies or fate. The powers that be just wouldn't stand for that. They see themselves as the guardians of world "order." They feel a sacred obligation to maintain "stability" throughout the imperial domains, which now means most of planet Earth—regardless of what voters may think. The Democratic front-runners know that "order" and "stability" are code words for American hegemony. They also know that voters, especially Democratic ones, see the price of hegemony in Iraq and just don't want to pay it anymore.

So the Democratic front-runners must promise voters that they will end the war—with not too many ideologically laden ifs, ands, or buts—while they assure the foreign-policy establishment that they will never abandon the drive for hegemony in the Middle East (or anywhere else). In other words, the candidates have to be able to talk out of both sides of their mouths at the same time.

No worries, it turns out. Fluency in doublespeak is a prime qualification for high political office. On Iraq, candidates Dennis Kucinich and Bill Richardson don't meet that test. They tell anyone and everyone that they want "all" US troops out of Iraq, but they register only 1–4 percent in the polls and are generally ignored in the media. The Democrats currently topping the polls, on the other hand, are proving themselves eminently qualified in doublespeak.

Clinton: "We got it right, mostly, during the Cold War"

On July 10, 2007 Hillary Clinton declared forthrightly: "It is time to begin ending this war. . . . Start bringing home America's troops . . . . within ninety days." Troops home: it sounds clear enough. But she is always careful to avoid the crucial word *all*. A few months earlier she told a *New York Times* interviewer: "We have remaining vital national security interests in Iraq. . . . What we can do is to almost take a line sort of north of, between Baghdad and Kirkuk, and basically put our troops into that region." A senior Pentagon officer who has briefed Clinton told National Public Radio commentator Ted Koppel that she expects US troops to be in Iraq when she ends her second term in 2017.

Why all these troops? We have "very real strategic national interests in this region," Clinton explains. "I will order specialized units to engage in narrow and targeted operations against al-Qaeda and other terrorist organizations in the region. They will also provide security for US troops and personnel and train and equip Iraqi security services to keep order and promote stability." There would be US forces to protect the Kurds and "our efforts must also involve a regional recommitment to success in Afghanistan."

Perhaps that's why Clinton has proposed "that we expand the Army by 80,000 troops, that we move faster to expand the Special Forces."

Says her deputy campaign manager Bob Nash, "She'll be as tough as any Republican on our enemies." And on our friends, he might have added, if they don't shape up. At the Take Back America conference in June 2007 the candidate drew boos when she declared that "the American military has done its job. . . . They gave the Iraqi government the chance to begin to demonstrate that it understood its responsibilities. . . . It is the Iraqi government which has failed." It's the old innocent-Americans-blame-the-foreigners ploy.

More important, it's the old tough-Americans-reward-friends-who-help-America ploy. We should *start* withdrawing some troops, Clinton says, "to make it clear to the Iraqis that . . . we're going to look out for American interests, for the region's interests." If the Iraqi government is not "striving for sustainable stability . . . we'll consider providing aid to provincial governments and reliable nongovernmental organizations that are making progress."

Clinton's message to the Iraqi leaders is clear: You had your chance to join "the international community," to get with the US program, and to reap the same benefits as the leaders of other oil-rich nations—but you blew it. So, now you can fend for yourselves while we look for new, more capable allies in Iraq and keep who-knows-how-many troops there to "protect our interests"—and increase our global clout. The draw-down in Iraq, our signal that we've given up on the al-Maliki government, "will be a first step towards restoring America's moral and strategic leadership in the world," Clinton swears.

"America must be the world's leader," she declared in June 2007. "We must widen the scope of our strength by leading strong alliances which can apply military force when required." And, when necessary, cut off useless puppet governments that won't let their strings be pulled often enough.

Hillary is speaking to at least three audiences: the voters at home, the foreign-policy elite, and a global elite she would have to deal with as president. Her recent fierce criticism of the way President Bush has handled Iraq, like her somewhat muddled antiwar rhetoric, is meant as a message of reassurance to voters, but also to our elite—and as a warning to foreigners: The next President Clinton will be tough on allies as well as foes, as tough as the old cold warriors. "We got it right, mostly, during the Cold War. . . . Nothing is more urgent than for us to begin again to rebuild a bipartisan consensus," she said in October 2006 in a speech that cut right to the bottom line: "American foreign policy exists to maintain our security and serve our national interests." That's what the bipartisan consensus has always believed.

Obama and Edwards: Don't Tread on Us

That seems to be what Barack Obama, another loyal member of the foreign-policy establishment, believes too. "The single most important job of any president is to protect the American people," he affirmed in a major foreign-policy statement in April 2007. But "the threats we face . . . . can no longer be contained by borders and boundaries. . . . The security of the American people is inextricably linked to the security of all people." That's why the US must be the "leader of the free world." It's hard to find much difference on foreign policy between Clinton and Obama, except that he is more likely to dress up the imperial march of US interests in such old-fashioned Cold War flourishes.

That delights neoconservative guru Robert Kagan, who summed up Obama's message succinctly: "His critique is not that we've meddled too much but that we haven't meddled enough. . . . To Obama, everything and everyone everywhere is of strategic concern to the United States." To control everything and everyone, he wants "the strongest, best-equipped military in the world. . . . A twenty-first-century military to stay on the offense." That, Obama says, will take at least 92,000 more soldiers and Marines—precisely the number Secretary of Defense Robert Gates has recommended to President Bush.

Like Hillary, Barack would remove all "combat brigades" from Iraq, but keep US troops there "for a more extended period of time"—even "redeploy additional troops to northern Iraq"—to support the Kurds, train Iraqi forces, fight al-Qaeda, "reassure allies in the Gulf," "send a clear message to hostile countries like Iran and Syria," and "prevent chaos in the wider region." "Most importantly, some of these troops could be redeployed to Afghanistan . . . . to stop Afghanistan from backsliding toward instability."

Barack also agrees with Hillary that the Iraqi government needs a good scolding "to pressure the Iraqi leadership to finally come to a political agreement between the warring factions that can create some sense of stability. . . . Only through this phased redeployment can we send a clear message to the Iraqi factions that the US is not going to hold together this country indefinitely. . . . No more coddling, no more equivocation."

But Obama offers a carrot as well as a stick to the Iraqis: "The redeployment could be temporarily suspended if the parties in Iraq reach an effective political arrangement that stabilizes the situation and they offer us a clear and compelling rationale for maintaining certain troop levels. . . . The United States would not be maintaining permanent military bases in Iraq." What, however, does "permanent" mean when language is being used so subtly? It's a question that needs an answer, but no one asks it—and no answer is volunteered.

John Edwards offers variations on the same themes. He wants a continuing US troop presence "to prevent a genocide, deter a regional spillover of the civil war, and prevent an al-Qaeda safe haven." But he goes further than either Obama or Clinton in spelling out that we "will also need some presence in Baghdad, inside the Green Zone, to protect the American Embassy and other personnel."

Around the world, Edwards would use military force for "deterring and responding to aggressors, making sure that weak and failing states do not threaten our interests, and . . . maintaining our strategic advantage against major competitor states that could do us harm and otherwise threaten our interests." His distinctive touch is to stress coordinated military and civilian efforts for "stabilizing states with weak governments. . . . I would put stabilization first." "Stabilization" is yet another establishment code word for insuring US control, as Edwards certainly knows. His ultimate aim, he says, is to ensure that the US will "lead and shape the world."

Running for the Imperial Presidency

The top Democrats agree that we must leave significant numbers of US troops in Iraq, not only for selfish reasons, but because we Americans are *so* altruistic. We want to prevent chaos and bring order and stabilization to that country—as if US troops were not already creating chaos and instability there every day. But among the foreign-policy elite, the US is always a force for order, "helping" naturally chaotic foreigners achieve "stability." For the elite, it's axiomatic that the global "stability" that keeps us secure and prosperous is also a boon for the people we "stabilize." For this to happen in Iraq, time must be bought with partial "withdrawal" plans. (It matters little how many foreigners we kill in the process, as long as US casualties are reduced enough to appease public opinion at home.) This is not open to question; most of the time, it's not something that even crosses anyone's mind to question.

Well, perhaps it's time we started asking such questions. A lost war should be the occasion for a great public debate on the policies and the geopolitical assumptions that led to the war. Americans blew that opportunity after the Vietnam War. Instead of a genuine debate, we had a few years of apathy, verging on amnesia, toward foreign affairs followed by the Reagan revolution, whose disastrous effects in matters foreign (and domestic) still plague us. Now, we have another precious—and preciously bought—opportunity to raise fundamental issues about foreign policy. But in the mainstream, all we are getting is a false substitute for real public debate.

With an election looming, the Democrats portray themselves as the polar opposite of the Republicans. They blame the Iraq fiasco entirely on Bush and the neocons, conveniently overlooking all the support Bush got from the Democratic elite before his military venture went sour. They talk as if the only issue that matters is whether or not we *begin* to withdraw *some* troops from Iraq sometime next year. The media report this debate in excruciating detail, with no larger context at all. So most Americans think this is the only debate there is, or could be.

The other debate about Iraq—the one that may matter more in the long run—is the one going on in the private chambers of the policy makers about what messages they should send, not so much to enemies as to allies. Bush, Cheney, and their supporters say the most important message is a reassuring one: "When the US starts a fight, it stays in until it wins. You can count on us." For key Democrats, including congressional leaders and major candidates for the imperial presidency, the primary message is a warning: "US support for friendly governments and factions is not an open-ended blank check. If you are not producing, we'll find someone else who can."

The two sides are hashing this one out in a sometimes strident, sometimes relatively chummy manner. The outcome will undoubtedly make a real difference, especially to the people of Iraq, but it's still only a dispute about tactics, never about goals, which have been agreed upon in advance.

Yet it's those long-range goals of the bipartisan consensus that add up to the seven-decade-old drive for imperial hegemony, which got us into

Vietnam, Iraq, and wherever we fight the next large, disastrous war. It's those goals that should be addressed. Someone has to question that drive. And what better moment to do it than now, in the midst of another failed war? Unfortunately, the leading Democratic candidates aren't about to take up the task. I guess it must be up to us.

December 2007

31

THE PERFECT STORM OF CAMPAIGN 2008

War, Depression, and Turning-point Elections

Steve Fraser

Will the presidential election of 2008 mark a turning point in American political history? Will it terminate with extreme prejudice the conservative ascendancy that has dominated the country for the last generation? No matter the haplessness of the Democratic opposition, the answer is yes.

With Richard Nixon's victory in the 1968 presidential election, a new political order first triumphed over New Deal liberalism. It was an historic victory that one-time Republican strategist and now political critic Kevin Phillips memorably anointed the "emerging Republican majority." Now, that Republican "majority" finds itself in a systemic crisis from which there is no escape.

Only at moments of profound shock to the old order of things—the Great Depression of the 1930s or the coming together of imperial war, racial confrontation, and deindustrialization in the late 1960s and 1970s—does this kind of upheaval become possible in a political universe renowned for its stability, banality, and extraordinary capacity to duck things that matter. The trauma must be real and it must be perceived by people as traumatic. Both conditions now apply.

War, economic collapse, and the political implosion of the Republican Party will make 2008 a year to remember.

The Politics of Fear in Reverse

Iraq is an albatross that, all by itself, could sink the ship of state. At this point, there's no need to rehearse the polling numbers that register the no-looking-back abandonment of this colossal misadventure by most Americans. No cosmetic fix, like the "surge," can in the end make a difference—because large majorities decided long ago that the invasion was a fiasco, and because the geopolitical and geo-economic objectives of the Bush administration leave no room for a genuine Iraqi nationalism which would be the only way out of this mess.

The fatal impact of the President's adventure in Iraq, however, runs far deeper than that. It has undermined the politics of fear which, above all else, had sustained the Bush administration. According to the latest polls, the Democrats who rate national security a key concern have shrunk to a percentage bordering on the statistically irrelevant. Independents display a similar "been there, done that" attitude. Republicans do express significantly greater levels of alarm, but far lower than a year or two ago.

In fact, the politics of fear may now be operating in reverse. The chronic belligerence of the Bush administration, especially in the last year with respect to Iran, and the cartoonish saber-rattling of Republican presidential candidates (whether genuine or because they believe themselves captives of the Bush legacy) *is* scary. Its only promise seems to be endless war for purposes few understand or are ready to salute. To paraphrase Franklin Delano Roosevelt, for many people now, the only thing to fear is the politics of fear itself.

And then there is the war on the Constitution. Randolph Bourne, a public intellectual writing around the time of World War One, is remembered today for one trenchant observation: that war is the health of the state. Mobilizing for war invites the cancerous growth of the bureaucratic state apparatus and its power over everyday life. Like some overripe fruit this kind of war-borne "healthiness" is today visibly morphing into its opposite—what we might call the "sickness of the state."

The constitutional transgressions of the executive branch and its abrogation of the powers reserved to the other two branches of government are, by now, reasonably well known. Most of this aggressive overreaching has been encouraged by the imperial hubris exemplified by the invasion of Iraq. It would be shortsighted to think that this only disturbs the equanimity of a small circle of civil libertarians. There is a long-lived and robust tradition in American political life always resentful of this kind of statism. In part, this helps account for wholesale defections from the Republican Party by those who believe it has been kidnapped by political elites masquerading as down-home, "live free or die" conservatives.

Now, add potential economic collapse to this witches' brew. Even the soberest economy watchers, pundits with PhDs—whose dismal record in predicting anything tempts me not to mention this—are prophesying dark times ahead. Depression—or a slump so deep it's not worth quibbling about the difference—is evidently on the way, indeed is already under way. The economics of militarism have been a mainstay of business stability for more than half a century; but now, as in the Vietnam era, deficits incurred to finance invasion only exacerbate a much more embracing dilemma.

Start with the confidence game being run out of Wall Street; after all, the subprime mortgage debacle now occupies newspaper front pages day after outrageous day. Certainly, these tales of greed and financial malfeasance are numbingly familiar. Yet, precisely that sense of *déjà vu* all over again, of Enron revisited, of an endless cascade of scandalous, irrational behavior affecting the central financial institutions of our world suggests just how dire things have become.

Enronization as Normal Life

Once upon a time, all through the nineteenth century, financial panics— often precipitating more widespread economic slumps—were a commonly accepted, if dreaded, part of "normal" economic life. Then the Crash of 1929, followed by the New Deal Keynesian regulatory state called into being to prevent its recurrence, made these cyclical extremes rare.

Beginning with the stock market crash of 1987, however, they have become ever more common again, most notoriously—until now, that is— with the dotcom implosion of 2000 and the Enronization that followed. Enron seems like only yesterday because, in fact, it was only yesterday, which strongly suggests that the financial sector is now increasingly out of control. At least three factors lurk behind this new reality.

Thanks to the Reagan counterrevolution, there is precious little left of the regulatory state—and what remains is effectively run by those who most need to be regulated. (Despite bitter complaints in the business community, the Sarbanes-Oxley bill, passed after the dotcom bubble burst, has proven weak tea indeed when it comes to preventing financial high jinks, as the current financial meltdown indicates.)

More significantly, for at least the last quarter-century, the whole US economic system has lived off the speculations generated by the financial sector—sometimes given the acronym FIRE for *finance, insurance, and real estate*. It has grown exponentially while, in the country's industrial heartland in particular, much of the rest of the economy has withered away. FIRE carries enormous weight and the capacity to do great harm. Its growth, moreover, has fed a proliferation of financial activities and assets so complex and arcane that even their designers don't fully understand how they operate.

One might call this the sorcerer's apprentice effect. In such an environment, the likelihood and frequency of financial panics grow, so much so that they become "normal accidents"—an oxymoron first applied to highly sophisticated technological systems like nuclear power plants by the sociologist Charles Perrow. Such systems are inherently subject to breakdowns for reasons those operating them can't fully anticipate, or correctly respond to, once they're under way. This is so precisely because they never fully understood the labyrinthine intricacies and ramifying effects of the way they worked in the first place.

Likening the current subprime implosion to such a "normal accident" is more than metaphorical. Today's Wall Street fabricators of avant-garde financial instruments are actually called "financial engineers." They got their training in "labs," much like Dr Frankenstein's, located at Wharton, Princeton, Harvard, and Berkeley. Each time one of their confections goes south, they scratch their heads in bewilderment—always making sure, of course, that they have financial life rafts handy, while investors, employees, suppliers, and whole communities go down with the ship.

What makes Wall Street's latest "normal accident" so portentous, however, is the way it is interacting with, and infecting, healthier parts of the economy. When the dotcom bubble burst, many innocents were hurt, not just denizens of the Street. Still, its impact turned out to be limited. Now, via the subprime mortgage meltdown, Main Street is under the gun.

It is not only a matter of mass foreclosures. It is not merely a question of collapsing home prices. It is not simply the shutting down of large portions of the construction industry (inspiring some of those doom-and-gloom prognostications). It is not just the born-again skittishness of financial institutions which have, all of a sudden, gotten religion, rediscovered the word "prudence," and won't lend to anybody. It is all of this, taken together, which points ominously to a general collapse of the credit structure that has shored up consumer capitalism for decades.

Campaigning Through a Perfect Storm of Economic Disaster

The equity built up during the long housing boom has been the main resource for ordinary people financing their big-ticket-item expenses—from college educations to consumer durables, from trading-up on the housing market to vacationing abroad. Much of that equity, that consumer wherewithal, has suddenly vanished, and more of it soon will. So, too, the lifelines of credit that allow all sorts of small and medium-sized businesses to function and hire people are drying up fast. Whole communities, industries, and regional economies are in jeopardy.

All of that might be considered enough, but there's more. Oil, of course. Here, the connection to Iraq is clear; but, arguably, the wild escalation of petroleum prices might have happened anyway. Certainly, the energy price explosion exacerbates the general economic crisis, in part by raising the costs of production all across the economy, and so abetting the forces of economic contraction. In the same way, each increase in the price of oil further contributes to what most now agree is a nearly insupportable level in the US balance of payments deficit. That, in turn, is contributing to the steady withering away of the value of the dollar, a devaluation which then further ratchets up the price of oil (partially to compensate holders of those petrodollars who find themselves in possession of an increasingly worthless currency). As strategic countries in the Middle East and Asia grow increasingly more comfortable converting their holdings into euros or other more reliable—which is to say, more profitable—currencies, a speculative run on the dollar becomes a real, if scary, possibility for everyone.

Finally, it is vital to recall that this tsunami of bad business is about to wash over an already very sick economy. While the old regime, the Reagan–Bush counterrevolution, has lived off the heady vapors of the FIRE sector, it has left in its wake a deindustrialized nation, full of superexploited immigrants and millions of families whose earnings have suffered steady erosion. Two wage earners, working longer hours, are now needed to (barely) sustain a standard of living once earned by one. And that doesn't count the melting away of health insurance, pensions, and other forms of protection against the vicissitudes of the free market or natural calamities. This, too, is the enduring hallmark of a political economy about to go belly-up.

This perfect storm will be upon us just as the election season heats up. It will inevitably hasten the already well-advanced implosion of the Republican Party, which is the definitive reason 2008 will indeed qualify as a turning-point election. Reports of defections from the conservative ascendancy have been emerging from all points on the political compass. The congressional elections of 2006 registered the first seismic shock of this change. Since then, independents and moderate Republicans continue to indicate, in growing numbers in the polls, that they are leaving the Grand Old Party. The *Wall Street Journal* reports on a growing loss of faith among important circles of business and finance. Hard-core religious right-wingers are airing their doubts in public. Libertarians delight in the apostate candidacy of Ron Paul. Conservative populist resentment of immigration runs head on into corporate elite determination to enlarge a sizeable pool of cheap labor, while Hispanics head back to the Democratic Party in droves. Even the Republican Party's own elected officials are engaged in a mass movement to retire.

All signs are ominous. The credibility and legitimacy of the old order operate now at a steep discount. Most telling and fatal perhaps is the paralysis spreading into the inner councils at the top. Faced with dire predicaments both at home and abroad, they essentially do nothing except rattle those sabers, captives of their own now-bankrupt ideology. Anything, many will decide, is better than this.

Or will they? What if the opposition is vacillating, incoherent, and weak-willed—labels critics have reasonably pinned on the Democrats? Bad as that undoubtedly is, I don't think it will matter, not in the short run at least.

Take the presidential campaign of 1932 as an instructive example. The crisis of the Great Depression was systemic, but the response of the Democratic Party and its candidate Franklin Delano Roosevelt—though few remember this now—was hardly daring. In many ways, it was not very different from that of Republican President Herbert Hoover; nor was there a great deal of militant opposition in the streets, not in 1932 anyway, hardly more than the woeful degree of organized mass resistance we see today despite all the Bush administration's provocations.

Yet the New Deal followed. And not only the New Deal, but an era of social protest, including labor, racial, and farmer insurgencies, without which there would have been no New Deal or Great Society. May something analogous happen in the years ahead? No one can know. But a door is about to open.

VIII

BACK TO THE FUTURE?

September 2006

32

KATRINA STARTED AT GROUND ZERO

David Rosner and Gerald Markowitz

Nothing else worked that day. The President was flying haplessly around the country looking distinctly unpresidential; the Vice President was in a bunkered panic. The military couldn't scramble armed jets, and anything else that could go wrong did. But one thing worked, and it worked splendidly—the New York City, as well as federal, public health system.

While the World Trade Center was burning fiercely and about to become a vast cloud of toxic smoke and ash, public health officials were already mobilizing. Within hours, hospitals had readied themselves to receive the injured; hundreds of ambulances were lined up along the West Side Highway awaiting word to race to the scene; the city's public health department had opened its headquarters to receive hundreds of people stricken by smoke inhalation, heart attacks, or just pure terror; the Department of Health had already begun providing gas masks and other protective equipment to doctors, evacuation personnel, and first responders of all sorts. From bandages and surgical tools to antibiotics and radiation detection equipment, the federal Centers for Disease Control readied immense planeloads of emergency supplies, ferrying them up to New York's LaGuardia Airport aboard some of the few planes allowed to fly in the days after September 11.

Despite the general panic and the staggering levels of destruction, even seemingly inconsequential or long-range potential health problems were attended to: restaurants were broken into to empty thousands of pounds of rotting food from electricityless refrigerators, countertops, and refrigeration rooms; vermin infestations were averted; puddles were treated to stop mosquitoes from breeding so that West Nile virus would not affect the thousands of police, fire, and other search-and-rescue personnel working at Ground Zero.

In the face of a great and unexpected catastrophe, this is the way it was supposed to be—and (for those who care to be nostalgic) after five years of the Bush administration's Global War on Terror, not the way it's ever likely to be again. One of the great ironies of 9/11 will pass unnoticed in the various memorials and remembrances now descending upon us: in the wake of the attacks, as the Bush administration claimed it was gearing up to protect us against any further such moments by pouring money into the Pentagon and the new Department of Homeland Security, its officials were also reorienting, privatizing, militarizing, and beginning to functionally dismantle the very public health system that made the catastrophe of 9/11 so much less disastrous than it might have been.

It took no time at all for the administration to start systematically undercutting the efforts of experienced health administrators in New York and at the national Centers for Disease Control. By pressing them to return the city to "normal" and feeding them doctored information about dust levels—ignoring scientific uncertainties about the dangers that lingered in the air—the administration lied to support a national policy of denial.

Bush-style Safety

Putting in place a dysfunctional bureaucracy would soon undermine the public's trust in the whole health system in downtown Manhattan. In the process, it also effectively crippled systems already in existence to protect workers, local residents, and children attending school in the area. As a result, what promised to be an extraordinary example of a government bureaucracy actually working turned into a disaster and later became the de facto model for the federal response to Hurricane Katrina.

Here's how it worked. First, Karl Rove and George Bush saw an opportunity—mounting the pile of World Trade Center rubble—for a public relations coup in devastated Manhattan that could instantly reverse the President's distinctly unpresidential day on 9/11 and his administration's previously weak polling numbers. Second, Washington pushed New York mayor Rudolf Giuliani and local officials to get with the program and reopen Wall Street (which the 9/11 attacks had shut down) faster than was advisable.

Third, city officials were told by administration emissaries that, despite the pall hanging over Ground Zero, all was well with the air and water in lower Manhattan and normal life should resume.

Finally, although nearly the entire city could, for months to come, smell the rancid comingling of burning plastics, asbestos, lead, chromium, mercury, vinyl chloride, benzene, and scores of other toxic materials as well as decaying human flesh, Bush's appointees in the Environmental Protection Agency (EPA) continually bombarded city officials with reports claiming that the air was certifiably "safe" to breathe. As EPA Administrator Christy Whitman put it on September 16, "There's no need for the general public to be concerned." To this day we do not know the extent of contamination or level of exposure to which residents, workers, and students in the area were (and are still being) subjected.

Everyone got on the bandwagon: the President mounted the pile of rubble without respiratory protection, signaling to firemen, policemen, and volunteers that he-men shouldn't worry about the towers having become a toxic wastepile the likes of which the developed world hadn't seen since Chernobyl. Under the goading of EPA officials, even the venerable New York City Department of Health (despite internal dissention) began proclaiming lower Manhattan safe for the return of residents. (At that time, lower Manhattan's congressional representative Jerrold Nadler was arguing that it was still dangerously toxic.) The Board of Education, feeling the heat from the Giuliani administration—in turn, reacting to pressure from Washington—ordered schools just a few blocks from Ground Zero reopened and thousands of students were sent back to the neighborhood.

New Yorkers, complaining of stinging and watery eyes, knew this was not, in any conventional sense, a "safe" area. Karl Rove and the President, however, were focused on solidifying the Republican Party's hold on the nation. In that context, the question of the possible effects on the lives and lungs of a few hundred thousand New Yorkers was a minor matter.

The policy worked like a charm—at least initially. The clearing of the pile was accomplished with miraculous speed. City authorities had estimated it would take two to three years, but thousands of city employees, undocumented workers, and volunteers labored feverishly and often without protection, in part inspired by the patriotic fervor that gripped Americans. The 1.8 million tons of debris was gone in a mere eight and a half months.

And, miraculously, the President's poll numbers, down in the toxic dumps just weeks before the 9/11 attacks, rose dramatically.

Residents of the area, at first wary that their apartments had been polluted, began to accept official reassurances and soon streamed back to the co-ops of Battery Park City and the lofts north and south of the Trade Center site. Despite their fears, parents, clinging to the consoling pronouncements that poured from the EPA, the city administration, and even the Department of Health, sent their children back into what some were calling a "war zone."

The Bush administration's triumph in bringing "normalcy" back to the area around Ground Zero would, however, turn out to be a victory of style over substance—of a sort that would become far more familiar to Americans in the years ahead. Just as the challenging questions and assessments of intelligence analysts and State Department experts would be ignored or drowned out by administration pronouncements on supposed Iraqi weapons of mass destruction as well as Saddam Hussein's alleged links to al-Qaeda, so, in those first weeks, the EPA's official pronouncements of safety trumped the skepticism of scientists at Mount Sinai and other area medical schools, reporters like Juan Gonzalez of the *Daily News*, and even local residents and politicians all of whom knew something was wrong. "The mayor's office is under pressure" to reopen lower Manhattan, reported one official who worried that the city's own Department of Environmental Protection felt the air was not suitable to breathe.

Before long, parents of children in the neighborhood were engaged in screaming matches with local officials who had the hapless task of carrying out policies they didn't necessarily support. As it happened, they were all correct in their fears. Class action lawsuits from over 7,000 residents and workers subsequently led to the discovery of documents showing how intense pressure from Mayor Giuliani had indeed led the Department of Health to certify areas in lower Manhattan safe so that they could be reopened for residents and businesses.

Style over Substance
What began with the dismantling of an effective public health response at Ground Zero later spread to the entire national and local public health systems. From September 12, 2001 on, public health professionals called ever more vigorously for resources to revamp a sagging health infrastructure of

hospitals, emergency services, disease-reporting systems, and preventive health care—in essence, the country's first line of defense against all sorts of health catastrophes, whether caused by terrorism or not.

As state after state faced fiscal crises, what public health departments got was "yo-yo funding," up one year, down the next. What they did not get from the Bush administration were adequate resources to face a more dangerous world—to make sure we knew when a strange disease pattern was emerging or where increased reports of peculiar symptoms might indicate a terrorist plot. The public health community never got sufficient equipment to detect higher-than-expected levels of radiation emanating from a container at some port, nor sufficient lab facilities and trained epidemiologists to track local outbreaks of disease. Instead, it got funding for a high-profile, showcase, mass smallpox inoculation campaign for a disease that may not even exist on the planet, and ineffective, color-coded public-warning systems that made everyone cynical about any alert that might come from public officials.

In general, administration officials worked doggedly in the public health arena to create great media images that drew attention away from real, if sometimes humdrum, reforms that might have cost money. In the meantime, such public health basics as laboratories, well-baby clinic care, and inoculation campaigns were quietly drained of money badly needed for a war-gone-wrong in Iraq. Administration cronies with no particular skills or experience in emergency management were put in charge of FEMA and on scientific panels at the Centers for Disease Control. As in other areas, administration officials evidently hoped that nothing revealing would happen on their watch and that they could slide away into history before anyone realized the public's health was in danger.

Then Hurricane Katrina blew into town, allowing the world to see just how unprepared they were. From a public health point of view, Katrina was the dark underside of the 9/11 experience. From lack of emergency power supplies for hospitals to an inability to collect dead bodies (in some cases for months), administration-managed public health services proved hopeless and helpless in New Orleans—which increasingly meant anywhere in the US. If that was what Katrina could do, what would happen if terrorists actually released a dirty bomb in the middle of Atlanta, Los Angeles, or Houston? Would the public health community even have the crucial equipment available to detect the nature of such an attack, much less respond quickly? Would anyone be lining up the ambulances, passing out the medications, checking those restaurants and puddles this time around, no less organizing an orderly evacuation of residents?

In the wake of September 11, the public health community saw its sanest initiatives stifled and its priorities distorted. While money is now less available for the inoculation of babies from the real threats of rubella, mumps, and measles, as hoped-for funds to prevent as many as 350,000 children from getting lead poisoning are no longer on anyone's agenda, as federal funds to support health education have been rescinded, and as (unbelievably enough) money needed to protect US ports from dirty bombs or bioterrorism has all but vanished, Katrina victims still wander the nation wondering whether they will be able to see a physician.

For the next 9/11, when it comes to public health, don't think New York, Ground Zero, 2001; think New Orleans, August 29, 2005. Think: "Brownie, you're doing a heck of a job . . ." Then sit back amid the disaster and wait for the private charities to appear, wait for FEMA to send in the mobile homes.

March 2007

3 3

ON NOT FORGETTING NEW ORLEANS

Rebecca Solnit

Riflemen and Rescuers

On March 5, 2007, Hillary Clinton and Barack Obama went south to compete for the limelight on the forty-second anniversary of Bloody Sunday, the day in March 1965 when Alabama law enforcement drove civil rights demonstrators off the Edmund Pettus Bridge and back into Selma. Somehow, the far larger and more desperate attempt of a largely African-American population to march across a bridge less than two years ago, during the days after Hurricane Katrina, and the even more vicious response, has never quite entered the mainstream imagination. Few outside New Orleans, therefore, understand that the city became a prison in the days after 80 percent of it was flooded (nor has it fully sunk in that the city was flooded not by a hurricane but by the failure of levees inadequately built by the US Army Corps of Engineers).

According to a little-noted *Los Angeles Times* report from that moment, "Authorities in St Bernard Parish, to the east, stacked cars to seal roads from the Crescent City." Not only were relief supplies and rescuers kept out of the city, but many who could have rescued themselves or reached outside rescue efforts were forcibly kept in. The spectacle of the suffering and squalor of crowds trapped without food, water, or sanitation in sweltering heat that so transfixed the nation was the result not just of incompetence, but of malice. While the media often tended to portray the victims as largely criminals, government officials shifted the focus from rescue to the protection of property and the policing of the public. There's no way to count how many died as a result of all this.

The Mississippi-straddling Crescent City Connection Bridge was closed to pedestrians by law enforcement from Gretna, the mostly white community across the river. They fired their guns over the heads of women and children seeking to flee the dire conditions of the Superdome and Convention Center, as well as the heat and thirst of the devastated city, driving back thousands attempting to escape their captivity in squalor. There have been no consequences from any of these acts, though Congressional Representatives Cynthia McKinney and John Conyers have denounced them as hate crimes and called for investigations, and the Reverend Lennox Yearwood said, "Can you imagine during 9/11, the thousands who fled on foot to the Brooklyn Bridge, not because they wanted to go to Brooklyn, but because it was their only option? What if they had been met by six or eight police cars blocking the bridge, and cops fired warning shots to turn them back?"

During my trips to the still-half-ruined city, some inhabitants have told me that they, in turn, were told by white vigilantes of widespread murders of black men in the chaos of the storm and flood. One local journalist assured me that he tried to investigate the story, but found it impossible to crack. Reporters, he said, were not allowed to inspect recovered bodies before they were disposed of. These accounts suggest that, someday, an intrepid investigative journalist may stand on its head the media hysteria of the time (later quietly recanted) about African-American violence and menace in flooded New Orleans. Certainly, the most brutal response to the catastrophe was on the part of institutional authority at almost every level down to the most local.

These stories are important, if only to understand what New Orleans is recovering from—not just physical devastation, but social fissures and racial wounds in a situation that started as a somewhat natural disaster and became a socially constructed catastrophe. Nothing quite like it has happened in American history. It's important to note as well that many racial divides were crossed that week and after—by people who found common cause inside the city—by, for instance, the "Cajun Navy" of white boat-owners who got into flooded areas to rescue scores of people.

Former Black Panther Malik Rahim says that he witnessed a race war

314

beginning in Algiers (next to Gretna) where he lived and that it was defused by the young, white bicycle medics who came to minister to both communities; since then the organization Rahim co-founded, Common Ground Collective, has funneled more than 11,000 volunteers, mostly white, into New Orleans.

Parades and Patrols

New Orleans may have always been full of contradictions, but post-Katrina they stand in high relief. For weeks in February 2007, parades wound past rowdy crowds in the uptown area as part of the long carnival season that leads up to Mardi Gras. Since June 2006, camouflage-clad, heavily armed National Guardsmen have been patrolling other parts of the flood-ravaged city in military vehicles, making the place feel as much like a war zone as a disaster zone—and perhaps it is. (On March 8, 2007, for instance, a Guardsman repeatedly shot in the chest a 53-year-old African-American with mental problems. He had brandished a BB gun at a patrol near his home, in which he had ridden out Katrina, in the Upper Ninth Ward.) New Orleans's poverty was, and is, constantly referenced in the national media; and the city did, and does, have a lot of people without a lot of money, resources, health care, education, and opportunity. But its people are peculiarly rich in networks, roots, traditions, music, festive ritual, public life, and love of place, an anomaly in an America where, generations ago, most of us lost what the depleted population of New Orleans is trying to reclaim and rebuild.

I've long been interested in ruins, in cities and civil society in the wake of disaster, and so I've been to New Orleans twice since Katrina hit and I've tried to follow its post-catastrophe course from afar the rest of the time. On this carnival season visit, even my own response was contrary: I wanted to move there and yet was appalled, even horrified, by tales of institutional violence that people passed on to me as the unremarkable lore of everyday life.

If New Orleans is coming back, it's because a lot of its citizens love it passionately, from the affluent uptowners who formed Women of the Storm to massage funding channels to the radical groups such as the People's Hurricane Relief Fund dealing with the most devastated zones. Nationally, there have been many stories about people giving up and leaving again because the reopened schools are still lousy and crime is soaring; the way people are trickling back in has been far less covered.

Of a pre-storm white population of 124,000 more than 80,000 were back by the fall of 2006, while about the same number of African-Americans had returned—from a pre-storm population of 300,000. Though some have chosen not to return, many are simply unable to, or are still organizing the means to do so. Other roadblocks include the shuttering of all the housing projects in the city, including some that sustained little or no damage in the floods. A few have been occupied by former residents demanding the right of return. It's little noted that not all those who are still in exile from the city are there by choice. And while, once again, the mainstream media story of exile has been grim—that evacuees from New Orleans have brought a crime wave to Texas, for instance—one longtime Austin resident assures me that they've also brought a lot of music, public life, and good food.

I visited New Orleans eleven months ago, during Easter Week 2006, and it was then a ghost town, spookily unpopulated, with few children among the returnees; ten months later, after more than fifty of its schools had reopened, there were dozens of high-school marching bands in the pre-carnival parades. But the bands were mostly monochromatic—all white or all nonwhite—and thirty of the reopened schools are charter schools. Of course, in the slogan "Bring Back New Orleans" lurks the question of how far back to bring it. Once the wealthy banking powerhouse of the South, New Orleans had been losing economic clout and population for decades before Katrina hit and already seemed doomed to a slow decline.

With Katrina, no one can say what the future holds. Many fear the city will become just a tourist attraction or that it will simply go under in the next major hurricane. The levees and floodwalls are being rebuilt, but not to Category 5 hurricane levels, and the fate of the Mississippi River Gulf Outlet, the shipping shortcut that funneled the storm's surge right into New Orleans, is still being debated. The Associated Press just reported that more than thirty of the pumps installed in 2006 by the US Army Corps of Engineers to drain floodwater are defective. (The manufacturer is a crony of Jeb Bush's and, like so many looters of the rebuilding funds, a large-scale donor to the Republican Party.)

The city's major paper, the *Times-Picayune*, recently revealed that the maps people have been using to represent the amount of wetlands buffer south of the city are seventy-five years out of date and there are only ten years left to save anything of this crucially protective marshscape, which erodes at the rate of 32 football fields a day.

Signs of Life in the Lower Ninth

That doesn't mean people aren't trying all over the city. It's easier, however, to get out the power tools than to untangle the red tape surrounding all the programs that are supposed to fund rebuilding or get governmental agencies at any level to act like they care or are capable of accomplishing a thing.

"Are you trying to rebuild?" I asked the woman who'd come into NENA, the Lower Ninth Ward Neighborhood Empowerment Network Association in the part of New Orleans most soaked by the floods Katrina caused. She politely but firmly corrected me, "I am *going* to rebuild."

I ran into this kind of steely will all through my eight days exploring the city. NENA's office in a small stucco church building in the heart of the Lower Ninth, the neighborhood of black homeowners that sustained several feet of water for weeks after the storm, is full of maps and charts. The most remarkable is a map of the neighborhood itself with every home being rebuilt marked with a green pushpin. They are lightly scattered over the map, but there are green dots on nearly every block and clusters of them in places, about 150 in this small neighborhood that looked as dead as any place imaginable not so very long ago.

When I visited the Lower Ninth six months after Katrina, the gaping hole where a barge had disastrously bashed through the levee above the Industrial Canal was still there, as were the cars that had been tossed like toys through the neighborhood when the water rushed in so violently that it tore houses into splinters and shoved them from their foundations. The Lower Ninth was a spooky place—with no services, no streetlights, no inhabitants.

That nothing had been done for six months was appalling, but so was the scale of reconstruction required to bring the place back to life. Throughout New Orleans, even homes that have no structural damage but were in the heavily flooded lowlands have severe water and mold damage. Along with the Ninth Ward, many more middle-class neighborhoods near Lake Pontchartrain also took several feet of water and they too are now but sketchily inhabited. Even the tacky condos in a row alongside the Southern Yacht Club on Lake Pontchartrain are still mostly wrecked, though some are being rebuilt. Sunken pleasure boats are still in the surrounding waters and one wrecked boat remained on the street in a devastated middle-class neighborhood nearby.

Across from NENA's headquarters was a FEMA trailer with a wheelchair ramp in front of one house. In front of another, right next door, a sign spray-painted on plywood read, "NO TRESPASSING NO DEMOLITION. WE ARE COMING BACK." And printed signs, scattered among those for demolition and building services, bore this message in red, "Come hell and high water! Restoration, revitalization, preservation of the Ninth Ward! Now and forever!" These signs mean something in a neighborhood so gutted and abandoned that many of the street signs disappeared, some of which have since been replaced by hand-painted versions.

That people are even making their own street signs is one sign of a city that has gotten to its feet. Or of citizens who have anyway. Failed by every level of government from the Bush administration and its still barely functional FEMA to the Louisiana bureaucracy with its red-tape-strangled Road Home program to the city government, people are doing it for themselves. NENA was founded by Patricia Jones, an accountant and Lower Ninth homeowner spurred into action by the dire situation, and it's co-directed by Linda Jackson, a former laundromat owner from the neighborhood. People are doing things they might never otherwise have done, including organizing their communities. Civic involvement is intense—but individual volunteers, no matter how many, from outside and local passion can't do it all. It's been said before that New Orleans represents what the Republicans long promised us when they spoke of shrinking government down.

The returnees, Jackson told me, are mostly doing their own rebuilding—but sheet-rocking and plumbing are far easier to master than the intricate bureaucracies applicants must fight their way through to get the funds that are supposed to be available to them. Even those who are not among New Orleans's large population of functional illiterates, or whose lack of electricity and money means that sending off the sequences of faxes required to set things in motion is arduous, or who lack the phones and money to make the endless long-distance calls to faceless strangers shuffling or losing their information have problems getting anything done—other than by themselves. Louisiana's Road Home program, for instance, is such an impenetrable labyrinth that the *Times-Picayune* recently reported, "Of 108,751 applications received by the Road Home contractor, ICF International, only 782 homeowners have received final payments." Rents have risen since the storm and home insurance is beyond reach for many of the working-class homeowners who are rebuilding. Others can't get the homeowner's insurance they need to get the mortgages *to* rebuild. In February, State Farm Insurance simply stopped issuing new policies altogether in neighboring and no less devastated Mississippi.

The disaster that was Katrina is often regarded as a storm, or a storm and a flood, but in New Orleans it was a storm, a flood, and an urban crisis that has stalled the lives of many to this day. Katrina is not even half over.

The Great Flood and the Great Divide

Volunteers have been flooding into New Orleans since shortly after the hurricane, and they continue to come. Church youth groups arriving to do demolition work were a staple for a while. This time around, I ran across a big group of Mennonite carpenters, some from Canada, doing rebuilding *gratis*.

Many young people—often just out of college and more excited, as several of them said to me, by "making a difference" than by looking for an entry-level job—have come to the city and many of them appear to be staying. Some have compared the thousands of volunteers to Freedom Summer, the 1964 African-American voter registration drive in the South staffed in part by college students from the North. Most of the volunteers in New Orleans are white, and one concern I heard repeatedly is that they may inadvertently contribute to the gentrification of traditionally black neighborhoods such as the Upper Ninth Ward. Others see the outreach of white activists as balm on the wounds inflicted by the racism apparent in the media coverage of, and the militarized response to, Katrina.

The Ninth Ward symbolizes the abandonment of African-Americans by the government in a time of dire need, and bringing it back is a way of redressing that national shame and the racial divide that went with it. But if it does come back, it will be residents and outside volunteers who do it. The government is still largely missing in action—except for the heavily armed soldiers on patrol and the labyrinthine bureaucracies few can navigate.

To rebuild your home, you need a neighborhood. To have a neighborhood, you need a city. For a viable city, you need some degree of a safe environment. For a safe environment, you need responsibility on the scale of the nation; so, every house in New Orleans, ruined or rebuilding, poses a question about the state of the nation. So many pieces need to be put in place. What will climate change—both increasingly intense hurricanes and rising seas—do to

New Orleans? Will its economy continue to fade away? Will the individuals who are bravely rebuilding in the most devastated areas have enough neighbors join them to make viable neighborhoods again? Will the city government improve itself enough to make a better place or will incompetence continue to waltz with corruption through the years? Will the nation revise its sense of what we owe our most significant cities (before my own city, San Francisco, undergoes the big one) or recognize what they give us? Will the solidarity of many antiracist whites across the country outweigh the racism that surfaced in Katrina and still lurks not far from the surface?

Despite its decline, New Orleans remains a port city and a major tourist destination. But it also matters because it's beautiful, with its houses—from shacks to mansions—adorned with feminine, lacy-black ironwork or white, gingerbread wood trim, with its colossal, spreading oaks and the most poetic street names imaginable; because the city and the surrounding delta are the great font from which so much of our popular music flows; because people there still have a deep sense of connection and memory largely wiped away in so many other places; because it is a capital city for black culture, including traditions that flowed straight from Africa; because, in some strange way, it holds the memory of what life was like before capitalism and may yet be able to teach the rest of us something about what life could be like after capitalism.

One of my friends in New Orleans was telling me recently about the generosity of the city; the ways that churches and charities kept the poor going so that poverty wasn't quite the abandoned thing it too often is elsewhere; the way that people will cook up a feast for a whole neighborhood; the ways the city never fully embraced the holy trinity of the convenient, efficient, and profitable that produce such diminished versions of what life can hold. The throws—glittery beads, cups, toys—from the carnival floats are a little piece of this. Life in New Orleans is grim in so many ways now, and all the beauty with which I end this letter coexists with the viciousness I began with. But the recovery of the city from this one mega-disaster could do much for the longer disaster that has so long now been part of our national lives—the social Darwinism, social atomization, the shrinking of the New Deal and the Great Society and the attacks on the very principle that we are all woven together in the fabric we call society. If New Orleans doesn't recover, we aren't likely to either.

We all owe New Orleans and those who suffered most in Katrina a huge debt. Their visible suffering and the visibly stupid, soulless, and selfish response of the federal government brought an end to the unquestionable dominance of the Bush administration in the nearly four years between New York's great disaster and this catastrophe. In China, great earthquakes were once thought to be signs that the mandate of heaven has been withdrawn from the ruling dynasty. Similarly, the deluges of Katrina washed away the mandate of the administration and made it possible, even necessary, for those who had been blind or fearful before to criticize and oppose afterwards.

One hundred and one years after my city was nearly destroyed by the incompetent response of the authorities to a major earthquake, we are still sifting out what really happened. In a hundred years, we may see Katrina as a crisis for the belief that the civil rights movement had moved us past the debacle on the Edmund Pettus Bridge—and as a crisis of legitimacy for a federal government that had done nothing but destroy for five years.

ACKNOWLEDGEMENTS

Because I'm too old for a lot of online chatter and have little patience with comments-wars, Tomdispatch wasn't designed for readers to post comments. As a result, my real adventure of recent years has largely been a private one— the letters that readers regularly send in to the site's email box from all over the world, as well as the US. (Those from tiny American towns sometimes come with population figures and tags like "living in red state hell.")

Perhaps because Tomdispatch started as an informal email for friends and kept something of that tone on going public, readers often respond directly, informally, and personally. From them, I get tips, personal histories, thoughtful critiques, suggestions for future directions for the site, and—most generous of all—entrée into worlds I would otherwise never know about: What it's like to be the mother of a son stationed in Iraq, or an Iraqi refugee, or a convoy commander in that country, to mention just three examples.

This is, believe me, a rare honor. I try, when I have a moment, to acknowledge as many letters as I can and indicate just how appreciative I am of the worlds being shared with me. Unfortunately, I can almost never reply in kind. So this is my moment to offer a deep, collective bow of thanks to all Tomdispatch letter-writers who have so generously opened windows into new worlds and new ways of thinking for me.

Because Tomdispatch is the sideline that ate my life and I'm often working as a book editor as well, I've made it a non-submission site. But rules are made to be broken. Every now and then someone wanders in through email—Rebecca Solnit with an essay that would become her book, *Hope in the Dark*, a pilot from Texas wanting to explain why the son of one of his neighbors died in Iraq, a retired Lieutenant Colonel in the Air Force who offered a critique of those chestfuls of medals American generals now regularly sport, a just-retired federal prosecutor commenting on the case of outed CIA agent Valerie Plame. In each of those cases, I was so struck by what they sent in that I couldn't help myself. The next thing they knew they were writing "Tomgrams" (as the posts at the site are called). But normally, readers' striking thoughts remain for me alone. They are by now— I've come to say—the university of my later life.

So here's a fulsome thank you to Tomdispatch readers more generally for everything you've taught me, for the encouragement you've offered, for the sometimes fierce critiques you've sent my way, and let's not forget the eagle-eyed, just-after-the-fact copyediting and error-catching you've often done. I'm appreciative as well of the way so many of you have passed on Tomdispatches to friends, neighbors, colleagues, and those with whom you disagree, helping make the Web the fascinatingly viral place it is.

Next, I want to thank all the writers—there are now more than sixty of you—who have offered another form of generosity: contributing to Tomdispatch, living through my manic editing, and regularly coming back for more. Some of you are in this book; others, no less wonderful, will, I hope, be in future volumes. It's been a thrill to tag along on this journey with you.

Then, there are those I've come to know—mostly online—at other websites that I visit, quote, and link to regularly, that I learn from constantly, and that, in turn, repost Tomdispatch material; people like Jan Frel at Alternet, Victoria Harper at Truthout, Juan Cole at Informed Comment, Steve Shalom at ZNET, Eric Garris at Antiwar.com, Mark Karlin at Buzzflash, Tony Allison at Asia Times, Paul Woodward at The War in Context, Dave Gilson and Gary Moscowitz at *Mother Jones* magazine, Lew Rockwell at LewRockwell.com, Rick Shenkman at History News Network, Mike Tronnes at Cursor.org, David Swanson at Afterdowningstreet.org, Chris Cook at the Pacific Free Press, the editors of Commondreams… and, above all, the wonderful Joan Connell of the *Nation* magazine online, who has even turned me into a part-time blogger. And then there are so many others—bloggers, website contributors, you name it. Don't get me started. A bow of appreciation to all of you.

Tomdispatch would undoubtedly still be a nameless e-list if it weren't for Ham Fish of the Nation Institute, who had the idea of turning it into a website, then made it happen, and finally—with an always outstretched hand from the Institute's Taya Kitman—kept it going (while making me an Institute Fellow). So a special bow of thanks to both of them—and to Joe Duax, a young man in the regular business of saving an older one (who, when anything goes wrong online, knows he's doomed) from computer hell on Earth.

This book came into existence only because of Tom Penn. He had the idea for it, signed me on at Verso, offered wonderful suggestions, and made it happen in a quality way. What more could a writer and editor ask of another editor?

And what would I do without Nick Turse? Who would I talk to every morning? Where would I be? He knows what he's done for me over these years. No need to say more. (Except to offer thanks as well to that volunteer proofreader and superb site photographer, Tam Turse.)

For my wife, Nancy Garrity: Nothing would have been possible, absent you. You make my life matter.

A NOTE ON SOURCING

One of the glories of the Internet is that it offers the first democratic form of footnoting. Previously, if you wanted to explore the footnotes in a book or article, you basically had to be a scholar or, at the least, have access to a very good library. The Web, which offers the ability to "link" to other pieces—in fact, information of all sorts—online, has changed much of that. Now, most Tomdispatch.com pieces, if read at the website, are fairly heavily sourced. You can just click on a range of links to see where thoughts or information came from, or simply to head deeper into a subject. (One problem, however, is that a certain number of those links do go dead over time.)

Unfortunately, a set of long urls as footnotes in a book are awkward indeed, and largely useless as well. As a result, the essays in this book are, with a single exception, unfootnoted and unsourced. However, if you go to Tomdispatch and use either the search window or the website's month-by-month archives—both at the right of the main screen (www.tomdispatch. com/)—you can check out the original sourcing on any of these pieces any time.

ABOUT TOM ENGELHARDT

Tom Engelhardt created and runs the Tomdispatch.com website, a project of the Nation Institute where he is a Fellow. He is the author of a highly praised history of American triumphalism in the Cold War, *The End of Victory Culture*, and of a novel, *The Last Days of Publishing*. Many of his Tomdispatch interviews have been collected in *Mission Unaccomplished: Tomdispatch Interviews with American Iconoclasts and Dissenters*.

Tomdispatch.com is the sideline that ate his life. Before that he worked as an editor at Pacific News Service in the early 1970s, and, these last three decades, as an editor in book publishing. For fifteen years he was Senior Editor at Pantheon Books where he edited and published award-winning works ranging from Art Spiegelman's *Maus* and John Dower's *War Without Mercy* to Eduardo Galeano's *Memory of Fire* trilogy. He is now Consulting Editor at Metropolitan Books, as well as the co-founder and co-editor of Metropolitan's American Empire Project. Many of the authors whose books he has edited and published over the years now write for Tomdispatch.com. For a number of years, he was also a Teaching Fellow at the Graduate School of Journalism at the University of California, Berkeley. He is married to Nancy J. Garrity, a therapist, and has two children, Maggie and Will.

ABOUT TOMDISPATCH.COM

Tom Engelhardt launched Tomdispatch in November 2001 as an email publication offering commentary and collected articles from the world press. In December 2002, it gained its name, became a project of the Nation Institute, and went online as "a regular antidote to the mainstream media." The site now features Engelhardt's regular commentaries, as well as the original work of authors ranging from Rebecca Solnit, Bill McKibben, and Mike Davis to Chalmers Johnson, Michael Klare, Adam Hochschild, and Karen J. Greenberg. Nick Turse, who also writes for the site, is its associate editor and research director.

Tomdispatch is intended to introduce readers to voices and perspectives from elsewhere (even when the elsewhere is here). Its mission is to connect some of the global dots regularly left unconnected by the mainstream media and to offer a clearer sense of how this imperial globe of ours actually works.

CONTRIBUTORS

John Brown, a former Foreign Service officer who resigned from the State Department over the planned war in Iraq, is affiliated with Georgetown University, where he teaches a course, Propaganda and US Foreign Policy: A Historical Overview. Articles of his have appeared in Tomdispatch, the *Washington Post*, the *Guardian*, the *San Francisco Chronicle*, the *Nation*, the *Moscow Times*, and *American Diplomacy*. For several years he compiled the "Public Diplomacy Press and Blog Review" (named one of the "best blogs of 2006" by US World and News Report) for the University of Southern California Center on Public Diplomacy.

Ira Chernus is Professor of Religious Studies at the University of Colorado at Boulder and author of *Monsters To Destroy: The Neoconservative War on Terror and Sin*.

Noam Chomsky is the author of numerous best-selling political works. His most recent books are *Failed States: The Abuse of Power and the Assault on Democracy* and *What We Say Goes*, a conversation book with David Barsamian, both in the American Empire Project series at Metropolitan Books. *The Essential Chomsky* (edited by Anthony Arnove), a collection of his writings on politics and on language from the 1950s to the present, has just been published.

Judith Coburn has covered war and its aftermath in Indochina, Central America, and the Middle East for the *Village Voice*, *Mother Jones*, the *Los Angeles Times*, and Tomdispatch, among other media outlets.

Juan Cole teaches Middle Eastern and South Asian history at the University of Michigan. His most recent book is *Napoleon's Egypt: Invading the Middle East.* He has appeared widely on television, radio, and op-ed pages as a commentator on Middle East affairs, and has a regular column at Salon.com. He has written, edited, or translated fourteen books and has authored sixty journal articles. His weblog on the contemporary Middle East is Informed Comment.

Mark Danner, who has written about foreign affairs and politics for two decades, is the author of *The Secret Way to War, Torture and Truth, and The Massacre at El Mozote,* among other books. He is Professor of Journalism at the University of California at Berkeley and the James Clarke Chace Professor of Foreign Affairs, Politics, and the Humanities at Bard College. His writings on Iraq and other subjects appear regularly in the *New York Review of Books.* His work is archived at MarkDanner.com.

Mike Davis teaches urban history at UC Irvine. His most recent books are *Buda's Wagon: A Brief History of the Car Bomb, Planet of Slums,* and *In Praise of Barbarians: Essays Against Empire.*

Steve Fraser is a writer and editor, as well as the co-founder of the American Empire Project. He is the author of *Every Man a Speculator: A History of Wall Street in American Life.* His latest book is *Wall Street: America's Dream Palace.*

Greg Grandin is the author of a number of books, most recently *Empire's Workshop: Latin America, the United States, and the Rise of the New Imperialism.* He teaches history at NYU.

Karen J. Greenberg, the Executive Director of the Center on Law and Security at the NYU School of Law, is the editor of the *Torture Debate in America* and, with Joshua Dratel, *The Torture Papers: The Road to Abu Ghraib* as well as *The Enemy Combatant Papers: American Justice, the Courts and the War on Terror.*

Chad Heeter grew up eating fossil fuels in Lee's Summit, Missouri. He is a freelance writer, documentary filmmaker, and a former high school science teacher.

Dilip Hiro is the author of *The Iranian Labyrinth, Secrets and Lies: Operation "Iraqi Freedom" and After*, and, most recently, *Blood of the Earth: The Battle for the World's Vanishing Oil Resources*, all published by Nation Books.

Arlie Hochschild, a University of California, Berkeley sociologist, is the author of *The Commercialization of Intimate Life, The Time Bind and The Second Shift*, and co-editor (with Barbara Ehrenreich) of *Global Woman: Nannies, Maids and Sex Workers in the New Economy*.

Dahr Jamail, an independent journalist, is the author of *Beyond the Green Zone: Dispatches from an Unembedded Journalist in Occupied Iraq*. Over the last four years, Jamail has reported from occupied Iraq as well as Lebanon, Syria, Jordan, and Turkey. He writes regularly for *Tomdispatch.com*, Inter Press Service, *Asia Times*, and *Foreign Policy in Focus*. He has contributed to the *Sunday Herald*, the *Independent*, the *Guardian*, and the *Nation* magazine, among other publications. He maintains a website, Dahr Jamail's Mideast Dispatches, with all his writing.

Chalmers Johnson is the author, most recently, of *Nemesis: The Last Days of the American Republic*. It is the final volume of his Blowback trilogy, which also includes *Blowback* and *The Sorrows of Empire*.

Ann Jones, a writer/photographer, is working as a volunteer with the International Rescue Committee (IRC) on a special project for their Gender-Based Violence unit called "A Global Crescendo: Women's Voices from Conflict Zones." She is the author, most recently, of *Kabul in Winter: Life Without Peace in Afghanistan*.

Michael Klare, author of *Resource Wars* and *Blood and Oil: The Dangers and Consequences of America's Growing Dependency on Imported Petroleum*, is a professor of peace and world security studies at Hampshire College. His newest book is *Rising Powers, Shrinking Planet: The New Geopolitics of Energy*.

Bill McKibben is the author of a dozen books on the environment and related topics, most recently an essay collection called *The Bill McKibben Reader*. In 2007 he helped organize almost 2,000 demonstrations across the country, the first real outburst of citizen activism on climate change.

Ruth Rosen, historian and journalist, was a columnist for the *Los Angeles Times* and the *San Francisco Chronicle*. She teaches history and public policy at the University of California, Berkeley, and is a senior fellow at the Longview Institute. A newly updated edition of her book, *The World Split Open: How the Modern Women's Movement Changed America*, was published in January 2007.

David Rosner is Ronald Lauterstein Professor of Sociomedical Science and History at Columbia University and its Mailman School of Public Health.

Gerald Markowitz is Distinguished Professor of History at John Jay College and CUNY Graduate Center. They are the authors of ten books and scores of articles on occupational and environmental health and, most recently, *Are We Ready? Public Health Since 9/11*.

Rasha Salti, a Lebanese curator and writer who has published in the *London Review of Books* and elsewhere, splits her time between New York City and Beirut.

Jonathan Schell is the author of *The Fate of the Earth* and *The Unconquerable World*, among other books, as well as *The Seventh Decade: The New Shape of Nuclear Danger*. He is the Harold Willens Peace Fellow at the Nation Institute and a lecturer at Yale University.

Michael Schwartz, professor of sociology at Stony Brook University, has written extensively on popular protest and insurgency. His Tomdispatch book, *War Without End: The Iraq Debacle in Context*, will be published in

2008. His work on Iraq has appeared on numerous sites, including Tomdispatch, Asia Times, Mother Jones, and ZNET.

Rebecca Solnit, who lives in and loves the peninsular republic of San Francisco, is the author of the award-winning *River of Shadows: Eadweard Muybridge and the Technological Wild West, Storming the Gates of Paradise: Landscapes for Politics, A Field Guide to Getting Lost,* and the Tomdispatch-generated *Hope in the Dark: Untold Histories, Wild Possibilities,* among other books. She is now at work on a book about disaster, utopia, and civil society.

Nick Turse is the associate editor and research director of *Tomdispatch.com.* He has written for the *Los Angeles Times,* the *San Francisco Chronicle,* the *Nation,* the *Village Voice,* and regularly for Tomdispatch.com. His first book, *The Complex: How the Military Invades Our Everyday Lives,* an exploration of the new military–corporate complex in America, is part of the American Empire Project series.

Behzad Yaghmaian is the author of *Embracing the Infidel: Stories of Muslim Migrants on the Journey West* and *Social Change in Iran: An Eyewitness Account of Dissent, Defiance, and New Movements for Rights.* He is a professor of political economy at Ramapo College of New Jersey.

INDEX

Abdullah, King of Jordan 150
Abdullah, Abdul 153
USS *Abraham Lincoln* 31, 249, 250, 251
Abu Ghraib prison 97, 107, 127–30, 267
Advisory Committee on Cultural Property 113
Afghanistan 27, 75, 80, 83, 89, 97, 115, 117; bombing operations 166, 167, 168; casualties 15–16, 140, 238; conditions 136–7; Constitution 136; as failed state 247; GDP 241; lack of targets 262; peacekeeping 139–40; Taliban resurgence 139–40; women in 134–40
Africa xv, 102
after action reports 117
Ahmadinejad, Mahmoud 195
air power xviii, 160–72
Al Jazeera 97
Alencar, José 67
Algeria 100, 255
Ali, Salah 132
Al-Ali, Zaid 207–8
Ali Ahmed 151
Allawi, Iyad 30, 205–6, 212
Allbaugh, Joseph 279–81, 282
al-Qaeda xviii, 6–7, 60, 143; asymmetrical

warfare 263–4; and Latin America 62, 63; links to Iraq 250
American Council for Cultural Policy 112
American Friends Service Committee 125
Americanization 79
Amnesty International 126, 130–1
anthrax murders-by-mail 7
anti-imperialism 26, 32–5
Applebaum, Anne 77
arc of instability 240
Argentina 56, 61, 67, 68
USS *Arizona* 16
Arjomand, Said 113
Arkin, William 93–4
Arlen, Michael 123
Arlington Cemetery 16
Armitage, Richard 40
Armitage Associates 41
arms trafficking 60, 62, 75
Army Corps of Engineers 281, 316
art crimes 110
Ashcroft, John 12, 60–1
Asher, David 40
Asia-Pacific Economic Cooperation 50, 52
Asma 130–1
Associated Press 118, 121–2, 316

Association of Southeast Asian Nations
    (ASEAN) 50, 56–7, 101
asymmetrical warfare 262, 263–4
Australia 41, 55
Axis of Evil 29, 196

Babylon 114–15
Bacevich, Andrew 245
Baghdad xii, 17, 30, 80, 82, 83, 109–11,
    113, 119, 130, 152–3, 268–9, 276, 295
Bahrani, Zainab 115
Baker, James 207
Bamiyan 115
Barbour, Griffith & Rogers Inc. 280
Barbour, Haley 230, 280
Barnett, Corelli 72
Bay Mills News 79
BBC 97
Bechtel Corporation xiii, 205, 277, 281, 282
Bedeski, Robert 46
Begin, Menachem 261
Beijing Olympic games, 2008 45, 47
Beirut, siege of 173–83
Bennett, Brian 131
Bergen, Paul 72
Black, Ian 169
Blackwater USA xiii, 283
Blair, Tony 107
Bloomberg, Michael 15
Bodman, Sam 208
Bolivia 56, 68
Bolton, John 41
Boot, Max xii, 77–8, 239
Bosnia 83
Bourne, Randolph 299
Bouton, Marshall 76
Boyer, Paul 3
Brazil 55–6, 61, 67, 68
Bremer, L. Paul, III 83, 204–6, 277–8

British Empire 26, 29
Brokaw, Tom 4–5
Brookings Institute 117, 119, 120
Brown, John 77–81
Brown, Michael 280
"Brownie, you're doing a heck of a job!"
    246–7
Brooks, David 27
budget cuts 285
Buenos Aires 61
Burkeman, Oliver 14
Burki, Shahid Javed 38
Burkina Faso 136
Burns, John 109
burqa, the 135
Bury the Chains (Hochschild) 35
Bush, George 31, 112
Bush, George W.; commitment to preserve Iraqi
    oil 107, 240; comparison with Napoleon
    248–56; declares war on terror 9;
    electoral victory 260–1; European tour,
    2005 54; faith in military power
    xiv–xvii; fundraisers 280; and Iran
    71, 196; Iraq policy 239–40; on Iraqi
    heritage 108; and Koizumi 42; and
    the liberation of Afghan women 135,
    139; and linkages to 9/11 12;
    mendacity 267; and nation-building
    85; popularity in wake of 9/11 xiv,
    308–10; privatization of morality 287;
    reaction to news of World Trade
    Centre attacks 18; reading ix; and
    rhetoric 257–71; Taiwan policy 48
    and torture 236–7, 268; use of language
    235–47, 258; version of capitalism 282–3
Bush, Laura 135
Bush Doctrine, the 217–18
Byelorussia 84
Byrd, Robert 125

cakewalk 240
Card, Robert G. 282
Carroll, James 162, 238–9
Carter, Jimmy 201, 218
Casey, General George W., Jr. 127
casualties; Afghanistan 15–16, 140, 238;
 Beirut 179; civilian war dead 16, 117,
 118–19, 120–2, 125, 237–8, 269–70;
 compensation 118; counting 117–19; the
 Holocaust 16; Iraq 15–16, 16, 238; Iraqi
 116–25, 269–70; Vietnam War 16, 237;
 World War Two 16, 49, 165, 237
CBS 267
Center for Defense Information 95
Center for International Policy 64
Center for Strategic and International Studies
 92
Center for Sustainable Agriculture 222
Center on Budget and Policy Priorities 285
Centers for Disease Control 307, 308, 310
CH2M Hill 277, 281, 282
Chávez, Hugo 56, 61, 68, 99–101, 100
Chechnya 17
Chen Shui-bian 44–6, 48
Cheney, Dick xiv, xix–xx, 11, 69, 201–2,
 235, 277
Chernus, Ian 291–7
Chery Automobile Company 53
Chiang Kai-shek 44
Chicago Tribune 8, 90–1, 93
Chile 56, 65–6, 67
China; American insults towards 39–40;
 American trade 37–8; and ASEAN 56–7;
 debt 39; defense spending 102–3;
 economic growth 36, 37–9, 48, 57; EU
 trade 37–8, 53–4; fifth Defense White
 Paper 46; foreign exchange reserves 39,
 101; GDP 37, 38, 101; international
 relations 52–9; Japanese aid 51; Japanese

invasion of 164; and Japanese remilitariza-
 tion 41; Japanese trade 37–8, 51–2; and
 Latin America 55–6; military threat 54–5;
 oil diplomacy 102; population 38–9;
 reemergence of 37; relations with
 America decline 47–9; relations with
 Japan 49–52, 57; rise of 101–3; and
 Russia 98; space program 55; and
 Taiwan 44, 45–7; trade with Iran 52–3;
 and Venezuela 101
China-Africa Forum, 2006 102
China Business Weekly 53
China Institute of International Studies 102
Chirac, Jacques 54, 55
Chomsky, Noam 71–6
Christian fundamentalism xv, 287–90
Christian Science Monitor 118
Chronicle of Higher Education 121
Chu, Hope 207
Churchill, Winston 88
CIA xvii, 6, 37, 184, 243
Ciudad del Este, Paraguay 61–3, 69–70
Clarke, Richard 12
climate change xix, 33, 225–8, 229–31
Climate of Fear: Sexual Violence and Abduction
 of Women and Girls in Baghdad (HRW)
 130
Clinton, Bill xii–xiii
Clinton, Hilary 292–4, 313
cluster munitions 124
CNN 62, 97, 118
Coalition Provisional Authority 119, 276,
 278, 279–80
Coburn, Judith 116–25
Cody, Edward 56
Cohen, Ariel 81
Cohen, William 59
Cole, Juan 206, 239, 248–56
collateral damage xix, 19, 120–2, 166, 238

Colombia 64–5

Colossus (Ferguson) 29

Common Ground Collective 315

Congo, the 17, 83

Conrad, Joseph 87

Convention on the Elimination of All Forms of Discrimination Against Women 136

Conyers, John 314

Cornell University 222

Counter-terrorism Fellowship Program 66

Craddock, General Bantz 59, 61, 63, 69

Crespo, Daniela 283

Creveld, Martin van 73

Croddy, Jack xii

Cruikshank, Paul 72

Crumpton, Henry A. 171

Cuba 56, 67, 75–6

Cuban Missile Crisis 5

Curtis, John 110, 114

Daily News 310

Damascus 147, 149, 156, 176

Dances with Wolves (film) 81

Daniel, Jamal 280

Danner, Mark 243, 257–71

Darfur 17

Daschle, Tom 130

Davis, Mike xiv, 225–8, 244

Deans, Phil 42

Declaration of Independence 78

decapitation 240

Defense Advanced Research Projects Agency 32

Defense Intelligence Agency 49

Defense Science Board task Force on Strategic Communication 108

democracy 245, 246, 265

Democracy Now! 283

democracy promotion 74–6

Democratic Party, Iraq policies 291–7

Department of Defense 64, 214–19, 241, 281

Department of Energy 215–16

Department of Health 307

Department of Homeland Security x, 66, 79–80, 241, 283, 308

Dewbury, LLC 281

Downing Street Memo 266

drugs 60, 62, 67

Duarte, Nicanor 69

East Asia 36–7

Ebadi, Shirin 74

economic collapse 300–4

economic distress 284–90

Editor and Publisher 121

Education for Peace in Iraq project 118–19

education funding 285

Edwards, John 295

Egypt 148; Napoleon's invasion of 248–56

Ehrenreich, Barbara 246

Emerson, Gloria 122–3

Emmanuel, Kerry 230

empathy 286–8

empires 26–7

Energy Task Force 202

Enron 300

Environmental Protection Agency 309, 310

EOS 227–8

Erlanger, Steve 161

European Union 37–8, 53–4, 98

Event Source 277

Exterminate All the Brutes (Lindqvist) 86–7

extraordinary rendition 243

Factbook 2003 (CIA) 37

failed states 247

Failed States (Chomsky) 76

Falluja   107, 121, 124, 167–8, 254
Federation of Oil Unions   211–12
Feith, Douglas   xv, 61–2, 92–3
FEMA   279–81, 281, 310, 317
Ferguson, Niall   28–9
fertilizer   222–3
financial malfeasance   300–2
Financial Times   38
Fisher, Richard   55
Fisk, Robert   111
five wars of globalization   60
Fleischer, Art   10
Fluor Corporation   277, 278–9, 281
food, energy costs   220–4
Forbes, Jack D.   79
Foreign Assistance Act, 1961   65
Foreign Claims Act   118
Foreign Policy   60
Foreign Policy Disconnect, The (Page and
    Bouton)   76
Foz de Igua u, Brazil   67
France   54; Napoleon's invasion of Egypt
    248–56
France 24   97
Franks, General Tommy   117, 235
Fraser, Steve   298–304
Freedom Summer   319
Freedom Tower, the   14–15, 18–21
Freeh, Louis   62
Friedman, Thomas   9–10, 27
Frist, Bill   129–30
Funabashi, Yoichi   56–7
Funai Electric Company   38
Future of Iraq project   202

Gabler, Neal   6
Gandhi, Mahatma   26
Ganji, Akbar   74
Garlasco, Mark   120

Garner, Jay   112–13
Gates, Robert   294
Gazprom   98
George III, King   20–1
George Washington University   122
Gettleman, Jeffrey   117
governmental redistribution   284–6
Ghadbhan, Thamir   208
Gibson, Maguire   112
Giuliani, Rudolf   308, 310
Global Policy Forum   203
Global Security Organization   114
global warming   33, 225–8, 229–31
globalization   31, 275
Gonzales, Alberto   235
Gonzalez, Juan   310
Goss, Porter   49
Graham, Bob   9
Graham, Bradley   92–3
Grand Army Plaza, New York City   17
Grandin, Greg   59–70
Great Britain   35, 41
Green, Michael   41
Greenberg, Karen J.   141–6
Greider, William   39
Griffith, Lanny   280
Ground Zero   3, 5, 7, 13, 15, 16, 20
Guantánamo   x, xvii, 97, 141–6, 243–4
Guardian   14, 112, 128, 129, 169, 276
guerrilla warfare   255–6
Guernica   164
Gulf Research Center   99
Gulf War, First   29–30, 97, 111, 112, 166,
    218
gunboat diplomacy   86–95
Guterman, Lila   120, 121

Haditha   97
Hague Convention for the Protection of

Cultural Property in the Event of Armed Conflict 112
Haifa 175
Hajjarian, Saeed 74
Halliburton xiii, 205, 277, 280, 281, 282
Hamad, Salim 149–50, 152
Hamas 62
Hamza, Abeer Qassim 126–7
Hardin, Luke 129
Haret Hreyk 180–1
Harper's 123
Harriman, Ed 277–8
Harris, Rear Admiral Harry B., Jr. 142, 143
Hassan, Ali 153
Hastert, Dennis 235
Hayden, Michael V. xvii
healthcare 75
Heart of Darkness (Conrad) 87
Hearts and Minds (HRW) 123–4
Hersh, Seymour 129, 168, 267
Hertling, General Mark 117
Hezbollah 61, 62, 160, 161, 168–70, 174–5, 176, 178
Hiroshima 3, 162–3
History of Bombing, A (Lindqvist) 162
Hitchens, Theresa 95
Hochschild, Adam 35, 82–5
Hochschild, Arlie 284–90
Holland, Joshua 208
Holocaust, the 16, 161
Holocaust Museum, Washington 16
homeland 240–1
honor killings 126, 138
Hoover, Herbert 303
House of War (Carroll) 162
Howard, John 55
Hsu, Spencer S. 279
Hu Jintao 50–1, 55–6

Human Rights Watch 118, 120–1, 123–5, 128, 130, 131
Hurricane Catarina 225–8
Hurricane Katrina xix, 229, 230, 231, 240, 246, 275, 278, 278–9, 281–3, 308–10, 311, 313, 318, 321. *see also* New Orleans
hyperpower 19

Ignatieff, Michael 28–9, 239
Imperial Grunts: The American Military on the Ground (Kaplan) 78
imperial hubris 20–1
Imperial "war system" 25–35
imperialism 25–35, 239, 248–56
Independent 111, 132
India 26, 38
Indian Wars 77–81
Institute of Petroleum Engineers 201–2
intellectual property piracy 60
Intelsat 281
Intergovernmental Panel on Climate Change (IPCC) 226–7
International Monetary Fund 206–7
International Peace Cooperation Law (Japan 1992) 41
internet, power of ix–x
Iran 29; and American pop culture 190–1; anti-Americanism 185, 188–9; Chávez visits 100; democracy promotion 74; disappearances 187; effects of attack on 72; embassy hostage crisis 187, 189; the fall of the Shah 187–9; growing up in 184–6; interference in Iraq 71–2; Islamic Republic of 187–97; and Japan 52; nuclear development program 53, 73–4, 196; the Savak 184–5, 187; student protests 186–7, 194–5; threat of 72–4; trade with China 52–3
Iranian Workers Bulletin 74

Iran-Iraq war 189, 203, 207
Iraq; American policy on 27–8, 239–40;
  Baath Party 250; bombing operations
  124, 167–8; casualties 15–16, 16,
  116–25, 238, 269–70; comparison with
  Napoleon's invasion of Egypt 248–56;
  compensation payments 118; debt
  206–8; Democratic party policies 291–7;
  as failed state 247; foreign military
  power in 82–3, 90–1, 292–3, 294; GDP
  241; hired guns 283; impact of 299–
  300; insurgency 205, 212; intelligence
  failure 29–30; invasion planned 12, 262;
  Iranian interference in 71–2; lack of
  popular resistance 30; linkages to 9/11
  12; linked to al-Qaeda 250; looting of
  archaeological heritage 107–15; looting
  of National Museum 109–11, 113;
  media coverage 97–8; militias 151–2,
  153; Ministry of Religious Endowments
  109; model for future 80; motivation for
  invasion 261–2, 264–5; National Library
  111; occupation of 29–30, 96–7, 204–5,
  218, 255–6, 276; oil 113, 201–13; oil
  production 203–4, 206; photographs
  122–3; proposed petrochemical bill
  208–13; as pseudostate 82–5; reconstruction 205, 276, 276–9, 279; refugee crisis
  147–56; suffering 123–5; Tallil air base
  114; treatment of women 126–33; US
  bases xviii, 89–91, 241–2, 295; weapons
  of mass destruction 10, 29–30, 250,
  265–7; withdrawal timetable 75, 292,
  294–5, 295–6
Iraq Body Count (IBC) 117, 118, 119, 120
Iraq effect, the 72
Iraqi Study Group 208
Iraqi War Victims Fund 118
Iraqi Women Under Siege (Lasky) 132

Isacson, Adam 64
Ishihara, Shintaro 44–5
Israel 76; air power 161; bombing
  operations 168–72, 173–4; rocket attacks
  on 160, 161; siege of Beirut 173–83; as
  surrogate America 80

Jackson, Andrew 78–9
Jackson, Linda 317
Jacoby, Admiral Lowell 49
Jamail, Dahr 147–56
James, Caryn 4
Jamestown, Virginia 78
Japan; aid to China 51; Chinese military
  threat 55; constitutional reform 42–3;
  debt 39; Defense Agency 43; economic
  stagnation 37; foreign exchange reserves
  39; GDP 40; and Iran 52; nuclear
  weapons capability 43–4; population
  decline 38; rearmament 36, 39–40,
  40–2; relations with China 49–52, 57;
  and Taiwan 42–3, 44, 49; trade with
  China 37–8, 51–2; US Army First Corps
  garrison 43; war crimes 49–50; Yasukuni
  Shrine, Tokyo 50–1
Japan-United States Security Treaty 40
Jaramana refugee camp 150
Jefferson, Thomas 78, 80
Jin Riguang 102
USS John C. Stennis xix–xx
Johnson, Chalmers 34, 36–58, 89, 107–15,
  241
Jones, Ann 134–40
Jordan, Iraqi refugees 148, 149, 150
journalism, and value of life 17–18
Jubouri, Qasim 151
Judd, Terri 132
Jumaa, Hassan 212

Kabul 16, 17, 62, 139
Kagan, Robert 294
Kalkan, Erdogan 148
Kaplan, Robert 27, 77–8
Karabayev, Ednan 102
Karon, Tony 52
Karzai, Hamid 136, 137, 140
Kazakhstan 101
Keating, Frank 282
Keller, Bill xiii
Kelley, James 41
Kellog, Brown & Root 277, 278, 280, 281, 282
Kennedy, John F. 5
Kennedy, Robert 125
Khalilzad, Zalmay 127
Khamenei, Ayatollah Ali 195
Khatami, Mohammad 53, 191
Khomeini, Ayatollah 185
Kilian, Michael 93
Kimmitt, General Mark 123
Kissinger, Henry 262
Koh Se-kai 45
Koizumi, Junichiro 42, 42–3, 50–1
Komsolskya Pravada 99
Koppel, Ted 120, 292
Korean War 166, 167
Kosovo 89
Krauthammer, Charles 8, 239
Kristol, William 27
Kuchinich, Dennis 292
Kurds 30, 155, 294
Kyoto Protocol 75
Kyrgyzstan 101

Lancet 119, 120–1
language; euphemistic 235–47; sanitization of 166–7, 170–1; in time of war 257–71
Laos 166

Lasky, Marjorie 132
Latin America; American military aid 65–6; and China 55–6; demonization of 59–70; failure of American policy 68–70; internal enemies 66; poverty 68; rejects American leadership 66–8; terrorists and terrorism 59–70; tri-border region 61–3, 69–70
Latta, Rafiq 211
Lauder, Arthur 55
Leahy, Patrick 118, 125
Lebanon; bombing operations 164–5, 168–72, 173–4; Iraqi refugees 148, 149; rocket attacks from 160, 161; siege of Beirut 173–83
Lee Hsien-loong 45
Li Zhaoxing 53
Liao Xilong 102–3
liberty, as tyranny 251–2
Library of Korans 109, 111
Lien Chan 45
Life 7–8
life, news value of 17–18
Lindh, John Walker 243
Lindqvist, Sven 86–7, 162
LMI Government Consulting 215, 216, 217–18
London, Joshua E. 77
London Review of Books 277–8
Looting of the Iraq Museum, Baghdad: The Lost Legacy of Ancient Mesopotamia, The (Park and Schuster) 109–10
Los Angeles Daily News 10
Los Angeles Times 5, 93–4, 276, 313
Louisiana Purchase 28
Lundquist, Andrew 280

McCaffrey, General Barry 59
McCain, John 8
Machimura, Nobutaka 42

McKibben, Bill 229–31
McKinley, William 264–5
McKinney, Cynthia 314
Mahdi, Adel Abdul 212
Mahmudiya 126–7
Mallowan, Sir Max 114
Manchurian Candidate (film) 35
Mandelson, Peter 54
Manhattan, restoration of normalcy 307–10
Mardini, Adham 149, 154, 155
Markowitz, Gerald 307–12
Márquez, Humberto 111
Massood, Ahmed Shah 264
Mayer, Jane 202
Mehdi Army militia 151–2, 153
Mellor, William 102
Mendel, Colonel William 62
Mexican-American War 28
Meyerson, Harold 279
Miers, Harriet 235
migration 60
migration fraud 62
Military Commissions Act, 2006 268
military power xiv–xvii, 31
Miller, T. Christian 276
Mission Unaccomplished: Tomdispatch Interviews with American Iconoclasts and Dissenters (Engelhardt) 237
Mohammed, Khalid Shaikh 6
money laundering 60, 62, 68
Mori, Yoshiro 42
multipolarity 52–9, 96–103
Muslim Scholars Association 127
Muzidin, Salah 132
Myers, Norman 229–30

Naderi, Manizha 134–5
Nadler, Jerrold 309
Najaf 167–8

Na'n, Moisés 60
napalm 124
Napoleon Bonaparte 248–56
Napoleon's Egypt: Invading the Middle East (Cole) 249
Nash, Bob 293
Nasrallah, Hassan 174–5
Nation 169–70, 211
National Defense Authorization Act, 2006 65
National Energy Policy 280
National Intelligence Council 38
National Museum, Baghdad, looting of 109–11, 113
National Review 77
National Security Council 202
National Security Strategy of the United States of America xiii, 244–5, 262–3
National World War Two Memorial 16, 18
NATO 139–40
natural gas 98
Nature 230
NBC 4–5
Negroponte, John xvii
Neighborhood Empowerment Network Association (NENA) 316, 317
New Bridge Strategies 280
New Orleans xix, 229, 230, 231, 275, 278, 278–9, 281–3, 311, 313–21
New Rome, the xii, 239
New York Times 4, 4–5, 5, 6, 7, 8, 9, 14, 27, 89–90, 109, 117, 119, 120, 121, 122, 124, 161, 164–5, 227, 239, 246, 259, 292
New Yorker 129, 168, 202, 267
news reality 17–18
Newsday 118
Newsweek 239
Ngo Dinh Diem 30
Niger 136
Nightline 120

Nimrud Gold, the 110
9/11/2001 terrorist attacks xvi, 3–13, 261,
    264; memorial xix, 13, 14–21; public
    health response 307–10
Nixon, Richard 298
North American Free Trade Agreement
    (NAFTA) 57
North Korea 29, 36, 41
Northrop Grumman 280
Nouri al-Maliki 126, 211
nuclear weapons 3, 4–5, 29, 41, 42–4, 43–4,
    73–4, 162–3

Obama, Barack 294–5, 313
Off Target (HRW) 124
Office of Force Transformation 217
Office of Homeland Security 9
Office of Reconstruction and humanitarian
    Assistance (ORHA) 112–13
Office of Special Operations and Low
    Intensity Warfare Conflict 66
oil; African exports to China 102; American
    military consumption 214–19; Bushes
    commitment to preserve 107, 240; food
    production energy costs 220–4; Iranian
    trade with China 52–3; Iraqi 113,
    201–13; peak output 216–17; prices xii,
    xviii, 203–4, 215–16, 302; Production
    Sharing agreements 206, 207, 209–10;
    Russian production 98; Venezuelan
    exports 56, 100–1
Okinawa 51
Oklahoma City National Memorial 16
Olmert, Ehud 169, 175
Omdurman, battle of (1898) 87–8
One Percent Doctrine, The (Suskind) 10, 243
Onishi, Norimitsu 122
Ono, Yoshinori 42, 51
Operation Condor 65–6

Operation Summer Pulse '04 48
Osama bin Laden xvii, 11, 62, 63, 90, 264
Ozaki, Hotsumi 57

Page, Benjamin 76
Pakistan 89
Palestine 76
Palestinian Authority, the 83
Paraguay, tri-border region 61–3, 69–70
Parenti, Christian 211
Paris Club 207
Park, Milbry 109–10
Patriot Act, 2001 12
Patterson, Torkel 40
Paul, James 203
Paul, Ron 303
peacekeeping 41
Pearl Harbor 4, 11, 16
Pearl Harbor (film) 11
Pentagon, 9/11 terrorist attacks 7
People's Hurricane Relief Fund 315
Perrow, Charles 301
Persian Gulf 218
PetroChina 101
Petroleos de Venezuela SA 101
Phillips, Kevin 298
Pimentel, David 222
Pinochet, General Augusto 65–6
Plame, Valerie 268
Planet of the Apes (film) 13
Poland 26
Polk, William R. 108
Pollman, Brig. Gen. Robert 90–1
poverty 68, 284–90, 315
Powell, Colin 40, 49, 164, 245
presidential election, 2008 298–304
Press TV 97–8
preventive strikes 79
preventive war 244–5

Price, Niko 121
propaganda 258–9, 261
pseudostates 82–5
public health 307–12
Putin, Vladimir 98–9
Pyle, Richard 121

Qatar 89, 97, 99
Quadrennial Defense Review, 2005 49
Quadrennial Defense Review, 2006 60–1
Quantock, Colonel Dave 129
Quito, defense ministers meeting 66–7

Rahid, Eman Abdul 153
Rahim, Malik 314–15
rape 126–33, 137
Rapid Deployment Joint Task Force 201
Rapture, the 287–90
reality based communities 259–60
Reflecting Absence 14–16, 18–21
refugees 147–56, 183; environmental
    229–31
Refugees International 150
regime change 240
Reischauer, Edwin O. 36
Reiss, Michael 57
Republican Party 298, 300, 303
Reuters 278–9
rhetoric 257–71
Rice, Condoleezza xii, 73, 235, 244
Richardson, Bill 292
Riefenstahl, Leni 258–9
Rise of American Air Power, The (Sherry) 162,
    164
Roberts, Les 120
Robson, Eleanor 109
rocket attacks 160
Rogers, Ed 280
Roman Empire 238–9

Roosevelt, Franklin Delano 303
Rosales, Manuel 100
Rosen, Jay xiii–xiv
Rosen, Ruth 126–33
Rosner, David 307–12
Rove, Karl xv, 260, 264–5, 308
Rumsfeld, Donald; and China 49; faith in
    military power xv; and Latin America
    59, 64, 66–7; on the looting of the
    National Museum, Baghdad 109;
    militarization of space 94–5; planning
    model 11, 93–4; plans invasion of Iraq
    12, 262; use of language 235; visit to
    Asunci 69; and the war on terror 81
Russia 98, 98–9, 101, 103
Ruzicka, Marla 118
Rwanda 127

Sa'ad Hussein 152
Saba A 130
Saddam Hussein 10, 29–30, 189, 203, 206–7,
    250, 256, 266
Sagar, Abdel Aziz 99
Saida 182–3
Saint-Gaudens, Augustus 17
Sakoda, Robin 40
Salti, Rasha 173–83
San Francisco Chronicle 91, 95
Sanchez, Lieutenant General Ricardo 129
Sarbanes-Oxley bill 300–1
Satterfield, David xii
Saudi Arabia 89, 90, 99, 189
Say, Captain Horace 252
Sayada Zainab refugee camp 150
Scahill, Jeremy 283
Schell, Jonathan 25–35
School of the Americas 66
Schuster, Angela M. H. 109–10
Schwartz, Michael 201–13

Scowcroft, Brent 96
secret prisons 243
Segovia 281
self-determination 26
Sen, Basav 207
service 242–3
sexual terrorism 126–33
Shadid, Anthony 122, 169
Shaker, Huda 128–9
Shanghai Cooperation Organization 101–2
Sharon, Ariel 80
Shatz, Adam 169–70
Shaw Group Inc. 277, 281
Sheehan, Cindy 240
Shelby, Richard 8
Sherry, Michael 162, 164
shock and awe 240
Singapore 45
single-mother families 287
Sinopec Group 52–3
Sixty Minutes II (TV program) 267
slavery 35
Solnit, Rebecca xi
Soong, James 46
Sorrows of Empire, The (Johnson) 34, 89
South Africa, homelands 82, 83
Southcom 65–6, 67, 68
Southern Oil Company 205
Soviet Union 28, 33, 83–4
space, militarization of 94–5
Spanish Civil War 164
special 60–1
Spolar, Christine 90–1
stabilization 295
Star Wars (film) 5, 163
Star Wars missile defense system 41, 43
State Department 41
Stern, Jessica 61, 62
Sterngold, James 91

Studies on Persianate Societies 113
suicide bombers 159–60, 261
Sullivan, Martin 113
Summit of the Americas, 2006 68
supremacy by stealth 27
Suskind, Ron 10, 243, 259
Swadi, Amal Kadham 128
Syria 147–56

Tagiura 162
Taguba, Major General Antonio 129
Taguba Report, 2004 129
Taiwan 36, 39, 42–3, 44–7, 48, 49, 55
Tajikistan 101
Talat, Abu 156
Taliban, the xviii, 139–40
Tallil air base 114
Tavernise, Sabrina 122, 164–5
taxation 284–5
Teets, Peter B. 94
Telesur 98
television news coverage 97–8, 122, 123
Al-Temimi. Gahaith 212
Tenet, George 9, 235, 243, 268
Tennessean 5
terrorists and terrorism. see also war on terror;
    financing 60, 62; and the Iraq effect 72;
    Latin American 59–70; propaganda 261;
    tactics 159–60
"The 36-Hour War" 7
Time 52
Times-Picayune 316, 317
Titan Maritime 277
Tojo, General Hideki 50
Tokyo, WWII air raids on 162; Yasukuni
    Shrine 50–1
Top Gun (film) 163
Topeka Capital-Journal 5
Tops in the Blue tours 94

torture 267–8; definition of 236–7, 243–4
Torture and Truth (Danner) 267–8
"Transforming the Way the DoD Looks at
    Energy" (LMI) 217–18
Triumph of the Will (film) 259
tsunami, December 26, 2004 16
Turbiville, Graham 63
Turkey 97
Turnley, Peter 123
Turse, Nick 275–83
Tyre 165

Ukraine, the 84
Unconquerable World, The (Schnell) 25–6
unemployment benefits 285
UNESCO 112
UNICEF 139, 149
unipolarity xiii
unitary executive theory 245
United nation Security Council 40, 53
United Nations 75, 84, 127, 147
United Nations High Commissioner for
    Refugees (UNHCR) 147–9, 150, 154–5,
    156
United States Central Command (Centcom)
    201
United States of America; armed diplomacy
    88–94; balance of payments 302; checks
    and balances 242–3; China policy 39–40;
    China trade 37–8; Chinese distrust of
    57; Colombia policy 64–5; empire
    25–35, 238–9, 264–5; exceptionalism
    103; failure of Latin American policy
    68–70; GDP 37, 38; as the Great Satan
    188, 190–1; hegemony 96, 239, 292,
    296–7; image eroded 96–7; imperialism
    26–35, 239, 248–56; Iranian threat 72–4;
    Iraq policy 27–8, 239–40; and Iraqi oil
    201–13; and Japanese remilitarization

40–2; military aid to Latin America 65–6;
    military bases xviii, 32, 34, 39, 40, 89–92,
    218, 241–2, 295; military budget 32, 39,
    75, 103, 241; military machine 32, 35;
    military oil consumption 214–19; military
    power xiv–xvii; oil imports 100; power
    262–3; Putin on 98–9; realignment
    strategy 92–3; relations with China
    decline 47–9; and Russia 98–9; sense of
    vulnerability 3, 8, 11; small wars 78,
    251; and Taiwan 44, 45, 48–9; threat of
    war with Iran 196–7
Universal Declaration of Human Rights 136
"Up in the Air" (Hersh) 168
Ur 113–14
US Air Force Transformation Flight Plan 95
USA Today 239
USS *Maine* 16
Uzbekistan 17, 89, 101

Van Tine, Kirk 282
Vanden Heuval, Katrina 245
Variety 5
Venezuela; Chinese trade agreements 56; and
    Latin America 67–8; news coverage 98;
    oil exports 56, 100–1; presidential
    election, 2006 100; purchase of Russian
    weaponry 100
Vietnam Memorial 16
Vietnam War 16, 30, 73, 90, 122–3, 163,
    166, 167, 237, 296
Vikan, Gary 113
Vladimirov, Major General Alexander 99

wages 286, 287, 302
Wall Street Journal 77–8, 281, 303
Wang Hongyi 102
war crimes 50, 127
war memorials 15–18

war on drugs 65

War on Terror. *see also* terrorists and
terrorism; achievement xvii–xviii;
declared x, 9, 10; defining 60–1; image
of 262; interpreting 77–81; origins 236;
Pentagon authority in 65; rhetoric and
257–71

Washington Post 4, 7, 8, 9, 56, 92–3, 120,
125, 169, 279, 283

Washington Times 171

wealth transfer 284–90

weapons of mass destruction; anthrax
murders-by-mail 7; Iraqi 10, 29–30, 250,
265–7

Weekly Standard 27

Wen Jiabao 51

Western Hemisphere Institute for Security
Cooperation 66

Whitman, Christy 309

Wilkes, Sybella 148, 150

Wilkinson, Larry 245

Wolff, Rick 287

Wolfowitz, Paul xv, 9–10, 11, 204, 235, 267

women; abduction 130–1, 138; in
Afghanistan 134–40; detainees 127–30;
education 138–9; Islamic duty 132;
self-immolation 138; trafficking 131,
138; treatment of 126–33

Women, Infants, and Children Supplemental
Nutrition Program 285

Women for Afghan Women 134

Women of the Storm 315

Women's Rights Association 131

Woolsey, R. James 4, 62

working hours 287

world, end of the 289

World Trade Centre 3–13. *see also*
9/11/2001 terrorist attacks; 1993 terrorist
attack 6; casualties 15–16; memorial
xix, 14–21

World War One 163

World War Two 16, 28, 42, 49, 162–3,
163–4, 165, 201, 237, 255

Wright, Ann 242

Yaghmaian, Behzad 184–97

Yarmouk refugee camp 149–50

Yearwood, Reverend Lennox 314

Yugoslavia 89, 127

Zacaria, Fareed 239

Zanganeh, Bijan 53

al-Zarqawi, Abu Musab 250

al-Zawahiri, Ayman xvii

Zhaair, Mayada 131

Zimansky, Paul 109

Zinn, Howard 237–8